PRINCIPLES OF COST-BENEFIT ANALYSIS IN A CANADIAN CONTEXT

Peter G. C. Townley
Acadia University

Prentice Hall Canada Inc.
Scarborough, Ontario

Canadian Cataloguing in Publication Data

Townley, Peter G.C.
   Principles of cost-benefit analysis in a
Canadian context

ISBN: 0-13-636713-5

1. Cost effectiveness. I. Title.

HD47.4.T68 1998 658.15'54 C97-930782-1

 © 1998 Prentice-Hall Canada Inc., Scarborough, Ontario
A Division of Simon & Schuster/A Viacom Company

Prentice-Hall, Inc., Upper Saddle River, New Jersey
Prentice-Hall International (UK) Limited, London
Prentice-Hall of Australia, Pty. Limited, Sydney
Prentice-Hall Hispanoamericana, S.A., Mexico City
Prentice-Hall of India Private Limited, New Delhi
Prentice-Hall of Japan, Inc., Tokyo
Simon & Schuster Asia Private Limited, Singapore
Editora Prentice-Hall do Brasil, Ltda., Rio de Janeiro

ISBN 0-13-636713-5

Acquisitions Editor: Sarah Kimball
Senior Marketing Manager: Ann Byford
Production Editor: Kelly Dickson
Editorial Assistant: Melanie Meharchand
Copy Editor: Matthew Kudelka
Production Coordinator: Deborah Starks
Cover Design: Monica Kompter
Cover Image: © Barrett & MacKay '96
Page Layout: Arlene Edgar

1 2 3 4 5 RRD 02 01 00 99 98

Printed and bound in the USA.

Visit the Prentice Hall Canada Web site! Send us your comments, browse our catalogues, and more
at **www.phcanada.com**. Or reach us through e-mail at **phcinfo_phcanada@prenhall.com.**

Every reasonable effort has been made to obtain permissions for all articles and data used in this
edition. If errors or omissions have occurred, they will be corrected in future editions provided
written notification has been received by the publisher.

To C.A.T.

Contents

PART IV   CASES

CASE 1   The Northumberland Strait Fixed Crossing Project   *243*

PART V   CONCLUSION

Errors and Conflicts   *311*

Preface

*Just because you **can** build it does not mean that you **should** build it.*

INTRODUCTION

Although most economists have a healthy sense of humour, there is little to laugh about concerning the state of public sector project evaluation in Canada—as a joke, it has become rather stale. Cost-benefit analyses are rife with fundamental errors: counting as benefits items that are actually costs, double-counting benefits, ignoring opportunity costs, and assessing multiplier effects as benefits willy-nilly. These errors are not matters of great economic debate: they are so basic that one wonders how this situation came about. Attempts by supporters to justify projects on the bases of *job creation* and *regional economic development* are also vexing, related matters.

One source of this problem may be that although many economics students take courses in cost-benefit analysis, they do not generally become involved in project evaluation after they graduate. While economists are usually employed to deal with complex problems, in practice much cost-benefit analysis is performed by non-economists. The idea of people with little or no knowledge of economics indulging in project evaluation is only slightly less disturbing than the thought of economists performing open-heart surgery or building bridges. Also worrisome is that these analyses are prepared for bureaucrats and politicians whose knowledge of economics may be quite limited or even nonexistent. There are exceptions, of course.

A related source of the problem may be that many courses in cost-benefit analysis are taught only at the senior undergraduate and masters levels, require significant prerequisites in microeconomic theory, and are aimed beyond the fundamentals toward formal welfare economics. This is fine, and there are some excellent fourth-year and graduate texts available, such as Boardman, Greenberg, Vining & Weimer (1996) and Zerbe & Dively (1994). Yet in delivering cost-benefit analysis courses at this level, we are excluding the very people who may evaluate projects frequently in their later, working life: economics majors and engineering, political science, biology, and commerce students.

If the practice of cost-benefit analysis is to improve, it must be taught to potential practitioners at a level that they can grasp given their limited exposure to economics. Only after they have mastered the basics will they be able to pursue advanced topics in the field. Also, the methods of cost-benefit analysis must become more accessible to decision-makers—the people who hire consultants to conduct public sector project evaluations. It would be preferable if these people, instead of having to accept consultants' reports at face value, were able to distinguish good from poor methodology.

For these reasons this textbook has been written in such a way that only an introductory-level course in microeconomics is required as a prerequisite. It is meant to be a textbook that all students—whether in universities, colleges, government, or consulting firms—can read and appreciate. It may also serve as a foundation for those who wish to go further in the study of those fields of economics that are related to cost-benefit analysis: microeconomics, public finance, welfare economics, and econometrics. As well, this textbook may be used as a supplement for courses in public finance, public administration, and policy analysis at the undergraduate and graduate levels. Ultimately, we hope this textbook will prepare readers to participate on project evaluation teams and to assess the cost-benefit analyses of others.

FEATURES

There already exist several cost-benefit analysis textbooks aimed at second- and third-year students. Their core material is similar to what can be found in this textbook. There are differences in coverage, and some texts treat some subjects in a more agreeable manner than others; but in general, these textbooks distinguish themselves from each other and from this one mainly in regard to the approaches taken.

The premise that guided the writing of this text is that students learn more from their own mistakes and from the errors of others than from learning only "correct" methodology. ("Susie did seven years in penitentiary for selling drugs" has more force than "Johnnie stayed out of the student pub and got straight A's.") Therefore, although proper methodology is presented here, an effort has been made throughout this text to point out common methodological errors and potential pitfalls—forcefully, and sometimes with humour.

This approach is emphasized in the context of three recent, major Canadian projects: the Northumberland Strait Fixed Crossing (the PEI Fixed Link), the proposed Trans Labrador Highway, and the Rafferty-Alameda Dams. A chapter is devoted to each. In discussing these projects we do not limit ourselves to presenting the actual cost-benefit analyses. More important, we also provide critiques of these evaluations in which we expose and explain their methodological errors. For whatever reason, students seem to retain more easily the principles of cost-benefit analysis when they are presented in the context of actual, if flawed, evaluations. Moreover, these cases will help students appreciate more the theory they will have learned in earlier chapters.

ORGANIZATION

As textbooks should complement professors and not the other way around, instructors are advised to examine the organization of this textbook before assigning chapters in numerical order or deciding whether to deal with all of them. What works in some circumstances may not work in others. The topics and order of presentation in this textbook are the result of an iterative process the author began over a decade ago in his course, but much depends on the economics courses students have taken beforehand, and how much they have retained. For the sake of flexibility in course design and organization, the chapters and cases are independent of one another to the extent that it is feasible. Still, readers with no instructor to guide them should be assured that chapters flow from one to the next in a methodical fashion.

This textbook has five parts. Part 1 consists only of Chapter 1, in which detailed chapter-by-chapter descriptions may be found. The main purpose of this chapter is to explain to readers why studying cost-benefit analysis is worthwhile and what it is all about. Indeed, efforts have been made throughout the text to make readers feel part of the process.

Part 2 consists of Chapters 2 through 4. Discounting techniques, alternative investment criteria, and a review of competitive markets are covered in these chapters. As students work through the end-of-chapter problems for the first two of these chapters, they will have the opportunity to develop additional skills with spreadsheet software packages such as Excel, Lotus 1-2-3, and Quattro Pro. Some instructors may wish to omit the material in Chapter 4 because of its introductory level. However, they might note the reasons why this separate chapter devoted to competitive markets and instances of market failure has been included. First, students whose major is not economics often enrol in cost-benefit analysis courses two or three years after taking introductory microeconomics. They will have forgotten much of the earlier material, and it should be appreciated that these students may not have been very interested in it when they took it—after all, they chose *not* to become economics majors. Second, economics majors sometimes become so engrossed in the intricacies of microeconomic theory, mathematical economics, and econometrics that they lose sight of some of the basics. For example, students' appreciation of the information that market prices convey may have dulled. Moreover, senior economics students advise us that their memory of introductory material has a half-life measured in heartbeats. These students feel that reviewing this material is worthwhile—and not many instructors make it a practice to discourage reading! Therefore, even if it may not be necessary to devote lecture time to this material because of course prerequisites, it is recommended that students be instructed to review this chapter.

Part 3 consists of six chapters, which deal with the essence of standard cost-benefit analysis: the measurement of welfare change, shadow pricing, items to count and not to count, public sector enterprise pricing, intangibles, and dealing with risk and uncertainty. The cost-benefit analyst's role as a provider of information and economic perspectives to decision-makers is emphasized. Quite deliberately, each chapter in Part 3 is more complex than the last. Some boxes in these chapters are used to present examples or extensions of the main discussion; others contain mathematical derivations of results, which some students may find useful. Throughout, instructors may prefer to add or delete material. For example, professors especially interested in the evaluation of environmental projects will want to augment the material in Chapter 9 on intangibles. Those involved with health projects will wish to add related material instead. Some instructors may wish to add discussion of the use of distributional weights. Instructors of students who have already studied public sector pricing models may wish not to devote lecture time to it. Still, reading this material will help students put it into the perspective of cost-benefit analysis. In Chapter 6, which is devoted to issues related to shadow pricing, only the weighted-average approach for determining what discount rate to use for project evaluation is presented. As this is not the only method—and there is certainly a vast literature on alternatives—instructors may wish to augment this material. Again, this textbook is meant to *complement* instructors' approaches (not vice versa), all the while laying a foundation for students.

Part 4 consists of three cases devoted to recent Canadian projects. The Northumberland Strait Fixed Crossing ("The Fixed Link"), the proposed Trans Labrador Highway, and the Rafferty-Alameda Dams are presented. The analyses of these projects offer an assortment of methodological errors; critiques of all three studies are provided. Instructors may wish to discuss additional cases. Because students have covered the theory by this stage, they should be able to assess actual analyses independently.

Part 5 consists of a concluding chapter. The economic objectives of project evaluation are compared to other objectives: political, job creation, and regional development. The confusion of *cost-benefit analysis* with *economic impact assessment* as a source of error is discussed, and a list of common errors, suggestions, and warnings is provided. We hope this chapter will leave students with a sense that what they have learned is important. It is.

ACKNOWLEDGMENTS

Parts of this textbook have been used across Canada in draft form for the past three years, and the instructors who assigned them or based lectures on them have provided much-valued criticism. Students, too, have been generous with their comments and suggestions. While retaining property rights to all errors, the author wishes to express his appreciation to the following individuals, who provided comments, help, and information: Lorraine Begley, Åke Blomqvist, Neil Bruce, Bev Dahlby, Jim Davies, Donald Deacon, Graham Harris, John Houtsma, Wade Locke, Amy MacFarlane, Senator Heath MacQuarrie, Melvin McMillan, The Honourable Pat Nowlan, Peter Penashue, Greg Quinn, David Robinson, Annette Ryan, Jim Sentance, Yvan Stringer, Gary Tompkins, Danielle Townley, Terry Veeman, Rhys Williams, and David Young.

A draft of this textbook was formally reviewed (anonymously) by four individuals. Their reviews were thorough and helpful—strikingly so—and their efforts are much appreciated. Thanks, too, to editors Sarah Kimball, Mclanie Marie Meharchand, Kelly Dickson, and Matthew Kudelka of Prentice Hall Canada.

Finally, thank you, Robin Boadway. May you cross the link on windless days.

PART I

INTRODUCTION

CHAPTER 1

COST-BENEFIT ANALYSIS

A QUANDARY

The Rafferty-Alameda Dams in Saskatchewan, the Northumberland Strait Fixed Crossing that links New Brunswick and Prince Edward Island, and the Oldman River Dam in Alberta have much in common. First, all three are public sector projects and were subjected to environmental review (a process that included economic assessment); second, all three resulted in federal court action brought by opponents; third, all three are considered environmentally questionable; and fourth, all three are economically suspect. Clearly, there is cause for concern regarding the state of public sector project appraisal and related decision-making in Canada.

Sometimes economic evaluations of proposed policies and projects are stand-alone, but often appraisals of proposed projects like dams and bridges are performed within the framework of an environmental review process. The term "environmental" has been interpreted quite broadly to include all possible impacts a project may have on society and the natural environment. (The 1984 legislation that provides guidelines for environmental assessments and reviews is reproduced in the appendix to this chapter.) All of this suggests that the range of inquiry of the review process is broad; and that the quantity of information available to decision-makers—many of whom are professional politicians—can be vast. It follows that if the process is flawed, it is often in large part because of the poor quality of information and analysis conveyed to decision-makers by those charged with rendering "expert advice" in the relevant fields.

Our concern is with the quality of economic advice supplied. We begin with the types of questions posed by (and to) those who evaluate the economics of public sector projects and policies.

QUESTIONS

- Should an existing ferry service be replaced? If so, by a bridge or a tunnel?

- Should a dam be built for flood protection and irrigation? If so, how high should it be and when should construction begin?

- Should a roadway be widened in order that traffic may flow more quickly and safely?

- Should a hospital be closed?

- Should aircraft be forced to follow noise abatement procedures near airports?

- Should a town install meters in homes to monitor water use?

- Should seatbelts and smoke detectors be mandatory and cigarette smoking outlawed?

- What amount should the government allocate in total to medical research, and how should this sum be allocated among research on AIDS, breast cancer, and heart disease?

- Should a nuclear power, solar power, or wind power generating facility be constructed?

- Where should a landfill be located, or would a waste-to-energy project be more sensible?

LOOKING FOR ANSWERS

An individual or government confronting any of the above questions would, quite reasonably, wish to assess the consequences of both action and inaction. The relative merits of the alternatives would be assessed, perhaps according to legal guidelines and procedures, and a decision would be made. The actual political process might involve a plebiscite or referendum, or the decision might be made exclusively by elected officials or civil servants.

Economists, naturally, are concerned mainly with the economic aspects of assessments, not with the environmental assessment process *per se*. Informed decisions are desirable, yet every one of the above questions has an economic dimension that may not be appreciated by decision-makers. Indeed, given the broad scope of environmental reviews, it would be impossible for decision-makers to grasp all facets of a project at a professional level.

Consider a multipurpose dam project involving flood protection, irrigation, power generation, and the creation of a reservoir for recreation. The relevant questions would include these: Is construction desirable? If so, where? If so, how large? If so, concrete or dirt? If so, when should it be built? If so, what will be the impact on the environment? Obtaining answers to these questions involves seeking the advice of many professionals in a variety of fields: hydrology, geology, zoology, botany, soil science, engineering, architecture, biochemistry, physics, meteorology, sociology ... and economics. Indeed, a typical environmental review requires the input of people in all of the above fields—and others depending on the exact nature of the proposed project. Moreover, an economist usually cannot begin his or her work until answers have been obtained from those in other disciplines.

ECONOMIC ISSUES

What constitutes "an economist's work" in this setting? What kinds of advice can an economist offer decision-makers? One analytical method that brings economics into a broader decision-making framework is cost-benefit analysis. This is a body of methods and techniques for evaluating the social consequences of economic phenomena, policies, and projects. To this end, matters economic that may be addressed include the following:

- What are the costs and benefits to society of the proposed policy, law, or public sector project?
- Once identified, how do we measure social costs and benefits, especially elusive ones such as those associated with quality of life, life itself, time, and noise pollution?
- If costs and benefits occur at different times, perhaps over decades, how do we compare and aggregate them?
- How can this economic information be used for making decisions, and what are the implications for individuals and for society as a whole?

In essence, cost-benefit analysts attempt to determine from an economic perspective whether a proposed project or policy would enhance or diminish social well-being. Of course, there are other perspectives, and analysts should not expect the economic one always to dominate. Nevertheless, the more meticulous a cost-benefit analysis is, the more valuable it will be to decision-makers and, indeed, the more difficult it will be to ignore in the decision-making process.

ELEMENTS OF COST-BENEFIT ANALYSIS

Microeconomic theory provides most of the tools used in cost-benefit analysis. Most economists view this area as applied welfare economics, which in turn is a field within microeconomic theory. Costs are *opportunity costs*. At times, benefits are measured directly in markets; sometimes they are inferred from market behaviour. Although welfare economics provides its intellectual foundation, cost-benefit analysis is not as far-reaching. Moreover, the application of cost-benefit analysis is restricted to policies and projects with a limited impact on relative prices in the economy. And because it is an "applied" field, many of the tools of cost-benefit analysis have been developed to meet the needs of economists attempting to evaluate public sector projects like dams, bridges, and roads.

Time

Many projects involve high, "up front" architectural, engineering, and construction costs. It is not unusual for construction to require several years; only after completion does society reap any benefit. However, once built, a dam or road may yield net benefits for many decades. It is not unusual for cost-benefit analysts to deal with time horizons of 25, 50, or 100 years.

This time dimension does not create a problem once we appreciate that a dollar in, say, the year 1999 is not equivalent to a dollar in 2025. The process of reformulating costs and benefits incurred or enjoyed in different time periods so that they can be meaningfully compared and aggregated is the subject of Chapter 2. These same techniques are used in Chapter 3 to evaluate various rules for investment decisions.

Markets and Information

Chapter 4 is a review of the workings of competitive markets. Although the concepts should be familiar, they are presented again in this book because when viewed with project evaluation in mind they take on new relevance. Market behaviour, prices, the welfare properties of market equilibria, and instances of market failure are fundamental steppingstones in cost-benefit analysis.

Much informatiom is required to evaluate a policy or project. Markets provide information, but an understanding of markets is needed to decipher this information and to assess its validity and relevance. In certain circumstances, the market price of a good, service, or factor of production reveals its true value to society. In other circumstances, market prices overstate or understate true social values.

The significance and worth to the analyst of the information that market prices convey thus depends on that analyst's ability to comprehend the forces that generate prices and determine their properties. In fact, understanding prices and markets where they actually exist is essential for assessing the value of things for which prices and markets do *not* exist.

Measuring Social Well-being

Cost-benefit analysts seek to determine whether proposed projects and policies would ultimately benefit or disadvantage society. This requires venturing beyond positive economics into the normative—something that economists do with great care. This is the subject matter of Chapter 5.

To go beyond the value-free, "if/then" analysis of positive economics, we must make assumptions that have normative content. In other words, at least one value judgment—usually in the form of an assumption—underlies normative analysis. Because they treat their own values as no more relevant, valid, or important than anyone else's, economists insist that assumptions be stated explicitly. Also, good methodology requires that the dependence of conclusions on the underlying assumptions be stated and evaluated.

How and why do these complications arise?

If we wanted to know whether a proposed project would make a certain individual better or worse off, we could simply ask the person. Note two important things: in doing so we would be respecting the preferences of the individual; and we would not be attempting to measure the impact of the policy on the individual's well-being. If all people stated that a project would make them better off, or if all said that it would make them worse off, the analyst's lot would be an easy one, in that no measurement of well-being would be required and, importantly, no value judgment would be required on the part of the analyst.

If this state of bliss were the norm, there would be little need for cost-benefit analysis. Situations in which all people agree, however, are rare. Usually, a project makes some people better off and others worse off. To proceed with project evaluation when this is the case requires measurement and comparison of the impacts of the project on affected individuals. Such procedures should not be undertaken without an appreciation of the normative implications of doing so, and of the assumptions required—and thus the limitations of the analysis.

Economists rely on willingness-to-pay measures of how a project affects an individual's well being. If a project were to make an individual better off, we would want to know by how much. We would wish to know the answers to "What is the maximum this person is willing to pay to have the project proceed?" and "What is the minimum this person is willing to accept in compensation for forgoing the project?" If a project would cause a person to be disadvantaged, we would want to know "What is the minimum this individual would be willing to accept in compensation for tolerating the project?" and "What is the maximum this individual would be willing to pay to prevent the project?" In both contexts, these are the ***compensating variation*** and ***equivalent variation*** questions.

Sometimes these questions can be asked directly. At other times, the answers can be inferred from individuals' behaviour in markets. Once the analyst has assessed the extent to which every individual's well-being—measured in dollars—would be affected by a project, the next step is to assess the impact on society's well-being.

An analyst could simply sum all of the positive (better off) and negative (worse off) dollar figures to arrive at society's total. If positive, the analyst might opine that the project would make society better off; if negative, the project would make society worse off. However, we should not fall into the trap of thinking that such a procedure does not require a value judgment. To treat the valuations of individuals equally—to assume that a dollar loss to one person can be offset exactly by a dollar gain to another—is to assume that these individuals value dollars equally. This may not be true; a wealthy person may put much less weight on losing or gaining a dollar than a poor person.

The analyst could take into account these differential valuations and give, for example, the gains and losses of poor people two or three times the weight of those of a wealthy person. But this, too, requires a value judgment. Any weighting scheme related explicitly or implicitly to the distribution of society's income or wealth involves a value judgment. Like it or not, the outcome of the analysis hinges on the specific value judgment made.

When a project benefits some people and disadvantages others, aggregation problems arise. The dependence of the analyst's conclusions on the normative assumptions made is to be recognized and assessed.

Distortions

Market prices always convey information regarding the value of goods, services, and inputs. Whether the information conveyed reveals social costs and benefits is the crucial question. In markets distorted by taxes, subsidies, market power, quotas, and the like, prices will either overstate or understate social values. The same is true in markets where an interest rate is the relevant price. Still, such market information is valuable because it is possible for an analyst to adjust observed prices in a manner that takes into account existing distortions. The adjusted prices are called *shadow prices*. The theory of shadow pricing and Canadian practice in this regard are the subjects of Chapter 6.

Particularly important prices that may require adjustment in cost-benefit analyses are the wage rates paid to people employed on projects and the interest (discount) rates used to aggregate costs and benefits over time. When otherwise unemployed labour is hired to work on a project, attributing a shadow wage rate lower than the wage actually paid to workers is sometimes justified. That is, even though a specific employee may actually be paid, for example, $15 an hour to work on a project, it may be appropriate to impute a wage less than $15 an hour to the costs of the project in order to reflect the opportunity cost to society of employing this person. Similarly, observed market interest rates are distorted, especially by a variety of taxes. In order to ensure that the interest rate used in an analysis reflects the appropriate social value, adjustment is usually required.

Illusion, Delusion, and Confusion

It may seem surprising, but many decision-makers (and their consultants) with limited exposure to economics have great difficulty identifying the social costs and benefits of a project or policy. Worse, they can even have a problem distinguishing costs from benefits. Also, they tend to double-count benefits.

An example of double-counting benefits: If an irrigation project makes farming a particular parcel of land more profitable because of higher crop yields, we may assess the extra profits earned year after year *or* the increase in land value as a benefit, but not both. An analyst who makes the error of counting both as benefits has failed to appreciate that the additional annual profits will be capitalized into the value of the land. To count both is to count the increase in annual profits twice.

An example of costs being counted incorrectly as benefits: Suppose a road project will adversely affect a nearby wildlife population unless more conservation officers are hired. If more officers are not hired, the damage to the environment will be viewed, correctly, as a negative impact of the project, a cost. If the officers *are* hired, the environmental cost will be avoided through the incurrence of an alternative cost—that of paying the officers. In either case, it is clear that an economic cost should be attributed to the project.

Note, however, that such salary outlays have been viewed by some non-economists as benefits—not costs—of projects. Surely this is incorrect. If we were to count it as a benefit every time a public sector project hired a person, *and not as a cost*, we could justify all public works projects. When a firm hires a person, it is counted as a cost; when the public sector hires a person, should it not be treated as a cost as well? It is rather telling that similar confusion of costs and benefits does not usually arise with nonlabour factors of production such as steel girders and cement blocks.

The potential for errors of logic in cost-benefit analysis is great. Moreover, there seems to exist a bias toward exaggerating benefits and understating costs. What to count and what not to count—discerning fact from fiction—is the focus of Chapter 7.

Pricing Issues

Not all public sector projects produce **public goods**, which are defined as jointly consumed goods and services that people cannot be prevented from consuming even if they do not purchase them. Thus, while a charge cannot be imposed for the output of a streetlight, it *is* possible for a municipal authority to charge a price for the water it provides, and for a province's transport ministry to collect public-highway tolls. Whether a price *should* be charged is a valid question. If the answer is "yes," what should that price be?

Socially optimal prices exist. If the output of a public sector project is priced too low, overconsumption will result and decision-makers will be led to build wastefully large facilities. If such output is priced too high, consumption will be needlessly constrained and too-small facilities will be constructed. In either case, waste will result. Clearly, there is a connection between public sector pricing and investment decisions—they go hand in hand.

Optimal pricing becomes straightforward once the possible sources of complication are identified. For example, consider projects like power-generating plants, waterworks, and recreational facilities. The common theme here is that the demand for the output of these facilities is cyclical. For example, domestic electricity consumption rises and falls over the course of a 24-hour period and from winter to summer. Is a single price per kilowatt optimal over the entire cycle?

Another situation might involve a project where a public agency is able to separate what it charges consumers for its output into two parts. For example, a municipality could charge a membership fee for its recreational facilities plus a user fee to members each time they use the facility. What is the socially optimal pricing scheme in these circumstances? These problems and others are investigated in Chapter 8.

Intangibles

The benefits of road and bridge projects include the value people attribute to time saved. Some projects involve accident reduction and, thus, lives saved. Others involve reduced noise at the cost of the possibility of lives lost. Time, noise, and lives: How can we put a value on life?

A standard economist's response is: How can we not? If no price—no dollar value—is put on a person's life, it is either worthless or of unimaginable worth. "Priceless" may not imply "of infinite value" to an economist.

Suppose we said that lives are beyond price, infinitely precious. This would mean that almost no public sector project should be approved because it is difficult to think of many that do not expose construction workers to possible loss of life. Likewise, we could justify not only seatbelts but a total ban on vehicular traffic because people die in traffic accidents.

A price of zero on lives would lead to similarly bizarre policy prescriptions. For example, it might mean that it would be acceptable to fight a "War on Poverty" with real bullets. And why go to the expense of medical research if only lives are to be lost?

Both notions are quite absurd. Lives are neither worthless nor infinitely precious. People do risk their lives by skydiving, having unprotected sex, and working in dangerous professions. People also wear seatbelts, make their children wear proper sports equipment, and purchase smoke detectors. The reality is that life has a value somewhere between zero and infinity. The same is true for noise and time, for which no market prices exist.

Economists have developed methods for imputing dollar values—prices—to phenomena like lives saved, noise abated, and time saved. These methods require rigorous application of microeconomic theory and econometrics, as well as ingenuity. The historical and modern methods for getting to the crux of these evaluation problems constitute the subject of Chapter 9. To many, the valuation of intangibles is the area of cost-benefit analysis that yields the greatest intellectual challenge and satisfaction.

Risk and Uncertainty

Analysts are often asked to evaluate projects which involve costs and benefits that may stretch over several decades; yet they do not possess perfect foresight. Only in the future will the magnitudes of future costs and benefits become known. This suggests that future values must be forecast and contingencies assessed.

Lack of certainty imposes costs on individuals. For example, we observe people taking measures and incurring costs in insurance markets in order to protect themselves against risky situations. Most homeowners purchase insurance to protect themselves against the risk of fire. This suggests that the chance of fire imposes a cost on individuals, in that they are willing to pay money to avoid or to lessen its financial impacts.

Road construction costs can escalate unexpectedly, bridges and dams can deteriorate more quickly than expected, and nuclear generating plants can melt down. Can and should we apply a typical individual's attitude toward risk-taking to risky public-sector projects? This is the subject of Chapter 10. The brief answer—and it is not very satisfying—is that it depends on the situation. Practical methods for accounting for risk and uncertainty in cost-benefit analyses are also presented.

Cases, Critiques, and Warnings

We noted early in this chapter that the state of the practice of cost-benefit analysis in Canada leaves much to be desired. It is not unusual for very basic errors to be made in the analyses of projects involving costs running into billions of dollars.

A major cause of this phenomenon may be that there are too many non-economist consultants preparing "economic" evaluations for non-economist decision-makers. At the same time, even competent consultants must depend on or may choose to depend on government sources for information, especially regarding construction and operating costs for projects. Our principal concern is the methodology of cost-benefit analysis. Probably, good methodology is best learned by doing. Still, there is much to be learned from people who are practitioners of cost-benefit analysis. When they do something—or do not do something—that appeals strongly to common (and economic) sense, it is important to understand why they did what they did. When practitioners err, it is important to appreciate the source of the error—errors are great teachers.

Cases 1, 2, and 3 are presentations and critiques of three recent analyses: the Northumberland Strait Fixed Crossing, the Trans Labrador Highway, and the Rafferty-Alameda Dams projects, respectively. These analyses were chosen not because of geography, or type of project, but because of the variety of errors made in them. The purpose of these cases is to illustrate, within the context of real projects and analyses, the *dos* and *don'ts* of cost-benefit analysis. Provided in the final chapter is a list of common errors, warnings, and suggestions.

KEY TERMS

opportunity cost
compensating variation
equivalent variation
shadow prices
public goods

Appendix

Legislation

The following order is reproduced from *Canada Gazette* Part II, Vol. 118, No. 114, pp. 2794–2798 (11 July 1984).*

Environmental Assessment and Review
Process Guidelines Order
21 June 1984

Her Excellency the Governor General in Council, on the recommendation of the Minister of the Environment, pursuant to subsection 6(2) of the *Government Organization Act, 1979*, is pleased hereby to approve the annexed Guidelines respecting the implementation of the federal policy on environmental assessment and review, made by the Minister of the Environment on June 11, 1984.

GUIDELINES RESPECTING THE IMPLEMENTATION
OF THE FEDERAL POLICY ON ENVIRONMENTAL
ASSESSMENT AND REVIEW

Short Title

1. These Guidelines may be cited as the *Environmental Assessment and Review Process Guidelines Order.*

Interpretation

2. In these Guidelines,

   "Environmental Impact Statement" means a documented assessment of the environmental consequences of any proposal expected to have significant environmental consequences that is prepared or procured by the proponent in accordance with guidelines established by a Panel;

---

* *Source:* Privy Council Office. Reproduced with the permission of the Minister of Public Works and Government Services Canada, 1997.

"department" means, subject to sections 7 and 8,

   (a) any department, board or agency of the Government of Canada, and

   (b) any corporation listed in Schedule D to the Financial Administration Act and any regulatory body;

"initiating department" means any department that is, on behalf of the Government of Canada, the decision making authority for a proposal;

"Minister" means the Minister of the Environment;

"Office" means the Federal Environmental Assessment Review Office that is responsible directly to the Minister for the administration of the Process;

"Panel" means an Environmental Assessment Panel that conducts the public review of a proposal pursuant to section 21;

"Process" means the Environmental Assessment and Review Process administered by the Office;

"proponent" means the organization or the initiating department intending to undertake a proposal; and

"proposal" includes any initiative, undertaking or activity for which the Government of Canada has a decision making responsibility.

Scope

3. The Process shall be a self assessment process under which the initiating department shall, as early in the planning process as possible and before irrevocable decisions are taken, ensure the environmental implications of all proposals for which it is the decision making authority are fully considered and where the implications are significant, refer the proposal to the Minister for public review by a Panel.

4. (1) An initiating department shall include in its consideration of a proposal pursuant to section 3

   (a) the potential environmental effects of the proposal and the social effects directly related to those environmental effects, including any effects that are external to Canadian territory; and

   (b) the concerns of the public regarding the proposal and its potential environmental effects.

   (2) Subject to the approval of the Minister and the Minister of the initiating department, considerations of a proposal may include such matters as the general socio-economic effects of the proposal and the technology assessment of and the need for the proposal.

5. (1) Where a proposal is subject to environmental regulation, independently of the Process, duplication in terms of public reviews is to be avoided.

   (2) For the purpose of avoiding the duplication referred to in subsection (1), the initiating department shall use a public review under the Process as a planning tool at the earliest stages of development of the proposal rather than as a regulatory mechanism and make the results of the public review available for use in any regulatory deliberations respecting the proposal.

Application

6. These Guidelines shall apply to any proposal

   (a) that is to be undertaken directly by an initiating department,

   (b) that may have an environmental effect on an area of federal responsibility;

   (c) for which the Government of Canada makes a financial commitment; or

   (d) that is located on lands, including the offshore, that are administered by the Government of Canada.

7. Where the decision making authority for a proposal is a corporation listed in Schedule D to the *Financial Administration Act*, the Process shall apply to that proposal only if

   (a) it is the corporate policy of that corporation to apply the Process; and

   (b) the application of the Process to that proposal is within the legislative authority of that corporation.

8. Where a board or an agency of the Government of Canada or a regulatory body has a regulatory function in respect of a proposal, these Guidelines shall apply to that board, agency or body only if there is no legal impediment to or duplication resulting from the application of these Guidelines.

9. (1) Where, in respect of a proposal, there are two or more initiating departments, the initiating departments shall determine which of the responsibilities, duties and functions of an initiating department under these Guidelines shall apply to each of them.

   (2) Where the initiating departments cannot under subsection (1) agree to a determination, the Office shall act as an arbitrator in the making of the decision.

INITIAL ASSESSMENT

Initiating Department

10. (1) Every initiating department shall ensure that each proposal for which it is the decision making authority shall be subject to an environmental screening or initial assessment to determine whether, and the extent to which, there may be any potentially adverse environmental effects from the proposal.

(2) Any decisions to be made as a result of the environmental screening or initial assessment referred to in subsection (1) shall be made by the initiating department and not delegated to any other body.

11. For the purposes of the environmental screening and initial assessment referred to in subsection 10(1), the initiating department shall develop, in cooperation with the Office,

    (a) a list identifying the types of proposals that would not produce any adverse environmental effects and that would, as a result, be automatically excluded from the Process; and

    (b) a list identifying the types of proposals that would produce significant adverse environmental effects and that would be automatically referred to the Minister for public review by a Panel.

12. Every initiating department shall screen or assess each proposal for which it is the decision making authority to determine if

    (a) the proposal is of a type identified by the list described under paragraph 11(a), in which case the proposal may automatically proceed;

    (b) the proposal is of a type identified by the list described under paragraph 11(b), in which case the proposal shall be referred to the Minister for public review by a Panel;

    (c) the potentially adverse environmental effects that may be caused by the proposal are insignificant or mitigable with known technology, in which case the proposal may proceed or proceed with the mitigation, as the case may be;

    (d) the potentially adverse environmental effects that may be caused by the proposal are unknown, in which case the proposal shall either require further study and subsequent rescreening or reassessment or be referred to the Minister for public review by a Panel;

    (e) the potentially adverse environmental effects that may be caused by the proposal are significant, as determined in accordance with criteria developed by the Office in cooperation with the initiating department, in which case the proposal shall be referred to the Minister for public review by a Panel; or

(f) the potentially adverse environmental effects that may be caused by the proposal are unacceptable, in which case the proposal shall either be modified and subsequently rescreened or reassessed or abandoned.

13. Notwithstanding the determination concerning a proposal made pursuant to section 12, if public concern about the proposal is such that a public review is desirable, the initiating department shall refer the proposal to the Minister for public review by a Panel.

14. Where, in any case, the initiating department determines that mitigation or compensation measures could prevent any of the potentially adverse environmental effects of a proposal from becoming significant, the initiating department shall ensure that such measures are implemented.

15. The initiating department shall ensure

    (a) after a determination concerning a proposal has been made pursuant to section 12 or a referral concerning the proposal has been made pursuant to section 13, and

    (b) before any mitigation or compensation measures are implemented pursuant to section 13,

    that the public have access to the information on and the opportunity to respond to the proposal in accordance with the spirit and principles of the *Access to Information Act.*

16. The initiating department, in consultation with the Office, shall establish written procedures to be followed in order to make a determination under section 12 and shall provide the Office on a regular basis, with information, on its implementation of the Process with respect to the proposals for which it is the decision making authority.

17. The initiating department shall

    (a) ensure that federal-provincial, territorial and international agreements reflect the principles of the Process with respect to proposals for which it is the decision making authority; and

    (b) include in its program forecasts and annual estimates of the resources necessary to carry out the Process with respect to proposals.

Federal Environmental Assessment Review Office

18. It is the responsibility of the Office to

    (a) provide initiating departments with procedural guidelines for the screening of proposals and to provide general assistance for the development and installation of implementation procedures;

(b) assist the initiating department in the provision of information on and the solicitation of public response to proposals early enough in the planning stage that irrevocable decisions will not be taken before public opinion is heard;

(c) publish in summary form the public information provided to the Office by an initiating department on proposals for which it is the decision making authority and for which a determination under section 12 has been made; and

(d) inform the Minister on a periodic basis, in a report to be made public, on the implementation of the Process by initiating departments.

Other Departments

19. It is the role of every department that has specialist knowledge or responsibilities relevant to a proposal to

  (a) provide to the initiating department any available data, information or advice that the initiating department may request concerning

   (i) any regulatory requirements related to the project, and

   (ii) the environmental effects and the directly related social impacts of those effects; and

  (b) as appropriate, advocate the protection of the interests for which it is responsible.

Public Review

20. Where a determination concerning a proposal is made pursuant to paragraph 12(b), (d) or (e) or section 13, the initiating department shall refer the proposal to the Minister for public review.

21. The public review of a proposal under section 20 shall be conducted by an Environmental Assessment Panel, the members of which shall be appointed by the Minister.

22. The members of the Panel shall

  (a) be unbiased and free of any potential conflict of interest relative to the proposal under review;

  (b) be free of any political influence; and

  (c) have special knowledge and experience relevant to the anticipated technical, environmental and social effects of the proposal under review.

PART II

BACKGROUND

DISCOUNTING— DEALING WITH TIME

INTRODUCTION

Typical public sector projects such as dams, bridges, and hydroelectric facilities have similar life cycles of costs and benefits. Early in the life of a project, construction, architectural, engineering, and other capital costs are incurred, perhaps for several years. Only after the project has been built does society glean any benefit from it in the form of flood protection, irrigation, faster transportation, or cheaper power. However, this second stage can last decades, during which operating and maintenance costs may be relatively minor. Like factories, office buildings, and people, many public projects wear out; thus it is not unusual for a project to have a finite *economic life*. For example, planners believe that a bridge built across the Northumberland Strait to join New Brunswick and Prince Edward Island will last 100 years after construction; and the Rafferty Dam in Saskatchewan is expected to be serviceable for 50 years. In the final stage of a project's life, it may be that some of it can be sold for scrap. Or it could be that costs will be incurred if the project site must be returned to its pre-project state because of public safety or environmental considerations.

Analysts attempting to assess the economic viability of a project will, naturally, want to compare all of its benefits and costs whenever they occur during its economic life. Assuming that the analysts can measure all of the relevant benefits and costs of a project for each year of the project's life, they may be tempted to sum all of these benefits, and sum all of these costs, and then subtract the sum of costs from the sum of benefits. If the resulting dollar figure is positive, analysts may conclude that the project is economically viable and that society will be better off if it is built. If negative, they may draw the conclusion that the project is not worthwhile. If they do, they will be wrong.

Unfortunately, aggregating benefits and costs over time is not this easy: a fundamental danger is embedded in the process. A dollar value for, say,

1999 can be added to a dollar value for 2030 *only* if both values are measured in the same units. However, a dollar in 1999 is not worth the same as a dollar in 2030, not so much because of inflation but rather because society values dollars differently at different points in time. To sum them would be to add apples and oranges.

Yet we still want to aggregate costs and benefits even though they occur at different times. How else can we reach any conclusions regarding the merits of a particular project, or compare a project to another one that has a different stream of benefits and costs, or a different lifespan? Such conclusions can be reached, but the first step must be to express all costs and benefits in the same units; all must be measured in dollars as of a specific year. This procedure is called *discounting*, and the following example will demonstrate how it is performed.

FUTURE VALUES AND PRESENT VALUES

Meg McCafferty of North Battleford, Saskatchewan, has a decision to make. She has just won a lottery that offers her two choices: Option L, whereby she receives a lump sum (L_0) of $800,000 today; or Option I, whereby she takes her winnings in three instalments: $100,000 today ($I_0$), $300,000 a year from today (I_1), and $500,000 two years from today (I_2). Which option should she choose? Which has the highest value?

To simplify her problem, assume that interest income and lottery winnings are not taxed.

Meg knows that it would not be correct to compare the sum of the three instalments ($I_0 + I_1 + I_2$ = $900,000) to the single payment of $800,000; like most people, she is aware that receiving a dollar next year or the year after is not the same as receiving a dollar today. A dollar you can spend today is worth more than a dollar you have to wait until tomorrow to spend. What she must do is make the value of her options comparable by converting them into the same units.

Suppose that capital markets are perfect in the sense that Meg can borrow or save money at the same rate of interest, and suppose further that this rate of interest (denoted by i) does not change over time. Of course, these assumptions are heroic, but they allow us to concentrate more closely on the issue at hand. At a 10% rate of interest, $800,000 will grow to $880,000 ($L_0[1 + i]$) after one year and to $968,000 ($L_0[1 + i]^2$) two years from today. On the other hand, if she takes Option I and saves her first instalment, it will grow at 10% to $121,000 ($I_0[1 + i]^2$) after two years with interest compounding. Her second instalment will earn interest for one year and will be worth $330,000 ($I_1[1 + i]$) two years from today. Therefore, on the day she receives her third instalment (I_2), her nest egg will be $951,000 ($121,000 + $330,000 + $500,000).

Her two options can now be compared because both are stated as dollar amounts as of two years from today. The lump-sum option would be worth $968,000, whereas the instalment option would be worth only $951,000. Note, however, that this is true only if the interest rate she can earn on savings is 10%.

What she has calculated is the ***future value*** of each option. The subscripts used refer to the year a payment is received, generally denoted by t where t = 0 is the present, t = 1 is next year, and t = 2 is two years from now. The general formula for converting an amount today (X_0) into its future value after T years (X_T) using a constant interest rate (i) is $X_T = X_0(1+i)^T$. Thus, for the lump-sum option, $968,000 = $800,000(1.1)^2$.

For a stream of income (Y) lasting from year 0 to year N {Y_0, Y_1, Y_2, ... ,Y_N}, the future value (at t = N) is $Y_0(1 + i)^N + Y_1(1 + i)^{N-1} + Y_2(1 + i)^{N-2} + Y_3(1 + i)^{N-3} + ... + Y_{N-1}(1 + i) + Y_N$. Thus, for the instalment option using an interest rate of 10%, $951,000 = $100,000(1.1)^2 + $300,000(1.1) + $500,000$.

Note the importance of the interest rate used. At 5% interest, the future value of the lump-sum option (FV_L) is $882,000; at 15% interest, it is $1,058,000. At 5% interest, the future value of the instalment option (FV_I) is $925,250; at 15% interest, it is $977,250. Clearly, at an interest rate of 5%, Option I would yield a higher total than Option L after two years, whereas Option L would compound to a larger future value than Option I at interest rates of either 10% or 15%. One may verify that for all interest rates above 8.6%, the lump-sum option will yield a higher future value, whereas for interest rates below this threshold, the future value of the instalment option will be higher. This is evident in Figure 2.1, which illustrates the future value of each option as a function of the interest rate.

Although couched in an example, this general lesson should not be ignored: dollar values, regardless of when they occur, can be transformed into values as of some future year using simple compounding formulae. This means that dollar streams of different magnitudes and timing can be made comparable as of some specific future date.

The year chosen to compare any number of dollar streams is arbitrary. It need not be in the future. For project evaluation, cost-benefit analysts usually choose—as a matter of convenience only—the year the stream of costs and benefits attributable to a project begins. This year is treated as the "present" or the ***baseyear*** of the project and is denoted by t = 0. That is, analysts convert every cost and benefit in each year of a project's life into its ***present value*** and compare different dollar streams on this basis.

Returning to the lottery example, the lump-sum option consists of receiving $800,000 today. As today is the present, the present value of this option (PV_L) is simply $800,000. The instalment plan option consists of I_0, I_1, and I_2. I_0 is paid today, so its present value is $100,000. I_1 ($300,000) will be received a year from today, so it must be discounted one year to the present. Its present

FIGURE 2.1   Future Values

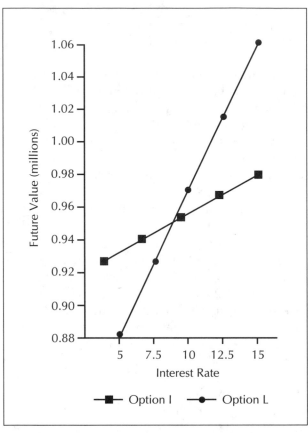

value is calculated by $I_1(1 + i)^{-1}$ which, using an interest (or *discount*) rate of 10%, yields $272,727. (Throughout this chapter, values will be rounded to the nearest dollar.) That is, $272,727 would grow to $300,000 in one year at a rate of interest of 10%. I_2 ($500,000) would have to be discounted backward in time two years to determine its present value—thus, $I_2(1 + i)^{-2}$, or $413,223. The present value of this option (PV_I) is simply the sum of the present values of its components: $PV_I = I_0 + I_1(1 + i)^{-1} + I_2(1 + i)^{-2} = \$785,950$.

Note that using present values to compare options gives exactly the same result as comparing future values as long as the same discount rate is used. In addition, which option has the higher present value depends on the discount rate used. Whereas the present value of Option L is always $800,000, the present value of Option I is $839,229 if the interest rate is 5%, and is $738,941 if the rate is 15%. Also, the lump-sum option will have the higher present value for interest rates greater than 8.6%, whereas the instalment

FIGURE 2.2   Present Values

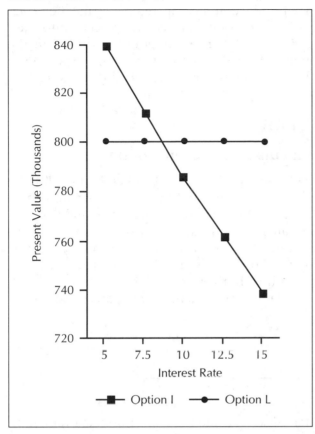

option will yield a higher present value for all interest rates below this threshold. This is illustrated in Figure 2.2, in which the present value of each option has been calculated as a function of the interest rate. Note, too, that at a given rate of interest, it does not matter whether present values or future values are used to rank these options: they yield the same answer.

Be aware that in choosing a particular option, Meg is not committing herself to a particular expenditure pattern. If she chooses to accept the lump sum of $800,000 today, she could spend it all now, let it compound for as many years as she likes, or spend it gradually over whatever time horizon she chooses. Any expenditure plan is feasible as long as its present value does not exceed $800,000. The expenditure pattern she chooses will depend on how much she prefers present consumption relative to future consumption. (One potential choice is the subject of an exercise at the end of this chapter.)

Again, dollar values can be moved backward or forward through time to a specific year so that they may be added and compared. As a rule, however, economists transform dollar values in whatever year they occur into their present values (as of t = 0). Because dollar amounts to be realized in the future are made smaller when transformed into present values, the procedure is called discounting and the interest rate used is called the discount rate.

DISCOUNTING FORMULAE

General Formulae for Calculating Present Value

Consider a stream of dollar values that begins at t = 0 and ends at t = T. If we call this stream X, it consists of X_0, X_1, X_2 through to X_{T-2}, X_{T-1} and, finally, X_T. Some of these values (X_t) may be positive, others negative, and still others zero. Now, let the discount rate during the first year (t = 0 to t = 1) be i_1, and let other interest rates over this time horizon (i_2, i_3, i_4 through to i_T) be defined similarly. In this way we allow for the possibility that the discount rate will not be constant over this time horizon.

The general formula for calculating the present value of this stream is

$$PV_X = X_0 + \frac{X_1}{(1+i_1)} + \frac{X_2}{(1+i_1) \cdot (1+i_2)} + \frac{X_3}{(1+i_1) \cdot (1+i_2) \cdot (1+i_3)} + \ldots$$
$$+ \frac{X_T}{(1+i_1) \cdot (1+i_2) \cdot (1+i_3) \cdot \ldots \cdot (1+i_T)}$$

Usually, however, a constant discount rate is used for project evaluation, which simplifies this formula considerably. At a constant discount rate i, the formula for calculating the present value of stream X reduces to

$$PV_X = X_0 + \frac{X_1}{1+i} + \frac{X_2}{(1+i)^2} + \frac{X_3}{(1+i)^3} + \ldots + \frac{X_T}{(1+i)^T}$$

For convenience, this can be written using a summation sign:

$$PV_X = \sum_{t=0}^{T} X_t \cdot (1+i)^{-t}$$

Be warned that throughout this chapter we use annual dollar values and annual discount rates for convenience only. This is usual for cost-benefit analysis but is quite arbitrary. Where circumstances warrant, any other time scale (daily, weekly, monthly, quarterly, and so on) can be used on the condition that the discount rate used is defined for the same time period. (The conversion of annual and monthly interest rates is the subject of an exercise at the end of this chapter.)

General Formulae for Calculating Future Value

The future value of the same dollar stream (as of year T) is very similar. For the constant-discount-rate case, each component is simply compounded to year T. The resulting formula is

$$FV_X = X_0(1+i)^T + X_1(1+i)^{T-1} + \ldots + X_{T-1}(1+i) + X_T$$

Note that future and present values are related according to $FV_X = PV_X(1+i)^T$.

Calculating the Future Value of a Constant Stream

Suppose that a person deposits R dollars in a savings account or RRSP every year from t = 1 to t = T (but not at t = 0), and that savings compound annually at a constant rate of interest, here denoted by r. What amount will this person have as soon as the final R dollars are deposited? What is being sought is the future value of a constant stream at a constant discount rate. Similar to the general formula for a future value, the future value in this special case is

$$FV_R = R(1+r)^{T-1} + R(1+r)^{T-2} + R(1+r)^{T-3} + \ldots + R(1+r) + R$$

This formula can be simplified by first multiplying both sides of the equation by $(1 + r)$ to form

$$FV_R(1+r) = R(1+r)^T + R(1+r)^{T-1} + R(1+r)^{T-2} \ldots + R(1+r)^2 + R(1+r)$$

Now, subtract FV_R from $FV_R(1 + r)$, noting that all but two right-hand-side terms cancel. The result, after simplifying the left-hand side of the equation, is

$$FV_R(r) = R(1+r)^T - R$$

Simplifying further yields the formula

$$FV_R = \frac{R[(1+r)^T - 1]}{r}$$

This can be a useful formula for people who wish to calculate what their savings will be at retirement age if they save a certain amount each year. For example, if T is the year that Nadine Belanger turns 65, and if she has saved $1,000 a year at 8% for 40 years, her last $1,000 deposit will bring the total to $259,057. Firms that sell RRSPs and the like sometimes refer to this as the "miracle of compound interest," although there is really nothing miraculous about it.

By rearranging this formula to

$$R = FV_R \cdot \frac{r}{(1+r)^T - 1}$$

Nadine could calculate how much she would have to save in each of these same 40 years to attain some target level of retirement wealth at year T. If her goal (FV_R) is $1 million, R will be $3,860 if her savings earn a rate of interest of 8%. What she has calculated is sometimes called a ***sinking fund***. Obviously, she will have to set aside less to attain the same goal if the period is longer than 40 years or if the interest rate is higher than 8%.

Calculating the Present Value of a Constant Stream

Although calculating the future value of a constant stream is useful for many personal applications, calculating its present value is more usual in project evaluation. Assume that an annual stream of A dollars begins at t = 1 (not at t = 0) and ends at t = T. At discount rate i, the present value of this stream (at t = 0) is

$$PV_A = A(1+i)^{-1} + A(1+i)^{-2} + A(1+i)^{-3} + \ldots + A(1+i)^{-(T-1)} + A(1+i)^{-T}$$

Multiplying both sides by (1 + i) to form $PV_A(1 + i)$, and subtracting PV_A from $PV_A(1 + i)$—similar to the future value case—yields

$$PV_A = \frac{A[1 - (1+i)^{-T}]}{i}$$

or, equivalently,

$$PV_A = A \cdot \frac{(1+i)^T - 1}{i(1+i)^T}$$

Rearranging the above and solving for A yields an ***annual amortization schedule***. For instance, a $100,000 mortgage at a rate of interest of 9.25% amortized over 25 years will require annual payments (beginning at t = 1) of $10,388. Another way of looking at this is to observe that an annuity which pays $10,388 annually for 25 years beginning at t = 1 has a present value of $100,000 when the discount rate is 9.25%.

Note that the above present value formula becomes very simple if this annual stream of A dollars beginning at t = 1 lasts forever (T → ∞):

$$PV_A = \frac{A}{i}$$

This formula should make a great deal of sense. If the interest rate is 10% and one had to set aside an amount of money today that would generate a payment of $8,000 per year forever beginning one year from today, the necessary amount would be $80,000.

If this infinite stream had started at t = 0, its present value would be the above *plus* A dollars to account for the first year's payment or receipt (at t = 0). If this stream had started at t = 5, its value as of t = 4 would be A/i, so to calculate its present value would require further discounting by the factor $(1 + i)^{-4}$—*not* $(1 + i)^{-5}$. Either general formula (for finite or infinite streams) always calculates the present value of the stream as of the year before the first payment is made or the first benefit is received.

Note, too, that the higher the discount rate, the smaller is the present value of this annuity. This should make sense, because the higher the interest rate, the less one would have to set aside initially in order to generate a given stream of A dollars annually.

An Example

The relationship between present and future values of a constant stream of money values is illustrated in Figure 2.3. A sum of $10 million is to be

FIGURE 2.3   An Example

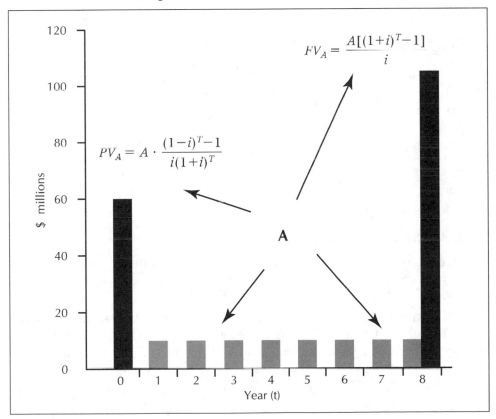

$$FV_A = \frac{A[(1+i)^T - 1]}{i}$$

$$PV_A = A \cdot \frac{(1-i)^T - 1}{i(1+i)^T}$$

received in each of eight years beginning at t = 1. The relevant formulae for calculating future and present values are shown.

Here A = $10 million and T = 8. To construct the graph, an interest rate of 7% (i = 0.07) was used. The resulting values are PV_A = $59.71 million and FV_A = $102.60 million . Note that $PV_A = FV_A \cdot (1+i)^{-T}$. That is, $59.71 million = $102.60 million $\cdot (1.07)^{-8}$.

SUMMARY

Being able to transform dollar values occurring in one year into dollar values as of a past or future year is necessary for cost-benefit analysis because projects typically have long economic lives. Fortuitously, the same techniques can be employed to calculate useful financial information: capitalized values, mortgage payments, and sinking funds.

Once the process of using a discount rate to move values backward and forward through time has been mastered, derivation of formulae from first principles to fit different circumstances becomes a simple technical exercise. Although calculation of net present values is the norm in cost-benefit analysis, an ability to calculate other values is required from time to time.

KEY TERMS

economic life
discounting
future value
baseyear
present value
sinking fund
annual amortization schedule

EXERCISES

2.1 Calculate the future value of each of Meg McCafferty's lottery options when the interest rate is 6% (i_1 = 0.06) during the first year and 10% (i_2 = 0.10) during the second year.

2.2 Calculate the present value of each of Meg McCafferty's lottery options when the interest rate is 6% during the first year and 10% during the second. Verify that the same option as in Exercise 2.1 is preferable.

2.3 Suppose that Meg McCafferty chooses Option L.

  a. At an annual interest rate of 10%, if she wants to spend these 800,000 dollars evenly over 10 years (10 payments) beginning next year, how much of it will she spend annually?

  b. At an annual interest rate of 10%, if she wants to spend this amount evenly over 10 years (10 payments) beginning immediately, how much of it will she spend annually?

2.4 a. You are considering taking out a 20-year mortgage of $100,000 at a monthly interest rate of 0.75% (i = 0.0075). Payments begin the month after you receive the mortgage. Calculate your monthly mortgage payment.

  b. If interest compounds monthly, what is the equivalent annual interest rate?

2.5 An aged relative has died and left you an inheritance consisting of an annual allowance of $1,000 beginning immediately and lasting another 25 years (for a total of 26 payments).

  a. The interest rate you can earn by saving this money is 5%. If you let this allowance accumulate, what amount will you have on the date of the last payment?

  b. Suppose that you are impatient to buy the most expensive car you can afford with your inheritance. You can borrow against your future inheritance payments at 11%. How much is your inheritance worth now, in the present?

CHAPTER 3

TIME-STREAM EVALUATION AND INVESTMENT CRITERIA

INTRODUCTION

A public sector project is *economically viable* if it makes society as a whole better off, and the data required to make this determination include assessments of social benefits, social costs, and a social discount rate. In the private sector, on the other hand, an investment project is *financially viable* if it is profitable for the firm undertaking it. Here the relevant data are private benefits (revenues), private costs, and the rate the firm chooses to discount future costs and revenues.

Although in special circumstances economic viability and financial viability can be the same, they are unlikely to be for the kinds of projects cost-benefit analysts usually assess. For example, a dam that offers flood protection generates no revenue because this protection is not sold. Although it would not be financially viable, it still generates social benefits and thus may be economically viable. Because social costs and benefits are more broadly defined than private ones, private sector project evaluation (or capital budgeting) is a special form of cost-benefit analysis.

In this chapter we do not dwell on the differences between economic and financial viability; we leave the measurement of social costs, benefits, and discount rates to later chapters. The issue we wish to address here is this: Given an appropriate discount rate, if analysts know the time stream of a project's benefits and costs, how do they determine whether the project is viable? Note that we do not distinguish the project in question as lying in the domain of the public sector or the private sector because, for the purposes of this chapter, it does not matter. We are concerned with investment criteria—the viability and ranking of projects—not with the type of investment itself. (Because the distinction between public and private is not relevant at this stage, readers may find it easier to cope with the following material if they think in terms of a firm trying to make a financial decision that involves a stream of revenues and costs over some time horizon.)

Let us think, then, of an analyst being handed a set of data for assessment. The time horizon of the project, denoted by T, will be determined (either finite or infinite), as will a stream of benefits from the starting date of the project, t = 0, until its completion. This stream will be denoted by {B_0, B_1, B_2, ... , B_T}. B_t, the benefit in year t, may be positive or zero. The cost of the project in year t will be denoted by C_t, and the stream of project costs will be given by {C_0, C_1, C_2, ... , C_T}. Costs, too, may be zero or positive in any time period. With this information, we can define the net benefit attributable to a project in year t as $B_t - C_t$, and the time stream of net benefits over the project's life as {$B_0 - C_0$, $B_1 - C_1$, $B_2 - C_2$, ... , $B_T - C_T$}. The net benefit in any year can, of course, be zero, positive, or negative. The last datum required is the discount rate to be used for project evaluation. This will be denoted by i, and we will assume (although we need not) that it is constant over the life of the project.

What do we do with this data? How can we use it to assess the viability of a project or to rank it among other potential investment projects? In practice, several investment criteria are used in both the private and the public sector. The choice sometimes depends on specific circumstances. At other times, it seems to be a matter of ignorance and/or tradition. What follows is a critical examination of some of these possible investment criteria.

THE NET PRESENT VALUE CRITERION

To Assess the Viability of Projects

Given the above data, we can calculate the present value of the stream of net benefits attributable to the project under consideration. If we call this the net present value of the project, NPV, its general formula is

$$NPV = (B_0 - C_0) + \frac{(B_1 - C_1)}{(1+i)} + \frac{(B_2 - C_2)}{(1+i)^2} + ... + \frac{(B_T - C_T)}{(1+i)^T}$$

What does it mean if the net present value of a project is positive? To answer this question, consider a simple private sector example where $B_0 = 0$, $C_0 = \$100$ million, and $B_t - C_t = \$15$ million annually beginning at t = 1 and lasting forever (T → ∞). That is, a $100 million outlay this year generates a never-ending annual net benefit of $15 million beginning next year. Further assume that capital markets are perfect in that the firm can borrow and lend money at the same rate of interest, here assumed to be 10% (i = 0.1). Also assume for the moment that this firm has $100 million at its disposal with which to finance the initial outlay.

Recall from Chapter 2 that the present value of a constant annual stream of A dollars beginning at t = 1 and lasting forever at a constant rate of interest (i) is A/i. Therefore, the net present value of this project (in millions of dollars) is

$$NPV = -100 + \frac{15}{0.1} = 50$$

thus positive.

Should the firm proceed? As usual in economics, this depends on what alternatives are available to the firm. If it spends $100 million on this project, the possibility of using that money for any other purpose is precluded: there is an opportunity cost. Even if this project is the only real investment opportunity available to this firm, it could always save this $100 million and earn a rate of interest of 10%. If it does, this sum could generate a stream of interest payments of $10 million per year forever beginning at t = 1. The present value (NPV^*) of this alternative in millions of dollars is

$$NPV^* = -100 + \frac{10}{0.1} = 0$$

That is, the present value of $100 million is $100 million. Saving any sum merely maintains it in terms of its present value. No surplus or profit is earned.

On the other hand, if the firm undertakes this project, a real investment opportunity, it will earn a profit (measured as a present value) of $50 million. Thus the return from the project exceeds, by $50 million, what the firm could earn by saving that money. Put another way, note that $150 million— not $100 million—would have to be saved at t = 0 to achieve the same time stream of net revenues that the project generates.

If this were a public project, the present value of social benefits would exceed the present value of social costs by this same amount. Society would reap a net benefit by undertaking the project. This is the essence of the net present value criterion.

What if the firm has to borrow $100 million to finance this project? This does not change the answer, because the opportunity cost of these funds is already embedded in the calculation. The present value of the loan is simply C_0. Whether the firm uses its own funds or borrows them, the same opportunity cost is incurred (given our assumption of perfect capital markets). When the firm borrows, this cost is obvious. When it uses its own funds, at the very least it forgoes the opportunity to earn interest on them.

A positive net present value thus indicates that a project is viable. It is worthwhile to undertake because, if private, it is profitable, and if public, it bestows a net benefit on society. If the net present value of a public sector project is zero, undertaking the project will neither enhance nor diminish social welfare.

Firms avoid unprofitable projects (NPV < 0). As governments sometimes undertake projects that have negative present values, we should make the implications of doing so clear.[1] When a public sector project with a negative net present value is undertaken, the resources used are worth more to society than what is produced. Social costs exceed social benefits, with the result that society as a whole is made worse off. Society's scarce resources have been wasted.

Why do governments undertake projects that are not viable according to this criterion? This is a troublesome question. It may be ignorance, or a rejection of the criterion, or it may simply be that political objectives override economic ones. The point here is that when a project with a net present value of, say, −$750 million is undertaken, the wealth of the country is decreased by $750 million. This is akin to reducing Toronto's SkyDome to rubble or dynamiting all government buildings on Parliament Hill. Wealth is destroyed.

Ranking Projects According to Net Present Value

Ranking Mutually Exclusive Projects

Every project with a positive net present value is economically viable and, if undertaken, will enhance social welfare. That being said, there are two situations where not all viable projects can be undertaken and some ranking or ordering of priorities is necessary.

The first situation arises when different projects are *mutually exclusive*—that is, when the construction of one project precludes proceeding with any other project under consideration. Example: A government is considering building a dam on a river to enhance irrigation and to provide flood protection, and does not know which of a small dam, a medium-size dam, or a large dam would be best. Obviously, only one dam can be built. The way to proceed would be to treat each dam as a separate project and to calculate the net present value of each. The time stream of costs and benefits of these dams may differ substantially, especially if construction time varies greatly according to size. Once calculated, the dam project with the highest net present value will be ranked first, and the dam project with the lowest net present value will be ranked last. Of course, if the net present value of all three projects is negative, a fourth mutually exclusive alternative—construct no dam—will dominate.

Another example of mutually exclusive projects involves choosing the optimal starting date for a project. Consider a project that involves widening a roadway from two lanes to four lanes. If population and traffic patterns are changing according to some trend, it may be that the net present value of starting the project in 1998 is different from the net present value of starting the project in 1999, 2000, or 2001, when all net present values are measured as of the same baseyear. Obviously, if the road is widened in 1999, the same project cannot be undertaken in 2001. In these circumstances, it is appropriate to treat the starting dates as mutually exclusive and to choose the alternative with the highest positive net present value.

Using the net present value criterion to rank mutually exclusive projects presents no unusual problems. When we choose the project that generates the highest positive net present value, society is guaranteed the largest increase in social welfare.

Ranking with a Budgetary (Capital) Constraint

Although every project with a positive net present value is economically viable, a government may not have the fiscal wherewithal to finance all of them. Consider Table 3.1, which shows the characteristics of ten (not mutually exclusive) projects. Dollar figures are measured in millions, and PV_B and PV_C denote the present value of benefits and costs, respectively. These projects are ranked from most to least expensive (perhaps from largest to smallest). Note that each is economically viable.

Now suppose that the government is unable to undertake all of these projects because of a budget (or capital) constraint. For illustration, let that budget constraint be $100 million. That is, the government is only prepared to commit itself to undertaking a project or group of projects for which the present value of costs does not exceed this amount.

TABLE 3.1 Ranking Without a Budgetary Constraint

Project	PV_B	PV_C	NPV	Rank
A	200	100	100	1
B	170	90	80	2
C	155	80	75	4
D	146	70	76	3
E	120	60	60	5
F	90	50	40	7
G	85	40	45	6
H	57	30	27	9
I	55	20	35	8
J	20	10	10	10

Because not all economically viable projects can be undertaken, ranking alternatives becomes important. The last column of Table 3.1 ranks these projects according to net present value. Project A ranks highest on this basis, so a government may decide to proceed with it. If it does, its budget will be exhausted and no other project will be possible.

This method of ranking is fundamentally flawed, because the concept of opportunity cost has been ignored. Letting the government's $100 million earn interest is not the next-best alternative use of these funds in this case. By choosing Project A, we would be forgoing the net benefits to society that another feasible project or combination of projects would have generated. Ranking projects according to the net present value of each fails to account for this.

The correct procedure when a capital constraint exists is to examine all alternative ways of spending the available funds. For instance, Project A is feasible, but one alternative would be to undertake both Project B ($90 million) and Project J ($10 million). The ten combinations of Projects A through J that would just satisfy the government's budget constraint and are shown in Table 3.2.

Notice that when combinations of projects rather than individual projects are ranked in this manner, Project A, although the best individual project, ranks only seventh-best. Undertaking the *combination* of Projects D, I, and J would be the best way for the government to spend its $100 million.

Where a government budget constraint exists, the proper procedure is to rank according to net present value all combinations of projects that satisfy the constraint. For every budget constraint, there can be a different ranking. Although this procedure can be tedious, it is the only way to ensure that the project or combination of projects chosen yields society the largest net benefit possible.

TABLE 3.2   Ranking With a Budgetary Constraint

Project Combinations	PV_B	PV_C	NPV	Rank
A	200	100	100	7
B and J	190	100	90	10
C and I	210	100	110	3
D and H	203	100	103	5
D, I, and J	221	100	121	1
E and G	205	100	105	4
E, H, and J	197	100	97	8
F, G, and J	195	100	95	9
F, H, and I	202	100	102	6
G, H, I, and J	217	100	117	2

THE BENEFIT-COST RATIO CRITERION

To Assess the Viability of Projects

The general formula for calculating the net present value of a project is

$$NPV = (B_0 - C_0) + \frac{(B_1 - C_1)}{(1+i)} + \frac{(B_2 - C_2)}{(1+i)^2} + \ldots + \frac{(B_T - C_T)}{(1+i)^T}$$

which may be written as

$$NPV = \sum_{t=0}^{T} \frac{(B_t - C_t)}{(1+i)^t} = \sum_{t=0}^{T} \frac{B_t}{(1+i)^t} - \sum_{t=0}^{T} \frac{C_t}{(1+i)^t} = PV_B - PV_C$$

A popular investment criterion involves calculating the benefit-cost ratio of a project, PV_B/PV_C. If the net present value of a project is positive, its benefit-cost ratio must be greater than one. This criterion can be used to assess the economic viability of projects. Net present value and benefit-cost ratio criteria are equivalent in this regard. If the ratio is less than one, a project's net present value must be negative, and an analyst will conclude that it is not viable.

Ranking Projects According to Benefit-Cost Ratios

Ranking Mutually Exclusive Projects

Although the benefit-cost ratio criterion can be used to determine the economic viability of a particular project, it does not rank projects well. Table 3.3 is Table 3.1 augmented by two columns to show the benefit-cost ratios of Projects A through J, and how this criterion would rank them.

TABLE 3.3   Ranking by Benefit-Cost Ratio

Project	PV_B	PV_C	NPV	Rank	B/C	B/C Rank
A	200	100	100	1	2.00	4
B	170	90	80	2	1.89	9
C	155	80	75	4	1.94	7
D	146	70	76	3	2.09	3
E	120	60	60	5	2.00	4
F	90	50	40	7	1.80	10
G	85	40	45	6	2.13	2
H	57	30	27	9	1.90	8
I	55	20	35	8	2.75	1
J	20	10	10	10	2.00	4

Now assume that these projects are mutually exclusive; they may be different-sized dams or airports, such that if one is built, none of the other nine can be. If we were to decide which project to construct on the basis of the benefit-cost ratio criterion, Project I would be chosen. If the net present value criterion were used, Project A would be chosen. Different criteria yield different answers. Which is correct?

The basic problem with the benefit-cost ratio criterion is that it cannot rank projects rationally when they differ according to scale. Here, Project A is five times more costly to construct than Project I so, likely, it is on the order of five times larger. If Project A is built, society will reap a net benefit of $100 million, while if Project I is constructed, society will gain a surplus of only $35 million. Project I does not contribute as much to the well-being of society.

A common argument is, "Yes, but Project I costs only $20 million, so society saves $80 million." This is true, but we should consider the value of this saving to society. As only one project can be built—they are mutually exclusive—the next-best alternative use of this money would be to save it at the going discount rate. It would earn interest, but the present value of this benefit would be just $80 million. That is, the present value of any amount saved is just the amount saved. Its value is maintained, but no surplus is created.

To make this clear, consider making Projects A and I comparable by treating Project I as a combination-project: part project ($20 million) and part saving ($80 million). It is now scaled to the same cost as Project A. The present value of its benefits would be $135 million ($55 million plus $80 million), and the present value of its costs would be $100 million ($20 million plus $80 million), the result being a net present value of $35 million.

Note that the net present value of Project I is still only $35 million, combination-project or not. Only if we actually built Project I five times over would it dominate Project A. This, of course, is impossible, since these "duplicates" would also be mutually exclusive. To summarize: using the benefit-cost ratio criterion to rank mutually exclusive projects can lead to poor investment decisions if our objective is to maximize social well-being.

Ranking with a Budgetary (Capital) Constraint

It is sometimes thought that the benefit-cost ratio criterion will rank projects correctly if a budget constraint is in force. This is not true. Assume now that Projects A through J are *not* mutually exclusive, and reimpose a capital constraint of $100 million. The benefit-cost ratio ranking (Table 3.3) would lead us to build Project I first and Project G second; together, these would exhaust $60 million of the budget. Project D is ranked third, but is too expensive, leaving us with Project J, which costs only $10 million. The next-highest-ranked affordable project is Project H. Projects I, G, and J plus H exactly exhaust the available funds and yield a total net present value of just $117 million.

However, from Table 3.2, constructing the combination of Projects D, I, and J— for the same $100 million—would yield society a net benefit of $121 million. Using the benefit-cost ratio criterion would lead us to choose an inferior combination of projects.

Returning to Table 3.2, note that if we were to rank all feasible combinations of projects using benefit-cost ratios, the result would be the same ranking as that given by the net present value criterion. The ratio criterion works in this case because all combinations of projects are of the same scale, $100 million. This, however, is a special case, and because of its pitfalls we recommend that the benefit-cost ratio criterion not be used. Indeed, as calculating it requires the same information as for calculating a project's net present value, there is no advantage to using it—only the risk of being led astray.

THE INTERNAL RATE OF RETURN CRITERION

The internal rate of return of a project is that discount rate which causes the net present value of the net benefit stream to be zero. If we denote it by ρ, it is the value which, for the general case, solves

$$0 = (B_0 - C_0) + \frac{(B_1 - C_1)}{(1+\rho)} + \frac{(B_2 - C_2)}{(1+\rho)^2} + \ldots + \frac{(B_T - C_T)}{(1+\rho)^T}$$

A project's internal rate of return is related to its net present value in the following way (where the discount rate is denoted by i):

If $\rho > i$, NPV > 0;

if $\rho < i$, NPV < 0; and,

if $\rho = i$, NPV = 0.

Recall our example involving a $100 million outlay at t = 0 that generates a never-ending annual net benefit of $15 million beginning at t = 1. Using a discount rate of 10%, the net present value of this project is $50 million. To calculate its internal rate of return, $0 = -100 + 15/\rho$. Therefore, ρ is equal to 0.15 (15%). The internal rate of return thus has a straightforward interpretation: the firm in question can earn either a 15% rate of return by investing in this project, or a 10% rate of interest by saving the same amount. The choice is clear: for a project that is not viable—say, with an internal rate of return of 6%—if the firm must pay 10% on borrowed funds (or save the necessary funds at an interest rate of 10%), it would be better off to reject this project.

Because the decision comes down to comparing two rates of return, ρ and the discount rate, the internal rate of return criterion is quite popular. It is easy to understand. Unfortunately, as with the benefit-cost ratio criterion, its use is not problem-free.

In what follows, we use simple examples to demonstrate that it is quite possible for the internal rate of return criterion to give no meaningful answer, or to rank projects differently from the net present value criterion. This presents difficulties, because the net present value criterion is consistent with maximizing social well-being. The internal rate of return criterion is not recommended for use. Still, many people in both the private and the public sector still use the internal rate of return criterion to make investment decisions, so it is important for analysts to be aware of its failings.[2]

Problem 1: Multiple Discount Rates In the general formulation of net present value, it is possible to have a different discount rate in each year of the project's life (i_1, i_2, i_3, ... , i_T). It is more common to use a single discount rate for project appraisal; even so, if a government's monetary policy is causing real interest rates to change over time in some predictable fashion, the use of variable rates is justified. This raises the possibility, however, that a project's internal rate of return could be greater than some of these discount rates and less than others. Use of this criterion requires that ρ be compared to a single discount rate—but which one?

Problem 2: Multiple ρs In our simple example above, ρ was unique, yet this need not be the case. Consider a project that lasts only three periods where $B_0 - C_0 = -\$1$ million; $B_1 - C_1 = +\$2,200,000$; and $B_2 - C_2 = -\$1,207,500$. The internal rate of return of this project is the solution to the following quadratic equation:

$$-1,000,000 + \frac{2,200,000}{1+\rho} - \frac{1,207,500}{(1+\rho)^2} = 0$$

Unfortunately, there are two solutions, 5% and 15%. Even if the discount rate is unique, to which of these internal rates of return should we compare it?

As it turns out, the net present value of this project is positive for all discount rates between 5% and 15%, and is negative for all discount rates higher or lower than this range. However, just calculating the internal rate of return would not reveal this fact. In the presence of multiple ρs, the only way to appraise the economic viability of a project is to retreat to the net present value criterion.

The existence of multiple internal rates of return is not uncommon, because such rates often are the roots of quadratic or higher-ordered equations. An intuitive explanation for why the above project has two internal rates of return is that the net benefit stream switches sign from negative to positive to negative again. This is not unusual, especially for any project that involves clean-up costs at the end of its economic life. The greater the number of times any net benefit stream changes sign, the greater the number of internal rates of return. Indeed, if the net benefit stream of a project changes sign, say, four times, it is possible for the project to have as many as four different internal rates of return. A project such as starting a ferry service may have multiple internal rates of return because major refitting will be required periodically. If the cost of this is large, the net benefit in the years of refitting may be negative. Thus, this net benefit stream may be generally positive, but punctuated in some periods with negative values. Generally, every switch of signs can add another internal rate of return solution.

Problem 3: Bias to Short-lived Projects   Consider the following two projects. Project R is a two-period project involving an outlay of $10 million at t = 0 in return for $13.5 million at t = 1. Project S lasts forever. The same outlay of $10 million at t = 0 generates an infinite stream of $1.08 million in net benefits beginning at t = 1. Using a discount rate of 8%, the net present values of these projects are

$$\text{NPV}_R = -10 + 13.5/1.08 = \$2.5 \text{ million}$$

and

$$\text{NPV}_S = -10 + 1.08/0.08 = \$3.5 \text{ million}$$

On the basis of the net present value criterion, Project S would be preferred to Project R.

Solving for internal rates of return,

$$-10 + 13.5/(1+\rho_R) = 0, \text{ which yields } \rho_R = 35\%$$

and

$$-10 + 1.08/\rho_S = 0, \text{ which yields } \rho_S = 10.8\%$$

On the basis of the internal rate of return criterion, Project R would be preferred.

This ranking problem can have serious implications, especially if these projects are mutually exclusive or if decision-makers must deal with a $10 million budget constraint. If the internal rate of return criterion were used in this situation, society would forgo the superior project, S.

Problem 4: Bias Against Large Projects   Project X costs $10 million at t = 0 and generates an annual net benefit of $2 million beginning at t = 1 and lasting forever. Project Y is ten times as large, costing $100 million and generating an annual net benefit stream of $15 million beginning at t = 1 and lasting forever.

Calculating internal rates of return, $\rho_X = 20\%$ and $\rho_Y = 15\%$. If society's discount rate is, for example, 10%, both projects are viable. If Projects X and Y are mutually exclusive, X will be chosen over Y on the basis of the internal rate of return criterion.

However, when net present values (in millions of dollars) are calculated, $NPV_X = 10$ and $NPV_Y = 50$. Again, both are viable, but Project Y will be preferred to Project X on the basis of the net present value criterion.

The essence of this problem is that the internal rate of return criterion, like the benefit-cost ratio criterion, does not account for the opportunity cost of investment funds. Here, Project X would only be superior to Project Y if it could be repeated ten times, each time earning the same internal rate of return. However, this is not possible for mutually exclusive projects. If Project X is chosen, society will forgo a net benefit of $40 million, which is the difference between NPV_X and NPV_Y.

Problem 5: Bias Regarding the Timing of Benefits   Consider two projects, each of the same scale and time horizon. Project W's time stream of net benefits in millions of dollars is the following: -50 at t = 0, +85.6 at t = 1, and 0 at t = 2. Over the same three time periods, the time stream of net benefits for Project Z is -50, 0, and 100. Applying a social discount rate of 7%, $NPV_W = $30 million and $NPV_Z = $37.3 million. Under the net present value criterion, Project Z would be preferred to Project W.

The internal rate of return criterion, however, would reverse this ranking. Here, $\rho_W = 71.2\%$ whereas $\rho_Z = 41.4\%$: Project W would be preferred.

The problem in this instance is that the internal rate of return criterion is biased toward projects that provide benefits early in their economic lives as opposed to later. Calculation of a net present value converts all net benefits to their value as of t = 0, thereby preventing this bias—dollar values are transformed through time automatically.

To demonstrate that Project Z is superior, consider the project manager, at t = 1, borrowing $85.6 million against the future earnings of Project Z. At t = 2, this amount plus interest at 7% ($91.6 million) would have to be repaid out of the $100 million net benefit in that period. This act would transform Project Z's time stream of net benefits from {-50, 0, 100} to {-50, 85.6, 8.4} expressed in millions of dollars. Now compare this altered time stream—which has exactly the same net present value as the original!—with that of Project W, {-50, 85.6, 0}. The superiority of Project Z will be obvious.

OTHER INVESTMENT CRITERIA

The above three criteria are the ones most often used for public sector project evaluation. There are several others besides, which are used mainly in private sector investment decisions. Although their use may not be advisable, two additional criteria, which are sometimes used when uncertainty is of major concern, are described below.

The Cut-off Period Criterion

Given the uncertainty inherent in any investment project, a firm may be worried about the length of time it takes for its initial investment to be recouped. When it "short-lists" its investment alternatives, a firm may adhere to a rule that any project which does not recoup its initial cost within a speci-fied number of years will not be considered. If this limit is six years, the firm is said to have established a *cut-off period* of six years. The firm's rationale may be that it has confidence in its short-term forecasts of the returns to vari-ous projects, but lacks faith in predictions for years beyond this time-span.

Using a cut-off period is one way of dealing with uncertainty. Certainly, most people would agree that forecasts concerning next year are likely to be more accurate than those for ten years from now. Nevertheless, it is obvious that a firm adopting this decision rule may pass up projects that, over a longer period of time, will be more profitable. Presumably, firms using this criterion are aware of this possibility but are willing to pass on such oppor-tunities in exchange for less uncertainty.

Another reason a cut-off period may be used is because of legislation. For instance, a firm may be considering buying the patent (production rights) for a new product. If it makes this purchase, the firm will enjoy monopoly profits for the life of the patent only, not for the economic life of whatever factory is required to produce the new product. For example, if this period is seventeen years, a cut-off period of this duration may be appropriate.

The Pay-back Period Criterion

The *pay-back period* criterion is similar to the cut-off period criterion. Given a choice among projects, a firm employing this rule will favour the project that recoups the initial investment expenditure in the shortest period of time.

Table 3.4 below shows the time stream of net benefits of Projects K and L. According to the (not discounted) pay-back period criterion, Project K will be preferred to Project L because its initial outlay for $10 million will be recovered within three years, whereas the same expenditure for Project L would not be recouped until $t = 4$. Note that if a cut-off period of three years were the firm's policy, Project L would not even be considered.

TABLE 3.4   Net Benefits ($ millions)

$t =$	0	1	2	3	4	5	6	7	8	9	10
Project K	-10	2	3	5	5	5	0	0	0	0	0
Project L	-10	2	2	3	3	4	4	4	4	4	4

The drawback of using the pay-back period criterion is that the net benefits of alternative investments occurring after the preferred project's pay-back period are discounted entirely. It is noteworthy that, using a discount rate of 10%, the net present value of Project K is $4.58 million, whereas that of Project L is $9.67 million.

SUMMARY

A number of investment criteria are available to analysts. For public sector decision-making, however, the net present value criterion is the most suitable because it is consistent with maximizing social well-being. Injudicious use of the benefit-cost ratio and internal rate of return criteria can lead analysts astray. Indeed, when these criteria yield correct results, they mirror the net present value criterion. Note also that the same information is required regardless of which of these three criteria is applied. As using one criterion is no more convenient than using another, it is a simple matter of prudence to employ the net present value criterion in order to avoid the potential pitfalls of the others.

It is important to interpret carefully the net present value of a public sector project. If net present value is positive, the benefits of the project will exceed the value of the resources used in their next-best alternative uses. If negative, scarce resources will be wasted on the project, in that society will be forgoing their employment in ways that would have benefited society more.

KEY TERMS

economically viable

financially viable

cut-off period

pay-back period

EXERCISES

For Questions 3.1, 3.2, and 3.3 below, consider two projects, A and B. The time profile of net benefits of Project A, for which T = 17, is shown in Table 3.5. Project B's net benefits are −$200 million at t = 0, −$100 million at t = 1, then $43 million per year forever (T → ∞) beginning at t = 2.

TABLE 3.5   Questions 3.1–3.3

PROJECT A Year (t)	PROJECT A Net Benefit ($ million)
0	−235
1	−200
2	10
3	20
4	40
5	60
6	60
7	60
8	60
9	60
10	60
11	60
12	60
13	60
14	60
15	60
16	60
17	10

3.1 To observe the relationship between present value and the discount rate used, calculate PV_A using discount rates of 4%, 7%, and 10%.

3.2 Calculate PV_B using discount rates of 9%, 10%, and 11%.

3.3 To examine the sensitivity of present value to project life, recalculate PV_B at 10% but assume that the stream of annual benefits ($43 million) beginning at t = 2 lasts only to t = 100. Repeat this exercise for the cases when this stream ends at t = 75, t = 50, and t = 25.

For Questions 3.4, 3.5, and 3.6, consider two projects, C and D. The time profile of costs and benefits of Project C (for which T = 17) is shown in Table 3.6. Project D is much simpler. The stream of costs is $100 million at t = 0, $50 million at t = 1, and 0 thereafter. Project D's stream of benefits begins at t = 2 and is $23.22 million annually from that year forever.

3.4 Calculate the benefit-cost ratios of Projects C and D using discount rates of 4%, 7%, and 10%. Note how the ranking of these projects changes with the rate used.

3.5 Calculate the net present values of Projects C and D using discount rates of 4%, 7%, and 10%.

TABLE 3.6   Questions 3.4–3.6

Year (t)	Benefits ($ millions)	Costs ($ millions)
0	0	135
1	0	125
2	160	150
3	160	140
4	160	120
5	160	100
6	160	100
7	160	100
8	160	100
9	160	100
10	160	100
11	160	100
12	160	100
13	160	100
14	160	100
15	160	100
16	160	100
17	160	150

3.6 Calculate the internal rates (!) of return of Projects C and D. Note how the projects are ranked using this criterion compared to the rankings in Questions 3.4 and 3.5.

ENDNOTES

1. Governments may proceed with nonviable projects for a variety of reasons. For example, Prince Edward Island was guaranteed a year-round transportation link with the mainland when it entered Confederation in 1873. Although it may be true that no transportation option—ferries, a bridge, a tunnel, and so on—has a positive net present value, one must be chosen in order to satisfy the terms of the legislation. In such a circumstance, we would wish to choose the option with the smallest negative net present value. Governments sometimes support projects with negative net present values for what many people consider less valid grounds.

2. For a classic treatment of this topic, see Feldstein & Flemming (1964).

A REVIEW OF BASIC MICROECONOMICS

INTRODUCTION

Most factors of production used to build public sector projects are purchased in input markets. Similarly, some projects produce goods and services that are sold in output markets. These reasons alone would warrant a brief review of how competitive markets operate, and their properties. Other issues worth addressing as relevant to cost-benefit analysis are these: how decisions are made "at the margin," the price mechanism, and the concept of opportunity cost.

The conditions necessary for perfect competition are these:

1. The good or service is homogeneous; the output of one producer is in no way different from that of any other producer, nor is it perceived to be different. There are no questions regarding quality, and information concerning the technology used to produce the good or service is known perfectly and is available to all. Also, the commodity is a private good— that is, it exhibits rivalry in consumption. Thus, if one person consumes a unit of it, another person cannot consume that same unit, and individuals not paying for the item can be excluded from consuming it.

2. So many firms produce the good or service that no single firm has any control over its market price and the possibility of collusion is precluded. In other words, firms are *price-takers*.

3. So many households consume the good or service that no one household can manipulate the price it pays through its consumption decisions. Thus, households also behave as price-takers.

4. Firms are free to enter and exit the industry at will. There are no barriers to entry or exit; this ensures that a marginal firm earns only normal (zero) economic profits in long-run equilibrium.

An understanding of market-determined prices is necessary if we are to recognize and assess the costs and benefits of policies and projects. So is an understanding of the welfare properties of competitive markets. Even when the above competitive conditions do not hold, these properties serve as a useful benchmark for discussing public goods, economic externalities, and instances of market failure.

A COMPETITIVE OUTPUT MARKET

Demand and Marginal Benefit

Consider Figure 4.1, which shows a simple market diagram. The supply and demand curves are marked S and D, respectively. Output per period of time—a day, a week, a year, or any other suitable measure of time—is measured along the abscissa, and price per unit (P) is measured along the ordinate.

FIGURE 4.1   A Competitive Output Market

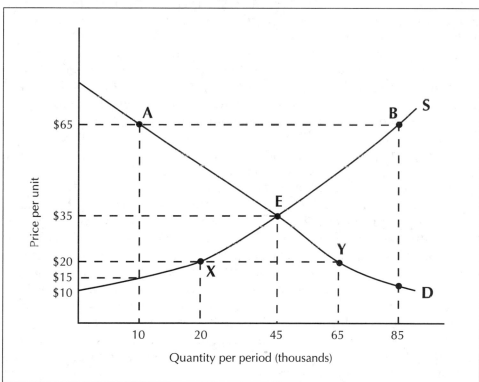

The demand curve shows the quantity consumers are willing and able to purchase at each price. So at $65 per unit, consumers will demand 10,000 units per period (point A), whereas at $20 per unit they will want to purchase 65,000 units (point Y). Households are assumed to be *utility maximizers*: the quantity a household demands at a particular price is the quantity that maximizes its utility (well-being) given its income, preferences, and the prices of other goods and services. The market demand curve shown is simply the horizontal summation of individual households' demand curves for the product. That is, it is formed by adding up every household's demand for the good at each price. Notice that as price rises, the quantity demanded falls; this is because consumers cannot afford as many units and because they will be inclined to switch consumption to substitute goods that are now relatively cheaper. Households are well aware that a dollar spent on one commodity is a dollar that cannot be spent on another.

On the diagram, note also that total expenditure on this good—and thus producers' total revenue—increases from $650,000 to $1,300,000 per period if the price of this good falls from $65 to $20 per unit. Here the proportional change in quantity demanded exceeds the proportional change in price, indicating that the demand for this good is quite sensitive to this price change. A measure of this sensitivity is the commodity's price elasticity of demand, which is the ratio of these proportional changes (−1.385).[1] This should suggest why total expenditure on this good increases when this price change occurs. Because the absolute value of this elasticity is greater than 1, demand is **price elastic** (or simply **elastic**), and a decrease in price will cause total expenditure on it to increase. (The reverse also holds.) If the price elasticity of this good has an absolute value of less than 1, demand for this good will be said to be (price) **inelastic**. If this is the case, demand will be relatively insensitive to price changes, and a fall in price will cause total expenditure on it to *decrease*. (The reverse also holds.)

In one extreme situation, demand would be absolutely insensitive to price changes—that is, perfectly inelastic. Here, price elasticity of demand would equal zero, and the demand curve would be drawn as a vertical line at the quantity consumed. This might be the case for a product such as insulin, which has no substitutes and is an absolute necessity for those who consume it. In the opposite extreme case, demand would be sensitive to price changes in the extreme—that is, perfectly elastic. Here, measured price elasticity would approach negative infinity, and the demand curve would be drawn as a horizontal line. Such a good would likely have a perfect substitute.

There is another way of viewing demand curves that is useful for the purposes of cost-benefit analysis. The height of the demand curve at any unit of output shows consumers' marginal benefit—the maximum they are willing to pay for that unit. That is, if households are presently consuming 9,999 units, the maximum amount any household will be willing to pay for the 10,000th unit will be $65. If households are presently consuming 64,999 units, the maximum amount any household will be willing to pay for the 65,000th unit will be $20. Marginal benefit decreases as consumption of a good increases because of consumers' diminishing marginal utility: as a household has more and more of a particular good or service, extra units of it become worth less and less to it.[2] Demand curves are sometimes called *marginal benefit curves*, and it is useful to think of them in this way.

Supply, Marginal Cost, and Opportunity Cost

A supply curve for a good shows the quantity producers are willing to produce and sell at each price. The upward slope of a typical supply curve indicates that producers will only expand production if given the incentive of a higher price. Firms are assumed to be *profit maximizers*. Therefore, in Figure 4.1, if the going price of the good is $20, firms will maximize profits by producing 20,000 units per period (point X). If the price is $65 dollars per unit, they will want to produce and sell 85,000 units (point B). Market supply curves are formed by horizontally summing firms' individual supply curves. In this way they are similar to market demand curves.

How producers respond to price changes is measured by the commodity's price elasticity of supply (the proportional change in quantity supplied ÷ the proportional change in price). As with demand, there are two limiting cases. In the first, supply is absolutely insensitive to price changes—perhaps because producers cannot respond to them within the given time frame. Here the elasticity of supply is zero, and a perfectly inelastic supply curve is drawn as a vertical line at the level of output firms are capable of producing. In the opposite extreme case, producers are profoundly sensitive to price changes: the elasticity of supply approaches infinity. Here, a perfectly elastic supply curve will be drawn as a horizontal line.

Instead of viewing supply curves horizontally, measuring the quantity supplied at each price, it is useful in cost-benefit analysis to interpret supply curves vertically. No producer will be willing to produce a given unit of output unless the price it fetches is at least as much as what the unit costs to produce. A profit-maximizing firm will expand production as long as price exceeds **marginal cost**, thereby adding to profits. The price of the last unit produced will be exactly equal to marginal cost. It follows that the height of a supply curve at a given unit of output is the *marginal cost* of producing that unit—that is, the minimum a producer (the one willing to accept the least) will be willing to accept for producing it. Thus, supply curves are marginal cost curves.

For example, in Figure 4.1, the minimum amount any producer will be willing to accept to produce the 20,000th unit is $20. Of course, this firm would be happy to accept more ... but not less. Similarly, the minimum amount any producer will be willing to accept to produce the 85,000th unit is $65. Here, the minimum price producers are willing to accept increases as output expands because the marginal cost of producing this commodity is increasing. This may be for several reasons. In a factory, increasing marginal cost may be associated with overtime wage rates. Or perhaps some input in the production process is fixed so that, as more and more variable inputs (inputs whose levels of use can be changed easily) are applied to this fixed input, the variable inputs become less and less productive. In the case of electricity production, it may be that the public utility providing power has a number of different ways of producing it. For low amounts of electricity, it may be cheapest to produce it at a nuclear power station; but as more and more electricity is required—exceeding the reactor's capacity—it may be necessary to use more expensive oil- or coal-burning generating plants.

This raises the following question: How exactly does one measure marginal cost, that is, the extra cost of producing one more unit of output? Why is this cost, for instance, $65 for the 85,000th unit in the diagram? To produce this unit requires resources that have alternative uses. Even if a company already owns these resources, it will not use them in one application if they can be used more profitably in another. That is, profit-maximizing firms will employ resources only in the most valuable, profitable ways. If they can be used (but are not) to produce something else worth more than $65, or if they could have been sold for more than this amount to another firm but are used instead to produce the 85,000th unit of the product in question, the firm is not maximizing profits. The value of these resources, or what they would earn in their next-best alternative use, is called their ***opportunity cost***, which is the only kind of cost economists recognize, because it reflects the true value of these resources to society.

As shall become evident, the calculation of opportunity cost need not be complicated. When firms purchase factors of production in competitive input markets, the prices they pay for those factors are their opportunity cost. The firm producing the 85,000th unit in the example will be unwilling to pay more than $65 for the inputs required. If it did it would suffer a loss, as a result of using the inputs to produce something worth less than what those inputs are worth. Both the firm and society in this sense would have wasted them.

Market Equilibrium

In Figure 4.1, if the price of this commodity is $65 per unit, producers will want to sell 85,000 units per period but consumers will be willing to purchase only 10,000 of them. An excess supply of 75,000 units will exist. Such a situation cannot persist: producers will cut both production and prices to clear this unwanted stock. Thus, excess supply of a commodity causes its price to fall. As output and price fall, there will be a movement along the supply curve from point B toward the point marked E. At the same time, falling prices will cause the quantity demanded to expand along the demand curve from point A toward point E.

On the same diagram, if the price of this commodity is $20 per unit, consumers will want to buy 65,000 units per period, but firms will be willing to produce only 20,000 of them. An excess demand of 45,000 units will exist. This situation, too, cannot persist. Given this shortage, consumers will bid up the price of the commodity, competing among themselves for the available supply, the same as what happens at a typical auction. Excess demand will cause prices to increase. As the price rises, some consumers will drop out of the competition, illustrated by a movement up the demand curve from point Y toward point E. At the same time, the rising price will induce firms to produce more, and thus production will move up the supply curve from point X toward point E.

Because excess demand drives prices up and excess supply drives them down, a market will only be in equilibrium when neither excess exists—that is, when the quantity supplied is equal to the quantity demanded. In Figure 4.1, this equilibrium occurs at a price of $35 per unit; only at this price does supply equal demand so that neither a surplus nor a shortage exists. In the absence of excess supply and excess demand, there is no market force that could cause the price to change from this level, given existing demand and supply conditions. Moreover, at any price above $35, excess supply will drive the price down; at any price below $35, excess demand will drive the price up. Equilibrium in economics can be thought of as a physical phenomenon: no force exists to move the market from its equilibrium position, but forces do exist to take it there.

Notice that for all units up to the 44,999th, the maximum amount consumers are willing to pay for each unit exceeds the minimum amount firms are willing to accept for producing each unit; marginal benefit is greater than marginal cost. Thus, we can think of these units being exchanged between firms and consumers in a series of mutually advantageous transactions. Only at the equilibrium does marginal benefit equal marginal cost. No unit beyond the 45,000th is produced because consumers will not be willing to pay as much as firms would require to produce it. Therefore, a net benefit— the difference between marginal benefit and marginal cost—is reaped from each unit produced (except the last). This is how competitive markets ensure that all units which do yield firms and consumers a net benefit are produced, and that none which would result in a net loss to them are produced. Supply curves show the marginal (opportunity) cost of each unit, and demand curves measure marginal benefit. Markets operate by employing resources in their most valued uses to produce those goods which consumers prize most. For instance, when the 10,000th unit is produced, its value to consumers is $65, whereas the resources used to produce it are only worth $15; a net gain of $50 is thereby yielded on this unit. On the other hand, if an 85,000th unit were produced, it would mean that resources worth $65 had been used to produce something worth only $15 to consumers. Competitive behaviour does not allow this kind of waste.

Welfare Properties of the Competitive Equilibrium

Figure 4.2 shows a generalized market diagram in which P_e and Q_e denote the equilibrium price and quantity, respectively, in this market. The height of the demand curve measures marginal benefit. The maximum consumers will be willing to pay for all units up to and including unit Q_e is given by the area

FIGURE 4.2   Consumer and Producer Surplus

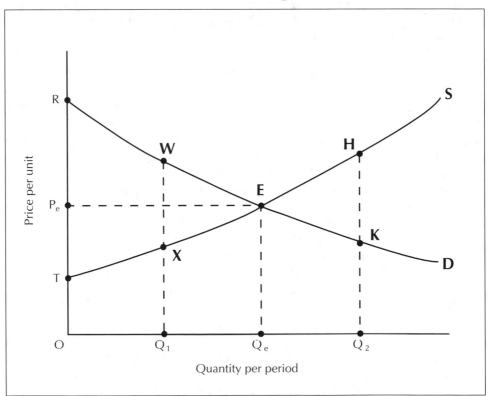

under the demand curve, $OREQ_e$. As the supply curve measures marginal cost, the cost of producing Q_e units of output is measured by the area under the supply curve, $OTEQ_e$.

The difference between the maximum consumers are willing to pay for these units and the minimum firms are willing to accept for producing them is given by the triangle RET—what we might call the ***social surplus***. The market forces of excess supply and excess demand will guide this market to the equilibrium that yields society this net benefit.

One can go further to determine how producers and consumers share this surplus. As above, the maximum consumers will be willing to pay for Q_e units of this product is given by area $OREQ_e$. In this market, each unit sells for P_e dollars, so what they actually pay in total is $P_e \cdot Q_e$, given by area OP_eEQ_e. The consumers' share of the total surplus is the difference between the maximum they are willing to pay and what they actually pay, measured by area REP_e. This amount is called the ***consumer surplus***. Also, as above, the minimum amount producers will be willing to accept for producing Q_e units is given by the area under the supply curve $OTEQ_e$. They actually receive more than this—what consumers actually pay—given by area OP_eEQ_e. The producers' share of this social surplus is the difference between the amount they actually receive and the minimum they are willing to accept, measured by area P_eET. This amount is called the ***producer surplus***, and is the difference between total revenues and total variable cost. Note that producer surplus and consumer surplus sum to what we have called the *social surplus*.

A feature of competitive markets is that they maximize the sum of producer and consumer surpluses. To see this, suppose that for some reason only Q_1 units are produced and consumed. Using the measures already identified, the total surplus associated with Q_1 units is given by the area between demand and supply curves up to that output, area RWXT. Compared to the market equilibrium, society would be forgoing a surplus measured by area WEX. Relative to the competitive equilibrium, this amount would be a net welfare *loss*, because it represents the net benefit of mutually advantageous trades that for some reason are not being consummated.

Suppose now that, perhaps by government decree, Q_2 units are produced. The total benefit consumers attribute to these units is again measured by the area under the demand curve up to that quantity, $ORKQ_2$. The total cost of producing these units is given by the area under the supply curve, $OTHQ_2$. Thus, the social surplus at this output, given by area RET minus area EHK, is *less* than what would have been obtained at the equilibrium output. This is because all units beyond unit Q_e cost more to produce than what they are worth to consumers.

Competitive markets maximize social surplus because they accommodate all transactions that are mutually advantageous, and reject any that are not.

This is to say that a competitive equilibrium is **Pareto optimal**. Another way to say this is that the resulting allocation exhibits allocative efficiency, or (more usually) that it is **efficient**. An allocation of resources is Pareto optimal (efficient) in this context if it is impossible to find another allocation (level of output) such that at least one economic agent is made better off and no other economic agent is made worse off. Any movement from Q_e units would result in a loss of social surplus, so that either consumers or producers, or perhaps both, would be made worse off. As it is impossible to increase or decrease production from Q_e so that someone gains and no one loses, Q_e, the competitive equilibrium, must be efficient. (This conclusion, however, requires that no external costs or benefits—topics to be discussed below—are associated with the production and consumption of this commodity.)

A COMPETITIVE INPUT MARKET

Much of what was stated above regarding competitive output markets also holds for competitive input markets, although demand and supply curves would be described differently. Take, for example, the labour market shown in Figure 4.3. Here, the demand-for-labour curve is labelled L^d, the supply-of-labour curve is marked L^s, and the axes, instead of measuring output and price, measure labour services per period and wage rates. The same market forces of excess demand and excess supply will guide this market to an equilibrium where L_e units of labour are hired per period and are paid a wage rate of w_e dollars.

The labour demand curve shows the amount of labour that firms are willing to hire at each potential wage rate. Another way to interpret it is to note that the height of the labour demand curve at a particular level of employment measures the maximum any firm will be willing to pay for an additional unit of labour. Certainly, a firm will not hire an additional unit of labour unless it is worth it—that is, unless the value of what this unit of labour produces is worth at least as much as the wage paid to it. An additional unit of labour produces extra output, which can be sold for a price in an output market. The extra revenue this additional unit of labour earns for the firm is the value to the firm of hiring this unit of labour, referred to as the **marginal value product of labour** (MVP_L), which is akin to a consumer's marginal benefit in an output market. As long as MVP_L is greater than the going wage rate—the firm's marginal cost of hiring labour—it will employ additional workers; this is because each unit of labour hired will add to the firm's profits. At wage w_e, no firm will hire labour beyond unit L_e, because the marginal cost of doing so (w_e) would be greater than the extra revenue this labour would generate. Profit maximization can thus be viewed in two equivalent ways. The first relates to expanding output as long as price

FIGURE 4.3   A Competitive Labour Market

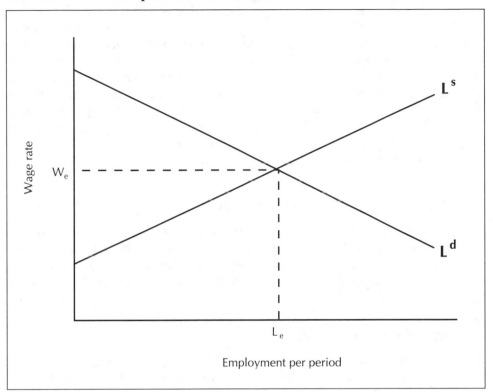

exceeds marginal cost. The second relates to continuing to hire labour (as a proxy for all variable inputs) as long as its marginal value product exceeds the wage rate. A firm can produce its profit-maximizing output only if it hires profit-maximizing amounts of inputs.

The supply-of-labour curve shows how much labour individuals are willing to supply at various wage rates. It arises from a trade-off that labourers face between income and leisure. They want leisure, but they also want income with which to buy other goods and services. This suggests that if we want people to work more, we must provide them with an incentive in the form of a higher wage. No person will put in an extra hour of work unless the wage paid in return is at least as much as the value he or she attributes to an extra hour of leisure. The height of the labour supply curve thus measures the opportunity cost of leisure at different levels of labour supply. In Figure 4.3, these labourers will ultimately supply L_e units of labour services because the wage they are paid for each unit (or hour) of work up to this level exceeds the opportunity cost to them of doing so. They will not supply labour beyond this point because the wage they earned would not be adequate compensation for the leisure they would have to forgo.

Thus, at the market equilibrium, all units of labour that generate a benefit to society (measured by the marginal value product of labour) in excess of the opportunity cost of employing them (measured by the height of the labour supply curve) have been hired. Employers and employees engage in mutually advantageous transactions of labour services, and the equilibrium is efficient. The market wage rate measures the opportunity cost of this input. It follows that if all input markets were perfectly competitive, the height of an output supply curve would truly measure the opportunity cost to society of producing a particular unit of output.

CHANGES IN DEMAND AND SUPPLY CONDITIONS

A particular price and quantity combination may form an equilibrium at one point in time; this does not mean that the equilibrium will last forever. An equilibrium exists for a particular set of supply and demand conditions, and these can change. How markets adjust to such changes is the subject of this section.

An Increase in Demand

Consider Figure 4.4, viewing first only the supply curve and the demand curve marked D_1. Given these conditions, this market will come to an equilibrium at price P_1 and quantity Q_1. Several factors may cause the demand for this product to increase—an increase shown by a rightward shift of the entire demand curve to the one marked D_2. That is, there are several reasons why consumers may demand more of this product at every price. They include the following:

1. The population may have grown.
2. The increase in demand could be for an input that a government requires to construct a project (this has much relevance to cost-benefit analysis).
3. The price of a substitute good may have increased.
4. The price of a complementary good may have decreased.
5. Consumers' preferences may have changed in the direction of this commodity.
6. If this good is a *normal* good, demand for it will increase if incomes increase.
7. If this is an *inferior* good, demand for it will increase if incomes decrease.[3]

FIGURE 4.4   An Increase in Demand

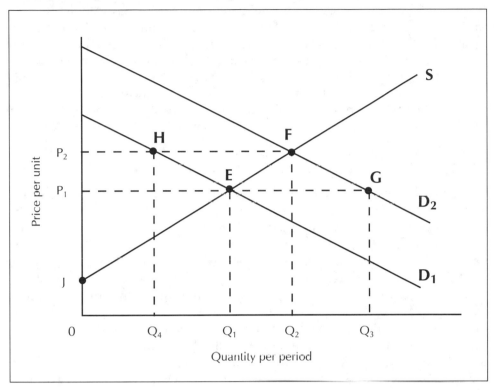

If, for whatever reason, demand increases as shown, excess demand will exist at price P_1. At this price, consumers will wish to consume Q_3 units (at point G), whereas firms will be willing to produce only Q_1 units (point E). This excess demand will cause the price of the commodity to increase until supply and demand are brought into balance again. At the new equilibrium (point F), the market-clearing price will be P_2, and Q_2 units of this good will be produced and consumed per period. We leave it to the reader to consider those situations involving a *decrease* in demand (say, from D_2 to D_1).

Using this framework and Figure 4.4, we can identify a number things that will be of interest for project evaluation.

Changes in Producer Surplus

Supply conditions do not change in Figure 4.4 (that is, the supply curve does not shift). Nevertheless, firms are better off because they are selling more of this good at a higher price. The question is this: By how much are they better off? The standard measure for this is the increase in producer surplus.

At the initial price, P_1, revenues are given by area OP_1EQ_1; the minimum firms will be willing to accept for producing Q_1 units is measured by the area under the supply curve, $OJEQ_1$. Firms' producer surplus at P_1 is thus given by area P_1EJ. At price P_2, revenue will expand to area OP_2FQ_2; the minimum firms will be willing to accept to produce Q_2 units grows to area $OJFQ_2$. Firms' producer surplus at price P_2 is, therefore, given by area P_2FJ. This increase in producer surplus, the wedge P_2FEP_1, is a measure of producers' gains. Notice that if the price had fallen from P_2 to P_1, this same change in producer surplus would have been applied to measure their loss.

The Opportunity Cost of Inputs Used on a Project

In Figure 4.4, let D_1 be the demand for some input by everyone in the economy except the government. If the government now requires $Q_2 - Q_4$ units of this input for a public project, total demand will shift to D_2. In an undistorted economy, the supply curve S will measure the marginal cost of producing this input both to firms and to society.[4]

Notice that when the government enters this market, the price of the input is pushed up from P_1 to P_2, so consumption of it by nongovernment parties falls from Q_1 to Q_4. Therefore, what the government project uses for the project actually comes from two sources: quantity $Q_1 - Q_4$ comes from displaced demand; and the balance of the government's requirements ($Q_2 - Q_1$ units) is the result of new supply. The cost of displaced demand is measured under the demand curve by the area Q_4HEQ_1. This is the value nongovernment demanders place on these units—the maximum they are willing to pay for them. The cost of newly supplied units is measured under the supply curve, area Q_1EFQ_2. Thus, the total opportunity cost to society of using $Q_2 - Q_4$ units of this input on a public project is the sum of areas Q_4HEQ_1 and Q_1EFQ_2, and the per unit cost of these units lies between P_1 and P_2. If the government's input requirements are small compared to those of nongovernment sources, price P_1 will approximate the true opportunity cost to society of each unit used on the public project.

An Increase in Supply

Figure 4.5 illustrates an improvement in supply conditions. Observe first only the demand curve and the supply curve marked S_0. Given these conditions, this market will come to an equilibrium at price P_0 and quantity Q_0. Several factors could cause the supply of this product to increase—an increase shown by a rightward shift of the entire supply curve to the one marked S_f. In other words, there are several reasons why firms will be willing to supply more output at every price. They include the following:

1. The number of firms may have increased, perhaps attracted by above-normal profits.
2. The increase in supply may have been produced by a newly constructed government project (this has much relevance to cost-benefit analysis).
3. The price of a product that is a substitute in production may have decreased.[5]
4. The government may have legislated (increased) a per unit subsidy on this product, or reduced a per unit tax.
5. The price of inputs used in the production of this product may have decreased.
6. There may have been some technological improvement in how this commodity is produced.
7. For an agricultural product, this increase in supply may be a reflection of favourable climate conditions.

FIGURE 4.5   An Increase in Supply

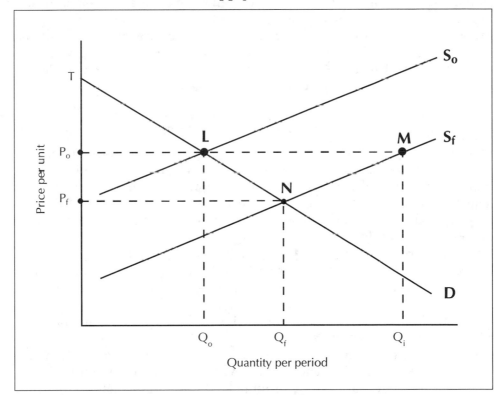

If supply increases as shown, excess supply will exist at price P_o. At this price, producers will want to produce Q_i units (at point M), whereas consumers will be willing to purchase only Q_o units (point L). This excess supply will cause the price of the commodity to decrease until supply and demand are equal. At the new equilibrium (point N), the market-clearing price will be P_f, and Q_f units of this good will be produced and consumed per period. Again, we leave it to the reader to consider what will happen when supply *decreases* instead.

Changes in Consumer Surplus

This framework and Figure 4.5 can be used to identify one important measure of welfare change used broadly in cost-benefit analysis. Consumers are made better off because the price of the good illustrated falls. The change in their consumer surplus can be used to assess their change in benefits.

At price P_o their consumer surplus—the difference between the maximum they are willing to pay for Q_o units and what they actually pay for them—is given by area TLP_o. When the price of the commodity falls to P_f, their consumption of it increases to Q_f units per period and their consumer surplus increases to an amount represented by area TNP_f. It follows that the increase in their consumer surplus arising from this price decrease is measured by the wedge P_oLNP_f. Had the price of this commodity risen from P_f to P_o, this same area—now signifying a loss of consumer surplus—could have been applied to measure the amount by which consumers were made worse off.

Short-run and Long-run Supply

How much a firm's costs change as it expands or contracts output depends on how much freedom it has to change the level and combination of the inputs it uses. Usually, this is a function of how much time it has to make adjustments. Given enough time, a firm that wishes to expand production may add machinery, build a larger factory, or add to its existing facility. For periods of shorter duration, this may be impossible and some of its inputs, typically capital, may be considered fixed. To expand output, a firm's only recourse in such situations is to hire more variable factors of production such as labour and materials, and to apply them more intensively to its existing capital stock.

A firm, therefore, must make production decisions both for the short run (that is, over a period of time when at least one factor of production is fixed) and for the long run (that is, over a period of time during which all factors are variable and it is free to choose whatever combination of inputs it desires to produce a particular volume of output). As any profit-maximizing firm wants to produce a given level of output at the least cost, and as it has more flexibility in the long run than in the short run, it follows that short-run costs can never be less than long-run costs.

Short-run marginal cost is the incremental cost incurred when production is expanded by one unit when capital, for example, is fixed. Here, the capital and labour combination used to produce this output need not be optimal (cost-minimizing). **Long-run marginal cost** is the incremental cost of producing an additional unit of output when the firm is free to change all inputs—that is, when it is free to choose the cost-minimizing combination of inputs. For every level of output there exists a cost-minimizing combination of inputs to produce it. In the long run a firm can choose this combination because it is free to select the optimal level of capital. In the short run this option is not available to it.

Short-run supply curves measure short-run marginal cost. For this reason they slope upward, because to expand output a firm must apply additional units of variable inputs such as labour to some fixed input such as capital. As it does so, the extra output each unit of labour yields eventually falls, because each such unit has less and less capital to work with. This phenomenon, called **the law of diminishing productivity**, is the reason why short-run marginal cost must eventually increase.

In the long run, average cost can increase, decrease, or remain the same depending on the existence of decreasing, increasing, or constant returns to scale. That is, at constant factor prices, a doubling of all inputs may cause total cost to more than double, or less than double, or simply double. To maximize profits in the long run at any output price, firms will choose to produce at a scale that minimizes long-run average cost. If a facility of optimal size exists, firms will choose it in the long run.

In the long run, firms are free to enter or exit an industry. If above-normal profits are being earned, firms will enter the industry. This will cause supply to expand and the price of the commodity to decrease. Entry will continue until the marginal firm just earns zero economic profits. If losses are being incurred, firms will exit, thereby driving up the commodity's price. The long-run equilibrium price—the one at which no firm has an incentive to enter or exit the industry—will be the lowest feasible price. This is not only because normal profits exist at the margin, but also because firms will have had time to choose the optimal amount of capital (scale) with which to produce their profit-maximizing output. By not choosing this amount, they would be inviting competitors to undercut them.

Be aware, however, that the existence of above-normal profits or losses does not signal efficiency or inefficiency. Efficiency depends only on whether the marginal benefit to society of the last unit produced is equal to that unit's marginal cost of production to society.

In a competitive industry in which all firms have access to the same technology and face the same input prices, an increase in industry input will involve the entry of additional firms, each choosing the optimal combination of inputs. If factor prices do not change as industry output changes, and if the quality of the factors does not change, the long-run equilibrium price will not change, and the industry's long-run supply curve will be perfectly elastic. If factor prices do increase as industry output expands, the long-run supply curve will be upward sloping—albeit more elastic than the industry's short-run supply curve. This reflects each firm's ability to choose inputs optimally.

MARKET FAILURE

If all markets were perfectly competitive and certain other conditions were satisfied, there would be no rationale for government intervention in markets. The resulting allocation of resources would be Pareto optimal—that is, it would be impossible to rearrange consumption, or to reallocate inputs, or to change the mix of products produced in the economy, so that at least one person would be better off and no person would be worse off.

For the well-being of economists in general and cost-benefit analysts in particular, perhaps it is just as well that the conditions necessary for perfect competition often do not hold, and that sometimes competitive behaviour does not result in a socially optimal allocation of resources. In such situations markets are said to fail.

Markets may fail for several reasons. Most obviously, they may fail because there is no competition, as in the case of a monopoly. As will be discussed in detail in later chapters, a profit-maximizing monopolist will produce less than what is efficient. And competitive insurance markets may fail. One possible reason: Insurers may possess less information about insurees' individual likelihoods of having accidents than the individuals themselves. As a result, mutually advantageous insurance sales may end up not being transacted. Below, we focus on two sources of market failure that are of particular relevance to cost-benefit analysis: externalities, and public goods.

Externalities

Consumers will purchase additional units of a good as long as their private marginal benefit exceeds the price they pay. People are assumed to be motivated by self-interest only; they do not care if their consumption makes someone else better off or worse off. For example, when people plant gardens they do so for their own benefit, even though neighbours or passers-by may also benefit. In the same vein, smoking is a consumption activity that imposes an external cost on others. A problem arises in either case because individuals making private consumption decisions weigh only their own benefits of consumption against the product's cost to them, its price; in this sense they ignore any potential benefits or costs to the rest of society.

Similarly, it may be that the costs an individual firm incurs to produce a product measure all of the costs of its production to society. If so, the marginal cost the firm bears will be identical to the marginal cost of production to society as a whole. This is not the case, however, if this productive activity creates pollution, which imposes additional costs on the rest of society. Because polluting firms do not pay this extra cost, it is not reflected in the market price of the goods they produce.

Competitive markets accommodate only private costs and private benefits; these are the only ones self-interested households and firms take into account when they make private consumption and production decisions. Utility-maximizing households will want to consume more and more of a particular product as long as their private marginal benefit exceeds the product's price; and profit-maximizing firms will want to increase production as long as the price they receive is greater than the private marginal cost of production. In this way, competitive markets come to an equilibrium at which the private marginal benefit of the last unit produced is equal to its private marginal cost of production, and both are equal to the product's price. If an external cost or benefit exists, this equilibrium will not be efficient.

The Case of an External Cost

The case of a negative externality on the supply side of a market is illustrated in Figure 4.6, in which the supply curve, $S\{MC_p\}$, shows firms' private marginal costs, and the demand curve, $D\{MB_s, MB_p\}$, shows households' private marginal benefits of consumption. Competitive forces have caused this market to come to an equilibrium (point B) at the price and quantity combination denoted by P_c and Q_c. Now suppose the firms in this example are polluters. Besides these firms' private costs, there will be an external cost imposed on society. The social marginal cost curve, MC_s, measures both private and external costs; thus, the difference between MC_p and MC_s is the marginal external cost of pollution at each level of output. If there is no externality on the demand side of this market—unlike the cases of gardening and smoking cigarettes—the height of the demand curve will measure not only households' private marginal benefit of consumption but also society's marginal benefit; this is why $D\{MB_s\}$ and $D\{MB_p\}$are the same in the figure.

From a social perspective, consumption and production of this good is warranted only as long as the marginal benefit to society from consuming it exceeds the marginal cost to society of producing it. Therefore, at the

FIGURE 4.6 An External Cost

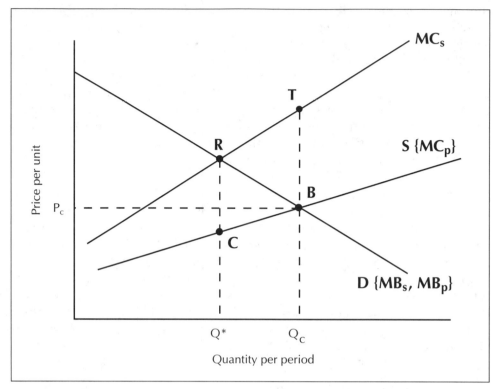

social optimum, $MB_s = MC_s$, yielding a socially optimal output of Q^* units. Note that competitive behaviour causes too much to be produced.

The welfare loss associated with this externality can be measured in relation to the social optimum. The cost to society of producing the units between Q^* and Q_c is measured by the area under MC_s between these two output levels, Q^*RTQ_c. The total benefit to society of consuming these units is measured under the demand curve, area Q^*RBQ_c. The net welfare (efficiency) loss that ensues when competitive firms produce these units is thus given by area RTB.

Note that one possible way to eliminate this distortion is to levy a *corrective* tax on this good. For example, a per unit tax equal to RC dollars in Figure 4.6—the extent of the marginal external cost at the socially optimal output—would cause the supply curve to shift upward parallel by this amount (not shown), so that it intersected with the demand curve at point R. Although firms do not take into account external costs, they will react to a corrective tax, in this case by reducing output from Q_c to Q^*. Note that at the new equilibrium, the price, gross of tax, will reflect the true social marginal cost (and benefit) of this good.

The Case of an External Benefit

Nova Scotia still has elm trees. To keep them, municipal and county governments operate spraying programs to protect these trees against Dutch Elm disease. Consider the case of a town trying to decide how frequently and widely to spray. Presumably, it will expand its program as long as the marginal benefit the town is perceived to gain from spraying exceeds its marginal cost. In Figure 4.7, the town's marginal benefit and marginal cost curves are labelled MB_T and MC_T respectively. It will, then, expand its spraying program to S_T units per period (point K).

However, when this town sprays for Dutch Elm disease, the adjacent areas also benefit. The spread of the disease is impeded not only within the town but outside it—that is, there is an external benefit. When the marginal benefit to the town of spraying and this marginal external benefit to outlying areas are summed, the total is represented by the curve MB_S. From a social perspective, and assuming no external costs of spraying, this activity should

FIGURE 4.7   An External Benefit

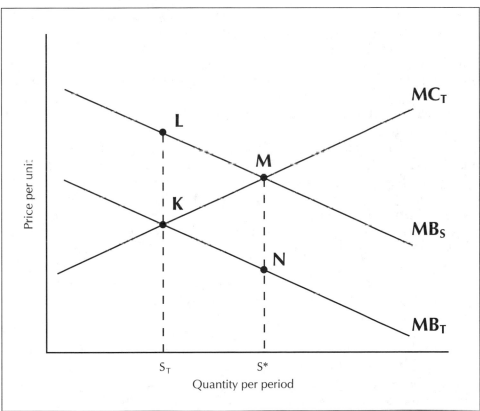

be expanded as long as MB_S exceeds MC_T—here, to the quantity marked S^*. However, because the town paying for the spraying does not take into account *all* of the benefits of its activity, spraying will be limited to S_T units and society will not reap the net social benefit it would have gained had the spraying been expanded to S^* units. The benefit society forgoes is given by area $S_T LMS^*$; the cost it avoids is given by area $S_T KMS^*$. The net welfare loss due to this externality is thus measured by the triangle KLM.

Where positive externalities exist, a government may employ a number of corrective measures—if the affected parties themselves cannot negotiate the optimal output. In Figure 4.7, note that a corrective subsidy equal to MN dollars, exactly equal to the marginal external benefit at the socially optimal output, would cause output to expand from S_T to S^*, thus eliminating any welfare loss.

The important point is that in the presence of externalities, either positive or negative, competitive equilibria will not be efficient; this raises the possibility of a role for government. Potential corrective measures are discussed in more detail in Chapter 8.

Public Goods

One of the conditions specified above for a market to be perfectly competitive is that the good or service in question must be private. This means two things: First, the good must exhibit rivalry in consumption. Thus, if one person consumes a particular unit of the good, no other person can consume the same unit. Second, exclusion must be feasible. Thus, a person can be deprived of consuming a good if he or she does not pay for it. Most goods and services fit this description: hamburgers, haircuts, airline tickets, beer, and so on. Some, however, do not.

Consider, for example, a streetlight. It exhibits **nonrivalry** in consumption because one person's use of it does not deprive any other person of the use of it. Also, it exhibits **nonexclusion**, because no one can be prevented from using it. The same holds true for national defence. Although both goods and services exhibit these properties, all are called **public goods**.

Competitive markets will not simply fail to produce efficient quantities of public goods—they will not produce them at all. When individuals cannot be excluded from consuming public goods, they will not volunteer to pay for them; and any private sector firm producing a public good will earn zero revenue. This is why governments provide public goods—they can finance the costs of producing them through taxation.

This question remains: What is the socially optimal quantity of a public good that a government should produce? The answer is the same as for a private good: output of a public good should be expanded as long as the marginal benefit society reaps from consuming it exceeds its marginal cost of production to society. This calculation, however, is not straightforward.

To arrive at the demand curve for a private good, and thus its marginal benefit curve, we gather individuals' demand curves and then sum them horizontally. This procedure is illustrated in Figure 4.8 for a two-person society. At a price of $4 per unit, person 1 demands 1 unit (read off D_1), whereas person 2 demands none (read off D_2). Society's total demand is thus 1 unit

FIGURE 4.8   Aggregating Demand for a Private Good

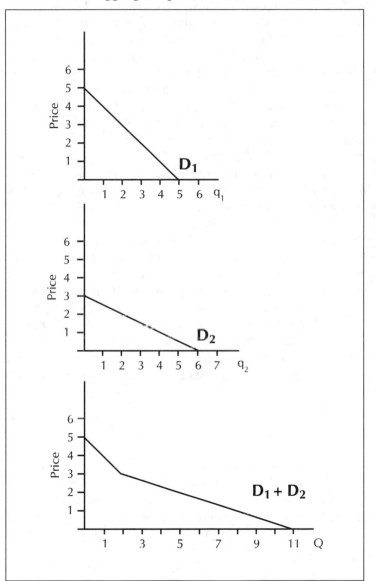

per period (on the aggregate demand curve $D_1 + D_2$). At a price of $1 per unit, person 1 demands 4 units and person 2 demands 4 units in the same period. Total demand at $1 is thus 8 units. This procedure—horizontal addition of every individual's demand at each separate price—yields an aggregate demand curve. In this example, if the marginal social cost of producing this good is constant at $2 per unit, the socially optimal output is 5 units per period. Of these units, person 1 would consume three and person 2 would consume two, and both people would pay $2 for every unit they consume.

Now consider the same two-person economy, except now the individual demand curves shown are for a public rather than a private good. It makes no sense to say that at $2 per unit each person will consume 4 units so that total demand is 8 units; this is because, as there is nonrivalry in consumption, each person will consume the same 4 units, not different ones. They consume this good jointly. To calculate society's marginal social benefit (or demand) curve—and thus its total willingness to pay—for a public good requires *vertical*, not horizontal, addition of individuals' demand curves. This procedure is illustrated in Figure 4.9.

The maximum person 1 is willing to pay for the first unit of the public good is $4. The maximum person 2 is willing to pay *for this same unit* is $2.50. Therefore, their combined total willingness to pay for this unit is $6.50. For this public good, we have now determined one point ($MB_1 + MB_2$) on society's demand curve, or marginal benefit curve. For a second unit, person 1's marginal benefit is $3 and person 2's marginal benefit is $2. It follows that the social marginal benefit of the second unit is $5. We repeat this procedure for all other relevant levels of output to form the entire social demand curve for this public good.[6] If the marginal social cost of producing this public good is constant at $2 per unit, the socially optimal output is 4 units per period. Person 1 and person 2 will consume these same 4 units jointly. However, neither person will pay for his or her consumption directly, because of nonexclusion. Therefore, the total cost of providing this public good (and many others that are the outputs of public sector projects) will have to be financed by taxation.

SUMMARY

Prices determined in competitive markets provide important information for project analysis. In the absence of government intervention, the price of a good or service always reveals the private marginal benefit and private marginal cost of the product. There is no co-ordinating role for government; self-interested firms and consumers interact to yield this result. The same is true of input markets.

FIGURE 4.9 Aggregating Demand for a Public Good

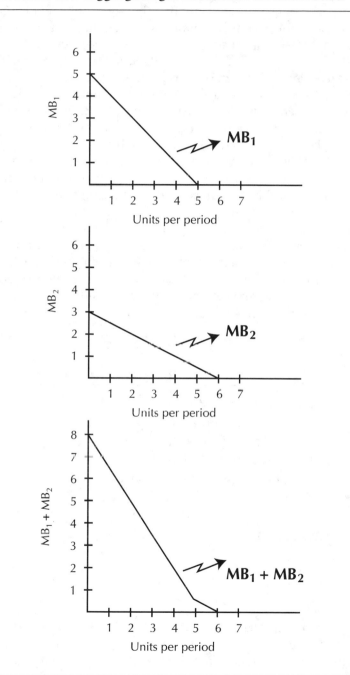

In the absence of externalities, a competitively determined price also reveals the social marginal benefit and social marginal cost of the good or service. In these circumstances, the quantity actually produced and consumed is efficient: markets accommodate all mutually advantageous trades, and the resulting equilibrium is Pareto optimal. If output is either smaller or larger than this amount that maximizes the sum of consumer and producer surpluses, a net welfare loss results. The same holds for competitive input markets.

If an external cost or benefit exists in a market, the competitive equilibrium will be inefficient. In the presence of a negative externality (an external cost) emanating from either side of the market, too much of the good will be produced and a net welfare loss will ensue. If a positive externality (external benefit) is associated with the consumption or production of a good, less than what is socially optimal will be produced and a similar net welfare loss will result. In either case, there is a potential role for government.

Markets will fail completely in the case of public goods, if only because consumers don't have to pay for what they consume of them. This implies that the public sector must provide them. Public goods exhibit both nonexclusion and nonrivalry in consumption. If the output of a public project exhibits nonrivalry, this will have implications for how it should be priced; if it exhibits nonexclusion, this will have implications for how its production must be financed.

KEY TERMS

price elastic	efficient
elastic	marginal value product of labour
inelastic	short-run marginal cost
marginal cost	long-run marginal cost
opportunity cost	law of diminishing productivity
social surplus	nonrivalry
consumer surplus	nonexclusion
producer surplus	public goods
Pareto optimal	

EXERCISES

4.1 Consider a competitive market for a private good that is free of externalities. Demand for the good is given by $Q_d = 90 - P$. Supply is given by $Q_s = 2P$. All inputs are purchased in perfectly competitive markets.

    a. What is the total benefit to society of the equilibrium output produced?

    b. What is the value of the resources used to produce the equilibrium quantity?

    c. What consumer surplus accrues to consumers at the equilibrium?

    d. What producer surplus accrues to producers at the equilibrium?

4.2 Consider a competitive market for a private good that is free of externalities. Demand for the good is given by $Q_d = 200 - 2P$. Supply is given by $Q_s = P - 10$. The government decrees a price floor of $80 supported by an overall quantity limit (quota) of 40 units per period. Calculate the efficiency (net welfare) loss per period caused by this policy.

4.3 Consider a competitive market for a private good that is free of externalities. Demand for the good is given by $Q_d = 100 - 2P$. Supply is given by $Q_s = 2P - 20$. The government legislates a $10 per unit subsidy on this good to be paid to producers. Calculate the impact of this subsidy on the well-being of consumers, on the well-being of producers, and on the government's budget. Calculate also the efficiency (net welfare) loss caused by this subsidy.

4.4 Consider a competitive market for a private good. No externality exists on the demand side, and demand for the good is given by $Q_d = 180 - P$. There is a negative externality created by production of this good. Supply (MC_p) is given by $Q_s = 2P$. The marginal external cost (MEC) increases with production according to $MEC = 0.1 \cdot Q_s$.

    a. Calculate the efficiency (net welfare) loss associated with this externality at the competitive equilibrium.

    b. Calculate the corrective per unit tax that would eliminate this loss (that is, cause the socially optimal output to be produced and consumed).

4.5 The social marginal cost of producing a public good is $20 per unit. Society consists of three individuals. Persons 1, 2, and 3 value the public good according to the following marginal benefit schedules: $MB_1 = 60 - Q$, $MB_2 = 110 - 3Q$, and $MB_3 = 150 - 2Q$, where Q denotes the number of units of the public good provided. Calculate the optimal level of provision of this public good.

ENDNOTES

1. This measure serves our purpose but is only one way of calculating a commodity's price elasticity of demand. See any introductory or intermediate microeconomics textbook for "arc" and "point" measures of elasticity.

2. A weaker assumption would be that of a diminishing marginal rate of substitution between goods. Both assumptions yield the same result: an individual's willingness to pay for successive units of a good or service decreases.

3. If an individual's income changes, his or her demand for a good can increase, decrease, or be unaffected. If an increase in income causes demand for a good to increase, it is called a *normal* good. If we define a

good's income elasticity of demand to be the proportional change in quantity demanded ÷ the proportional change in income, a normal good is characterized by a *positive* income elasticity of demand. If *negative*, an increase in income will cause the quantity demanded of the good to decrease, thus revealing it to be an *inferior* good. If the demand curve for a good or service does not change as income changes, its income elasticity of demand is zero.

4. We deal with pricing inputs in distorted markets in Chapter 6.

5. For example, if land can be used to produce either wheat or barley, and the price of barley falls, farmers will be inclined to shift out of barley production and into wheat production, and the supply curve for wheat will shift outward.

6. Of course, this depends on whether individuals reveal their willingness to pay for a public good truthfully. If individuals believe they will be taxed according to their response, one would expect them to understate their marginal benefit. If they believe that the amount they will have to contribute to financing the public good is not related to their statement of marginal benefit, they will tend to overstate the desirability of the public good. For treatments of this preference revelation problem and the implications of voting processes in this regard, see Chapter 6 of Boadway & Wildasin (1984), Chapter 6 of Stiglitz (1986), or Chapter 3 of Musgrave & Musgrave (1984).

PART III

ASSESSING COSTS AND BENEFITS

CHAPTER 5

THE MEASUREMENT OF
WELFARE CHANGE

INTRODUCTION

The essential question that cost-benefit analysts are charged with answering is this: "Would the construction of a particular public-sector project (or the implementation of a particular policy) make society better off?" To answer this question we must weigh the social benefits of the proposed action against its social costs. For this, we need a method for assessing a project's impact on all affected individuals and then aggregating those impacts. Broadly, we would like to rank various social states. This is the meat of welfare economics, and it forms the theoretical basis of cost-benefit analysis. However, to fashion a social-preference ordering (ranking) from individuals' preference orderings is a formidable task. Because of measurement and aggregation problems, in order to carry it out we must make rather strong assumptions. Simplifying assumptions, whatever their context, limit the robustness of the conclusions reached. Analysts must bear in mind that while the tools of cost-benefit analysis are powerful, they are also limited.

THE PARETO IMPROVEMENT CRITERION

A town consisting of H households has a main thoroughfare that is pleasantly wide. At present, automobiles are allowed to use the entire width of the road, and this makes bicycling through town a risky endeavour. When cars and bicycles meet, bicycles—and cyclists!—lose. The town council is considering whether to designate part of this roadway for bicycles only; this would limit the width available for automobile traffic. Should the council create this bicycle path (right-of-way)?

A typical household in the town has a preference ordering represented by a utility function, $U(x_1, x_2, x_3, ..., x_N)$, which is defined over goods, services, and leisure: everything that yields utility to this family. If the bicycle path is created, this household's utility will change by amount ΔU.

The town's decision would be simple if either $\Delta U_h \geq 0$ for every family in the town ($h = 1, 2, 3, \ldots, H$) and $\Delta U_h > 0$ for at least one family; or if $\Delta U_h \leq 0$ for every family in the town, and $\Delta U_h < 0$ for at least one family.

If the former were true, creating the bicycle path would make at least one family better off and no family worse off. Here, proceeding with the project would yield a **Pareto improvement.** It would unambiguously increase the welfare of the citizenry. Relative to the status quo (no path), the new situation (having a path) would be **Pareto superior**.

If the latter were true, obviously the right-of-way should not be created. Proceeding with it would unambiguously decrease social welfare; the new situation would be **Pareto inferior** vis-à-vis the status quo.

Most decisions, however, are not this easy. Some families will realize a net benefit if the path is created ($\Delta U > 0$), but others may be made worse off ($\Delta U < 0$)—especially drivers who like a lot of room to manœuvre. Still others may not care one way or the other ($\Delta U = 0$). We may be tempted to think that the way to solve this policy problem is to sum all of these utility changes ($\Delta U_1 + \Delta U_2 + \Delta U_3 + \ldots + \Delta U_H$) to yield the town's change in welfare ΔW^*. Then, if $\Delta W^* > 0$, create the bicycle path; if $\Delta W^* < 0$, do not; and, if $\Delta W^* = 0$, the right-of-way will neither add to nor detract from the town's welfare.

But this approach is not possible. First, a household's utility function only ranks alternative consumption bundles or situations; it is an *ordinal* measure, not a cardinal one. A household may prefer having a bicycle path, or prefer not having a bicycle path, or be indifferent; but no meaningful units can be attached to utility levels or changes in utility. A utility function can be used to assign numbers to various consumption bundles for the purpose of ranking them according to a household's preferences; but for this, any numbering system that does not change a household's preference ordering (ranking) will suffice. So saying that a household attaches a utility level of 3.5 to not having a bicycle path and 6 to having a path tells us no more than if the numbers assigned had been, respectively, 0.8 and 1,000. All that can be known in either case is that this family prefers having a bicycle path to not having one. Comparing a utility increase of 2.5 ($6 - 3.5$) against one of 999.2 ($1,000 - 0.8$) is a meaningless exercise.

The second problem arises from the first: if utility cannot be meaningfully measured, there can be no comparisons of utility between households. As there is no unique measure of utility, summing arbitrary numbers is meaningless. Creating the path may make one family worse off and another better off, but summing their changes in utility yields just one more meaningless number. Indeed, it would be worse than comparing apples and oranges, because at least fruit can be counted. The bicycle path may cause one household's utility to increase by 5 and another's to decrease by 5, but there is no way of knowing whether these changes in utility cancel each other out, because we don't know whether they mean the same thing to the two different households.

This is why the **Pareto improvement criterion** is so appealing. A project or policy satisfies this criterion if it makes at least one person better off and makes no person worse off. Notice that in invoking this criterion we are trying neither to measure utility nor to make comparisons of it between households. Unfortunately, the Pareto improvement criterion is not very useful for project or policy evaluation. In the above example, it could be that creating a bicycle path is favoured by 3,000 families and opposed by one family. If we followed this criterion, the path would not be created. Clearly, adherence to the Pareto improvement criterion would cause the rejection of many worthwhile projects and policies. So some other way of measuring and aggregating individuals' or households' changes in utility must be found if we are to determine a particular project's impact on social welfare.

WILLINGNESS-TO-PAY MEASURES

Although we would prefer to measure directly the change in utility a project causes each household, this is not possible. One way to proceed is to transform changes in utility into something that *can* be measured in meaningful units—that is, transform an ordinal measure into a cardinal one. Although we could use donkeys, apples, or bales of hay—any *numeraire* would do—dollars are the most convenient yardstick. Economists use willingness-to-pay measures to accomplish this conversion.

For example, consider a family who will be better off if the path is built. A question we might put to them is, "What is the maximum amount you are willing to pay to have the bicycle right-of-way created?" The answer, a positive dollar amount, is this family's **compensating variation**. Note that this is a proxy for this family's change in utility, not its *actual* change in utility. For instance, if the family's answer is $500, this means that if the path is created and if, simultaneously, its income is reduced by this amount, it will be as well off as if it had kept its money and gone without the path. Thus, one possible measure of the benefit this family attributes to a bicycle path is its compensating variation—$500.

Another family, perhaps not bicyclists, may not want the town to designate a bicycle right-of-way. It may feel that reducing the road space available for automobiles may make driving through town a more harrowing experience. The establishing of a bicycle path would make it worse off. The appropriate compensating variation question for this family is, "What is the minimum amount you are willing to accept in order to induce you to tolerate the proposed bicycle right-of-way?" This family's answer, too, will be expressed in dollars, but it should be treated as a negative amount. Notice that if the path is created and, simultaneously, this family is given the number of dollars it stated as its compensating variation, it will be as well off as if it had been given no lump-sum payment and the path had not been created.

Compensating variation and utility changes are related in the following way: for a particular household, h, if its compensating variation $CV_h > 0$, then $\Delta U_h > 0$; if $CV_h < 0$, then $\Delta U_h < 0$; and if $CV_h = 0$, then $\Delta U_h = 0$.

In general terms, if implementation of a policy or construction of a project would take an economy from social state A to social state B, the appropriate compensating variation question for people who would gain from this change is, "What is the maximum amount you are willing to pay to achieve state B?" The appropriate question for people who would lose is, "What is the minimum amount you are willing to accept in order to induce you to tolerate state B?"

There is a second willingness-to-pay measure that serves as a proxy for utility changes, *equivalent variation*. Whereas compensating variation questions are always stated so that the new situation (having a path) is the end result, equivalent variation questions are framed in such a way that the new situation is forgone, thus leaving society with the status quo (not having a path). The appropriate equivalent variation question to a family who would benefit from a bicycle path is then, "What is the minimum amount you would be willing to accept to forgo the bicycle path?" This dollar figure should be recorded as a positive amount.[1] So, if this family's answer were $700, it would mean that starting from the position of having a path, it would feel a loss of utility worth this amount to them if the right-of-way were eliminated. The appropriate equivalent variation question to a household that would be made worse off if the path were created is, "What is the maximum amount you are willing to pay in order to prevent part of the roadway from being designated a bicycle path?" The answer should be recorded as a negative amount.

Equivalent variation and utility changes are related in the following way: for a particular household, h, if its equivalent variation $EV_h > 0$, then $\Delta U_h > 0$; if $EV_h < 0$, then $\Delta U_h < 0$; and if $EV_h = 0$, then $\Delta U_h = 0$.

In general terms, if implementation of a policy or construction of a project would take an economy from social state A to social state B, the appropriate equivalent variation question for people who would gain from this change is, "What is the minimum amount you are willing to accept to forgo achieving state B?" The appropriate question for people who would lose from the change is, "What is the maximum amount you are willing to pay to prevent state B from becoming reality?"

COMPENSATION TESTS AND THE POTENTIAL PARETO IMPROVEMENT CRITERION

Because compensating variation and equivalent variation are measured in dollars, both can be aggregated. Aggregate compensating variation, denoted by CV, is $CV_1 + CV_2 + CV_3 + \dots + CV_H$. Similarly, aggregate equivalent variation,

EV, is $EV_1 + EV_2 + EV_3 \ldots + EV_H$ (for the same H households). Note that implicit in this formulation is that each household's compensating variation and equivalent variation are given the same weight as every other household's.

Take the situation, first, where every household's compensating variation is either positive or zero, and at least one household's is positive. Given the relationship between an individual household's compensating variation and its change in utility going from the status quo to the new situation, creating the bicycle path would result in a Pareto improvement. The same is true for equivalent variation.

Now suppose that the compensating variations of some households (bicyclists) are positive while those of others (drivers) are negative. If their sum, CV, is positive, it means that the gains to bicyclists if the path were built would exceed the losses to drivers who would be made worse off. Hypothetically, then, it is possible for bicyclists to compensate drivers for their losses if the path is built and still be left better off. If this is possible, creating a bicycle right-of-way would achieve what is called a ***potential Pareto improvement***, and the proposal is said to pass this compensation test.

We may be tempted, therefore, to treat CV > 0 as a sign that the project or policy in question is welfare-improving. Some caution is required, however. First, only hypothetical—not actual—compensation is required to satisfy the ***potential Pareto improvement criterion***. Indeed, in many circumstances it may be impossible to pay actual compensation to losers. This leaves open the possibility that some households will be left worse off and some will be made better off if the project proceeds. That is, without actual compensation, a Pareto improvement (with no one made worse off) will not result.

Thus, CV > 0 may not mean that the project or policy will cause social welfare to increase. Ultimately, we would like the sign of aggregate compensating variation to indicate accurately the direction of welfare change, but without compensation it may be that the utility losses of losers will exceed the utility gains of winners even when CV > 0.

The problem is that although every household measures its gain or loss in dollars, these dollars may not be valued equally by all households. For example, if a government takes $100 from household 1 and gives it to household 2, these dollar values will cancel, as will their two compensating variations. But will the corresponding utility changes cancel? It may be that household 1 is poor and household 2 is wealthy. A loss of $100 to household 1 may cause it great distress, while an extra $100 may not enhance the well-being of household 2 by much at all. That is, the former's loss of utility may greatly exceed the latter's increase in utility. Such a transfer would cause an overall welfare loss even though aggregate compensating variation is zero. If the transfer is from household 2 to household 1, the former's loss of utility may be much smaller than the latter's gain. We expect that the higher a household's income, the less value it attaches to each additional dollar of income: the marginal utility of income diminishes as income increases. Only if households value an extra dollar (or the loss of a dollar) equally—that is, only if they have identical marginal utilities of income—will CV > 0 truly signal an increase in welfare if actual compensation is not paid.

This leads us to a critical assumption that is usually made in cost-benefit analysis. In the absence of compensation, a government is assumed to be using tax and transfer policies to ensure a "perfect" distribution of income, one under which the marginal utility of income of every household (individual) is equal.[2] This assumption is, of course, heroic. Indeed, it is the source of much criticism of cost-benefit analysis.[3] At the same time, many economists agree that if a government wishes to redistribute income, it is best advised to do so directly through a tax-and-transfer system rather than through other forms of intervention, including project selection.[4]

In any case, the assumption of equal marginal utilities of income—that a dollar is a dollar is a dollar, to whomever it accrues—is common in cost-benefit analysis, and is made here explicitly. A common rationalization for it is that governments in countries like Canada do engage in income redistribution. Although their efforts likely do not result in equality of marginal utilities of income, policy tenets such as progressive taxation are in this spirit. However, it would be difficult to make this argument in countries where income distribution is heavily skewed—say, where 5% of the population owns 95% of the country's wealth. In such circumstances, we would want to assign weights to households' compensating variations differently, according to income.[5]

When the assumption that households' marginal utilities of income are equal is invoked, CV > 0 for a project satisfies the potential Pareto improvement criterion for welfare change, in that it would be hypothetically possible for winners to compensate losers and still be left better off. If CV < 0, this criterion is not satisfied. In the above example, this would mean that the gains of bicyclists from having a path would be less than the losses of drivers who oppose it. If the path were created, a welfare loss would ensue.

Aggregate equivalent variation, denoted by EV and equal to $EV_1 + EV_2 + EV_3 + \ldots + EV_H$, forms the basis of a second compensation test. Subject to the same proviso regarding the distribution of income, if EV > 0 for a project, it passes the potential Pareto improvement criterion. Recall the equivalent variation questions for those who would benefit and for those who would lose if the path (the new situation) were not built. If EV > 0, the minimum amount bicyclists would require in compensation for forgoing the right-of-way exceeds the maximum amount drivers would be willing to pay to prevent its creation. Because the latter could not afford to compensate the former to forgo the path, and still be left better off, designation of part of the roadway as a bicycle path would increase social welfare.

If EV < 0, people who do not want the project or policy could afford to compensate those who do want it, and still be left better off. The proposed project would, therefore, fail this compensation test and the potential Pareto improvement criterion.

Together, CV > 0 and EV > 0 thus ensure that proceeding with a project will cause a welfare improvement. The project satisfies a double-compensation test: winners would be able to compensate losers if the project were built, and losers would not be able to afford to compensate winners for forgoing the project. That is, bicyclists could afford to compensate drivers for tolerating the path, but drivers could not afford to compensate bicyclists for going without it. It follows that if the path does not exist, create it; if one does exist, retain it.

Therefore, if state A represents the status quo and state B is the new situation (with the project or policy), and if the economy is at A, a potential Pareto improvement will ensue if it moves to B; and if the economy is at B, a loss of welfare will ensue if it moves to A. Thus, whichever measure is used, EV or CV, the project should be built.

If EV < 0 and CV < 0, the project or policy should be rejected. The former means that people who would gain by remaining at state A (the status quo) can afford to compensate those who do *not* want to remain there; and if we start from state B, those who wish to move to state A can afford to compensate those who would lose by doing so. Viewed from either starting point, state A dominates; the project does not cause a potential Pareto improvement. In this example, bicyclists could not afford to compensate drivers for tolerating the path, and drivers could afford to compensate bicyclists for forgoing it. If the bicycle right-of-way does not exist, do not build it; if it exists, get rid of it.

There are, however, two other possibilities. A third situation occurs where CV > 0 and EV < 0. Using states A and B as above, this means that if the economy is currently at state A, going to state B would cause a potential Pareto improvement; and if at B, going to A would cause a potential Pareto improvement. In other words, moving in either direction causes a potential Pareto improvement. In the context of the example used above, if no path exists, build one; if a path exists, get rid of it. Obviously, this situation provides little guidance for those charged with determining policy.

It is possible for the combination of CV > 0 and EV < 0 to occur in aggregate, but is it reasonable at the level of an individual? Perhaps, but it would seem somewhat rare. For example, consider marriage. The decision rule would be, "If single, get married; if married, get divorced." (We might well dub this the "Gay Divorcée–Vacillating Bachelor syndrome.") Another example would be that of an individual choosing between facing toward or facing away from the sun. It could come down to this: "If facing the sun, turn 180 degrees;

if facing away from the sun, turn another 180 degrees"—perpetual motion inevitably leading to much dizziness ... but at least an even tan. However unlikely this case may be at the level of an individual, analysts must still watch out for it when applying aggregate measures—that is, in situations where cost-benefit analysis is usually applied.

The fourth (and last) possibility arises when EV > 0 and CV < 0. The former is interpreted to mean that if at state B, moving from that state would cause a welfare loss. The latter means that if at state A, moving from that state would cause a welfare loss. Whatever the starting point is—having the project or not having the project—any change would fail the potential Pareto improvement criterion. Thus, if a bicycle right-of-way exists, retain it; if one does not exist, do not create one. This case is not far-fetched. Townley (1991) shows the circumstances in which a society with no public pension plan would choose not to initiate one (CV < 0), and in which if it did have such a plan, it would choose to retain it (EV > 0).

The third and fourth situations above can occur and are the essence of the Scitovsky Paradox (or Reversal).[6] Note that in either case, CV and EV separately give different assessments of the desirability of the proposed project. To the problem of avoiding a decision that reduces social welfare, Scitovsky's solution is to apply a double-criterion: if CV and EV are positive, proceed with the project; if EV and CV are negative, reject it. When CV and EV have different signs, compensation tests do not offer definitive guidance to analysts. Whether creation of the bicycle right-of-way would cause a welfare increase or decrease is not known.

CONSUMER SURPLUS, EV, AND CV

Compensating variation and equivalent variation are the best available measures of welfare change given that it is impossible to measure directly the impact of a project on a household's utility. Survey methods can be used to pose the relevant compensating variation and equivalent variation questions. Unfortunately, it is sometimes not easy to obtain truthful answers to the questions these calculations involve.

Take, for example, a family of bicyclists who would gain if the town were to create a bicycle right-of-way. The appropriate compensating variation question is, "What is the maximum amount you are willing to pay to have the path created?" If this household thinks it will be charged or taxed according to the benefit it states, it will likely understate its true compensating variation. This family may even be inclined to answer zero dollars, indicating that it would reap no benefit at all. If it thinks that compensation would be forthcoming, it may even state that the path would make it worse off. In doing so, this family would be behaving rationally, as a *free rider*.[7] It would be count-ing on other households to answer truthfully and, it follows, to finance any costs involved or compensation. This family wants the bicycle path, but also wants to avoid paying for it. As all bicyclists will have the same incentive to understate their preferences for a path, it may not be created. Individual rationality is not the same as social rationality.

On the other hand, if this household thinks that the amount it would have to pay for a path is independent of its answer to the compensating variation question, it will tend to overstate its willingness to pay for it. The right-of-way may then be created even though the project is truly not justi-fied. Answers to the relevant equivalent-variation questions could be simi-larly biased, especially if households think actual compensation would be paid to them.

However, households *do* reveal their preferences in markets, and the measurement of welfare change arising from changes in incomes and prices can often be applied to project and policy evaluation.

Income-induced Changes in Benefits

Suppose that a family's income increases by $500. Obviously, it is made bet-ter off. Indeed, if this family were asked the relevant compensating variation question ("What is the maximum you are willing to pay for a $500 increase in income?") and the relevant equivalent-variation question ("What is the minimum you are willing to accept to forgo a $500 increase in income?") the answer would be the same: $500. All this is rather obvious, but it will be useful for the analysis to follow to note that there are two ways to measure the change in benefits when income changes.

The first is to note the change in income itself; the second is to calculate this household's total change in expenditure. When income falls, either we can count the fall in income as the loss of benefits, or we can calculate the total decrease in the family's expenditures. For an economy, either the aggregate change in income or the aggregate change in expenditures will measure society's change in benefits caused by an income change.

Price-induced Changes in Benefits

Consider the simple market demand curve for good X shown in Figure 5.1. Initially the price of the good is P_1, and X_1 units of it are consumed each period. As described in Chapter 4, the maximum consumers are willing to pay for these units is given by the area under the demand curve, marked a + b + d. The amount they actually pay for X_1 units is $P_1 \cdot X_1$ dollars, represented by the area b + d. Therefore, their consumer surplus when the price of X is

FIGURE 5.1   Change in Consumer Surplus

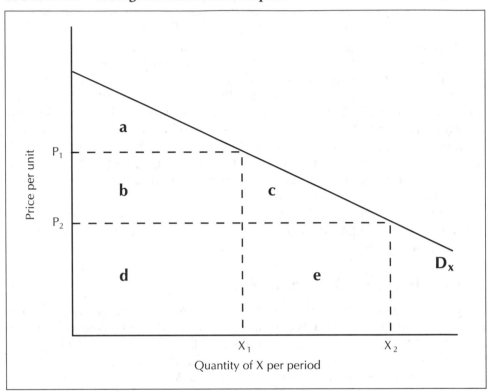

P_1 is given by area a. If the price of this good decreases to P_2, consumers will be unambiguously better off because they will now consume X_2 units per period and consumer surplus will expand. Their consumer surplus when the price of X is P_2 is given by area a + b + c. This price decrease will cause society's consumer surplus to increase by the amount indicated by area b + c. This is one possible measure of this society's total change in benefits when this price change occurs.

Yet compensating and equivalent variations of this price decrease are still the preferred measures of its impact on benefits. If a change in consumer surplus (ΔCS) is to be used to measure a benefit change, we will want to know its relationship to CV and EV. The relationship is this:

1. For a normal good, $EV > \Delta CS > CV$.

2. For an inferior good, $EV < \Delta CS < CV$.

3. $EV = \Delta CS = CV$, if the income elasticity of demand for the good is zero.

This means that if the demand for the output of a project is independent of income, the change in consumer surplus that results if its price changes will exactly measure compensating and equivalent variations. In practice, changes in consumer surplus provide a reasonable approximation of these measures as long as the absolute value of income elasticity of demand for the good in question is small.[8]

Another Way to Measure Price-induced Changes in Benefits[9]

Using ΔCS, area b + c in Figure 5.1 measures consumers' total change in benefits when the price of good X falls from P_1 to P_2. It is often convenient, however, to measure this change in benefits another way. Note that when the price of this commodity falls, demand for its substitutes decreases and demand for its complements increases. That is, society's expenditure pattern changes. Yet as income has not changed, total expenditure cannot have changed.

Consider the case of three goods shown in Figure 5.2. Good X is some commodity, good Y is assumed to be a substitute of X, and good Z is a composite commodity (representing expenditure on all other goods and services in the economy, here assumed to be a complement of X. When the price of X decreases as shown, the demand curve for Y shifts to the left (D_{Y1} to D_{Y2}), while the demand curve for Z shifts to the right (D_{Z1} to D_{Z2}). Consumption of X increases from X_1 to X_2, consumption of Y decreases from Y_1 to Y_2, and consumption of the composite commodity increases from Z_1 to Z_2.

Initial expenditures on X, Y, and Z are shown by areas b + d, f + g, and h, respectively. After the price of X falls and the other two demand curves shift, total expenditures on X, Y, and Z are shown by areas d + e, f, and h + j, respectively. As income has not changed, any change in expenditure on X must be offset by changes in expenditure on Y and Z. This means that the following must be true:

$$b + d + f + g + h = d + e + f + h + j$$

Rearranging this equality yields,

$$b = e - g + j$$

and adding c to both sides yields

$$b + c = (c + e) - g + j$$

FIGURE 5.2 An Alternative to ΔCS

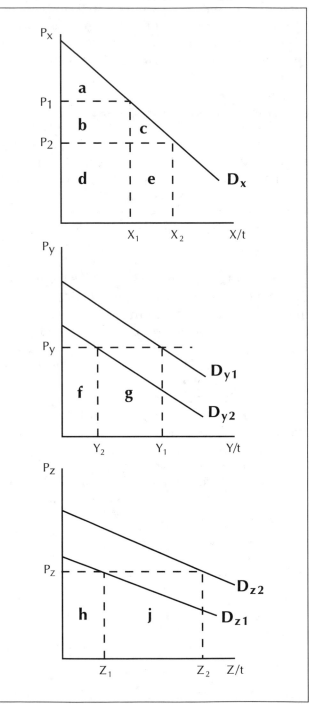

Note that the term on the left-hand side of this equation is simply the change in consumer surplus induced by this price decrease. The right-hand side of the equation provides another way of measuring this surplus that holds intuitive and practical appeal. The first term on the right (in parentheses) measures the total amount consumers are willing to pay for the extra $X_2 - X_1$ units this price decrease allows them to consume. It is their *total increase in benefit* from consuming more good X. The second term on the right is negative because less of good Y is consumed now. This decrease in expenditure measures their *total loss of benefit* from consuming less good Y, like that induced by a decrease in income. Similarly, the third term on the right is positive because more of the composite commodity is consumed. This increase in expenditure measures their total increase in benefit from consuming more of good Z. This change in benefits can, therefore, be measured either by the change in consumer surplus, which is a *net benefit* measure, or by looking at all affected markets and calculating the *change in total benefits*. Having two ways to calculate changes in benefits when a price increases or decreases will be useful for double-checking measurements of welfare change.

MEASURING WELFARE CHANGE IN MARKETS

In the example above, only the change in benefits induced by a price decrease was examined. But, as production of X and Z have increased while that of Y has decreased, total costs of producing each good have also changed. The change in welfare caused by this price decrease is the change in benefits less the change in resource costs.

Measuring changes in resource costs is less complicated than measuring changes in benefits. Figure 5.3 shows the supply curve for a commodity. As described in Chapter 4, the height of this supply curve at a particular unit of output measures the marginal cost of producing that unit. To calculate the total cost of producing Q_1 units, we must sum the marginal costs of producing each unit of output. This total cost is given by the area under the supply (marginal cost) curve, $OwvQ_1$. Under this same procedure, the total cost of producing Q_2 units is given by area $OwrQ_2$. It follows that the cost to society of producing an extra $Q_2 - Q_1$ units is given by area Q_1vrQ_2. If production *falls* from Q_2 units to Q_1 units, this same area will represent a cost (resource) saving to society.

Welfare Change When Related Markets Are Not Distorted

First, assume that all three goods can be produced at constant marginal cost and that all three markets are undistorted. *Undistorted* means simply that the price of each good is equal to its marginal cost to society. Figure 5.4 is

FIGURE 5.3   Changes in Resource Costs

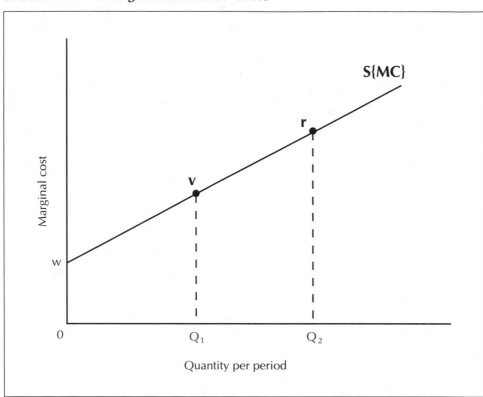

Figure 5.2 with marginal cost curves added. Let P_2 measure the marginal cost of producing X, and let P_y and P_z, respectively, measure the marginal costs of producing Y and Z. The additional cost of producing $X_2 - X_1$ units of X is thus given by area e; the resource (cost) saving when production of Y is decreased by $Y_1 - Y_2$ units is given by area g; and the extra cost to society of producing $Z_2 - Z_1$ units of Z is given by area j. The extra resource cost (ΔC) induced by this decrease in the price of good X is, therefore, $e - g + j$.

Recall that the change in benefits (ΔB) caused by this price decrease is $\Delta B = c + e - g + j$. The resulting change in welfare (ΔW) is equal to $\Delta B - \Delta C$ and, therefore, can be written as

$$\Delta W = [c + e - g + j] - [e - g + j]$$

or, market by market in alphabetical order,

$$\Delta W = [c + e - e] + [-g + g] + [j - j]$$

**FIGURE 5.4   Welfare Change When Markets
Are Not Distorted**

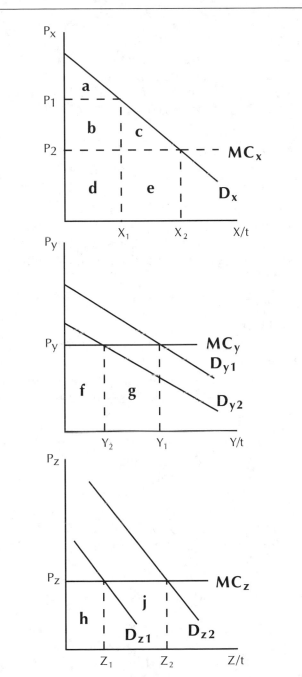

Note that in the markets for Y and Z, whatever changes have occurred have not caused any change in welfare. The reduction of benefits due to decreased consumption of Y is exactly matched by the decrease in the cost of producing this good. Extra consumption of Z yields a benefit, but the value of this extra benefit is exactly offset by the increased cost of producing it. This is true for any related market that is undistorted—the change in benefit is matched by the change in cost, so that no welfare change is yielded in that market.[10] Only in the market for X is the benefit of extra consumption not matched by an equal increase in costs. The total welfare change is, thus, $\Delta W = c$.

Welfare Change When Related Markets Are Distorted

Examine Figure 5.5, which shows markets for goods J, K, and L. L is a composite commodity representing all goods and services in the economy except for J and K. Initially, the price of J is P_1, and J_1 units of it are consumed. The market for good K is distorted because the price it is sold for, P_k, is less than the marginal cost to society of its production, MC_k. This distortion could be caused by an external cost associated with its production, such as pollution, or by a per unit subsidy. Whatever the source of this distortion, K_1 is the number of units of K currently being consumed each period. The market for the composite commodity is not distorted ($P_L = MC_L$). For this situation, assume that both K and L are substitutes of good J.

Now suppose that the price of J increases from P_1 to P_2, perhaps because a per unit tax is levied on it. The quantity demanded of it decreases to J_2 units, and the demand curves for K and L shift from D_{k1} to D_{k2} and from D_{L1} to D_{L2}, respectively. Consumption of goods K and L thus increases to K_2 and L_2 units per period, respectively.

The change in total benefits caused by this price increase may be separated according to market. In the market for J, consumers suffer a loss equal to $k + m$, the maximum they were willing to pay for the $J_1 - J_2$ units that they no longer consume. In the markets for K and L, they reap gains of n and r, respectively, because their expenditure on both of these commodities has increased. The total change in benefits (ΔB) occasioned by this price increase is, thus, $n + r - (k + m)$.

Changes in resource costs may also be stated for each market. There is a resource saving in the market for J given by the area under MC_J, m. More resources, however, have been expended to produce both K and L. Measuring under MC_k and MC_L, these extra resource costs are given by areas $q + n$ and r, respectively. ΔC, the extra resource cost associated with this price increase, is therefore $q + n + r - m$.

The resulting change in welfare ($\Delta W = \Delta B - \Delta C$) can also be shown market by market. In the market for J it is $[-(k + m) + m]$, thus $-k$; in K it is $[n - (q + n)]$, thus $-q$; while in the market for L it is $[r - r]$, thus zero. Therefore, $\Delta W = -(k + q)$.

**FIGURE 5.5   Welfare Change When a Related
Market is Distorted**

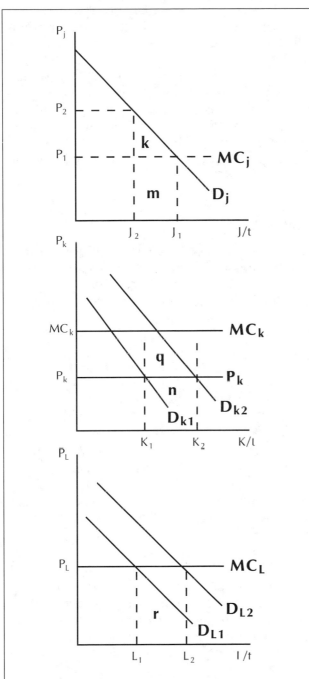

Notice that because the market for the composite commodity is not distorted, changes in costs and benefits in this market can be ignored—they cancel out. However, the same is not true of the market for K. Here, the extra cost of producing K is not equal to the benefit of this extra consumption because consumers ascribe a lower value to these units than what they cost to produce.

It is important to appreciate that when we are measuring the welfare change caused by a price change in a given market, we can ignore the impact of that change on all related markets that are not distorted. Only if a related market is distorted will the change in welfare not be restricted to the market where the change originated.[11] This is important for project evaluation, because it indicates which impacts of a project analysts may not ignore and which they may ignore.

A BRIDGE-FERRY EXAMPLE

The following fictional case is an elaboration of Layard's (1972) classic example and will draw on the techniques developed in this chapter and in Chapters 2, 3, and 4. Many features of it will be applicable to the (nonfictional) Northumberland Strait Fixed Crossing project, to be discussed in Case 1.

The Proposed Project

In the distant land of Fredonia, many Fredonians make a trip each year to a holy shrine located in the mountains of that country. However, to reach their destination they must traverse a deep gorge through which a raging river riddled with rapids runs.

Currently, the only way to make this trip is by a privately owned ferry service. The Government of Fredonia is considering construction of a bridge to span the gorge. Although the distance is not great—if built, people would walk across—it would be both difficult and expensive to construct.

The ferry is owned by a monopolist who charges $5 per person per crossing. Annual demand for trips by ferry is steady at 130,000. The marginal cost of a ferry trip is a constant $3 per trip, so the ferry owner's operating costs are $390,000 per year. The Government of Fredonia levies a 50% tax on corporate profits.

Travellers would be willing to pay an extra $6 per trip if they could cross by bridge because it would be faster—there would be a time saving. If the bridge were built, the government would not charge people to cross it and 240,000 trips would be made year after year forever. Also, if the bridge were built there would be no demand for ferry trips. The ferry has a scrap value of $825,000.

FIGURE 5.6 Bridge-Ferry Example—No Toll

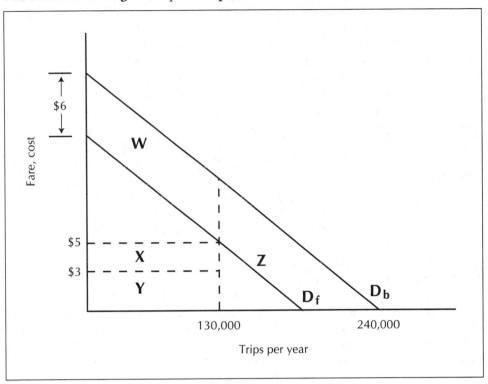

The bridge would take one year to build and would thus open to traffic at the beginning of t = 1. It would cost $20 million to construct, but it would last forever without requiring any maintenance. Assume that the demand curves for ferry and bridge trips are both linear and stable, and that the social discount rate in Fredonia is 10%. These demand curves are illustrated in Figure 5.6.

The cost-benefit analyst's task is to advise the government as to whether the bridge would add to or subtract from the well-being of the country.

The Party-by-Party Approach

One way to approach this problem is to separate those who would be affected by the proposed bridge into parties and then assess the impact of the project on each of them. First, there are those people who currently make 130,000 trips by ferry every year and who would switch to the bridge if it were built. They represent *diverted traffic*. Second, if the bridge were built, 110,000 extra trips would be made. This is *generated traffic*. Third, there is the monopolist *ferry owner*, who would be put out of business. Finally, there is the *government*. It would pay for bridge construction, and its tax revenues would decrease because of the demise of the ferry business.

The net gains to *diverted traffic* would derive from two sources. Currently these people pay $5 per trip, a cost that would fall to zero. As they make 130,000 trips annually, they would enjoy a fare saving of $650,000 each year. This is shown by the marked area X + Y. Also, they would enjoy a time saving, which they value at $6 per trip; this would yield a total time saving valued at $780,000 per annum. This is shown by the area marked W. The net benefit of the bridge to this group is, thus, $1.43 million annually beginning at t = 1 and lasting forever (areas W + X + Y). At a discount rate of 10%, the present value of this benefit to diverted traffic is $14.3 million.

Generated traffic would gain consumer surplus if the bridge were built. This is shown by area Z on the diagram. The maximum amount this generated traffic would be willing to pay for the first trip made by the one of them who values it the most is $11 (the height of the demand curve for ferry trips at 130,000 trips). As the price of a bridge crossing is zero, this amount would be the consumer surplus attributable to that single trip. The consumer surplus attributable to the last generated trip made (the 240,000th) is zero. As it has been assumed that this demand curve is linear, area Z is a triangle of area (1/2 · 110,000 · 11 =) $605,000. The annual benefit to generated traffic is thus $605,000 beginning in year t = 1 and lasting forever. The present value of this annual benefit to generated traffic is $6.05 million.

The *ferry owner* would lose. Total annual revenues and costs from operating the ferry are $650,000 and $390,000, respectively. The difference, the monopolist's before-tax annual profit, is represented by area X. After taxes, the monopolist's profit is thus $130,000 per year. The present value of this loss is thus $1.3 million. On the other hand, at t = 1 the monopolist could sell the ferry for $825,000. This amount must be discounted by one year to arrive at a present value of $750,000 for the ferry. The present value of the ferry owner's net loss if the bridge is built would thus be $550,000.

The *government* would lose more. The bridge would cost $20 million to build, and it would lose tax revenue from the ferry owner equal to $130,000 per year (beginning at t = 1). The present value of this lost tax revenue at 10% is $1.3 million, bringing the present value of the government's loss to $21.3 million.

The net present value of this project may now be calculated. Counting net benefits as positive and net losses as negative, it is $14,300,000 + $6,050,000 − $550,000 − $21,300,000 = −$1.5 million. That is, if the bridge were built, society would suffer a net loss of $1.5 million. As the net present value of the project is negative, the cost-benefit analysis indicates that the bridge should not be constructed. The above calculations are summarized in Table 5.1.

TABLE 5.1   The Party-by-party Approach

Party	Item	Value	Present Value	NPV
Diverted traffic	Annual fare saving	+$650,000 (@)		
	Annual time saving	+$780,000 (@)		
	TOTAL — Diverted Traffic	+$1.43m (@)	+$14.3m	+$14.3m
Generated traffic	Annual consumer surplus	+$605,000 (@)	+$6.05m	
	TOTAL — Generated Traffic		+$6.05m	+$6.05m
Ferry owner	Annual loss of fares	−$650,000 (@)		
	Annual cost saving	+$390,000 (@)		
	Annual tax saving	+$130,000 (@)		
	Subtotal of annual items	−$130,000 (@)	−$1.3m	
	Scrap Value of ferry (at t = 1)	+$825,000	+$750,000	
	TOTAL — Ferry Owner		−$550,000	−$.55m
Government	Annual tax loss	−$130,000 (@)	−$1.3m	
	Capital cost of bridge	−$20.0m	−$20.0m	
	TOTAL — Government		−$21.3m	−$21.3m
TOTAL				**−$1.5m**

Another Approach

There is a more direct method of calculating the net present value of this project. Instead of assessing the *net* benefit or *net* loss to each affected party, we can examine the change in *total* benefits in the economy caused by the project and net out the change in *total* resource costs it imposes on the economy—without considering to whom they accrue.

Consider first the question of resource costs. Annually, $390,000 worth of resources are used to operate the ferry (area Y in Figure 5.6). If the project proceeds, society will benefit from this resource saving, which has a present value of $3.9 million. Resources are also liberated when the ferry is sold. The present value of this saving is $750,000. The present value of the cost of building the bridge is $20 million. Therefore, the total increase in resource costs if the bridge were built would be $15.35 million.

To calculate the economy's total change in benefits, first observe *diverted traffic*. The maximum these travellers are willing to pay for 130,000 trips by ferry is the total area under the demand curve marked D_F. The maximum these same travellers are willing to pay for the same number of trips by bridge is the area under the demand curve for bridge trips, marked D_B. Their *change in total benefits* is, therefore, given by area W in Figure 5.6. This is simply the time saving offered by the bridge, and the present value of this benefit is $7.8 million.

The change in total benefits to *generated traffic* is easier to calculate. They take no ferry trips and therefore do not benefit from it. Their total annual benefit from the bridge would be the maximum they would be willing to pay to take 110,000 trips (240,000 − 130,000) each year, given by area Z in Figure 5.6. The present value of their change in total benefit is thus $6.05 million.

The increase in total benefits that would accrue to this society if the bridge were built is, then, $13.85 million ($7.8 plus $6.05 million). The increase in total resource costs is $15.35 million. The net present value of the bridge using this method is, therefore, -$1.5 million. These calculations are summarized in Table 5.2.

Note that although these two approaches yield the same answer, the latter requires less information than the former. Consider what is left out. First, corporate taxes are ignored—they are, after all, merely a transfer between the ferry owner and the government. Any dollar exchanged in this manner has a net present value of zero: a loss of a dollar to the party that surrenders it is cancelled by the benefit of a dollar to the party that receives it. Second, the monopolist's profits are ignored. Recall that in the party-by-party approach, area X in Figure 5.6 measures the monopolist's loss of before-tax profits should the bridge be built. This area also appears as part of the fare savings to diverted traffic, area X + Y. Of this area, only Y, representing the resource cost of operating the ferry, is relevant from an economywide perspective.

The main difference between the approaches is that the *change in total benefits minus change in total resource costs* method ignores all transfers, whereas the

TABLE 5.2   Change in Total Benefits *Minus* Change in Total Resource Cost Approach

Type	Item	Value	Present Value
Change in total benefit (ΔB)	Diverted traffic	+$780,000 (@)	+$7.8 m
	Generated traffic	+$605,000 (@)	+6.05 m
ΔB			+13.85 m
Change in total cost (ΔC)	Capital cost (bridge)	+$20m	+$20 m
	Scrap value (ferry)	−$.825m (t = 1)	−$.75 m
	Resource saving (ferry)	−$390,000 (@)	−$3.9 m
ΔC			+$15.35 m
ΔB − ΔC	**Net present value**		**−$1.5 m**

party-by-party approach does not. This does not mean that one approach is superior to the other: they are equivalent. Note that for a government that is concerned with the distribution of costs and benefits, the party-by-party approach is appropriate. Perhaps the most useful aspect of this equivalence is that it gives cost-benefit analysts a way of double-checking their calculations. It is not often in economics that a method of verification exists. Here one does, and it is recommended that both approaches be used to verify calculations.

A Common Error

In the above example, the net present value of the bridge is negative. It would not be unusual for someone to suggest that this loss could be avoided if travellers were charged a toll to cross the bridge. Is this thinking correct?

Suppose now that if the bridge were built, travellers would be charged a $5 toll per trip, exactly what they currently pay to cross by ferry. Is the bridge now a feasible project? Figure 5.7 is similar to Figure 5.6 and shows the impact of this toll. If this bridge toll were levied, only 190,000 trips would be made each year. That is, the number of generated trips would be reduced to 60,000 per year.

FIGURE 5.7   Bridge-Ferry Example—with Toll

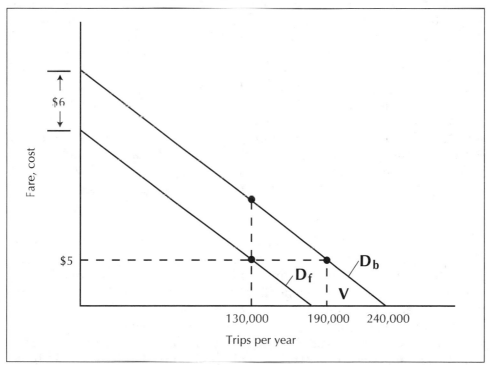

Using the *change in total benefits minus change in total resource costs* method, note that the present values of the increase in total resource costs and the change in total benefits to diverted traffic are still $15.35 million and $7.8 million, respectively.

The change in total benefits to generated traffic is, however, no longer $6.05 million. The maximum these people would be willing to pay for the trips they would now take each year is given by the area under the demand curve for bridge trips between 130,000 trips and 190,000 trips. This annual change in total benefits is $480,000. Its present value is thus $4.8 million. The net present value of the bridge when travellers are charged a bridge toll of $5 is, thus, −$2.75 million. Clearly, the project is even less attractive when a toll is charged. (In Exercise 5.9 you will be verifying this result using the party-by-party approach.)

Why does charging no toll yield a higher net present value than charging a toll? The answer is that the marginal cost to society of a person crossing the bridge in the absence of congestion is zero. Therefore, zero dollars is the socially optimal bridge toll. When a toll is charged, it causes dollars to be transferred from travellers to the government; but since the loss to travellers is a gain to the government, these gains and losses cancel out. The other impact, however, is that 50,000 fewer trips are made each year (the difference between 190,000 trips and 240,000 trips). The annual benefit to society of these trips is given by the area under D_B, shown by area V in Figure 5.7. That is, the maximum travellers would be prepared to pay for these trips is $125,000. The extra cost to society if they were taken would be zero. Therefore, charging $5 per crossing when the actual opportunity cost to society per crossing is zero results in an annual welfare loss of $125,000. Note that the present value of this loss is $1.25 million, which is exactly the difference between the net present value of the bridge with no toll and the net present value of the bridge *with* this toll.

In the absence of other distortions in the economy, any departure from socially optimal pricing always induces a welfare loss. Not charging the socially optimal price for the output of a project can only cause its net present value to be less than otherwise. (This is not necessarily true when distortions exist in related markets—a topic we address in Chapter 8.)

SUMMARY

The Pareto improvement criterion yields clear answers regarding whether a particular project or policy would make society better or worse off. Its strengths are that it requires neither measurement of utility changes nor interpersonal comparisons of utility. Unfortunately, its usefulness is limited, because any project that would cause even a single person to be worse off would fail this criterion. However, to go beyond the Pareto improvement criterion when a project makes some people better off and others worse off, we must measure utility changes, and apply a method for aggregating and thus comparing these changes across individuals. Willingness-to-pay measures—compensating variation and equivalent variation—fulfil this role.

Yet when we aggregate individuals' compensating and equivalent variations, we cannot avoid making value judgments. When we give every person's compensating and equivalent variations the same weight as everyone else's, we are making the value judgment that every person values income changes the same—that marginal utilities of income are identical. In doing so we are ignoring the distributional consequences of a project or policy—that is, we are assuming that one person's gain of a dollar will be offset by another's loss of a dollar. Yet to assign different weights to individuals' compensating and equivalent variations requires some other value judgment.

Aggregate compensating and equivalent variations are used to determine whether a project meets the potential Pareto improvement criterion. This criterion differs from the Pareto improvement criterion in that it allows for the hypothetical possibility that people who would be made better off by a project could pay compensation to those who would be made worse off. Actual compensation need not be paid for this criterion to be met. Moreover, a double-criterion must be met in order to avoid any Scitovsky Reversal.

The appropriate compensating and equivalent variation questions can be asked; however, this is sometimes not necessary. Where markets exist, changes in consumer surplus approximate compensating and equivalent variations for price changes. In both distorted and undistorted markets, changes in consumer surplus and information regarding the opportunity costs of any resources used or saved can be gathered by analysts to measure welfare changes. Indirect impacts of a change in one market on related, undistorted markets can be ignored.

These tools can be used in actual project evaluation. In particular, the net present value of projects can be assessed two ways: the *party-by-party* approach and the *change in total benefits minus change in total resource costs* approach. As these approaches will yield the same answers, a method of verifying results exists.

KEY TERMS

Pareto improvement
Pareto superior
Pareto inferior
Pareto improvement criterion
compensatory variation
equivalent variation
potential Pareto improvement
potential Pareto improvement criterion
free rider

EXERCISES

5.1 Residents of Pleasantville currently commute by train to and from Metropolis, where many of them work. It has been proposed that this railway line be terminated—residents who chose to would have to commute by either car or bus. Mr. A looks forward to the day when the train no longer runs, because the noise it makes upsets him. Mrs. B wants to keep the train because it is the fastest and cheapest way for her to get to work.

    a. What is the appropriate compensating variation question for Mr. A?
    b. What is the appropriate equivalent variation question for Mr. A?
    c. What is the appropriate compensating variation question for Mrs. B?
    d. What is the appropriate equivalent variation question for Mrs. B?

5.2 Residents of Hog's Hollow currently commute by either bus or car to and from Gotham City, where many of them work. It has been proposed that a railway line be operated between these centres. Mr. C looks forward to the day when the train runs, because it will be faster and cheaper than either bus or car travel. Mrs. D does not want the train service because she thinks it will destroy the bucolic ambience of Hog's Hollow.

    a. What is the appropriate compensating variation question for Mr. C?
    b. What is the appropriate equivalent variation question for Mr. C?
    c. What is the appropriate compensating variation question for Mrs. D?
    d. What is the appropriate equivalent variation question for Mrs. D?

5.3 Does satisfaction of the Pareto improvement criterion imply satisfaction of the potential Pareto improvement criterion? Explain.

5.4 Does satisfaction of the potential Pareto improvement criterion imply satisfaction of the Pareto improvement criterion? Explain.

5.5 Suppose that for a change from state A to state B, $CV > 0$ and $EV > 0$. If actual compensation is paid to losers, the change to state B will increase social welfare regardless of the distribution of income. Discuss.

5.6 Suppose there are three goods: A, B, and C (a composite commodity). Goods A and B are complements, and goods A and C are substitutes. If the price of good A increases, households consume less of A and their total loss of benefits is the consumer surplus they lose in the market for A. Using your own diagrams, find the equivalent (three-market) expression for this change in benefits.

5.7 Consider the markets for goods R, S, and T shown in Figure 5.8. Initially, the market for good R is not distorted and households purchase R_1 units of R for price P_1 each; the market for good S is distorted and households consume S_1 units of S for price P_S each; and the market for good T, a composite commodity, is undistorted where households consume T_1 units of T for price P_T each.

FIGURE 5.8

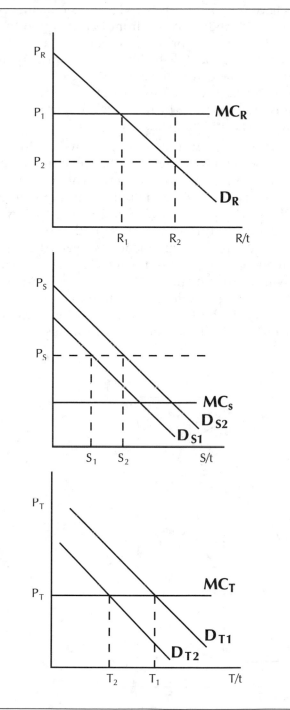

Now suppose that the government subsidizes each unit of good R so that its price to consumers falls to P_2. As goods R and S are complements, the demand curve for good S will shift outward from D_{S1} to D_{S2} so that S_2 units will be consumed each period at price P_S. As goods R and T are substitutes, the demand curve for good T will shift inward from D_{T1} to D_{T2}, so that T_2 units of good T will be consumed at price P_T.

Calculate the change in welfare caused by this price decrease. In what circumstances will this price decrease increase welfare? Provide an intuitive explanation of why this could happen.

5.8 Figure 5.9, which shows a map of Ricardo Island, renowned for its retirement and rest homes for economists. Travellers between the towns of Oz and Id are served by a government-operated ferry. The retirement home in Oz caters to monetarists only, while the retirement home in Id is exclusively for Keynesians. These retired economists like to travel back and forth on the ferry if only to hurl insults at each other.

Between Id and Oz, 10,000 ferry trips are made each year. The fare is $5 per trip, and the annual operating cost of the ferry is $70,000. The operating loss is covered by the government.

The government is considering the immediate termination of the ferry service and sale of the ferry. The ferry could be sold for $20,000. The government would replace the ferry service with a bus service

FIGURE 5.9

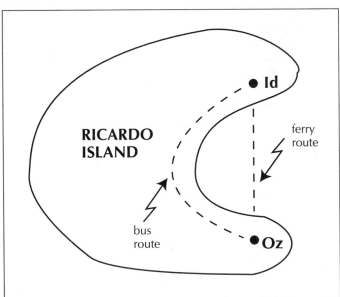

immediately and forever. No passenger is indifferent between the two modes of transportation—each person would be willing to pay $3 more per trip to travel by ferry.

It is estimated that if the ferry service were terminated and if bus passengers were charged $5 per bus trip, only 4,000 trips would be made annually. Total bus fares would exactly cover the operating costs of the bus service. Assume that the capital cost of the bus is zero, that it has no alternative use, and that it will last forever without maintenance. Assume also that the demand curves for ferry trips and bus trips are linear.

On the basis of the net present value criterion, you must decide whether to replace the ferry service with a bus service. The social discount rate is 10%.

a. Perform this evaluation. In doing so, set out the costs and benefits (properly discounted) in a methodical way. A diagram will aid your analysis.

b. If you used the *party-by-party* approach in **a**, repeat your analysis using the *change in total benefits minus change in total resource costs* approach here. If you used the *change in total benefits minus change in total resource costs* approach in **a**, repeat your analysis using the *party-by-party* approach here.

c. Using either approach, calculate the net present value of this project using discount rates of 7% and 4%.

5.9 The net present value of the bridge-ferry project described in this chapter when a five-dollar bridge toll is charged is −$2.75 million. Verify this answer using the party-by-party approach.

ENDNOTES

1. We adopt the convention of Boadway & Bruce (1984). This is to be contrasted with that of Mishan (1976).

2. Of course, if society does not place equal weight on the well-being of households, the optimal distribution of income will not be characterized by equal marginal utilities of income. To begin to address this and associated issues in welfare economics is beyond the scope of this text. See Boadway & Bruce (1984) for a full treatment.

3. See Blackorby & Donaldson (1990).

4. See Raynauld, Stringer & Townley (1994).

5. The subject of distributional weights is treated in Sugden & Williams (1978) and Boardman, Greenberg, Vining & Weimer (1996). Although the subject of some criticism, see Weisbrod (1968) for a method of calculating

a set of weights. No exposition is provided here as it seems likely that disparate distributions of income are most likely to be found in less developed countries where, perhaps, most projects—such as dams and hydroelectric facilities—would have a significant impact on relative prices and production. In such circumstances, general equilibrium analysis rather than cost-benefit analysis is presumably the more appropriate evaluation tool.

6. See Scitovsky (1941).

7. Although the term "free rider" applies appropriately enough to bicyclists in this example, it is meant to be used more broadly. For example, a person who regularly watches PBS television programming but does not respond to pleas for contributions may be regarded as a free rider.

8. See Willig (1976) regarding this approximation.

9. The following is an expanded version of Boadway & Wildasin's (1984, pp. 35–37) treatment.

10. This is true given the assumption of constant marginal costs in this example. If marginal cost in a related market is not constant, this result is a valid approximation only for small price changes.

11. Implicitly, price changes in related markets are assumed to be negligible.

CHAPTER 6

CORRECTING MARKET DISTORTIONS: SHADOW PRICES, WAGES, AND DISCOUNT RATES

INTRODUCTION

The construction of a typical private-sector investment project such as a factory or an office building requires inputs such as cement, steel, and labour. The cost to the investing firm of these inputs is what it actually pays for them: the bills it receives from cement and steel suppliers and its total wage bill (including any benefits). The relevant input prices for a private sector analyst are just the price of steel per girder, the price of cement per cubic yard, and the relevant wage rate(s)—each input's market price.

Construction of a typical public-sector investment project such as a dam or bridge also requires inputs such as cement, steel, and labour. Is it appropriate for a cost-benefit analyst to use the market prices of these inputs to cost them? That is, even if a government agency actually pays market prices for these inputs, do these prices reflect the opportunity cost to society of employing them on a public sector project? Are these the prices that should be used for the purpose of evaluating the project?

The best answer we can give is that it depends on the circumstances. In all situations we wish to evaluate the true opportunity cost of the inputs used on a project—their value to society in their next-best alternative uses. Sometimes observed market prices reflect the opportunity cost of inputs. In other circumstances market prices—prices actually paid—understate or overstate true values. That is, input and output markets can be distorted so that market prices do not convey true economic values. In these instances it is necessary to correct observed prices—that is, to calculate *shadow prices*.[1] In this chapter we discuss how to determine the shadow prices of inputs such as steel and plywood when their markets are distorted by taxes, subsidies, and other forms of government intervention. Treated separately are shadow wage rates and the shadow price of output produced in distorted markets.

An important related matter for cost-benefit analysts is the choice of discount rate to be used in project evaluation. To evaluate private sector investment projects, firms use discount rates that reflect market interest rates among other factors. But credit and capital markets are distorted, and for this reason, we must adjust these interest rates when evaluating public sector projects.

In order to understand why it is sometimes necessary to reject observed market prices in favour of shadow prices, it is worthwhile to review first the circumstances in which it is *not* necessary—that is, the circumstances in which market prices *are* shadow prices.

COMPETITIVE INPUT AND OUTPUT MARKETS

In Chapter 4 the properties of competitive equilibria were enumerated. When a market is perfectly competitive and neither external benefits nor external costs exist, the equilibrium quantity produced and consumed is socially optimal. This arises out of self-interested behaviour. Profit-maximizing firms expand production as long as the price of output (P) exceeds the minimum they are willing to accept to produce an additional unit, their marginal private cost (MC_p). Utility-maximizing consumers expand consumption of a good or service as long as the maximum they are willing to pay for an additional unit, their marginal private benefit (MB_p), exceeds the price of the good. Therefore, in a competitive equilibrium, all units for which $MB_p \geq MC_p$ are produced and, importantly, no units for which $MB_p < MC_p$ are produced; that is, $MC_p = P = MB_p$. In the absence of externalities, there is no divergence of social (MC_s) and private costs, nor of social (MB_s) and private benefits. When firms and consumers are acting only in their own self-interest, the market forces of excess demand and excess supply guide a competitive market to an equilibrium in which all units for which $MB_s \geq MC_s$—and none for which $MB_s < MC_s$—are produced and consumed. The allocation is Pareto optimal such that, in equilibrium, $MC_s = P = MB_s$.

We are interested in the properties of equilibrium prices. For example, suppose the market in question is for some input—say, sheets of 3/4-inch plywood. Further, suppose that this market is perfectly competitive and that there exists no externality—or other distortion such as taxes or subsidies—in the production or consumption of plywood. Many public sector projects require plywood. If the market price of a sheet of plywood is $45, and if 15,000 sheets are required, some government agency (or the construction firm it hires) will pay $675,000 for the plywood. In these circumstances, what the agency actually pays for the plywood is its true opportunity cost.

Note that if the government agency's extra demand induces an increase in plywood production, $45 per sheet will reflect the marginal social cost of the product—the opportunity cost of the resources used to produce an extra sheet of plywood. If some of the government's demand is diverted from other users of plywood, $45 per sheet will reflect their marginal benefit—the value of a sheet of plywood in its next-best (nonproject) alternative use. Regardless of where the plywood comes from, new supply or displaced demand, the market price of the plywood—the price per unit the government actually pays—will reflect its true value to society and thus the opportunity cost of using it for the project.

The above may seem obvious, but the properties of competitive prices are sometimes overlooked. For example, suppose that construction of a bridge over a body of water will mean that ferries that once transported goods and passengers will no longer be needed. This represents a resource saving, and an analyst would wish to assess the value of this benefit. Note that if a ferry is sold in a competitive market, the price it fetches will reveal its true value, a benefit to the bridge project. And (although it depends on the number of potential purchasers) if the ferry was auctioned, market prices in this context would more or less reflect its true worth. However, what if instead of selling the ferry, the government agency simply transfers it to another route? The benefit of this resource saving is no less real, even though government coffers are not expanded. In this case it would be necessary to impute a value, and the simplest way would be to determine what the ferry would have sold for had it been offered for sale in a competitive market. This merely requires some homework: studying existing markets for used ferries. Although an approximation, the quest is still to determine the maximum someone would be willing to pay for the ferry, even if this requires the analyst to impute market values.

Note that the above applies to market prices where external costs or external benefits exist *if the government has intervened with corrective taxes or subsidies*. In the presence of an external cost, the appropriate tax will raise the price of the good to consumers so that the tax-inclusive (gross-of-tax) price will reflect the marginal social cost of the product. In the presence of an external benefit, the appropriate subsidy will cause the price consumers pay to decrease and the price firms receive to increase, thereby inducing the socially optimal amount of the good to be produced and consumed. That is, corrective taxes and subsidies yield "correct" prices. It is when taxes and subsidies not designed to correct distortions are levied that adjustments may be required.

SHADOW PRICING IN OUTPUT AND (NONLABOUR) INPUT MARKETS

Distortionary Taxes

Consider again the market for sheets of 3/4-inch plywood, but now suppose that included in the market price is either a per unit tax or an *ad valorem* tax. In this situation the price consumers pay for the product is not the price firms keep. For example, if consumers pay $45 per sheet and the per unit tax is $8, suppliers retain $37 per sheet. If we denote the consumers' price by P_c, the firms' price by P_f, and the per unit tax by τ, then $P_c - \tau = P_f$. That is, P_c is the gross-of-tax price and P_f is the net-of-tax price.

The case of a per unit tax is illustrated in Figure 6.1, in which D is the demand curve for this input, S is the supply curve for this product before the tax is levied, and S_T is the supply curve when firms take the per unit tax into account. The vertical distance between S and S_T is τ. Recall that in the absence of externalities, the height of D measures the marginal social benefit of this input and the height of S measures the marginal social cost of producing it. With the tax in place, a market equilibrium exists at the point marked A where X_e units of the input are produced and consumed. Firms receive price P_c per sheet from customers, remit τ per unit to the government (shown by distance AB), and retain price P_f, with which they pay their factors of production.

FIGURE 6.1   A Per Unit Tax

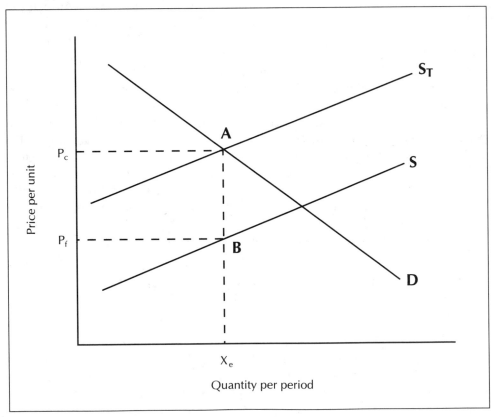

Now suppose that a government agency requires plywood for a project. In Figure 6.2 this increase in demand is represented by the rightward shift of the demand curve from D to D_G. The horizontal distance between these two demand curves measures the government agency's input requirement, which we will denote by X_g, the number of sheets it needs for the project. This causes a new equilibrium to be established at the point marked C. Total production increases from X_e to X_f, the price consumers pay increases from P_c to $P_c{'}$, and the price firms retain per unit rises from P_f to $P_f{'}$.

Note that consumption by nonproject demanders has fallen from X_e to X_c because the price they pay has increased. Thus, the government's requirement of X_g units arises from two sources: $X_f - X_e$ units of new supply and $X_e - X_c$ units from displaced demand. This two-source phenomenon would not matter if this market were undistorted, because at the margin, consumers' marginal benefit (the maximum they are willing to pay for these units) would be exactly equal to firms' marginal cost (the least they are willing to accept to produce them). Here, however, this is not true.

FIGURE 6.2 Project Demand with a Per Unit Tax

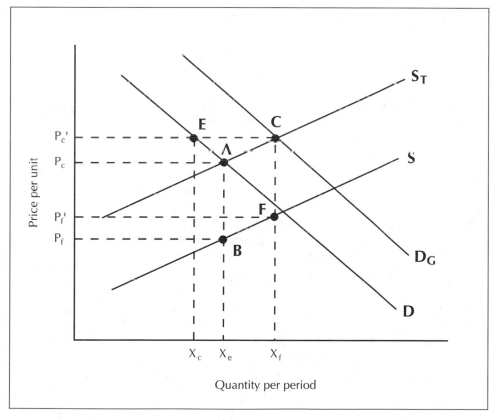

The tax has driven a wedge between consumers' and firms' valuations of this input. Consumers now consume $X_e - X_c$ fewer units than before the project's demand requirements were met. The value of this *displaced demand* to consumers is the maximum they are willing to pay for these units, given by the area under the demand curve $X_c EAX_e$. In their next-best alternative use, these units would be utilized by nongovernment consumers. Therefore, this amount is the opportunity cost of employing these units on the project. Also, resources are used to expand production from X_e to X_f in order to satisfy the *new supply* part of the government's requirement. The opportunity cost of these units is given by area $X_e BFX_f$ under S, which measures the resource cost to society of producing these additional units. Therefore, as the government agency's requirement derives from two sources, the total opportunity cost of the units used on the project is the sum of opportunity cost $X_c EAX_e$ from displaced demand and opportunity cost $X_e BFX_f$ from new supply.

If we ignore the (slight) increase in prices from P_c to P_c' and from P_f to P_f', we can calculate the (approximate) shadow price of this input, denoted by P_G, as

$$P_G = P_f \cdot \frac{X_f - X_e}{X_g} + P_c \cdot \frac{X_e - X_c}{X_g}$$

or, slightly differently, as

$$P_G = P_f \cdot \frac{X_f - X_e}{X_g} - P_c \cdot \frac{X_c - X_e}{X_g}$$

if we follow convention by expressing displaced demand as a negative amount $(X_c - X_e)$, in which case the *minus* sign is needed between the two terms on the right-hand side of this expression.

BOX 6.1

Example

In the plywood example described, the gross-of-tax price, P_c, is $45, the net-of-tax price, P_f, is $38, and the government requires 15,000 sheets. If 12,000 result from expanded production and 3,000 from displaced demand, the shadow price of plywood will be $39.40 per sheet. The total cost an analyst will assess the project for this input is $591,000, even though a cheque will be issued for the full purchase price of $675,000.

Regardless of which expression is preferred, the important point is that this shadow price is a weighted sum of the opportunity costs relevant to the two sources of the government's input requirement. In this situation there are two next-best alternative uses, thus two components of opportunity cost.

Note that the above shadow price depends crucially on the elasticities of supply and demand, for these determine the relative magnitudes of new supply and displaced demand and, it follows, where the shadow price will fall in the range between gross-of-tax and net-of-tax prices. (An equivalent expression for P_G in terms of elasticities is shown in Box 6.2.)

Four extreme cases are shown in Figure 6.3.

- In the figure marked (a), supply is perfectly inelastic ($\epsilon_s = 0$). The increase in demand from D to D_G induces no increase in production. Therefore, all of the project's requirements are satisfied by displaced demand, and the appropriate shadow price of the input is P_c, the maximum consumers are willing to pay for these units. Thus, $P_G = P_c$, the gross-of-tax price.

- In the figure marked (b), supply is perfectly elastic ($\epsilon_s \rightarrow \infty$). The increase in demand from D to D_G is satisfied completely by expanded production. Therefore, none of the project's requirements is satisfied by displaced demand and the appropriate shadow price of the input is P_f, the minimum firms are willing to accept to produce these additional units—their opportunity cost. Therefore, $P_G = P_f$, the net-of-tax price.

BOX 6.2

Elasticity Formula

The equation for P_G may be expressed in terms of demand and supply elasticities. If we denote

$$\Omega = \frac{X_c}{X_f}$$

and ϵ_d and ϵ_s to be, respectively, the elasticities of demand and supply, then

$$P_G = \frac{P_f \cdot \epsilon_s - \epsilon_d \cdot \Omega \cdot P_c}{\epsilon_s - \epsilon_d \cdot \Omega}$$

where P_c and P_f denote gross-of-tax and net-of-tax prices, respectively.

FIGURE 6.3   Extreme Cases

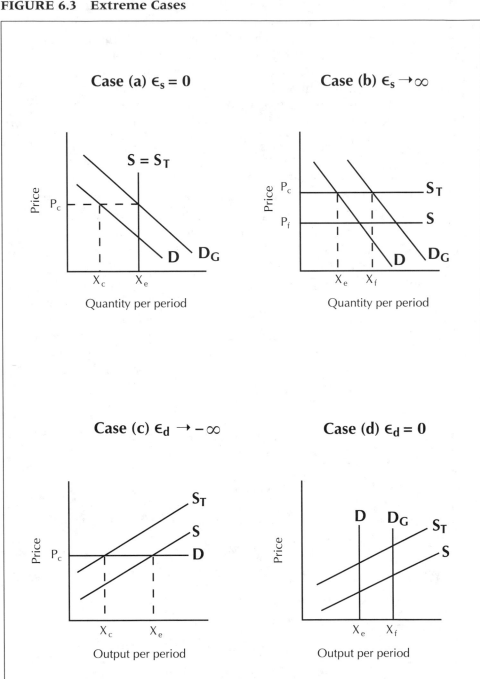

- In the figure marked (c), demand is perfectly elastic ($\epsilon_d \to -\infty$). That is, any upward pressure on the input's price causes the quantity demanded to decrease dramatically. As all project demand is satisfied by displaced demand, $P_G = P_c$, the gross-of-tax price.

- In the case marked (d), nonagency demand is perfectly inelastic ($\epsilon_d = 0$). That is, regardless of any upward pressure on prices caused by the agency's demand, nonagency users will continue to consume X_e units. As there is no displaced demand, the agency's requirements must be satisfied by new supply. The opportunity cost of this new production is simply its resource cost, measured by the height of S. Therefore, $P_G = P_f$ the shadow price of the input is its net-of-tax price.

Although these extreme cases are unusual, there may be circumstances where they are reasonable approximations.

In case (a), where supply is perfectly inelastic, it may be that the input is so specialized that only so many are available. For example, very few high-altitude construction cranes exist, perhaps because they are very expensive to manufacture and their use is so specialized. If such a crane is employed on a public sector bridge project, it follows that it cannot be simultaneously used in the construction of private sector skyscrapers.

In case (b), the entire input requirement may derive from new supply because of idle capacity in the input-producing industry. The agency's demand would apply no upward pressure on prices and, therefore, would cause no nonagency demand to be displaced.

In case (c), perfectly elastic demand implies that the input has perfect substitutes. We suppose a requirement may exist that only locally produced inputs be used on government-financed projects. If the agency's demand puts upward pressure on the prices of these inputs, local private sector demanders may switch to inputs produced elsewhere.

In case (d), perfectly inelastic demand implies that the input is a necessity. This situation may be difficult to imagine, but we might consider a remote location where households obtain water supplies from private wells. Suppose that the project in question requires water for its labourers, to mix cement, to cool machinery, or for any other function. If households are unwilling or unable to sell the agency any of their water, the agency will have to drill its own wells. Therefore, this input will derive completely from new supply.

Distortionary Subsidies

The calculation of shadow prices when markets are subsidized is quite similar to the case of distortionary taxes. (Indeed, we will employ the same notation so that the formulae will be identical.) The general situation of a market distorted by a per unit subsidy is illustrated in Figure 6.4. In this figure, S is the before-subsidy supply curve; its height measures marginal social cost. Supply curve S_S is the supply curve when the per unit subsidy is taken into account. D is the nonagency demand curve for the commodity, and its height measures the marginal social benefit for these consumers.

In the absence of any project (agency) demand for this input, an equilibrium exists at the point marked V. For output X_e, consumers pay price P_c per unit. Suppliers receive this price per unit from consumers plus a per unit subsidy from the government, denoted by σ and shown by distance WV. P_f, the suppliers' price, is thus the sum of P_c and σ. Here, $P_f > P_c$, the exact opposite of the tax case.

Now suppose that a government agency requires some of this input for a project. In Figure 6.4 this increase in demand is represented by the rightward shift of the demand curve from D to D_G. The horizontal distance between these two demand curves measures the government agency's input requirement for the project, which, again, we will denote by X_g. This causes

FIGURE 6.4   A Distortionary Input Subsidy

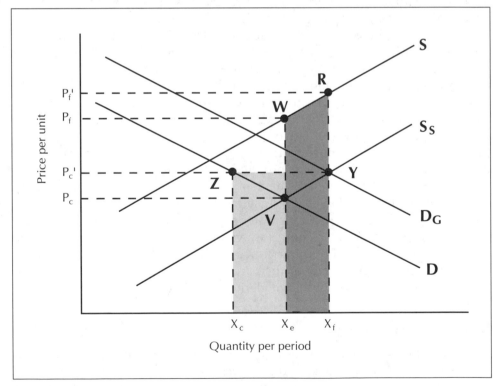

a new equilibrium to be established at the point marked Y. Total production increases from X_e to X_f, the price consumers pay increases from P_c to $P_c{'}$, and the (total) price firms receive per unit rises from P_f to $P_f{'}$.

Note that consumption by nonproject demanders has fallen from X_e to X_c because of the price increase. As with the tax situation, the government's requirement of X_g units arises from two sources: $X_f - X_e$ units of new supply and $X_e - X_c$ from displaced demand. Again, that the agency's input requirement is met by a combination of two sources would not matter if this market were undistorted because at the margin, consumers' marginal benefit of these units would be exactly equal to firms' marginal cost. As with taxes, however, this does not hold in the presence of distortionary subsidies.

The subsidy causes consumers' and firms' valuations of this input to differ. Consumers now consume $X_e - X_c$ fewer units than before the project's demand requirements were met. The value of this *displaced demand* to consumers is the maximum they are willing to pay for these units, given by area X_cZVX_e. In their next-best alternative use, these units would be used by nonagency demanders. This, then, is the opportunity cost of employing these units on the project. Also, resources are used to expand production from X_e to X_f in order to satisfy the balance of the government agency's input requirement. The opportunity cost of these units is given by the area under S between X_e and X_f, here area X_eWRX_f. Therefore, as the government agency's input requirement derives from two sources, the total opportunity cost of the units used on the projects is the sum of the opportunity costs X_cZVX_e from displaced demand and X_eWRX_f from new supply.

Note that because the subsidy causes consumers' valuations of marginal units to be less than suppliers', units of the input for a project deriving from displaced demand are worth less than any that must be produced anew to satisfy the project's requirements. That is, the subsidy has already caused overproduction from a social perspective, into the range of output where the resources required to produce additional units of this product are worth more than what they are used to produce. The maximum consumers are willing to pay for additional units (read off D) is less than what they cost society to produce (read off S).

We have denoted prices and quantities identically in the subsidy and tax situations for good reason: the formulae for calculating the shadow price of this input, P_G, are exactly the same as those used in the tax situation. The only difference is the relative magnitudes of P_c and $P_f{'}$.

Moreover, the same elasticity relationships hold. In the extreme cases where supply is perfectly inelastic ($\epsilon_s = 0$) or demand is perfectly elastic ($\epsilon_d \rightarrow -\infty$), the agency's demand for the input must be satisfied entirely by displaced demand. The opportunity cost of these units is their value in their next-best alternative use—in the hands of nonproject consumers. Therefore, they should be shadow-priced at the artificially low consumers' price P_c. Here what the agency actually pays suppliers for the input is the cost that should be recorded in the cost-benefit analysis. If either supply is perfectly elastic ($\epsilon_s \to \infty$) or demand is perfectly inelastic ($\epsilon_d = 0$), the quantity nonagency demanders consume will not be affected by the project. Therefore, the entire amount demanded for the project will derive from new production. In this scenario the opportunity cost of these units will be the value of the resources used to produce them. This is measured by the height of S. It follows that the appropriate shadow price will be P_f, the price consumers and the agency pay *plus* the subsidy. The drain on the agency's budget will be only P_c per unit; however, the higher price P_f should be used as the shadow price in the cost-benefit analysis in order to reflect the true opportunity cost of the required input.

In all situations we must evaluate the opportunity cost of an input "at source." If the input derives from more than one source, opportunity cost at each source must be evaluated and summed. By dividing this total opportunity cost by the number of units required for the project, we arrive at the shadow price of the input.

Price Supports and Exchange Rate Controls

Consider Figure 6.5, which illustrates a market for which a government has legislated a support price (price floor) at price P_j. To prevent the excess supply that would otherwise exist at this price, and to maintain the support price, the government may have decreed that no more than output Q_j be produced each period. Perhaps a quota for total production has been set by a marketing board or similar body. (This is the case with many agricultural products in Canada such as milk, eggs, chicken, and turkey.) Note that at quantity Q_j, marginal cost is given by MC_j.

Now suppose this commodity is an input and that some of it is required for a public sector project. If the total quota, Q_j, is not lifted, the amount required by the project cannot but derive from displaced demand. Here the opportunity cost of the units acquired for the project is the maximum that nonagency consumers are willing to pay for them. At the margin this amount is price P_j per unit. On the other hand, if the quota is increased in a one-time fashion to satisfy the project's requirements, the resource (opportunity) cost of the units newly produced will be their marginal cost, MC_j.

Instead of an input, now suppose that this commodity is an output and that the project increases production of it, perhaps as a result of improved irrigation. If extra units are produced, their value on domestic markets will be zero, because producers will not be allowed to violate the quota system by selling them. Only if those extra units are exported will extra revenue accrue to producers. In either case, some benefit will occur if enhanced irrigation causes costs of production to fall.

FIGURE 6.5   Price Supports and Exchange Rate Controls

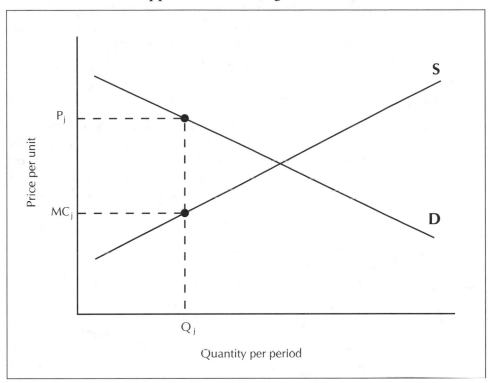

Now interpret Figure 6.5 to illustrate a distorted foreign exchange market. Instead of allowing the value of the domestic currency to fall to its equilibrium level, it may be that a government has adopted a policy of overvaluing its currency. Such a policy will result in its imports being cheaper than otherwise, and its exports more expensive. On foreign exchange markets, there will be excess demand for foreign currencies—a demand the government may satisfy for a time by running down its reserves of foreign currencies. However, these foreign reserves will be exhausted sooner or later. At that point, the government will be able to purchase additional imports only by exporting more; in such situations it is not unusual for the government to impose currency controls in addition to tariffs.[2] The result is an excess demand for foreign (or hard) currencies.[3]

Consider now a project that produces goods for export, or produces goods that are substitutes for imports. Such a project will allow more goods to be imported. Given the scarcity of such imports that policies have created, the value attributed to the project should be shadow priced at the artificially high rate. On the other hand, when a project in such a country requires imported inputs, they can only be acquired at the expense of other imports, and their opportunity cost will be correspondingly high. Tariffs should be treated in the same way. When a shadow exchange rate is used in project evaluation, projects that produce exports and import substitutes are encouraged, and those that require foreign inputs are discouraged.[4]

Monopoly

Figure 6.6 illustrates a monopoly. D represents the market demand curve, MR represents the monopolist's marginal revenue schedule, MC is the monopolist's marginal cost schedule, and AC is the monopolist's average cost curve. A profit-maximizing monopolist will produce Q_M units (where MR = MC) and charge consumers price P_M, the maximum they are willing to pay for the marginal unit.

FIGURE 6.6   Monopoly

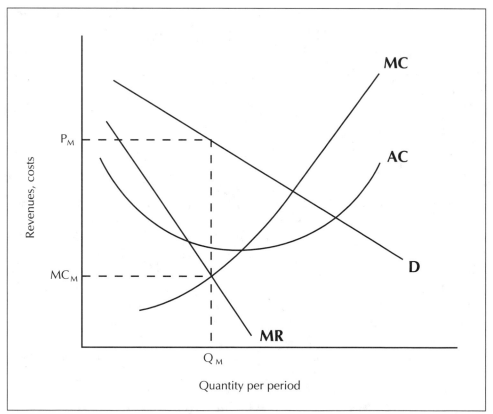

If the monopolist produces an input required by a project, the public agency will pay the monopolist's price of P_M per unit. Nevertheless, the shadow price an analyst should use to evaluate the project can lie anywhere between P_M and MC_M. If the monopolist's output does not increase in response to the agency's demand, it must be that the project's input requirement derives from displaced demand and thus should be priced at P_M so as to reflect its value in its next-best alternative use. However, if the monopolist expands production in order to satisfy project requirements, these units should be shadow priced at MC_M, the value of the resources used to produce them. If project requirements are satisfied by a combination of these two sources, the appropriate shadow price is a weighted average of P_M and MC_M, the weights being the proportions of the project's requirements derived from each source.

Subsidized Output

Quite often the output of a public sector project cannot be sold, perhaps because it involves the production of a public good. In other situations, however, projects do result in new or increased output that is saleable in markets. In these circumstances we must assess the value of this output. Only if the output is sold on undistorted markets will the price it fetches reveal its social value.

Consider a proposed dam project that will enhance the irrigation of agricultural lands. If there is a competitive market for water, it will be simple to assess how much farmers will be willing to pay for it. Often, however, water is not priced—that is, it is not bought and sold in a market. When this is the case, the benefits of enhanced irrigation must be calculated indirectly.

Presumably this irrigation will lead to increased output of (let us suppose) cereal crops. We might then calculate the annual increase in affected farmers' revenues, deduct any annual increase in resource costs, and thus assess the annual benefit of the irrigation as the increase in farmers' profits. This would seem an appropriate methodology. But what if these crops are currently subsidized?

This situation is illustrated in Figure 6.7. The market demand curve for this grain is shown by D. If the grain is not subsidized, the market supply curve is S, and the height of this supply schedule measures the marginal cost of production. A per unit subsidy, however, will cause supply to shift outward to the schedule marked S_S. A market equilibrium will thus be established at point A, and Q_e tons of this grain will be produced each period. Consumers will pay price P_1 per ton. In addition to this price, farmers will receive a subsidy per ton shown by the distance AB, and the total price they receive per ton will be P_2.

FIGURE 6.7   Subsidized Output

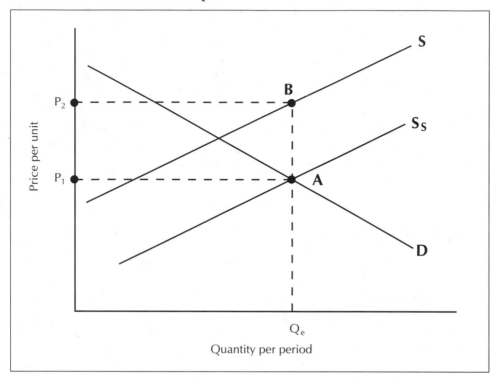

Now consider an irrigation project that shifts the supply curve of this good slightly to the right (assuming this increase in supply is small relative to the size of the existing market). Farm revenues will increase by P_2 times the number of extra tons of grain produced. This, less any additional costs, will yield the farmers' extra profits arising from the project—their benefit. However, this procedure will overstate these irrigation benefits—a common error made in analyses of such projects. Although farmers will receive price P_2 for each extra ton they produce, the social value of this increased output will be the maximum consumers are willing to pay for it. The correct measure is given by the height of the demand curve at point A. Price P_1 is the proper measure, and it should be used as the shadow price of this output.[5]

SHADOW WAGE RATES

Rationale and Measurement

Public sector projects employ labour and pay labourers market wages. Indeed, governments often justify projects on the basis of job creation, paying less heed than most economists would like to whether these "make work" projects actually enhance social welfare. If labour markets functioned perfectly, market wages (including all benefits[6]) would reflect the true opportunity cost of hiring labour for a project. Of course, if labour markets functioned perfectly, anyone willing to work at the market wage would be employed. This, obviously, is not the case, and labour markets are distorted by a number of factors. This is why analysts must calculate the shadow price of labour, the ***shadow wage rate***.

Labour hired on a public sector project can be drawn from three sources: people hired away from employment elsewhere in the economy; people drawn into the labour force by the project; and people involuntarily unemployed. To assess the economic cost of employing people on a project, we must assess the opportunity cost of labour from each source.

When an individual leaves another job to come to work on a public sector project, the value of the output he or she had been producing is forgone. In a well-functioning labour market, the value of this output is best measured by that individual's gross wage (including all employment benefits). We know from Chapter 4 that a profit-maximizing firm will expand employment as long as the value of the marginal product of labour exceeds the wage rate. In other words, a marginal worker just earns the value of what he or she produces. Because psychic benefits or costs from working on the project may differ from those experienced in the previous employment, and because the project wage rate may reflect compensation for moving from the previous job to the project site, the appropriate measure of the opportunity cost of hiring this type of person is simply the gross-of-tax wage (including benefits) paid to him or her by the project. Denote this wage by w_1.

Sometimes projects employ people who are drawn into the labour force by the prospect of working on the project. These people are said to be voluntarily unemployed. For example, world fairs, Olympic games, and the like often draw people out of retirement, and encourage young people to take time off school to work at the event, especially if they have the skills required to work as interpreters for guests coming from around the globe. The opportunity cost of hiring these people is the minimum amount required to induce them to work. As these people had revealed themselves to be unwilling to work at the market wage, and as they must forgo alternative nonmarket activities in order to work on the project, the best measure of their opportunity cost is the net-of-tax wage the project pays them.[7] Denote this wage rate by w_2.

The third source of project labour is the ranks of the involuntarily unemployed—that is, people who are willing to work at the market wage but are unable to find a job. It seems to be the view of some that the opportunity cost of a project hiring this type of labour is zero or negligible.[8] This is not so; to assume this we would have to believe that people involuntarily unemployed put no value on their time, which is something they forgo when they are hired by the project. Presumably these people put a positive value on leisure time even though they are prepared to work at the market wage. Perhaps, as well, they are involved in nonmarket activities such as hunting, fishing, and gardening, all of which contribute to the well-being of their families, and all of which they must forgo once hired by the project. For these reasons, some positive opportunity cost must be imputed to this type of labour.

To assess this opportunity cost we would like to know the minimum amount these people would be willing to accept as an inducement to take employment. Denote this by w_3. Realistically, the best we can do is establish a range of possible values for w_3. We know that these people are willing to work for the existing net-of-tax wage rate, as they are involuntarily unemployed. This, then, is an acceptable upper bound on the opportunity cost of hiring them. Also, this opportunity cost must be higher than the value they put on leisure time, which is the least they are willing to work for (sometimes called their *reservation* wage).[9] Unfortunately, we cannot observe this lower bound. Hughes (1981) uses 20% of the market wage as the value of leisure time forgone; although this is quite arbitrary, it may be sensible to use this or some other some arbitrary lower bound for sensitivity analysis. That is, we might calculate the net present value of the project using a variety of values for w_3 between the net-of-tax wage rate and 20% of the actual wage rate paid.

Assuming that values for w_1, w_2, and w_3 are determined, and letting α_1, α_2, and α_3 denote, respectively, the proportions of those hired by the project drawn from other employment, from outside the labour force, and from the ranks of the involuntarily unemployed, the shadow wage rate (w_s) for project evaluation is given by

$$w_s = \alpha_1 \cdot w_1 + \alpha_2 \cdot w_2 + \alpha_3 \cdot w_3,$$

where $\alpha_1 + \alpha_2 + \alpha_3 = 1$. That is, if L labourers of like job skills are hired by the project, even though the project's total wage bill—the amount workers receive—is $w_1 \cdot L$, an analyst should assess a lower labour cost equal to $w_s \cdot L$.

Even so, we must exercise caution when pricing labour below its market wage when a project employs otherwise unemployed workers. First, if a project causes a decrease in unemployment in one region, inflationary pressures may well be created.[10] If a government responds to these pressures with contractionary monetary and/or fiscal policies, unemployment may be created elsewhere in the economy, thus wholly or partly offsetting employment gains in the region where the project is situated. Second, to deal with unemployment governments implement a variety of policies in addition to public sector projects. Thus, a project may be credited with reducing unemployment in a region, even while ongoing fiscal and monetary policies are also playing a role in its reduction. Ignoring these other factors may result in the underpricing of labour.

These warnings aside, note that the shadow pricing of labour favours projects in regions of high unemployment. For example, even if carpenters would be paid the same wage on a project in British Columbia as on a project in Newfoundland, the opportunity cost of labour for project evaluation will be less in the region with the higher unemployment rate. (See the next section for a discussion of two methods for calculating shadow wage rates that have been used in project evaluation in Canada; and see Box 6.3 for a special situation, in which the shadow wage is the wage actually paid even when unemployment is high.)

Hughes and Gardner Pinfold Methods

As job creation in depressed regions of the country has been the rationale for many public sector projects, it is worthwhile examining one method actually used to assess the opportunity cost of labour. Hughes (1981) provides a method for calculating this datum based on work by Havemen & Krutilla (1968).

Hughes calculates the social opportunity cost of hiring labour (or shadow wage) in locale i to be

$$SOCL_i = P_i \cdot W_i + (1 - P_i) \cdot V \cdot W_i$$

where

W_i	$\equiv$	the wage rate paid workers on the project
U	$\equiv$	the actual unemployment rate in locale i
U^B	$\equiv$	the historical minimum unemployment rate in the area
U^M	$\equiv$	the historical maximum unemployment rate in the area
V	$=$	the proportion of the wage paid that represents the opportunity cost of hiring involuntarily unemployed labour (assumed by Hughes to be 0.20).
P_i	$\equiv$	the probability of hiring a person who is already employed
$(1 - P_i)$	$\equiv$	the probability of employing an (involuntarily) unemployed person. And where

$$P_i = 1 - 0.5 \cdot [\sin(\pi\frac{U - U^B}{U^M - U^B} - \frac{\pi}{2}) + 1]$$

Note that

$$\pi\frac{U - U^B}{U^M - U^B} - \frac{\pi}{2}$$

is a radian value.

Gardner Pinfold (1993) further refines the Hughes formula in its analysis of the Northumberland Strait fixed crossing project. Instead of assuming, as Hughes does, that the opportunity cost of hiring unemployed labour is 20% of the wage rate, they adjust this value for unemployment insurance benefits and the tax rate on these benefits. For V, they solve

$$W \cdot (1 - t_w) = V + UI \cdot (1 - t_{ui})$$

where UI denotes unemployment insurance benefits as a percentage of the wage rate (assumed to be 57%), t_{ui} denotes the tax rate on unemployment insurance benefits (assumed to be 15%), and t_w denotes the tax rate on wages (assumed to be 20%). Gardner Pinfold thus arrives at a value of V equal to 36% of the wage paid by the project.[11] To the extent that the opportunity cost of hiring unemployed labour is the minimum amount these individuals are willing to accept, and that this amount is influenced by unemployment insurance benefits and tax rates, the Gardner Pinfold approach would appear to be somewhat less arbitrary than that of Hughes.

Still, a number of criticisms can be made of this method for calculating shadow wage rates. First, combining notations, P_i is equivalent to α_1 and $(1 - P_i)$ is the same as α_3. This means that the Havemen & Krutilla–Hughes–Gardner Pinfold method implicitly sets α_2, the proportion of labour drawn into the labour force by the project, equal to zero. This seems unlikely. In high-unemployment areas it would not be unusual for the labour force to have previously shrunk by reason of the "discouraged worker" effect. Also, it may be that female participation rates have been low in these areas simply because the likelihood of finding employment has been slight. If participation rates increase in response to the project, we would expect α_2 to be greater than zero.

Second, this shadow wage formulation applies (apparently) to an aggregate of all labour types, whereas calculation of shadow wages skill level by skill level would be more appropriate. For example, if a project requires high-beam construction workers and only so many exist, those we hire to build our public sector bridge towers must necessarily be drawn away from private sector projects such as skyscrapers. None would be drawn from the unemployed; all would be attracted from previous employment. Indeed, in the case of the Northumberland Strait fixed crossing project, Fiander-Good Associates (1987), on the advice of officials of the Department of Regional Industrial Expansion, used a base-case shadow wage equal to the wage rate actually paid to labourers constructing the bridge. This was consistent with the project drawing skilled construction workers away from other employment both in the Maritimes and across the country. On the other hand, Gardner Pinfold (1993, p. 19), using the above formulation, calculates the

BOX 6.3

Shadow Wages in Dual Economies[12]

Consider a dual, underdeveloped economy consisting of a rural sector and an urban sector. The rural sector is characterized by overemployment. That is, an extended family may be working a too-small plot of land so that the marginal product of labour in the rural sector is extremely low, hovering about the subsistence level. Denote this marginal productivity by M.

The urban sector—where a project will be built—suffers from high unemployment, and the probability of having a job in the city is denoted by ø (ø < 1). This unemployment is caused by market imperfections that result in the market wage rate, the one the project pays and denoted by W, being greater than what would cause the urban labour market to clear.

If a project is to be built in the urban sector, workers will migrate from the rural sector in the hope of obtaining employment. The first simplifying assumption of this analysis is that for every job the project creates, 1/ø workers will migrate from the farm to the city, thus causing the urban sector rate of unemployment to be constant despite the project. That is, if ø = 50%, for every job the project creates two people will migrate to the urban sector.

The second simplifying assumption is that rural workers are risk-neutral. That is, they will migrate to the city so long as the expected wage they might earn on the project, ø · W, exceeds M, which is what they earn in the rural sector. In equilibrium—when migration ceases—ø · W = M.

To assess the social opportunity cost (shadow wage rate) of one job created in the urban sector, we must calculate the value of forgone rural production. As output M of rural output is forgone whenever a single worker migrates, and 1/ø workers migrate, the opportunity cost of one project job is M/ø.

But from the condition for migration equilibrium, W = M/ø. Therefore, the central conclusion of the analysis is that the wage actually paid workers on the project represents the opportunity cost of labour in this context. That is, the shadow wage and the market wage are identical.

Of course, this result hinges on the assumptions of the model. For example, if the flow of migration is impeded or if rural sector workers migrate at less than the assumed rate (perhaps because of risk averseness), the shadow wage will be less than the wage actually paid. Still, this simple model may have lessons for more developed countries. For example, it may be that a megaproject in one region of the country will attract more migration from high-unemployment regions than there are jobs created.

social opportunity cost of employing these people to be 36% of the wage rate. Although it may be reasonable to accept the latter estimate as it applies to unskilled, unemployed labour, it is difficult to justify its application to all employee skill classes.

Shadow wage rates should be calculated with caution. Governments of some Canadian provinces seem to believe that their hopes for development rest on public sector "high tech" infrastructure projects. It would seem reasonable that if they are not now "high tech," they must be "lower tech" and have labour forces correspondingly educated or trained. Therefore, construction of such projects will draw little labour from the ranks of their unemployed, and the appropriate shadow wage should approximate the wage rate actually paid. On the other hand, if a proposed project would require much unskilled labour in a high-unemployment area, a shadow wage rate below the market wage may be appropriate.

Analysts must assess shadow wages on a project-by-project basis. Application of any rule of thumb is to be resisted.[13]

CHOOSING A DISCOUNT RATE

Discounting procedures were introduced in Chapter 2 and their use in determining the economic viability of public sector projects was presented in Chapter 3. Recall the formula for net present value:

$$NPV = (B_0 - C_0) + \frac{(B_1 - C_1)}{(1+i)} + \frac{(B_2 - C_2)}{(1+i)^2} + \ldots + \frac{(B_T - C_T)}{(1+i)^T}$$

In this equation, "i" is the discount rate. As many public-sector projects are characterized by large initial costs followed by a stream of net benefits that may extend for decades, it is the magnitude of the present value of later net benefits relative to initial costs that determines whether a project is viable—that is, whether NPV > 0. For a given stream of annual costs and benefits, the higher the discount rate the less likely it is that this public investment criterion will be satisfied. At the other extreme, a discount rate of zero would imply that society weighs future net benefits and present-day costs equally. As has been demonstrated, net present value—and thus economic viability—is extremely sensitive to the choice of discount rate.

The literature on social discount rates is vast and complex. Indeed, a survey of this literature would be book-length itself. Moreover, an advanced knowledge of microeconomic theory and mathematical techniques is required to appreciate this literature—a knowledge that is beyond the level we have thus far required of the reader. Nevertheless, it is possible to appreciate the theory's rudiments, and its application to project evaluation in Canada.[14] In the following discussion we treat interest rate determination in a mythical, perfect, closed economy, and consider the distortions that make it necessary to adjust observed interest rates for project evaluation much as we do for shadow pricing. We then discuss the Canadian experience.

A Simple Model of Interest Rate Determination

Consider how firms might make investment decisions in a perfectly competitive economy if there were neither risk nor distortions of any kind (including taxes), and if they had access to perfect capital markets. If a firm ranked five potential investment projects—call them A through E—according to real rates of return (denoted by ρ) from highest to lowest, and listed the dollar amounts (denoted by I) required to finance each option, it might develop a menu of investment options such as the one in Table 6.1. (Note that we use ρ, which earlier denoted a project's internal rate of return, deliberately. Other names for this rate of return include the marginal efficiency of investment and the marginal efficiency of capital.)

By plotting the above ρ and I values, we could trace out an investment demand schedule for this firm. A possible schedule is shown in Figure 6.8.

Assume further that this firm can borrow or lend (save) at a real rate of interest i in perfect capital markets. Now consider whether project A is worthwhile undertaking. If the firm borrows I_A, $4 million, to finance this project, it will be profitable if $\rho_A > i$. That is, if the rate of interest it pays its bank (or what it pays on newly issued corporate bonds) is less than the rate of return the project would earn, 19%. Indeed, even if the firm had I_A dollars at its disposal, it would be worthwhile investing this sum, as the rate of return it would earn from the project would exceed what the same dollars could earn if saved. On the other hand, the project will not be profitable (financially viable) if $\rho_A < i$. A profit-maximizing firm will not borrow funds at, say, 8% in order to finance a project that earns a modest 5%. A firm will be indifferent to the real investment project if its rate of return is equal to the interest rate the firm faces.

TABLE 6.1 Investment Demand

Investment Project	Investment Dollars Required (I in millions)	Rate of Return (ρ)
A	$I_A = 4$	$\rho_A = 0.19$
B	$I_B = 4$	$\rho_B = 0.17$
C	$I_C = 6$	$\rho_C = 0.14$
D	$I_D = 9$	$\rho_D = 0.09$
E	$I_E = 10$	$\rho_E = 0.04$

FIGURE 6.8 Investment Possibilities

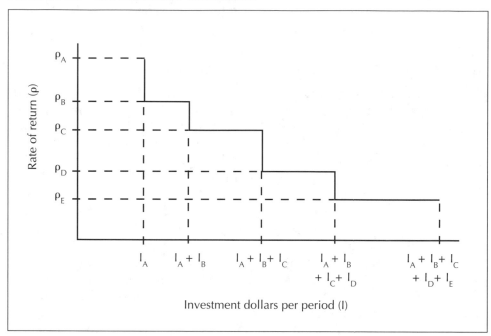

What is true for project A is true for less attractive investments, and what holds for the above firm holds for other firms. In the above example, for instance, if i = 10%, Projects A, B, and C will be viable; Projects D and E will not be. Therefore, this firm's total investment demand will be $14 million to finance these three projects. If i = 8%, Project D will also be viable, and total investment will increase to $23 million.

Profit-maximizing firms will undertake investment projects for which $\rho \geq$ i and invest in none for which $\rho <$ i. Figure 6.9 shows an aggregate investment demand schedule (also called a marginal efficiency of investment curve) and the equilibrium amount of investment (I_e) when the market rate of interest is i_e. Note the following: first, the investment demand schedule becomes smoother as individual firms' schedules are aggregated; second, there is a negative relationship between the rate of interest and total investment; and, third, i = ρ at the equilibrium.

Now consider a consumer who can allocate his or her consumption over the present and the future (assumed to be one year apart), and let δ denote this person's real marginal rate of time preference, a measure of impatience. Suppose that this individual, like the firms above, can borrow and save at real rate of interest i. Note that if this person saves an additional dollar in the present, 1 + i dollars will be available for additional consumption in the

FIGURE 6.9   Investment Demand

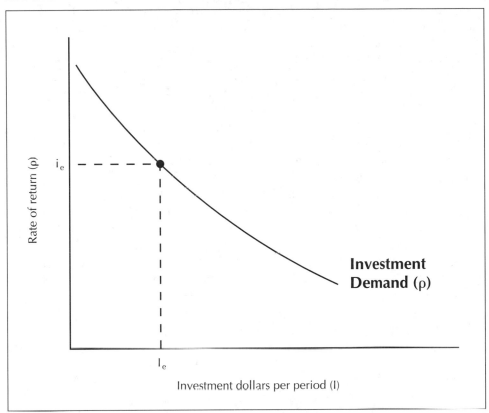

future. That is, the interest rate measures the rate at which this person *can* convert present into future consumption. Naturally, this person will have preferences regarding the relative merits of present versus future consumption. Indeed, most people require compensation in the future if they are to be induced to forgo present consumption. The least this person would be willing to accept in the future to induce him or her to forgo an additional dollar of present consumption is $1 + \delta$ dollars; this is what a marginal rate of time preference measures. Thus, δ measures the rate at which this person is *willing* to exchange present for future consumption.

If $i > \delta$ for a particular dollar, the reward from saving it exceeds its opportunity cost, and it will be worthwhile for the person to save this dollar. Thus, he or she will save all dollars for which $i > \delta$, and the higher the rate of interest, the greater will be the number of dollars saved. Moreover, as more and more dollars are saved, the value of present consumption will increase relative to future consumption. That is, as saving increases the individual will require more and more dollars in compensation for forgone present consumption. If i < δ for a given dollar, the reward for saving it will be less that the minimum the person is willing to accept to forgo present consumption. This dollar will not be saved. Furthermore, i < δ indicates that the individual's intertemporal utility will increase if he or she borrows against future income in order to increase present consumption.

Therefore, in aggregate we would expect net savings to increase as the interest rate increases. Also, in aggregate, δ is called the social rate of time preference. Figure 6.10 shows an aggregate savings schedule where we have netted the borrowing of those who much prefer present to future income out of the savings of those who choose to delay consumption. In equilibrium, when δ = i, S_e dollars will be saved per period.

In a simple closed economy, we can think of a market for loanable funds. The supply of funds is saving net of consumer borrowing, and interest rate increases will encourage increased saving. The demand for loanable

FIGURE 6.10   Aggregate Saving

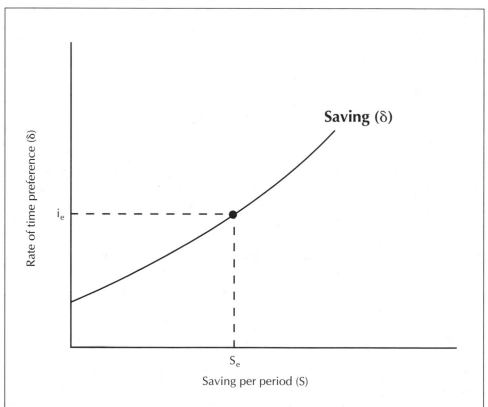

funds is aggregate investment demand, and the relationship between it and interest rates is negative. This simple market is illustrated in Figure 6.11.

Note that the height of the investment demand schedule at any dollar amount measures the lowest rate of return on investment (ρ) investors will accept if they are to be induced to invest those dollars. The height of the savings supply schedule at any dollar amount measures the least rate of return on savings interest (δ) savers will accept if they are to be induced to save those dollars. Investment will expand as long as $\rho \geq i$, and savings will expand as long as $i \geq \delta$, so it must be that in equilibrium, $\rho = i = \delta$. This equilibrium is shown in Figure 6.11, where the equilibrium rate of interest is i_e and the number of dollars saved and invested during the period is $\$_e$. At any rate of interest greater than i_e, savings will exceed investment demand. This excess supply of savings will tend to drive the interest rate down. At any rate of interest lower than i_e, there will exist an excess demand for loanable funds that will exert upward pressure on that rate.

FIGURE 6.11   Interest Rate Determination

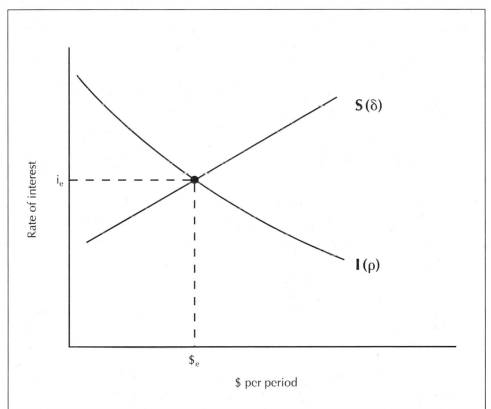

Of course, such a simple, perfect market does not exist. We have outlined one here in order to establish a benchmark, just as we outlined perfectly competitive input and output markets in order to form benchmarks for assessing shadow prices. Of importance here are the properties of the equilibrium (market) rate of interest.

Suppose that a government agency enters the above market in order to borrow funds with which to finance a public sector investment project. If the agency's project is small relative to total domestic investment, only modest upward pressure will be put on the equilibrium rate of interest. Such an increase will typically encourage new saving and discourage some private sector investment—marginal projects will no longer be viable. Thus, as long as neither the supply of savings nor investment demand is neither perfectly elastic nor perfectly inelastic, the agency's financing requirements will derive from two sources: displaced investment demand and new supply of savings. When private sector investment is displaced, the opportunity cost to society is the rate of return it would have earned (ρ).[15] When new savings are attracted, the opportunity cost is the value of forgone consumption (δ). Therefore, if we were to calculate the total opportunity cost of a government's requirement of G dollars with which to finance the project, it would be $\delta \cdot \Delta S - \rho \cdot \Delta I$, where ΔS denotes the increase in saving and ΔI denotes the decrease in domestic investment. If we denote i_s to be the social (shadow) rate of discount, the opportunity cost of the agency's borrowing is given by $i_s \cdot G = \delta \cdot \Delta S - \rho \cdot \Delta I$, where $\Delta S - \Delta I = G$. However, as $\rho = i_e = \delta$ in this market, $i_s \cdot G = i_e \cdot \Delta S - i_e \cdot \Delta I = i_e \cdot (\Delta S - \Delta I) = i_e \cdot G$. Therefore, the market rate of interest, i_e, will accurately measure the social discount rate, and a government in these perfect circumstances should discount future project costs and benefits at this rate, as it reflects the true cost to society of diverting the required funds from private sector investment and saving to the public sector.[16]

Distortions and the Weighted Average Approach

Of course, the above analysis will not do for a more realistic, distorted economy. Although there are myriad factors that can distort capital markets, taxation is a major culprit.

First, people who own firms are interested in after-tax rates of return, whereas ρ measures the *before*-tax rate of return. For example, if a corporation can borrow funds at an interest rate of 8%, then in the absence of risk and taxation all investment projects that earn at least 8% will be viable. Still assuming no risk, if a firm must pay a corporate income tax of 50%, then only projects that earn a before-tax rate of return of at least 16% will be feasible. Therefore, in equilibrium, $\rho > i$. If a public sector project now displaced investment demand, the opportunity cost rate of return to society of these funds, which is the gross-of-tax rate of return to investment, would be greater than the interest rate at which the agency could borrow.

Second, people pay income tax on interest earnings—that is, they forgo current consumption in return for a net-of-tax rate of interest on savings, revealed to be the least they are willing to accept in return for an additional dollar of saving. If a public sector agency acquires some of the required funds from new saving, the opportunity cost rate of return to society of those funds will be the net-of-tax rate of interest on savings, and this will be less than the rate at which the agency can actually borrow.

Third, we do not live in a closed economy. Governments in Canada borrow on international money markets. Indeed, some governments have borrowed so much abroad that a major worry of finance ministers is that rating agencies will downgrade their bonds.[17] When governments borrow abroad, the opportunity cost rate of return of the funds borrowed is the rate of interest required to induce foreigners to lend the required funds.[18]

If we denote the proportions of a public sector agency's financing requirement arising from displaced domestic investment, induced savings, and foreign borrowing, respectively, to be γ_I, γ_S, and γ_F, we can calculate a weighted-average (shadow) social rate of discount to be

$$i^* = i_g \cdot \gamma_I + i_n \cdot \gamma_s + i_f \cdot \gamma_F,$$

where i_g is the gross-of-tax rate of return to domestic investment, i_n is the net-of-tax return to domestic saving, and i_f is the rate of interest paid on foreign borrowing.[19]

Once again, when the financing requirements of a project derive from more than a single source, opportunity cost at each source must be assessed, and proportions determined and then aggregated.[20]

The Social Discount Rate in Canada

Because measurements of i_g, γ_I, i_n, γ_S, i_f, and γ_F are not likely to be perfectly accurate, economists typically conduct sensitivity analyses by calculating net present values for a variety of possible social discount rates. In its *Benefit-Cost Analysis Guide* (1976, p. 26), the Treasury Board provides the following guidance regarding the social discount rate to be used for project evaluation:

> Analysts are encouraged to calculate the net present values of benefits and costs for a range of social discount rates. We recommend the use of a social discount rate of 10 per cent, and of 5 and 15 per cent for sensitivity analyses. It should be noted that these are real, as opposed to nominal, discount rates.

The base rate of 10% the Treasury Board recommends is based on Jenkins (1973), who calculated a (weighted-average) social rate of discount of 9.5% using Canadian data for the years 1965–69. The results for 1965–74 appear in Jenkins (1977). Calculated values for i_g, γ_I, i_n, γ_S, i_f, and γ_F are set out in Table 6.2.[21]

TABLE 6.2   Jenkins' Results

Parameter	Description	Value
γ_I	Proportion from displaced domestic investment	0.75
γ_S	Proportion from increased domestic saving	0.05
γ_F	Proportion from increased foreign borrowing	0.20
i_g	Gross-of-tax return on domestic investment	11.45%
i_n	Net-of-tax return on domestic saving	4.14%
i_f	Interest rate on foreign borrowing	6.11%
i^*	Calculated social discount rate ($i^* = i_g \cdot \gamma_I + i_n \cdot \gamma_S + i_f \cdot \gamma_F$)	10.0%

Sumner (1980) and Burgess (1981) criticize Jenkins' calculations. Both conclude that if various biases were corrected, the recommended social discount rate would be significantly lower. Two of Sumner's arguments follow:

- The data on i_g used by Jenkins are inappropriate because private sector investors demand a rate of return that compensates them for risk-taking. That is, a private sector rate of return includes a risk premium. As we shall see, there are other methods we can use for accounting for risk and uncertainty when evaluating public sector projects. When one of these other methods is used, the social discount rate should not include a risk premium, because this would mean double-counting the cost of risk taking.

- Jenkins' calculation of i_g is biased upward because his data would generate average rates of return to private sector investment. What we wish to measure is the marginal rate of return of investment, because a public sector project will displace marginal private-sector projects. For example, if Projects A through D in Table 6.1 were feasible before the public sector project, their average (weighted) rate of return would be 13.43%.[22] However, if the public sector investment caused the marginal investment, Project D, to be displaced, the true opportunity cost rate to society would be its rate of return, 9%, which is much lower than the average rate.

Burgess (1981) goes further. Among his arguments are these:

- Because of measurement errors, Jenkins's calculation of γ_S is too low, and his estimate of i_S is too high.

- From his review of the literature, Burgess (p. 386) suggests that "incremental foreign funding will contribute somewhere between 1.75 and 2.5 times as much as displaced private investment in the determination of the social opportunity cost of resources withdrawn to finance a public project." That is, Jenkins's estimate of γ_F is understated, and his estimate of γ_I is overstated.

- Regarding i_F, Burgess cites other estimates of this datum in the literature and suggests that approximately 4.6% (compared to Jenkins's 6.11%) is more appropriate.

- Burgess notes that data on rates of return to private sector investment reflect both distortionary and corrective taxes. While this process (akin to shadow pricing) for calculating a social discount rate is necessary because of distortionary taxes, corrective taxes are part of true opportunity costs. For example, private sector firms use public goods such as highways. Ideally, a government would charge user fees that reflect the true cost of using public sector resources, but this is not always feasible. As some taxes paid by firms are substitutes for user fees but are included in estimates of the returns to private investment, these data overstate the opportunity cost of displaced private-sector investment.

Given his reservations, Burgess re-estimated the social discount rate for Canada. He concluded: "Our analysis ... leads to the conclusion that the appropriate social discount rate is in the order of 7 per cent" (1981, p. 393). Indeed, many economists agree with Burgess's estimate. For sensitivity analysis, it is suggested that net present values be calculated at rates of 4% and 10% as well.[23]

Nevertheless, some caution is warranted. Values for i_g, γ_I, i_n, γ_S, i_f, and γ_F are not set in stone, and it may be argued that the data used by Jenkins and Burgess are dated. As corporate and income tax rates change, so will i_g, γ_I, i_n, and γ_S. As foreign sources react to changing debt and deficit levels in Canada, i_f and γ_F will change. Also, as typical public-sector projects have long economic lives, future monetary and fiscal policies are likely important. Although this state of ignorance or lack of foresight may be frustrating, application of a base social-discount rate such as the Treasury Board's or Burgess's to all public sector projects, at the very least, encourages consistent evaluation of them.

SUMMARY

Prices in perfectly competitive, undistorted input and output markets reveal the social value and the opportunity cost of the input or output in question. If inputs for a project are purchased in such a market, the prices paid for the inputs represent their true opportunity cost. If a project produces a good that is sold on such a market, the market price it fetches is its marginal benefit to society. This is not the case if an input or output market is distorted by (non-corrective) taxes or subsidies, price- and/or quantity-setting government intervention, and market power.

When inputs for a project are purchased or a project's output is sold on distorted markets, observable market prices should be adjusted to take into account the source and impacts of the distortion; shadow prices should be calculated and used in the evaluation. In other words, even though market prices are actually paid or received, shadow prices should be used to calculate social costs and benefits.

When markets are distorted, each unit of the input (or output) used (or produced) by a project must be valued at source. In the case of nonlabour inputs, two sources are usual: displaced demand and new supply. The opportunity cost of a particular unit of an input will depend on its source and on the nature of the distortion.

In the case of labour, there may be three sources: previously employed labour, involuntarily unemployed labour, and voluntarily unemployed labour. The opportunity cost to society of hiring a person will depend on that person's situation. Unless all employees on a project were previously employed, the total wage bill actually paid will overstate the social cost of hiring them. Note that all things being equal, the use of shadow wage rates will typically favour high-unemployment regions competing with low-unemployment regions for the same project. Although rule-of-thumb formulae exist for calculating shadow wage rates, their use is to be resisted, because labour requirements are project-specific, not region- or province-specific.

Because capital and credit markets are distorted, unadjusted market interest rates should not be used to discount a project's costs and benefits. Although other methods exist to account for these distortions, we favour the shadow-pricing approach. Relevant here is the marginal valuation of funds from three different sources: displaced domestic investment, new saving, and foreign investment. For base-case scenarios, most analysts use either the Treasury Board's recommended 10% or Burgess's 7% real discount rate. Regardless of the base-case discount rate chosen, it is recommended that base-case calculations be supplemented by sensitivity analysis.

KEY TERMS

shadow price
shadow wage rate

EXERCISES

6.1 In the absence of taxes and subsidies, the demand and supply for steel girders per time period are given by $Q_d = 7,500 - 0.5P$ and $Q_s = 7P$, respectively. However, a per girder subsidy of $150 exists. One thousand girders are required for a project. Calculate the opportunity cost to society of these 1,000 girders and the shadow price of girders.

6.2 In the absence of taxes and subsidies, the demand and supply for bags of cement per time period are given by $Q_d = 1,500 - 10P$ and $Q_s = 140P$, respectively. Nevertheless, a tax of $2 per bag exists. Three hundred bags of cement are required for a project. Calculate the opportunity cost to society of these 300 bags and the shadow price of cement.

6.3 A dam project will cause a parcel of land currently used for agriculture to be flooded, and a reservoir will result. The crop currently being grown on this land is subject to an effective price support and quota scheme. The market price of this land has been assessed as a cost of the project. Is this appropriate?

6.4 Assume $U = 14\%$, $U^B = 6\%$, and $U^M = 16\%$. If a project pays labourers $15 per hour, what shadow wage rate will be attributed to this labour using Hughes's method? How would your answer change if some labour hired by the project were previously voluntarily unemployed?

6.5 If saving were perfectly elastic with respect to interest rates, what discount rate would be appropriate for project evaluation? If saving were perfectly inelastic with respect to interest rates, what discount rate would be appropriate?

ENDNOTES

1. Shadow prices are also called *accounting prices* in the literature.

2. For example, Canadians studying in Britain or Americans studying in Canada face few foreign currency problems. They can exchange one currency for another at most banks. However, this is not the case for students from nations with currency controls who wish to study in North America or Europe. These students must apply to their government or central bank for the foreign currency required for tuition, books, and living expenses if it is only legal for authorities to hold foreign currencies. As foreign exchange markets are not allowed to allocate currencies, an administrative mechanism is usually used to ration scarce foreign currencies.

3. It is also likely that a black market will form. Thus, one Deutschmark might purchase a given number of the local currency at the official exchange rate, but might fetch several times this number on the black market.

4. Given zero or falling tariffs in Canada and a currency that is allowed to respond to market forces, it is not usual or necessary to make foreign exchange adjustments when evaluating Canadian projects. However, it is necessary to do so when projects are being considered in a country whose currency is distorted on foreign exchange markets. Little & Mirrlees (1968) provides guidance concerning evaluation procedures in such circumstances. For an analysis of project evaluation techniques in less-developed countries, see Curry & Weiss (1993).

5. Another way of viewing this is to note that farmers receive price P_2, but included in that price is the per unit subsidy, a cost to the government. From a social perspective, it is necessary to deduct this extra cost.

6. That is, employers' contributions to Canada or Quebec Pension Plans, their share of Employment (formerly Unemployment) Insurance premiums, contributions to company pension plans, and the like—all costs of employing a person—should be included, as this is what employers pay in exchange for the value of what employees produce.

7. Note that before the project, these people were not paying income taxes on labour income. If employed by the project, they do. However, these taxes are simply a transfer and do not enter the calculus.

8. Dasgupta & Pearce (1972, p. 105) state: "If a project employs a resource which would otherwise have been unemployed, the true cost to society is (virtually) zero." Similarly, Pearce & Nash (1982, p. 108) opine that no opportunity cost is incurred.

9. It is likely that reservation wages are sensitive to the value of any transfers the unemployed receive. For example, a person may be willing to work for $100 per week in the absence of (un)employment insurance benefits, but will not work for less than $250 per week if he or she is receiving $130 per week in benefits. In the former case, the opportunity cost of hiring the individual is $100 less taxes. In the latter, the opportunity cost is $120 ($250 − $130) less taxes.

10. This would occur, for instance, if the preproject unemployment rate in a region, regardless of how high it seemed, was actually the natural rate of unemployment—that is, composed only of frictional and structural unemployment.

11. Gardner Pinfold (1993, p.19) calculates the shadow wage rate for ferry cost savings and bridge operating costs to be 32% of the wage paid, and to be 36% of the wage paid for bridge construction.

12. The following is based on a combination of Harberger's "Panama case" (1971) for assessing the social opportunity cost of labour in a dual economy and a linear version of Harris & Todaro's (1971) formal model of the relevant phenomena. An excellent synthesis of the formal (nonlinear) model can be found in Boadway & Bruce (1984).

13. In this context, analysts may find themselves at odds with those who have a political stake in job creation projects. Some analysts will treat the hiring of labour as a project cost; others will view it as a benefit. The difference appears to lie in what each party is attempting to maximize. Economists are concerned with social welfare as described in Chapter 5, but this may be inconsistent with political motives.

14. The basic model is Fisher's (1930), and extensions of it can be found in many intermediate and higher-level microeconomics texts.

15. In order to sell bonds with which to finance a project, a government must offer a sufficiently high rate of interest. As corporate bonds must compete with government bonds, the rate corporations must offer rises, thus crowding out those private sector projects which are not viable at the higher rate.

16. Sen (1961) demonstrates that even if capital markets were not distorted by taxation, market interest rates would not be efficient if people saving for bequests did not take into account all of the benefits of saving for bequests. This intergenerational externality arises when the benefit a saver's contemporaries feel when the saver's heir is made better off because of an inheritance is not taken into account. Because this external benefit is ignored, less is saved than what would be efficient.

17. When a government's bonds are downgraded, it means they will be treated as a riskier financial vehicle than before. To compensate potential bond buyers for this increased riskiness, a government must offer a higher rate of interest if it wishes to raise additional dollars, and this adds to the costs of borrowing.

18. Typically, Canadian governments borrow in foreign currencies: American dollars, Japanese yen, Deutschmarks, Swiss francs, and so on. Principal and interest payments are thus made in foreign currencies. Although the rates of interest on these bonds sometimes appear low relative to what is required to induce Canadians to purchase Canadian dollar-denominated bonds, allowance should be made for exchange rate risk. That is, if American dollars are borrowed, and then the Canadian dollar falls relative to the American dollar on foreign exchange markets, the effective rate of interest paid will be higher than otherwise.

19. For a critique of this method, see Feldstein (1972).

20. The distortions present cause the social cost of displaced investment to be much greater than that of forgone consumption. Moreover, this cost depends on what proportion of investment returns are consumed instead of reinvested. Those who wish to pursue this and other problems, and take a more mathematical approach to this topic, might begin their own search of the literature with Marglin (1963), Harberger (1972), and Feldstein (1972).

21. See Burgess (1991).

22. This is the solution to $(0.19) \cdot \$4$ million $+ (0.17) \cdot \$4$ million $+ (0.14) \cdot \$6$ million $+ (0.09) \cdot \$9$ million $\div$ the total investment, $\$23$ million.

23. If projects could be financed by nondistortionary taxation, it would be appropriate to discount public sector projects at the social rate of time preference. If a project were financed wholly by distortionary taxes and not by debt finance, it might be argued that this same rate should be used and that the deadweight loss of taxation should be assessed as a cost of the project.

CHAPTER 7

VALID VALUATIONS — PROBLEMS IN PROJECT EVALUATION

INTRODUCTION

This chapter presents a number of practical problems with which analysts must deal. Although the economics of the issues to be discussed may not seem complicated at first, tread carefully, as failure to understand these issues well is the source of many errors in "real life" cost-benefit analyses. Although a "perfect" cost-benefit analysis may never be conducted because of data and information constraints, the avoidance of fundamental errors in method seems a reasonable and practical objective.

Note that all errors, omissions, and incorrect inclusions in project evaluation do not create the same bias. Some will cause the net present value of a project to be understated; others will result in a project's viability being exaggerated. In the following, we will point out directions of possible bias and, when feasible, present "real world" examples of errors and error avoidance.

DEALING WITH INFLATION

In Chapter 6 the social discount rate to be used for project evaluation was described as *real* as opposed to *nominal*.[1] That is, the social discount rate described was net of inflation, whereas any observed market rate of interest has two components: a real rate of return and, in addition, an adjustment for (expected) price level changes.

For example, suppose that at t = 0 an individual is willing to save $100 for a year at an interest rate of 3% in the absence of inflation. Here, 3% is a real rate of interest; this individual is willing to forgo $100 of current consumption in exchange for purchasing power of $103 at t = 1. Now suppose that inflation has been steady at 5% for a number of years so that borrowers, lenders, buyers, and sellers all fully expect prices to increase by 5% between t = 0 and t = 1. This means that an item which costs $103 at t = 0 will cost

$108.15 at t = 1. When inflation is at 5%, to reap the same increase in purchasing power as with no inflation, a person saving $100 at t = 0 would have to earn an interest rate of 8.15%.

Note that if we denote the real rate of interest by i and the rate of general price inflation by ψ such that i = 0.03 and ψ = 0.05 above, $(1 + i) \cdot (1 + \psi)$ = 1.0815. Here, 8.15% is the *nominal* rate of interest required to achieve the same increase in purchasing power. If we denote the nominal rate of interest by i_n, then $(1 + i) \cdot (1 + \psi) = (1 + i_n)$.[2] Note that the present value of the real amount $103 at t = 1 discounted at the real discount rate of 3% is $100 at t = 0 and that the present value of the nominal amount $108.15 at t = 1, discounted at the nominal discount rate of 8.15%, is $100 at t = 0.

Now consider a project for which the stream of net benefits from t = 0 to t = T denominated in *real* dollars is $B_0 - C_0$, $B_1 - C_1$, $B_2 - C_2$, $B_3 - C_3$, ..., $B_T - C_T$. When we use a *real* rate of discount, i, to aggregate these net benefits, the net present value of the project is given by

$$NPV = (B_0 - C_0) + \frac{(B_1 - C_1)}{(1+i)} + \frac{(B_2 - C_2)}{(1+i)^2} + \dots + \frac{(B_T - C_T)}{(1+i)^T}$$

Suppose that steady inflation of ψ% per year is expected throughout the life of the project. Measured in nominal dollars, the net benefit stream will be $B_0 - C_0$, $(B_1 - C_1) \cdot (1 + \psi)$, $(B_2 - C_2) \cdot (1 + \psi)^2$, $(B_3 - C_3) \cdot (1 + \psi)^3$, ..., $(B_T - C_T) \cdot (1 + \psi)^T$. That is, net benefits in each year except the first will be inflated by ψ% compounding over time.

An analyst who wishes to assess the same project, but measure net benefits in nominal dollars, should use a nominal discount rate. The expression for net present value is, thus,

$$NPV = (B_0 - C_0) + \frac{(B_1 - C_1) \cdot (1+\psi)}{(1+i) \cdot (1+\psi)} + \frac{(B_2 - C_2) \cdot (1+\psi)^2}{(1+i)^2 \cdot (1+\psi)^2} + \dots + \frac{(B_T - C_T) \cdot (1+\psi)^T}{(1+i)^T \cdot (1+\psi)^T}$$

Note that all $(1 + \psi)$ terms cancel in the above expression. This means that the present value of the real net benefit stream discounted at a real discount rate is exactly equal to the present value of the nominal net benefit stream discounted at the corresponding nominal discount rate.

This would seem to suggest that an analyst will be indifferent as to whether all nominal values or all real values are used. There is, however, a major difference. Although the equivalence holds even if real interest and inflation rates vary over time (as long as the net benefit and nominal discount rate in every year are adjusted proportionately), to use all nominal values an analyst would have to forecast the inflation rate for every year of the project. This would be a formidable task even if it could be performed accurately. If inflation rates were not forecast perfectly, a source of error would be introduced into the calculation. On the other hand, using real net benefits and a real discount rate requires no information about rates of inflation. An analyst would be interested in changes in relative input and output prices over the planning horizon, but could safely ignore movements in the general price level.

Analysts are well advised to measure all benefits and costs in real (constant) dollars and to calculate net present values using a real discount rate. This has become the general practice in cost-benefit analysis, and the dollars of the year corresponding to t = 0 are typically the constant dollars chosen to express monetary values.

STARTING DATES, PLANNING HORIZONS, AND SCRAP VALUES

If a dam takes one year to build and is built in 1997, it will not be built in 1998 or 1999; if built in 2003, it was not built in 2001 or 2002. Presumably, a public sector agency could choose to build the dam in any of these years. Which one?

The key is that these are mutually exclusive projects. If the dam will have the same economic life regardless of when it is built (say 100 years), then it is simply a matter of comparing net present values *as of the same baseyear*. As a delay of one year will push construction costs, the first year of service, and the end of the dam's economic life all into the future by one year, discounting all values back one year will maintain the relevant comparisons.

This is not to say that the timing of a project is not important. Population changes—and thus changes in aggregate willingness to pay—can cause net present values to differ. For example, as a population ages, its willingness to pay for any age-related public facility like a retirement home will increase, while its demand for primary school space will dwindle. Expectations of new, cheaper construction technologies may also influence net present values. For example, nuclear reactors cost much less per unit of output to build in the 1990s than they did in the 1970s because of the introduction of modular designs. Presumably, had we as a society anticipated this change, we might have judged it worthwhile to postpone construction of the Point Lepreau power plant in New Brunswick. Although we do not expect perfect foresight, sometimes future developments are quite predictable within reasonable limits. As well, costs may differ because of shadow pricing. For example, if 2003 is expected to be a high-unemployment year relative to 2004, we would expect shadow wage rates to be lower in 2003 than in 2004.

All things being equal, the net present value of the 2003 dam will be greater than the net present value of the 2004 dam when we compare the two as of the same baseyear.

Another example: Consider an energy project that consists of a large solar-energy collection facility or a wind-power farm. The optimal starting date of this project will likely be sensitive to expected changes in oil and/or hydroelectricity prices. If these relative prices are expected to increase quickly in the near future, it may be best to build the solar or wind generators sooner rather than later. If these prices are not expected to increase for a decade, it may be best to delay construction.

Analysts typically do not choose the termination date (t = T) of a project, or determine its economic life. If engineers and architects say that a bridge will last 100 years after construction or that a dam will last 50 years, so be it. Indeed, given customary discount rates, it would be unusual if the net present value of such a project was sensitive to small changes in its economic life. For example, whether a bridge is expected to be serviceable for 80, 90, or 100 years after construction will usually have little impact on the sign or magnitude of the project's net present value.

Nevertheless, not setting the planning horizon (T) to the expected life of the project can lead to other errors. For example, in its 1987 analysis, Fiander-Good Associates assumed that the Northumberland Strait Fixed Crossing to replace the existing ferry service would take five years to construct and would last 100 years once built. However, part of the project proposal involved paying the bridge builder the annual subsidy the ferry service would have received and, in addition, allowing the operator to collect the tolls the ferry service would have collected for 35 years after construction. At the end of 35 years of service (after five years of construction), ownership of the bridge would revert to the federal government. Perhaps because of these factors, Fiander-Good Associates used a planning horizon of 40 years instead of the 105-year economic life of the project.

The problem this led to was that the bridge would still have 65 years remaining in its economic life at the end of the planning horizon. On this basis, Fiander-Good Associates calculated that the bridge would have a scrap value at year 40 of the project equal to 65% of what it cost to build, a benefit to the project ... which leads us to the issue of assessing scrap values.

A scrap (terminal) value should be determined the same way as any other economic value. An asset's value is its worth in its next-best alternative use. In the case of a steel bridge project, the next-best alternative use of girders is likely to be as scrap metal. If a competitive market for scrap metal exists, the price paid will reflect its economic value.

Fiander-Good Associates' method was not correct. Indeed, historical accounting methods like those it used result in a flaw that would cause every project to be deemed viable. Consider: If after 35 years of use the bridge is worth 65% of its original cost, then after five years of use it must be worth 95% of its original cost, and after one year of use it must be worth 99% of its original cost. Therefore, when it has just been built, it must be worth what it cost to build—it is economically viable. Using this method *assumes* economic viability instead of determining it.

Of course, the whole notion of selling a bridge for scrap before its usefulness has ended is silly, and so is the idea of expending resources to dismantle it. Our point is that this situation could have been avoided if the planning horizon of the project had been aligned with its economic life. Including dismantling costs and the scrap value of the steel girders discounted 105 years to the beginning of construction would have negligible effect on the net present value of the project.

Note that choosing a planning horizon based on the duration of a government's involvement or noninvolvement in a project misses this point: cost-benefit analysis is concerned with the costs and benefits of a project *to whomever they accrue*. As similar public-private partnerships are becoming more common, analysts should bear in mind that the government and the builder are both full members of society for the purpose of evaluation and, as such, should be treated symmetrically.

DEPRECIATION AND INTEREST CHARGES

Accountants routinely assess depreciation (capital consumption) allowances for firms' capital assets for tax purposes. For example, if a construction firm purchases earth-moving equipment, it may claim 30% of its cost annually until the allowance is exhausted. On the other hand, the full cost of computer software may be deducted in the fiscal year in which it is purchased. The rule of thumb is that the more durable the item, the lower the percentage of its cost that can be claimed each year.

For cost-benefit analysis, obviously if both the capital cost of a project and corresponding depreciation charges were included in net present value, the cost of the project would be overstated. That is, inasmuch as the sum of depreciation allowances reflects the initial capital cost, this cost would be double-counted. Therefore, analysts should include only capital costs and ignore depreciation.

Depreciation is also used incorrectly if it is calculated as the cost of a project's assets wearing out. For example, if a bridge costs $1 billion to build and is expected to last 100 years once built, an analyst may be tempted to assess a depreciation charge of $10 million per year. This, too, would result in double-counting whether the bridge was being maintained or not. Both situations are explained below.

Suppose that expenditures are being made regularly on the upkeep of the bridge. These costs may involve painting, repaving, periodic replacement of components, and other regular maintenance. All of these costs will be explicitly included in the net present value of the bridge. That is, explicit maintenance costs will be included precisely because the bridge is *not* being allowed to deteriorate. If depreciation charges are then added—costs meant to reflect the deterioration of the bridge when it is not in fact deteriorating—costs will be exaggerated. Here, actual expenditures on maintenance should be included, and bookkeeping depreciation charges should *not* be included.

Now suppose that the bridge is being allowed to deteriorate over time. If benefits are measured correctly, presumably they will be decreasing over time relative to what they would have been had the bridge been maintained. That is, the stream of benefits will be lower than otherwise. If depreciation costs were now calculated, they would charge again for that which was already being accounted for by the reduced benefits. Again, to include depreciation would be to overstate the costs of the project.

The inclusion of interest charges results in an error similar to that of calculating depreciation costs. Suppose a project costs $120 million, takes one year to construct, and is expected to last forever. If the rate of interest for financing the project is 7%, we may be tempted to assess an annual interest charge of $8.4 million each year of the project's life beginning at t = 1. Note, however, that the present value of this stream of interest charges is $120 million, which is the capital cost of the project. To count the capital cost *and* the interest charges would be to double-count. Be aware that how a project is financed is irrelevant: we are concerned only with resource costs. Interest payments, whether they are paid or not, and whatever period they are paid, are simply transfers between lenders and borrowers and, therefore, should not be part of the calculation.[3]

MARGINAL VERSUS AVERAGE COSTS

To assess a project, an analyst needs to know the opportunity cost of the extra resources allocated to construction of the project; in other words, he or she must know the marginal cost of whatever it is being produced. Sometimes, however, average rather than marginal costs are used, and this causes total costs to be understated or overstated depending on the underlying production technology.

For example, suppose a province is considering building a new highway. It may be that another highway has been constructed in the province and that the provincial Department of Transportation knows its length and what it actually cost to construct. Given these data, it may have determined that highways cost so many dollars per kilometre to construct. For example, that cost may be on the order of $1.5 million per kilometre—an average cost figure. So, if the proposed highway is to be 446 kilometres long, officials may think it appropriate to use a cost estimate of $669 million. Setting aside differences in topography, climate, and geography, this method of calculation will yield a correct measure of construction costs for the new highway only if marginal and average costs are identical. Yet these are not likely to be the same.

Suppose that the highway on which this cost estimate is based is longer than the proposed highway, and that construction of it proceeded from beginning to end without interruption. As there are sure to be fixed costs associated with highway construction, these costs would have been spread over more and more kilometres as it was built. This suggests that the average cost per kilometre fell as construction proceeded. In whatever context, if average cost decreases as quantity expands, marginal cost must be less than average cost. *Ceteris paribus*, average cost will not fall by as much on the proposed, shorter highway; from this, it follows that the use of average cost data from the first highway will result in understatement of the cost of the proposed highway. Note also that if the proposed highway were *longer* than the first, its total cost would be *over*estimated.

Or it may be that the proposed highway will be built in stages. At the beginning of each stage there may be startup costs, such as the costs associated with hiring labour and moving the required heavy equipment to the site. If so, marginal costs will tend to be high relative to the average cost of building a highway in a single stage. Here, the cost of the proposed highway will be underestimated.

These biases are difficult to avoid. Cost estimates for projects are often provided by the relevant government department or ministry, be it Public Works, Transportation, or Energy. As average cost data are readily available, and as marginal cost calculations may be time-consuming and expensive to make, it is not unusual for the former rather than the latter to be used. When they are, and when marginal project costs are not obtainable, it may be that the best an analyst can do is determine the direction of any likely bias and report as much. Cost estimates are just that—estimates—and should be subjected to sensitivity analysis in any case. If a potential bias exists because only average rather than marginal cost data are available, an analyst may be able to provide decision-makers with information regarding possible estimate bias in addition to the results of the sensitivity analysis.

INTERGOVERNMENTAL GRANTS

Most of us have driven by a highway construction project where large signs have been erected to inform the public of both provincial and federal governments' contributions to the financing of the project. In newspapers, federal, provincial, and municipal contributions to projects like libraries and hospitals are noted. A provincial treasurer or transportation minister will likely perceive the federal contribution to a highway project as a benefit; a mayor will perceive outside monies helping to build a town library in the same way. Are such financing agreements relevant to cost-benefit analysis? This is an important question, because many projects administered by provinces would not proceed without federal funding.

If analysts viewed every project from a national perspective, these grants could be ignored because they are simply transfers. Thus, if the federal government contributed x dollars to the cost of a provincial project, the benefit of x dollars to the province would be balanced by the cost of x dollars to the federal government. From a national perspective, the two amounts would cancel.

Suppose, however, that an analyst takes a more parochial, provincial view. That is, he or she—who may be an employee of a provincial government or of a consulting firm hired by a province—may wish to assess only those benefits and costs which accrue to the province in question, and ignore any costs or benefits accruing to other provinces or to the federal government. He or she might, then, be inclined to view a federal government grant of x dollars as a benefit (or, equivalently, as a reduction in costs) of x dollars. Indeed, in the calculation, treating the federal contribution in this manner might swing the net present value of the project from negative to positive.

Note that the analyst has ignored the opportunity cost of these dollars. For example, in spending this money on a highway project, the province will be forgoing the opportunity to spend it on schools. If the federal contribution is counted as a benefit to the highway project, it must also be counted as an offsetting cost. The two cancel each other.

If, on the other hand, the federal contribution is conditional on the monies being spent on a particular project, then an analyst could argue that there is no associated opportunity cost. That is, spending these dollars on a highway will not cause the province to forgo any alternative project or program; there will be no offsetting opportunity cost. This argument, however, requires us to believe that there is no possibility that the province will receive these monies in some other form. Inasmuch as the federal government seems committed to regional development and equal treatment of the provinces, it may be that should the province in question decide not to proceed with a highway project (for example), the federal government will feel obligated to help finance some other project.

The issue seems to be this: Just how "conditional" are conditional grants? Staying with the highway example, assume that the province in question accepts the federal funds. The next time the province appeals to the federal government for project funding, will the federal authorities object, citing the earlier financing? Will Ottawa tell the province that as it has just received x dollars, it will have to wait its turn, until other provinces' needs are addressed? If so, there is an opportunity cost associated with federal grants that offsets any perceived provincial benefit.

It is our view that intergovernmental grants should be ignored in project evaluation. Moreover, projects should be viewed from a national perspective. If an analyst wishes to calculate and report the municipal, provincial, and federal impacts of a project separately, so be it—as long as *all* costs and benefits are considered. That is, we think that there is almost always an opportunity cost associated with spending outside funds.

If the above view is taken, the likelihood of proceeding with projects that are not viable is diminished. Moreover, the provinces are then obliged to treat federal financing as a scarce commodity to be allocated accordingly. As a result, even if Ottawa is committed to the economic development of a particular region or province, projects will be financed according to their net present value rankings.[4] Presumably, waste will be avoided because only those projects which contribute the most to economic development will be financed. Projects that aren't viable without intergovernmental grants will not become artificially viable with them. The same applies *mutatis mutandis* to the relationships between provinces and lower levels of government such as cities, towns, counties, and townships.

SPILLOVER AND SECONDARY EFFECTS

Consider a multipurpose dam project on a river. If it is built, a reservoir will be created that will provide flood protection, a source of water for agriculture through irrigation ditches, and a recreation facility for boaters, wind surfers, and swimmers. The dam would likely have other impacts, including the following:

Impact I   The productivity of nearby agricultural lands would be enhanced, and farm profits would increase.

Impact II   The increase in agricultural production would lead to increased profits for firms that supply inputs to farmers, such as fertilizer and machinery.

Impact III The increase in agricultural production would lead to increased profits for firms that process agricultural outputs, such as millers and meat packers.

Impact IV   The recreation facility would lead to increased profits for local restaurateurs and hotel owners.

Impact V   The altered flow of water would cause downstream dredging to be required more frequently than otherwise for navigation.

Impact VI   The altered flow of water would be conducive to fish breeding, and thus would enhance a downstream freshwater fishery.

Impact VII   The increase in demand for construction workers would cause the wages of those workers to increase.

Some of the above impacts should be taken into account in a cost-benefit analysis. Others should be ignored. To wit, Impacts I, V, and VI should be part of the calculations, and the rest should not be.

Impacts to Count

Generally, only those impacts which would result in changes to physical production should be counted. Those involving redistribution of income would be counted elsewhere, or would be offset in some other manner and so should be ignored. Three situations where the direct or indirect impacts of the dam project should be counted, and four where they should not be, are described below. Common to Impacts I, V, and VI is a technological change. That is, the production possibilities of the economy would be changed by the dam, and result in changes in output.

Direct Impacts

Regarding increased farm output (Impact I), this benefit is attributable to enhanced water supplies. (Note that if water were priced, this benefit would be revealed in the market for water.) Land productivity would change— physically—and the increase in profits (the increase in revenues less any change in costs) would reflect the value of this water. Of course, any increase in the value of this land should not be counted, as it is simply a reflection of increased profits, which presumably would be counted as a benefit. (That is, either the increase in land values or the present value of the increased profits should be counted as a benefit, but not both.) Other direct impacts of the proposed dam would include flood protection and the recreation facility. Note, again, that these involve physical changes.

Negative Technological Spillovers

In the case of dredging for navigation (Impact V), the dam would cause a *negative technological spillover* (or externality). As the river would have to be dredged more often, this spillover would involve a real resource cost to the economy. Another example of such a spillover from this project relates to water quality: if downstream users had to treat (filter) the water more than otherwise for either drinking or industrial use, the resources they would have to expend for this purpose should be assessed as a cost of the project.

Again, there would be a physical impact that would alter the capability of the river to yield society utility. It would not matter whether those affected negatively were compensated by the government or by the builder, as this compensation would involve transfers only.

Positive Technological Spillovers

The impact on the downstream fishery (Impact VI) would be a *positive technological spillover*. A physical change would occur that would alter the production capabilities of the river. Fishery operators would enjoy increased profits as a result of some combination of increased revenues and decreased costs, and these extra profits would reflect the value of the dam to this activity.

Note that parties benefiting from this type of spillover would be willing to pay for the indirect benefits bestowed on them. Whether they would *actually* pay for these benefits is immaterial: they would exist, and would have to be assessed, with a willingness-to-pay measure if feasible.

Impacts Not to Count

Secondary impacts should not be counted if they are purely pecuniary (thus redistributive), or are offset in some manner, or are accounted for elsewhere in the analysis.[5]

Secondary Induced Benefits

Consider Impact II. The increase in agricultural production would be a *direct* benefit of the project. It would lead to increased demand for farm inputs and thus extra business for firms that supply items such as fertilizers and farm machinery. These are called *secondary induced benefits*.

Note that if increased farm profits are assessed as a benefit of the project, the value of the inputs required to produce more farm output in the form of tons of grain and/or head of livestock will have already been accounted for in the price of this output. To make separate provision for these secondary benefits would be to double-count.

For example, when a factory produces a car that is sold for $30,000, that car's value is $30,000. If we then added on the incomes of all of the inputs that go into the manufacturing process—wages, salaries, interest, rents, and profits—also as benefits of producing the car, we would soon arrive at a value of $60,000. When we use national income accounting methods to calculate GDP, we must avoid this error. We do so by either counting the value of final goods and services *or* summing the *value added* at each stage of production. Both methods yield the same total. One method is always used; both methods are never used.

Note that a project can result in induced secondary costs. Assume, for example, that a project involves terminating a rail service. Less fuel will be required, and there will be a chain reaction of reduced business for fuel retailers, fuel wholesalers, fuel refiners, and so on. When analyzing such a project, we count the resource saving using the same approach as we took just above to count resource costs.

Secondary Stemming Benefits

Consider Impact III. The increase in agricultural output would lead to increased production by firms that process agricultural outputs, such as millers and meat packers. These impacts are called *secondary stemming benefits*. Consider the following two situations.

Suppose that resources in the economy are fully employed. Example: For a meat-packing plant to expand in response to a project-induced supply of extra cattle, resources would have to be drawn away from other uses. In this way, there would be a gain of output in one sector and a loss of output elsewhere, with corresponding changes in income. Only if we are concerned with income distribution will we factor in this impact. If the distribution of income—especially across regions—is important to policy-makers, then it is appropriate to report these off-setting positive and negative impacts. Otherwise, their impact on the net present value of the project is assumed to be zero.

When resources are not fully employed, it may be argued that a net gain should be assessed to the expansion of a secondary activity, as there is no (wholly or partly) offsetting contraction of output elsewhere. For example, if employment increases in a secondary activity, and some of the labour hired was previously unemployed, it may be appropriate, when assessing the cost to the economy of employing these people,[6] to use a shadow wage rate that is less than the market wage rate. In such a situation, any increase in revenues in the secondary market would not be offset by the opportunity cost of the expanded activity.

Even so, secondary stemming benefits should not be assessed as a matter of course when resources are idle. This would be to assume that these resources would be unemployed over the entire life of the project. For typical long-lived projects, this is unlikely. We recommend, as a base-case assumption for project evaluation, that secondary benefits *not* be attributed to projects when resources are unemployed. An analyst who wishes to assess these benefits should be required to justify doing so—that is, provide evidence that unemployment would persist over the life of the project in the absence of the project.

Pecuniary Spillovers

Consider Impact IV. The reservoir would attract people for recreational activities, and the volume of business would increase in local restaurants. Examine first a situation where this increase in activity would *not* lead to price increases.

The increase in restaurant business near the reservoir does not represent any gain to society as a whole. If the reservoir is not built, people will eat elsewhere, either at home or in other restaurants. Alternatively, when people spend more on restaurant meals, because of their own budget constraints they must spend less on other goods and services. In this way, economic activity is transferred from one area to another. There would be distributional impacts as restaurateurs near the reservoir gain and those elsewhere lose, but there would be no overall expansion.

If restaurant prices increased in response to the new business, restaurateurs' profits (economic rents) would rise. But if the price of a particular meal increased by one dollar, those who paid it would be worse off by a dollar, and the restaurateur who received it would be better off by the same dollar. Again, this is simply redistribution, and has no impact on the economic viability of the project, or lack thereof.

Impact VII is another pecuniary externality. An increase in wages with no corresponding increase in output is a transfer and should not be counted. Employee gains are offset by employer losses.

Land Values

The dam project we are using as an illustration would cause land values to change. Sometimes this type of change reflects a real phenomenon—the production possibilities of the land in question change—but the value of the change is captured elsewhere in the analysis. And sometimes the change is illusory.

For example, the farmland the project would irrigate would increase in value because of its greater productivity. This would be a real benefit to society; but if annual increases in farm profits have already been attributed to the project, and because these increases would be capitalized into the value of agricultural lands, to count the increase in land values as a benefit of the project would be to double-count. That is, the increase in value of the land would reflect a real benefit, but that benefit would already have been counted.

The value of the nearby land on which the restaurant in our example is situated would also increase. Note, however, that the productive capability of this land would not change. Although the project would make the owner of this land better off, this change in land value would be a reflection of the enhanced profitability of the restaurant business and would be offset elsewhere. For example, if restaurant profits were to rise near the project site, they would fall elsewhere, as would the values of those businesses. Restaurateurs would be attracted to the project site, and we would expect their willingness to pay to increase for existing restaurants. On the other hand, the demand for restaurants located elsewhere would decrease correspondingly.

More generally, transportation and other projects may cause land values to change. This change should not be counted because it is offset elsewhere, or because it is accounted for elsewhere.

An example of an offsetting change: A new road is constructed that draws traffic away from an older road. Service stations along the new road flourish, and those along the original road decline. Increasing service station profits along the new road are offset by decreasing service station profits along the old road. Here, an increase in land values along one road is being offset by decreasing land values along the other.

An example of a land value change that would be accounted for elsewhere: Improved commuter service is proposed between a major business centre and some outlying town or village. Without this service, few people are willing to commute from the village to work in the city. Once the service is provided, people will find it more feasible to live in the country and work in the city. Once the service is established, demand for residences in the village will probably increase, and this will push up land values. But this change in land values should not be counted as a benefit of the project, for the following reason.

The demand for city residences will necessarily decline, as will property values in the city. But this change will not be offsetting: remember that people could have chosen to remain in the city, and the fact that they chose not to indicates that they are better off (remember that given the choice, people only move if doing so is utility-enhancing). This differential gain, however, will already have been counted. The principal benefit of the improved commuter service is time saved. People have a willingness to pay for time saved, and this primary benefit will have been attributed to the project. (The benefits of saving time are assumed in the main example of Chapter 5; methods for measuring this benefit will be discussed at length in Chapter 9.) The value of the land in the country increases, but it increases because it now takes less time to commute, which is a benefit already counted.

A key question is this: Will the productive capability of the land in the village change? As the ability of this land to deliver housing services (gardens, space, and so on) does not change, no benefit should be attributed to it.

THE USE OF MULTIPLIERS

Most public sector projects involve government expenditures, and first-year macroeconomics students are drilled in the theory and calculation of government expenditure multipliers. The basic idea is that if a level of government spends z dollars constructing "social infrastructure," GDP will expand by more than z dollars; the government expenditure is income to those it hires to construct the project, and this income triggers a series of new consumption expenditures as the new money circulates through the economy, through round after round of new spending. (This is the so-called "trickle down" or "spinoff" effect: the labourer on the project spends part of his or her new income on goods and services; this is new income to retailers of these goods and services, whose spending increases accordingly, and so on and so on.)

Several factors constrain the multiplier process. First, the greater the proportion of new income that is taxed away, saved, or spent on imports, the less will be spent on domestically produced goods and services that would "multiply through" the domestic economy. Second, the government expenditure must be financed. If taxes must be raised, this will have multiple contractionary effects on domestic production. If bonds are sold to finance the new expenditure, interest rates will rise and private sector investment will be crowded out, thus diminishing domestic production. Third, if the economy is fully employed, expansion of the public sector will simply draw resources from the private sector, causing inflation but no increase in output.

Multiplier effects are often used by politicians and other noneconomists to justify public sector projects that are not economically viable. Sometimes the process and justification are described vaguely in the context of job creation, as in, "For every job created by this project, six others will be created elsewhere." In other cases, the process is described as stimulating so many millions of dollars of economic activity in an area.

Should multiplier effects be included in cost-benefit analyses?

Note that multiplier and secondary effects are really two sides of the same coin. The difference is that usually, specific secondary effects are identified. A multiplier, on the other hand, is usually applied to total project expenditure to capture aggregate secondary effects. It follows that the reservations concerning (specific) secondary benefits also apply to (generic) multiplier effects.

First, as noted above, if resources in the economy are fully employed, a project cannot but draw resources away from other employment. The multiplier process depends on the factors of production hired by a project spending new income, thereby triggering rounds of expenditures. However, employees give up employment elsewhere to work on a public sector project. In that sense, they are exchanging one source of income for another. If they earn the same wage on the project as they did in their previous employment, their expenditures will not increase, and nor will the incomes of those from whom they buy goods and services. It follows that no secondary economic activity will be generated. When there is full employment, if the project lures these workers away from other employment through higher wages, inflation will result. That is, if the economy is fully employed, spending increases will lead to increases in the general price level with no corresponding increase in output.

If resources are unemployed, secondary impacts may result in a net increase of output. That is, secondary industries may hire unemployed labour and other factors of production in order to expand production in response to new spending. If this is what happens, this expansion will not be offset by contractions elsewhere. Nevertheless, analysts must be cautious about treating this as a benefit of the project. The Treasury Board's *Benefit-Cost Analysis Guide* provides excellent advice in this regard. It states (italics ours):

> The problem with using multipliers or calculating secondary benefits in circumstances where resources are unemployed is that in benefit-cost analysis one needs to eliminate consequences which are common to alternative courses of government action. Such consequences are irrelevant to the decision-maker who has to choose among alternative courses of action. In this respect, the alternative to undertaking a particular public project may be some other form of government expenditure, which would also employ otherwise-idle resources and have multiplier effects on income and price levels. In a broader context, reductions in taxes or increases in the money supply would similarly be alternatives to undertaking particular government expenditures. These policies would also have expansionary effects on income, employment and price levels. For these reasons, *it is recommended that the analyst avoid adding multiplier effects or secondary benefits to benefit-cost analyses of public projects in circumstances where unemployment is widespread.* (1976, p. 23)

This advice would seem to be straightforward, and the reasons cogent.[7] Yet some recent cost-benefit analyses include both secondary benefits and multiplier effects. (Examples: the Rafferty-Alameda Dams project in Saskatchewan, and the Trans Labrador Highway.) That this advice has been ignored is a serious matter, as many projects that would have been judged economically nonviable had secondary and multiplier effects not been included, have been deemed viable. The result: economic waste and the destruction of wealth. There are probably many reasons why these effects continue to be included erroneously. Rather than be uncharitable to governments or their consultants, or excessively cynical regarding political decision-making processes, it may be wise to consider instead the Treasury Board's thoughts on the matter:

The continued enthusiasm for secondary benefits and multipliers in benefit-cost analyses may represent a misplaced endeavour to incorporate effects which are entirely relevant in a different context. We have seen that these effects are often pecuniary effects, involving transfers of income from some areas and persons to others. We are therefore not indifferent to such pecuniary effects, although they are irrelevant in estimating what the implications of a project are for *total* production and consumption opportunities in the economy (that is, the efficiency effects of a project). (1976, p.24)

As a matter of course, secondary benefits and multiplier effects should *not* be included in cost-benefit analyses.

SUMMARY

Potential problems related to real versus nominal value, marginal versus average cost estimates, depreciation, interest charges, intergovernmental grants, multipliers, starting dates, planning horizons, and scrap values are important but easy to avoid. If an error of this type has been made in an analysis, it is usually not difficult to spot.

Errors caused by erroneous inclusion or exclusion of spillover and secondary effects are sometimes difficult to identify. Part of the problem is that the same cost or benefit can show up in many guises. Sometimes a flow of benefits appears also as a stock, as in the case of profits being capitalized into asset values. At other times, a distinct benefit or cost can also appear as a price change. For example, if a project causes transportation costs to decline because time is saved, the prices of goods in supermarkets may decrease. To count both the price decreases and the time saved as benefits is to double-count.

We cannot discuss every potential pitfall. We can classify and give examples of the ones we are aware of, but new varieties may well arise. (Additional, specific errors are identified in the cases provided later in this text.) As the potential for errors of logic seems boundless, analysts must be wary. "Is this really a benefit?" "Is this really a cost?" and "Is this accounted for elsewhere?" are questions that should be asked at each step of the analysis.

EXERCISES

Map 7.1 shows a river and surrounding lands. From the north, this river passes a recreation area (area A) on the west and agricultural land used for growing grain crops on the east (area D). Currently, the river is not being used to irrigate this agricultural land. The river then flows through area C,

MAP 7.1   **MAP 7.2**

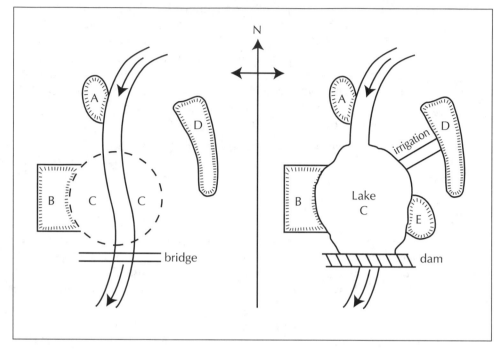

which is used to grow vegetables, although farmers in this area permit horseback riders to use this land free of charge. To the west of area C is area B, which is partly residential and partly commercial, the latter consisting of restaurants, grain merchants, millers, and so forth. The river then flows under a bridge and, farther south, courses out of the area of interest.

It has been proposed that a dam be built at the site of the bridge. This dam would transform area C into a lake (see Map 7.2), thereby destroying farmland. Area E would become suitable as a recreation area. Water from Lake C would be diverted via an irrigation ditch to area D, thus increasing its value as farmland. The physical attributes of area A would not be affected.

7.1 The proposed dam would cause area D farmland to become more productive. This would cause land values in this area to rise and crop revenues to increase. Discuss (explain) how an analyst might assess these impacts, if at all.

7.2 Because crop yields in area D will rise, the dam is expected to generate increased business economic activity in area B. That is, grain merchants' and millers' business volumes will expand. Discuss and explain how this phenomenon should be treated by an analyst.

7.3 Horseback riding in area C will no longer be possible if the dam is con-structed. As riders pay no fee to use area C, the analyst has ignored this item. Is this procedure correct or incorrect? Explain.

7.4 Farmers in area C are willing to relocate if the government pays them the market value of their land. The prices of the vegetables raised on this land are subsidized (and these subsidies are not corrective ones). Will the market value of these lands underestimate, overestimate, or accurately reflect the loss of this farmland to society? Explain.

7.5 New recreational lands in area E will compete with area A so that some users of A will go to E instead. If overall use of recreational lands does not change (the total from A is simply divided between A and E with no new users), should a benefit be attributed to this new recreation area? Explain.

7.6 Residents of area B who live close to area C will become owners of lake-front property if the dam is built. As lakefront property is generally more valuable than other property, the value of their homes will increase. Should any benefit be attributed to this phenomenon? Explain.

7.7 Some homes south of the dam were subject to flood damage, which will be eliminated when the dam is constructed. Based on the frequency and extent of this damage, an analyst has correctly attributed a benefit of $1 million to the project. Home insurance premiums will also fall, and owners of the houses previously prone to flood damage will be better off. From an analyst's perspective, does it matter whether the market for home insurance is perfectly competitive or monopolistic? Explain.

ENDNOTES

1. *Real* and *nominal* dollars are also called *constant* dollars and *current* dollars, respectively.

2. We take liberty here for convenience later. Whereas we would normally define $1 + i_n = 1 + i + \psi$ (where ψ is the expected rate of inflation), $(1 + i) \cdot (1 + \psi) = 1 + i + \psi + \psi i$. That is, the formula used overstates the nominal rate of interest by ψi. Thus, $(1 + i) \cdot (1 + \psi) \approx (1 + i_n)$ for small values of i and ψ.

3. We could, of course, count the interest charges both as a cost to the pro-ject and as a benefit to the lender if we were concerned with the distrib-utional impacts of the project.

4. Subject, of course, to the warning issued in Chapter 3 regarding the rank-ing of projects when project choice is subject to a financial constraint.

5. This is with the proviso that the analyst is not concerned with the redis-
    tributive impacts of a project. If he or she is, it will be necessary to
    report all such offsetting gains and losses.

6. See Chapter 6 regarding shadow pricing of inputs, especially the reser-
    vations expressed therein regarding the use of generic shadow-wage-
    rate formulae.

7. Both this statement and the following one from the Treasury Board's
    guide are reproduced with the permission of the Minister of Public
    Works and Government Services Canada, 1997. With respect to the first
    statement, we would modify it slightly to allow for the inclusion of sec-
    ondary and multiplier effects, but only if the analyst can argue convinc-
    ingly that the Treasury Board's reasons are not applicable to a specific
    project. Moreover, the analyst would have to justify the period over
    which the resources in question would have been unemployed if the
    project were not to proceed, to shadow price the relevant inputs, to
    count all secondary costs, and to use realistic multipliers. Such justifica-
    tion is so unlikely—and in any case, calculated impacts would be so
    minor—that our advice is to *not* calculate secondary or multiplier effects
    as a matter of course.

PUBLIC ENTERPRISE PRICING RULES

INTRODUCTION

Often the output of public sector projects can be sold. As is not the case with "pure" public goods, exclusion is possible, so that when the authorities choose to charge for the good or service provided, consumers must pay for it if they wish to consume it. Examples of facilities that produce such goods and services are hydroelectricity projects, theme parks, roads, recreation facilities, waterworks, and public transportation networks. In some cases public provision or regulation is warranted on efficiency grounds; in others, clearly intervention is not warranted. Even so, as some governments have chosen to participate in all of these areas, it is worthwhile examining the welfare implications of public sector pricing in a variety of circumstances.

Pricing and investment decisions go hand in hand. For example, to assess the viability of a hydroelectricity project, we must calculate its benefits and costs, and these will depend on the amount of electricity that will be consumed once the facility is constructed, which in turn will depend on how electricity is priced. If it is not priced optimally, the net present value of the project will be understated. Also, if the output of a public enterprise or a regulated one is not priced correctly, the facility constructed to produce this output may be either larger or smaller than what is socially optimal.

In a simple competitive market like the one outlined in Chapter 4, social welfare is maximized if, barring any externalities or other sources of market failure, a good or service is priced at its marginal cost. Because consumers will not purchase any unit for which their marginal benefit is less than its price, and firms will not produce any unit if its marginal cost exceeds its price, the price mechanism results in the marginal benefit of the last unit produced being just equal to its marginal cost. For all other units produced, marginal benefit will exceed marginal cost and society will reap a net benefit, the sum of producer and consumer surplus. Because social welfare is maximized at this price, if a government were to dictate a price either higher or lower than marginal cost, a welfare loss would ensue.

163

From all of this, it follows that a government can ensure that the net present value of a project is maximized by pricing its output at marginal cost. This implies that a pure public good, or any good or service that exhibits nonrivalry in consumption, ought to be provided free of charge, whether exclusion is possible or not.

For example, motorists using an uncongested highway should not be charged a toll—even if it were possible—if they bear all of the costs of their trips and thus impose no extra cost on society. To the extent that charging a toll would cause some people not to use this highway, social welfare would be diminished needlessly. Note that if demand is restricted by a toll in this manner, decision-makers may be led to build a two-lane highway or no highway at all when, had road use been priced optimally during the planning assessment stage, perhaps a four-lane highway would have yielded the highest positive net present value. Poor pricing decisions can lead to suboptimal public-investment decisions.

In the following situations, it is not obvious how to arrive at the marginal cost price for a project's output, or marginal cost pricing leads to other problems:

- There is a natural monopoly.
- Demand is cyclical.
- It is possible to charge two-part tariffs.

Usually these topics are covered only in pure microeconomics and public finance courses. We address them in this book—albeit in a rudimentary fashion—because of their implications for project appraisal. We also discuss a situation where it is better *not* to price a project's output at marginal cost.

NATURAL MONOPOLY

Many public utilities are natural monopolies, which are characterized by significant economies of scale. For example, the cost to a town of constructing a sewer system is large, but once in place, it costs relatively little to service an additional business or dwelling. As output is increased, these large initial costs are spread over more and more consumers, and this causes average cost to fall. Therefore, marginal costs (both to the firm and to society) must be less than average cost (AC), as shown in Figure 8.1. Given the market demand curve for this product (D), an unregulated monopolist will maximize profits by producing all units for which its marginal revenue (its private marginal benefit, given by MR) exceeds its marginal cost (MC). Having determined its profit-maximizing output (Q_m), the monopolist will charge the maximum price it can for it (P_m)—read off the demand curve at quantity Q_m. Its profit in this instance will be given by area P_mBAC.

FIGURE 8.1   Natural Monopoly

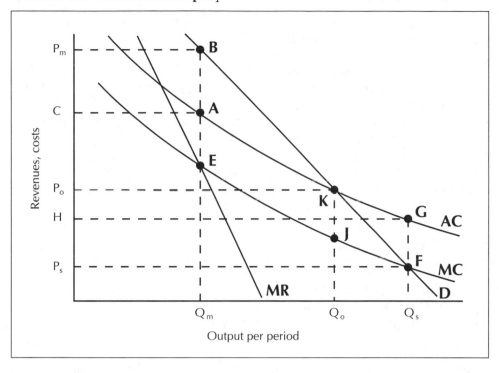

Society will suffer a welfare loss. As the height of the demand curve measures the marginal benefit to society of this good at each level of output, the monopolist will underproduce because, at Q_m, social marginal benefit (height Q_mB) will be greater than social marginal cost (height Q_mE). Units that would benefit society more than what they cost to produce (between Q_m and Q_s) will not be produced, and a welfare loss measured by area BFE will result. Here, the socially optimal output is Q_s, where the social marginal benefit of the last unit produced is exactly equal to its marginal cost to society.

To reduce or eliminate this welfare loss, a government could operate the firm as a public enterprise. If it does, presumably it will choose to produce the socially optimal output. This, however, will still leave it with a pricing problem. On the other hand, if the natural monopoly is a private concern, the government has at its disposal a menu of regulatory mechanisms that it may use to ameliorate the situation. These mechanisms can apply to either a public enterprise set up to produce the good or to a public agency charged with regulating a (private sector) natural monopoly. The properties of three possible regulatory responses to this problem are described below. Other responses exist—the literature on regulation is vast—but will not be discussed here, as the purpose of this section is merely to demonstrate the connection between pricing rules and public investment decisions.

Marginal Cost Pricing

To achieve efficiency in a market, we would have to set the product's price equal to its marginal cost at the optimal level of output. In Figure 8.1 this price would be P_s, where the demand curve (which shows both price and marginal social benefit) intersects the marginal cost curve. Certainly, consumers will want to consume Q_s units of this good per period at this price. However, MC < AC is a characteristic of natural monopoly; thus, by setting P_s = MC we would be setting P_s < AC, and a financial loss would result—in this case, of the magnitude shown by area $HGFP_s$.

To actually achieve output Q_s, then, we would have to pay a subsidy equal to $HGFP_s$ to the monopolist each period so that it did not incur a financial loss. In summary, if a marginal cost pricing rule is imposed, either on a public enterprise or by regulation, no welfare loss will ensue, but there will be a drain on the government's budget.

Average Cost Pricing

To avoid a financial loss, a government could order its agency to finance its own activities—that is, to behave as a nonprofit (or nonloss) enterprise. This would be equivalent to regulating a private sector monopoly by means of an average cost pricing rule.

In Figure 8.1 this would require that Q_0 units be produced and that they be sold for price P_0 each. There is no financial loss when this method is used; however, there is a welfare loss, because units between Q_0 and Q_s, for which marginal social benefit exceeds marginal social cost, are not produced. The extent of this welfare loss is given by area KFJ.

Thus, choosing between marginal cost and average cost pricing rules involves a trade-off between a welfare loss and a financial loss. Which loss to choose is an important decision for a cost-benefit analyst who is charged with assessing the viability of a public utility fitting the description of a natural monopoly. If a marginal cost pricing rule is to be imposed, the public project must be scaled to the size at which it will produce Q_s units per period at least cost.[1] If output is to be priced at average cost, presumably fewer resources will be required.

Emulating Perfect Price Discrimination

So far in this section, it has been assumed that *all* consumers will pay either p_m, p_s, or p_0 for every unit of the monopolist's output—that is, that the monopolist does not price discriminate. If this monopolist could price discriminate perfectly, each consumer would be charged the maximum he or she is willing to pay for each unit of the good or service. The conditions necessary for perfect price discrimination are these: the monopolist must be able to distinguish individuals on the basis of willingness to pay, and resale of the product must be either not feasible or preventable.

If a monopolist could price discriminate perfectly, and did, it would be because it is more profitable than not doing so. Important for our purposes is that if the monopolist could price discriminate perfectly, an efficient allocation of resources would result. As this applies to all monopolies, natural or otherwise, the veracity of both statements can be demonstrated for situations where marginal cost is constant.

Consider a simple example where there are N potential consumers, each of whom will purchase either one unit or nothing from the monopolist. These individuals have been ranked on the basis of willingness to pay. The maximum that person 1 is willing to pay for one unit (Q_1) is P_1, which is more than P_2, the maximum that person 2 is willing to pay for unit Q_2, and so on to P_N, which is the most person N is willing to pay for unit Q_N.

In the example shown in Table 8.1, N = 12 and the relationship between units and what people are willing to pay for them—the demand schedule—forms the first two columns. Marginal cost is assumed to be constant at $37 per unit, and total cost is shown in the third column. Suppose that this monopolist cannot price discriminate. This simply means that it will sell each unit it produces for the same price no matter who buys it. In these circumstances, the monopolist will maximize profits by expanding production as long as marginal revenue (the monopolist's marginal benefit)

TABLE 8.1   Monopoly

Q	P	TC	TR_n	MR_n	π_n	TR_d	MR_d	π_d
1	80	37	80	80	43	80	80	43
2	75	74	150	70	76	155	75	81
3	70	111	210	60	99	225	70	114
4	65	148	260	50	112	290	65	142
5	60	185	300	40	115	350	60	165
6	55	222	330	30	108	405	55	183
7	50	259	350	20	91	455	50	196
8	45	296	360	10	64	500	45	204
9	40	333	360	0	27	540	40	207
10	35	370	350	-10	-20	575	35	205
11	30	407	330	-20	-77	605	30	198
12	25	444	300	-30	144	630	25	186

exceeds marginal cost. Once the profit-maximizing output is determined, the monopolist will charge the highest price possible, a datum that can be read off the demand curve at that quantity.

The fourth through sixth columns of Table 8.1 show how total revenue (TR_n), marginal revenue (MR_n), and profits (π_n) change as output expands when this monopolist does not price discriminate. As $MR_n < MC$ for all units after the fifth, the monopolist will maximize profits by producing five units and pricing them at $60 each. At this output and price, the monopolist's profit is $115.

A welfare loss is incurred because some units that consumers would value more than what they would cost to produce are not produced. The value of any unit is simply the maximum any person is willing to pay for it. Therefore, society suffers a loss because units Q_6 through Q_9, for which price exceeds marginal cost, are not produced. If these units were produced, their value to society would be $P_6 + P_7 + P_8 + P_9$ ($190), whereas their cost would be only $148. This monopolist's actions, therefore, impose a welfare loss of $42 on society each period.

Now suppose that this same monopolist can charge every person a different price. Thus, it would charge person 1 $80, person 2 $75, and so on. Notice that the monopolist's marginal revenue schedule when it can discriminate perfectly (MR_d) is simply the demand schedule. Total revenue (TR_d), MR_d, and profits (π_d) in these circumstances are shown in the last three columns of Table 8.1. Here, the monopolist maximizes profits by producing nine units. Note that its profits are higher when it can price discriminate ($207) than when it cannot ($115).

Note well that society incurs no welfare loss when the monopolist can engage in perfect price discrimination. This is because the firm maximizes profits by producing the socially optimal output. It is true that the monopolist appropriates all consumer surplus in this situation, but this represents a transfer only.

Loeb & Magat (1979) demonstrate that this efficiency property of price discrimination can be put to good use for regulating a monopoly firm that cannot price discriminate. Consider a subsidy scheme whereby if a monopolist produces j units and sells them for P_j dollars each, it receives a subsidy from the government equal to $P_1 + P_2 + P_3 + ... + P_j - j \cdot P_j$ dollars. In the above example, if the monopolist were to produce four units, its subsidy would be $80 + $75 + $70 + $65 − $260 = $30.

The first four columns of Table 8.2 are identical to those of Table 8.1. The fifth column, S, shows how the Loeb-Magat subsidy increases as output increases. TR^* is the monopolist's total revenue when revenue from sales and the subsidy are summed. MR^* and π^* show the corresponding marginal revenue and profit schedules.

TABLE 8.2 Loeb-Magat Regulation

Q	P	TC	TR$_n$	S	TR*	MR*	π^*	$\pi^*(1-\tau)$	$\pi^* - t$
1	80	37	80	0	80	80	43	21.5	−107
2	75	74	150	5	155	75	81	40.5	−69
3	70	111	210	15	225	70	114	57.0	−36
4	65	148	260	30	290	65	142	71.0	−8
5	60	185	300	50	350	60	165	82.5	15
6	55	222	330	75	405	55	183	91.5	33
7	50	259	350	105	455	50	196	98.0	46
8	45	296	360	140	500	45	204	102.0	54
9	40	333	360	180	540	40	207	103.5	57
10	35	370	350	225	575	35	205	102.5	55
11	30	407	330	275	605	30	198	99.0	48
12	25	444	300	330	630	25	186	93.0	36

Notice that when this subsidy scheme is used, this nondiscriminating monopolist's marginal revenue schedule is transformed into the marginal revenue schedule that would exist if it were able to price discriminate perfectly—that is, the demand schedule. This results in the monopolist maximizing profits by producing the socially optimal output. This monopolist will produce 9 units of output and sell them for $40 each. It will receive $360 from sales and a subsidy of $180 from the government yielding a profit of $207, which, not surprisingly, is the same profit that would have been earned had it been able to price discriminate perfectly ($\pi_d = \pi^*$).

However, for the above case, a government may deem it inequitable or unreasonable to subsidize a monopolist that is already earning above-normal profits. It can overcome this problem by combining the Loeb-Magat subsidy scheme with either a proportional tax on the monopolist's profits or a lump-sum tax, perhaps in the form of a licensing fee. The column in Table 8.2 marked $\pi^*(1 - \tau)$ shows the monopolist's after-tax profits when a proportional tax (τ) on profits of 50% is levied in conjunction with the subsidy scheme. The column marked $\pi^* - t$ shows the monopolist's after-tax profits when a lump-sum tax (t) of $150 is levied with the subsidy. In neither case does the monopolist's profit-maximizing output (and thus price per unit) change. Here, the structure of the subsidy induces the monopolist to produce the socially optimal quantity, but neither tax is distortionary.

Note that in this example a lump-sum tax of $180 would be not only nondistortionary, but also neutral with respect to the government's budget—the government would be paying out in subsidies to the monopolist exactly what it collects in taxes from the monopolist. Thus, the Loeb-Magat subsidy scheme creates an incentive for the monopolist to expand output to the socially optimal level, yet the lump-sum (or proportional) tax that is coupled with it does not cause the firm to change output from that level.

The Loeb-Magat scheme and marginal cost pricing regulation both yield the same output and thus eliminate any welfare loss arising from monopoly. For a cost-benefit analyst, the size of the facility required to produce this output is the same regardless of which type of regulation is used. There is, nonetheless, an important difference. To formulate the exact price using the marginal cost pricing rule, regulators would have to know both cost and demand conditions as, figuratively, their target is the intersection of demand and marginal cost curves. To implement a Loeb-Magat subsidy scheme (with or without a nondistortionary tax), regulators need only know demand conditions.

The above example was of a situation where the monopolist earns a profit. However, it is not inevitable that a monopoly will earn a profit. An analyst evaluating a project that would become a government-operated monopoly when completed may find that it would incur a loss per period even when subsidized according to the Loeb-Magat formulation. As the monopolist's total revenue is measured by the entire area under the demand curve for its output and is, therefore, the total social benefit of the enterprise's output per period, such a project would not be economically viable. With this subsidy scheme, a financial loss signals a net social loss; a profit indicates a net social benefit.

TWO-PART TARIFFS

Some communities in depressed parts of the country seem to believe that public investment in theme parks would cure their economic ills. Most economists have concluded that if these were worthwhile projects, the private sector would build and operate them because what theme and amusement parks usually offer are private goods. If private firms do not provide them, it is because they are not viable. Here, if the public sector, for whatever reason, ventures where the private sector will not, resources will be wasted.

Despite negative net present values, governments do build and operate theme *cum* amusement parks. Given this reality, perhaps the role of an economist is to minimize social losses by pricing optimally.

Oi (1971) has provided the basic monopoly pricing model for theme parks, and the following discussion is based largely on his seminal work. As it would appear that his rules have sometimes been applied (misapplied?) by public sector agencies, we will augment Oi's analysis with a discussion of the welfare implications of pricing according to his model.

Assume that theme parks offer only one activity, rides, which can be provided at a constant marginal cost of C dollars per ride. We denote the quantity of rides by R. The individual whose demand curve for rides is shown in Figure 8.2 will take R^* rides per time period if rides are priced at marginal cost. Like Oi, we assume throughout that the income elasticity of demand for rides is zero.

Note that at this price this individual enjoys the consumer surplus given by area ABC. This is the maximum amount this individual will be willing to pay for the opportunity to purchase tickets for rides for C dollars each. A profit-maximizing monopolist will act on this information by charging this individual an admission fee equal to area ABC. If the monopolist does so, ABC will be the total profit it will earn from this individual. Although its revenues from rides will be the amount represented by area $0CBR^*$, this same amount will be its cost of providing R^* rides.

FIGURE 8.2   Two-part Tariffs—Homogeneous Demand

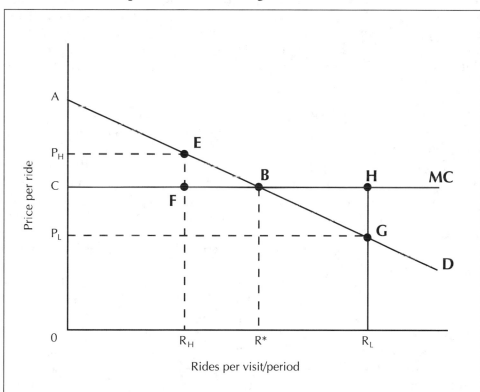

If the monopolist charges a price greater than marginal cost, say P_H, the maximum it will be able to charge this person for admission will be given by area AEP_H. Clearly, as the price of rides increases, consumer surplus and thus the maximum admission fee the individual is willing to pay decreases. If this two-part tariff is charged, the monopolist will earn a profit given by area AEP_H from admission, and a profit on rides shown by $0P_HER_H - 0CFR_H$. Therefore, the monopolist's total profit will be given by $ABC - EBF$, which is less than what would have been earned by charging ABC for admission and C dollars per ride.

If the monopolist charges this individual a lower price for rides, say P_L, it will be able to exact a higher admission charge, here equal to area AGP_L. If it does so, it will incur a loss on rides equal to $0CHR_L - 0P_LGR_L$. Total profit from admission and rides in this case is given by $ABC - BHG$—again, less than what would have been earned by pricing rides at marginal cost.

Therefore, a monopolist maximizes profits from an individual by pricing rides at marginal cost and charging the patron an admission fee equal to his or her consumer surplus at that price. From a welfare perspective, it matters only that rides be priced at marginal cost; any other price would cause rides to be either overconsumed or underconsumed. Because the admission fee is collected as a lump sum, any entrance charge between 0 dollars and ABC dollars will yield the same number of rides per period. The entrance fee is simply a transfer between patron and owner, and does not enter into the calculations.

If all individuals were identical, the theme park operator would maximize profits by pricing rides at marginal cost and appropriating everyone's consumer surplus as a lump-sum admission fee. Individuals, however, are not likely to demand rides identically.

Suppose that two equal-sized groups of patrons exist. Their demand curves are shown in Figure 8.3. If the monopolist could distinguish these individuals on the basis of willingness to pay, each would be charged C dollars per ride, but type 1 and type 2 people would be charged CZW and CXY dollars, respectively, for admission.

When the monopolist cannot price discriminate, there are two options for maximizing profits (although more are possible with other configurations of D_1 and D_2). One option is to charge park patrons C dollars per ride plus an admission fee of CXY dollars. That is, all of a type 2 person's consumer surplus will be appropriated, but only part of a type 1 person's. The monopolist's profit in this case will be twice CXY per pair of patrons.

A second option is to charge C dollars per ride and an admission fee of CZW dollars. Here, type 2 people will not pay the admission fee and thus will take no rides. This strategy will make sense to the park operator when $CZW > 2 \cdot CXY$. From a welfare perspective, this pricing strategy is inferior to

FIGURE 8.3 Two-part Tariffs—Heterogeneous Demand

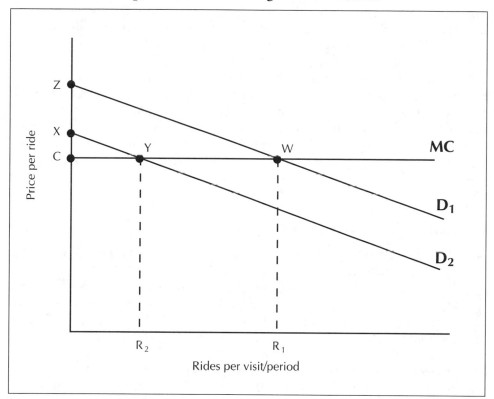

the previous one. Because the admission fee is simply a transfer, the social loss is every type 2 individual's consumer surplus whether it is appropriated by the monopolist or by the individual. Because type 2 people take no rides, neither the individuals nor the monopolist gets this surplus: this potential net benefit is lost to society.

There are other pricing possibilities when preferences differ across individuals. The monopolist's solution might involve pricing rides at more than marginal cost and charging a lower admission fee, or pricing rides at less than marginal cost and charging a higher admission fee. The exact two-part tariff also determines the number of people who enter the park: the number of park patrons is inversely related to the admission fee.

The analysis of profit-maximizing behaviour under a two-part tariff is quite complicated. Fortunately (?), the public sector agent need not perform it when attempting to set the socially optimal price of rides and an admission fee. First, to price rides at any price other than marginal cost invites a welfare loss. Second, to set an entrance fee that causes any individual not to enter the park results in another welfare loss. As the marginal patron in a multiperson setting would gain no consumer surplus, the socially optimal pricing scheme is to charge C dollars per ride and, unlike a profit-maximizing monopolist, charge nothing for admission to the park.

This should make absolute sense once we have cut through the complication of *being able* to charge an admission fee. If the park is not congested, the socially optimal admission fee is zero because the marginal cost of allowing one more person into the park is zero. Just because patrons *can* be excluded by means of an admission fee does not mean that they *should* be.[2] Of course, *no* admission fee is what would be charged if the market for theme parks were competitive.

PEAK LOAD PRICING

A town's recreation committee is considering building an outdoor tennis facility. It must determine how many courts, if any, it should build and what hourly rate to charge for court sessions. During the months of the year when the facility would be open, the committee expects weekend demand for court time to be much greater than weekday demand. Indeed, not all court space would be used on a typical summer weekday.

The committee could decide to charge the same fee per session every day of the week and build just enough courts to satisfy weekend demand. This strategy would minimize waiting time on weekends; but it would also maximize idle court space during the rest of the week. An alternative would be to charge weekend players more than weekday players. This would discourage weekend use and encourage weekday use; fewer courts would have to be built. Again, pricing and investment decisions go hand in hand.

The problem facing this committee is similar to those encountered by many operators of public (or regulated) enterprises—hydroelectricity facilities, telephone networks, water supply systems, and the like. For all of these, demand fluctuates in regular cycles. That is, there are times of peak demand and times of off-peak demand, but the capacity (or capital) of the facility cannot be adjusted instantaneously to ensure that price is continuously equal to long-run marginal cost. Also, it is either physically impossible or prohibitively expensive to store excess production from off-peak periods for consumption in peak periods.

In all of these situations, minimization of excess capacity and maximization of social welfare require that all consumers pay the marginal cost of producing whatever amount they consume. That is, prices must be used to equate marginal benefit and marginal cost in all parts of a demand cycle. If idle capacity exists in off-peak periods, off-peak users will derive no benefit if the capacity of the facility is expanded. Peak period users, on the other hand, stand to benefit if capacity is increased, and efficiency requires that the price they pay reflect this. The efficient pricing solution is, therefore, that off-peak users pay a lower price than peak users. For example, people who make long-distance telephone calls at midnight will pay less per minute than those who call at noon when connections are in higher demand.

Williamson (1966) has provided the standard model for determining exact peak and off-peak prices, and the following diagrammatic analysis of the simplest peak-load pricing problem is drawn from his work. Assume that over a demand cycle, there exist a single peak demand period and a single off-peak demand period. The peak and off-peak periods last fractions w_1 and w_2 of the cycle, respectively, so that $w_1 + w_2 = 1$. D_1 and D_2 are, respectively, the demand curves for the enterprise's output during peak and off-peak parts of the cycle; each has been drawn in Figure 8.4 as if it was independent of the other and as if its duration were the entire cycle. (As these demands occur at different times, to combine them on a single diagram requires that they exist within the same time dimension.)

The cost of expanding capacity enough to produce one more unit of output during a cycle is assumed to be constant and is denoted by β, and the extra variable cost of producing one more unit of output (denoted by b) is

FIGURE 8.4 Peak-load Pricing

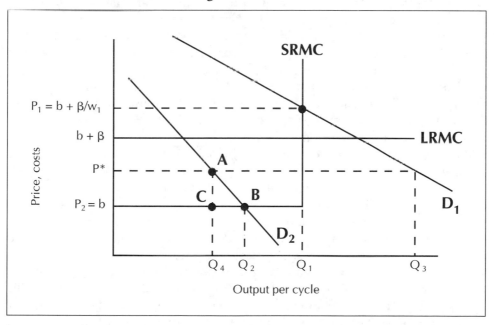

assumed to be constant up to capacity output. Therefore, long-run marginal cost (LRMC) is β + b. Given some capacity output, short-run marginal cost is equal to b dollars per unit up to this maximum output, at which point the short-run marginal cost curve (SRMC) becomes vertical to indicate that it is impossible to produce more without expanding capacity.

For the sake of efficiency in the off-peak part of the cycle, the price these users pay per unit (P_2) must equate their marginal benefit with marginal cost. As P_2 measures off-peak users' marginal benefit if the off-peak period were to last the entire cycle, the actual measure of their marginal benefit is $w_2 \cdot P_2$. As these consumers put no demand at all on capacity, the cost of them consuming one more unit of output over an entire cycle is b, SRMC. For their part of the cycle, this marginal cost is $w_2 \cdot$ b. Equating off-peak users' marginal benefit and marginal cost yields P_2 = b. That is, for every unit of output these individuals consume during their part of the demand cycle, efficient pricing requires that they be charged b dollars. In Figure 8.4, off-peak consumers would demand Q_2 units at this price.

During the peak part of the demand cycle, the cost of producing one more unit of output is β dollars for the extra capital required to expand capacity output by one unit, plus $w_1 \cdot$ b dollars for the variable inputs needed to produce it. (Note that β is not discounted by factor w_1 because this marginal capacity cost *is* for the entire cycle.) If the peak period were to last the entire cycle, price P_1 would measure peak users' marginal benefit. As it occupies only fraction w_1 of the cycle, their actual marginal benefit is less, $w_1 \cdot P_1$. Equating peak users' marginal benefit and marginal cost, $w_1 \cdot P_1$ = $w_1 \cdot$ b + β. Therefore, for every unit of output that peak-period users consume during their part of the demand cycle, efficiency requires that they pay P_1 = b + β/w_1. The output that peak users consume at this price during their part of the cycle determines the optimal capacity of the facility.

The results that p_2 = b, that p_1 = b + w_1/β, and that the optimal size of the facility should be that just capable of satisfying peak demand when peak use is priced optimally may also be derived mathematically. For this, see Box 8.1.[3] Although cast as a profit-maximization problem, the same results are obtained when welfare maximization is the objective.

Over an entire cycle, the total cost of production can be divided into $w_2 \cdot$ b $\cdot Q_2$ dollars for off-peak users and, further dividing peak-period costs into operating and capacity costs, $w_1 \cdot$ b $\cdot Q_1$ + $\beta \cdot Q_1$ dollars, respectively. Total revenue in the off-peak part of the cycle is $w_2 \cdot P_2 \cdot Q_2$. Since P_2 = b, revenues equal costs in the off-peak period. Total revenue in the peak part of the cycle is $w_1 \cdot P_1 \cdot Q_1$. As P_1 = b + β/w_1, this may be written as $w_1 \cdot$ b $\cdot Q_1$ + $\beta \cdot Q_1$. Thus, total cost is equal to total revenue during the peak part of the demand cycle as well.[4] Note that peak users pay for the entire capital cost of the facility; off-peak users pay for none of it. Intuitively, this is appropriate, because at the margin, only peak users would benefit if capacity were expanded.

BOX 8.1

Peak-load Pricing and Investment Rules

A competitive's firm's problem is to choose the peak (Q_1), off-peak (Q_2), and capacity (X) quantities so as to maximize profits. That is, maximize $w_1 \cdot p_1 \cdot Q_1 + w_2 \cdot p_2 . Q_2 - w_1 \cdot b \cdot Q_1 - w_2 \cdot b \cdot Q_2 - \beta \cdot X$ subject to $X \geq Q_1$ and $X \geq Q_2$.

Forming the Lagrangean function,

$$£(Q_1,Q_2,X,\lambda_1,\lambda_2) = w_1 \cdot p_1 \cdot Q_1 + w_2 \cdot p_2 \cdot Q_2 - w_1 \cdot b \cdot Q_1 - w_2 \cdot b \cdot Q_2 - \beta \cdot X + \lambda_1 \cdot (X - Q_1) + \lambda_2 \cdot (X - Q_2)$$

First-order necessary conditions to solve this problem are:

(1) $w_1 \cdot (p_1 - b) - \lambda_1 = 0$
(2) $w_2 \cdot (p_2 - b) - \lambda_2 = 0$
(3) $-\beta + \lambda_1 + \lambda_2 = 0$
(4) $\lambda_1 \geq 0$, $(X - Q_1) \geq 0$, $\lambda_1 \cdot (X - Q_1) = 0$, and
(5) $\lambda_2 \geq 0$, $(X - Q_2) \geq 0$, $\lambda_2 \cdot (X - Q_2) = 0$

If Q_2, demand in the off-peak period, is less than capacity output, X, then from equation (5), $\lambda_2 = 0$. Thus from (3), $\beta = \lambda_1$. As $\lambda_2 = 0$, (2) requires that $p_2 = b$. Using $\beta = \lambda_1$ in (1) requires that $p_1 = b + \beta/w_1$.

The optimal pricing rules are the same as those shown earlier diagrammatically. Also note that because λ_1 is non-zero, from (4) $X = Q_1$, yielding the optimal investment rule.

Figure 8.4 shows how the above prices and quantities would be determined optimally, and we can use it to examine the welfare implications of not pricing optimally. Take the situation where a public enterprise capable of producing Q_1 units of output has been constructed but, instead of charging peak users P_1 per unit and off-peak users P_2 per unit, an authority rules that every consumer must be charged the same price, perhaps in the belief that charging different prices is unfair. In Figure 8.4, let this price be denoted by P^*, which, reasonably, has been chosen to lie between the optimal prices, P_1 and P_2.

At this lower price, peak users will want to consume Q_3 units, but they will not be able to because the facility is capable of producing only Q_1 units. Although their consumption remains at Q_1, they will be better off because they now pay a lower price per unit. This, however, has no implication for social welfare because their saving is only a transfer between the enterprise and these individuals. (Nevertheless, if at the planning stage of this public enterprise authorities had decided to build a facility capable of producing more than Q_1 units because they had erroneously underpriced peak use, a welfare loss would be incurred because the marginal social cost of expanding capacity beyond this point would exceed its marginal social benefit.)

Off-peak users, on the other hand, will consume less at price P^*; their demand will fall from Q_2 to Q_4. They will thus be made worse off, as will society. The loss of benefit to these individuals is given by the area under their demand curve between these two quantities, Q_4ABQ_2. Because fewer units are produced, there is a resource saving equal to Q_4CBQ_2. Thus, a welfare loss represented by area ABC is incurred. Adjusting for the fact that the off-peak period lasts fraction w_2 of each cycle, this net welfare loss is $w_2 \cdot$ ABC per cycle.

When peak-load pricing rules are followed, consumers at every stage of a demand cycle pay the marginal cost of their consumption. When the output of the enterprise is priced uniformly, a welfare loss results instead. Off-peak users will be needlessly restrained from consuming the enterprise's product. Also, should the optimal pricing scheme not be used at the enterprise's planning evaluation stage, it is likely that a too-large facility will be constructed because uniform pricing exaggerates peak-period demand levels.

SECOND-BEST PRICING

The Rationale

Figure 8.5 shows a simple competitive market for a good that is distorted by a negative externality. In this particular situation the marginal cost to society (MC_s) of producing this good is greater than its marginal cost to producers (MC_p), perhaps because of pollution or congestion. Here, we assume no externality exists on the demand side. This means that the height of the demand curve measures the marginal benefit of this good both to society (MB_s) and to private consumers (MB_p)—there is no difference.

In any market, a competitive equilibrium is determined where $MB_p = MC_p$. That is, profit-maximizing firms will expand production as long as the price they receive exceeds their marginal cost ($P \geq MC_p$), and utility-maximizing households will demand more and more of this good as long as the marginal benefit they enjoy from consuming it exceeds what they pay for it ($MB_p \geq P$). Thus, at the competitive equilibrium, $MC_p = P = MB_p$. In Figure 8.5, the competitive equilibrium price and resulting quantity are shown by P_c and Q_c, respectively.

In Figure 8.5, because of this distortion the competitive equilibrium is not socially optimal. To maximize welfare in this market, only output for which $MB_s \geq MC_s$ should be produced and consumed. Here, the socially

FIGURE 8.5 **Corrective Taxation**

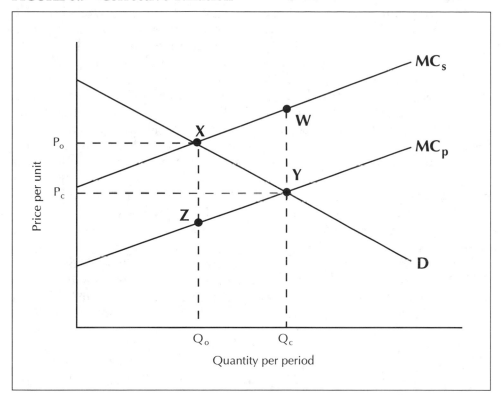

optimal output is shown by Q_o. When more than Q_o is being produced, units are created that society values less than what they cost society to make, and a welfare loss results. The extent of this welfare loss is measured by area XYW.

One way to correct this distortion is to levy a tax on this good equal to amount XZ per unit. Here, XZ is the marginal external cost of producing this good at quantity Q_o. This tax will cause the industry supply curve (MC_p) to shift up by this amount so that at the output Q_o, $MC_p + XZ = MC_s$. That is, a tax of this amount will eliminate the difference between private and social marginal costs at the optimal output. Now producers will only expand production as long as $P \geq MC_p + XZ$ and will thus produce quantity Q_o, the socially optimal output. Here, the distortion has been "internalized" because the tax has caused producers to take into account *all* of the costs of their productive activities, both internal and external to the firm.

Note that this corrective tax eliminates the welfare loss that competitive behaviour would have generated. The same kind of tax could have been used had the externality been on the demand side of the market instead of the supply side, such as in the case of cigarette smoking. If a positive externality distorts a market, so that $MC_p > MC_s$ and/or $MB_s > MB_p$, less than the socially optimal amount of the good or service in question will be produced. In these cases, a corrective subsidy equal to the marginal external benefit (the difference in either case) at the optimal output is appropriate.

Sometimes, however, it is not feasible or practical to use corrective taxes and subsidies to deal directly with distortions. For example, if a road is congested, it is because drivers entering it take into account only the private costs they incur by driving, such as their own fuel and time costs. By entering the highway, however, they may cause or increase congestion and thus impose an additional time cost on other drivers. That is, they do not take into account the external costs they impose on other travellers. In this situation $MC_p < MC_s$, the difference being the marginal external cost of congestion. The standard first-best solution would be to levy a toll (tax) equal to this marginal external cost as shown in Figure 8.5; but this remedy may not apply in this case.

The basic problem is that cars are moving too slowly because of congestion. To correct this by levying a toll may require setting up tollbooths. Yet forcing cars to stop at tollbooths slows down traffic, perhaps adding to congestion delays on balance. In some circumstances, then, implementing the first-best pricing solution may actually heighten the distortion.[5]

When it is not feasible to eliminate a distortion by a corrective tax or subsidy, it is sometimes possible to achieve a welfare gain by reducing the negative impact of the distortion by indirect means. Returning to the example of a congested road, if a corrective toll cannot be levied, the distortion (congestion) could be reduced by inducing some drivers to use public transportation. One way to accomplish this would be to subsidize transit fares, even though this would create a welfare loss in that market. The point is that if this subsidy causes the welfare loss existing because of congested roads to be reduced by more than the induced welfare loss in the market for public transit, an overall welfare gain results. That is, *not* pricing at marginal cost a good or service that *can* be controlled directly, in order to reduce a welfare loss in a related market that *cannot* be controlled directly, may be appropriate. This trading off of a welfare *loss* in one market where taxes and subsidies can be levied, for a welfare *gain* in a related, distorted market that cannot be controlled by direct means, is called "second-best pricing." It is second- rather than first-best because in the circumstances at hand, the welfare loss due to a distortion cannot be eliminated completely. Second-best pricing results in the smallest possible welfare loss when corrective taxes and subsidies are not feasible.

Optimal Departures from Marginal Cost Pricing

Case 1

Consider two goods that are substitutes, such as roads (R) and public transportation (T). The market for R is distorted; T is some related good that can be either taxed or subsidized directly, or T may be the output of a public enterprise. In Figure 8.6, the market for R is distorted by a negative externality so that too much of it is produced when T is priced at marginal cost. Here, D_T is the demand curve for good T, and D_R is the demand curve for good R *when T is priced at marginal cost*. For simplicity we will assume that both goods (or services) can be produced at constant marginal cost. Initially, T_0 units of T are being consumed per period at the undistorted price P_T, and R_0 units of R are being consumed at price P_R, which is less than the marginal social cost of producing this good (MC_s).

As T and R are substitutes in this situation, one way to reduce production of R (as it cannot be taxed directly) is to decrease the price of T, either through subsidization or by setting it directly, as in the case of a public enterprise. The resulting price is shown as $\bar{P}_T$. This decrease in price will cause the quantity demanded of good T to expand to amount T_f. Because R and T are substitutes, this will also cause the demand curve for R to shift inward from D_R to $\bar{D}_R$; as a result, the equilibrium quantity of good R will decrease from R_0 to R_f.

In the market for good T, a welfare loss has been created. The benefit to consumers when consumption is expanded from T_0 to T_f is measured by the area under its demand curve, $T_0 ac T_f$. The extra cost to society of producing these units is given by area $T_0 ab T_f$. Thus, the net welfare loss induced by pricing this good at less than marginal cost is given by the triangle abc.

In the market for good R, welfare has increased. Consumers of this product are worse off by the amount their expenditure on this good decreases, given by area $R_f de R_0$. At the same time, however, fewer resources are now being used to produce R; this resource saving is measured by area $R_f fg R_0$. Thus, the resulting net welfare gain in this market is rectangle dfge.

If dfge > abc, then social welfare has increased. That is, by introducing a distortion into the market for good T, we have reduced overall welfare losses. To find the optimal (second-best) price for good T, we decrease its price as long as the extra gain in the market for R exceeds the extra induced loss in the market for T; the second-best price for good T is the one that maximizes the difference between the areas corresponding to dfge and abc. The second-best quantity per period of the public enterprise's output will determine the size of facility required.

FIGURE 8.6   Second-best Pricing—Case 1

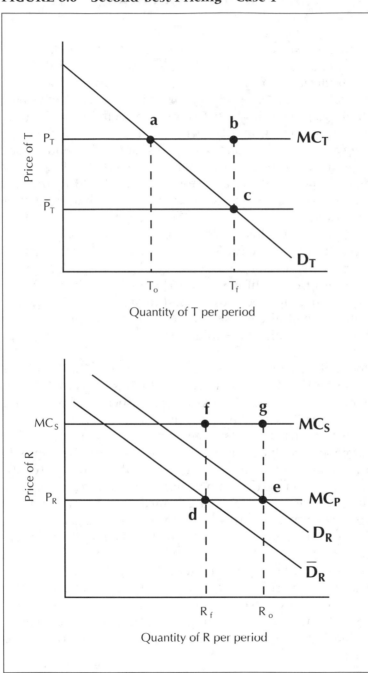

It is possible, of course, that second-best pricing will require us to provide good T free of charge. Indeed, in the case of public transit, if the second-best fare is very low, it may not even be worth collecting. Also, it could be that the second-best fare is negative. Although the prospect of bus drivers handing passengers loonies (a negative fare) as they board is difficult to imagine, it is a possible second-best solution.

Case 2

Figure 8.7 shows a situation where R and T are substitutes, but too little of good R is being produced and consumed because of a positive externality. Initially, good T is priced at marginal cost (P_T) and T_0 units of it are being consumed. At this price of T, the demand curve for good R is given by D_R so that R_0 units of it are being consumed at its distorted price P_R. Here the distortion exists because the marginal social cost of producing R (MC_s) is less than the marginal private cost of producing it (MC_p).

As too little of R is being produced and consumed, and direct subsidization of it is not feasible, the second-best solution involves raising the price of good T above its marginal cost. If the price of T is increased from P_T to $\bar{P}_T$, consumption of it will decrease from T_0 to T_f. At the same time, the demand curve for R will shift outward from D_R to $\bar{D}_R$, and consumption and production will increase from R_0 to R_f.

The resulting net welfare loss in the market for T is represented by area hjk. That is, the loss to consumers (T_fhjT_0) exceeds the resource saving to society (T_fkjT_0) by this amount. At the same time, however, a welfare gain shown by rectangle *lmnr* is realized in the market for R. Here, the gain to consumers because of their extra expenditure on good R (R_0mnR_f) exceeds the extra resource cost to society of producing these units (R_0lrR_f). Thus, society enjoys a net welfare gain represented by *lmnr   hjk*. The second best price of good T is the one that maximizes this difference and so minimizes the overall welfare loss.

Other Cases

Two corresponding cases not shown are when goods R and T are complements. We leave these as exercises for the reader, with the following directions: If too much (little) R is being produced and consumed because of a negative (positive) externality, the appropriate policy is to price good T above (below) its marginal cost. Obviously, if goods R and T are neither substitutes nor complements, pricing good T above or below its marginal cost will cause a net welfare loss in its market *without* any offsetting gain in the market for good R.[6]

FIGURE 8.7   Second-best Pricing—Case 2

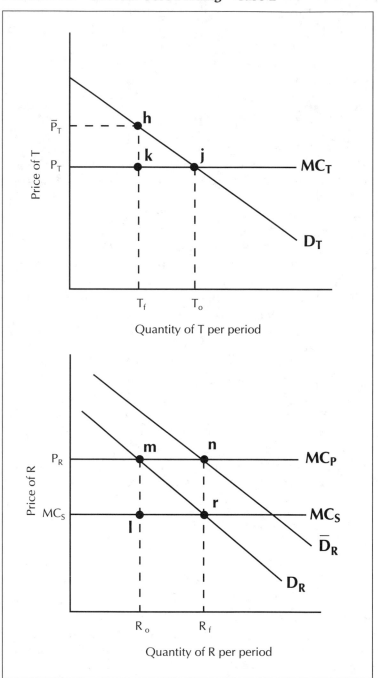

FROM PRICING TO PROJECT SELECTION

The above pricing rules are important in the context of cost-benefit analysis because they determine what the output of a public project should be in a particular time period. Ideally, we would want to construct a public project that is capable of producing this output in each period at least cost. If cost and demand conditions are stable, project capacity in one period will be optimal for all periods; a facility of optimal size will yield a higher net present value than any larger or smaller one.

However, the optimal level of output of a publicly provided good or service need not be the same over the life of the public investment project constructed to produce it. For good example, optimal output will not be the same every year in the life of a project if society's demand for it changes over time (which could mean several decades). Demand can change over time in a predictable fashion for many reasons: population growth or decline, changes in average income, changes in the age structure of the population, and so on. This suggests that ideally, we would wish to adjust the scale of the project or enterprise periodically to ensure that we produce the (changing) optimal output every period in its economic life.

For enterprises like public transit this may not be a problem, because a bus service can be expanded or contracted on short notice. Once a dam is built, however, its size is fixed for the duration of its economic life. A dam or bridge that is the optimal size for today's needs may be too large or too small a decade from now. The same may be more or less true for school buildings, retirement homes, and other age-related goods and services. The question for cost-benefit analysts is this: Does society build for today or for tomorrow?

Once a public project has been constructed, if its magnitude cannot be changed, and if multiples of it cannot be built during its economic life, and if demand for its output is changing in a predictable pattern over this same time period, it will likely be larger than optimal in some years and smaller than optimal in others. Choosing the best-sized facility, however, does not present a major problem. Each possible size can be treated as a mutually exclusive project—as in building a two-, three- or four-lane bridge. The one that yields the highest positive net present value will then be favoured.

Still, a warning is in order. An analyst who examines alternative structures only on the basis of size may end up overlooking other important factors. For example, a community may require a school that is capable of holding a given number of students today, yet at the same time be well aware that the student population will decline over the life of whatever size school is actually built. That is, what is optimal today will be too large tomorrow. (We ignore the possibility of portable classrooms.)

An analyst could rank different-sized schools of the same general architectural design, but in doing so he or she would be ignoring the fact that all schools capable of holding a given number of students need not be of the same design. Some buildings can only be used as schools, but other designs may have built-in flexibility—for example, they may incorporate non-stress-bearing walls that can be added or removed with relative ease. Perhaps this community knows that its elderly population will be swelling as its student population is shrinking, and that it may be worthwhile to consider designing the school in such a way that classrooms can be converted into spaces suitable for activities in demand by older citizens. Therefore, it would be appropriate for a cost-benefit analyst to consider not only schools of different sizes, but also schools of different structural design.

Although building flexibility into a particular structure adds to its initial cost, a school capable of being wholly or partly converted into a facility for retirees may contribute more to social welfare over the relevant time horizon. This same commonsense consideration may apply *mutatis mutandis* to other public sector projects.

SUMMARY

Public-sector pricing and investment decisions cannot be separated. Ultimately, the task is to choose the combination that maximizes social well-being given the situation and the existing constraints. Optimal pricing and investment yield the maximum net present value of a project that produces output that can be sold. If the net present value of a project is negative when pricing and investment decisions have been made optimally, no adjustment of either can make the project viable.

Although the rule has myriad forms, usually marginal cost pricing is optimal. However, when markets for related goods and services are distorted in ways that cannot be corrected directly, pricing the output of a public sector project greater or less than marginal cost can minimize welfare losses.

In times of changing demand conditions and technology, it may be physically impossible for the scale of a public sector project to be optimal during every year of its economic life. Still, some future events are predictable—even inevitable—and this information can be exploited at the planning stage.

EXERCISES

8.1. Consider the following problem from the theory of second-best pricing that is illustrated in Figure 8.8. The market for good Y is distorted, and its price cannot be controlled by a tax or subsidy directly. The marginal cost of producing Y is constant at 90¢ per unit, while the price of good Y

FIGURE 8.8

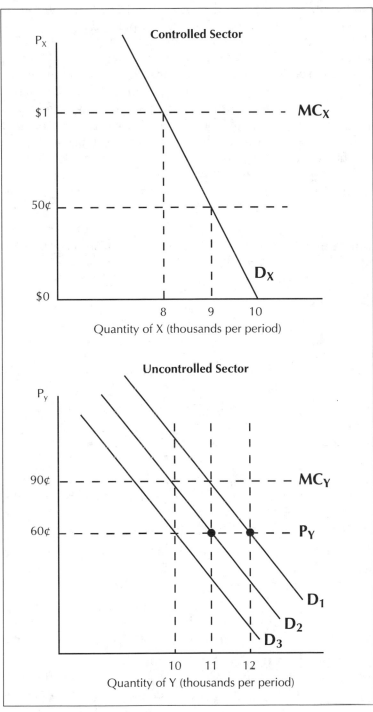

Quantity of X (thousands per period)

Quantity of Y (thousands per period)

is 60¢ per unit. This 30-cent distortion exists at all levels of output. Good X is the output from a public project (enterprise), and it can be produced at a constant marginal cost of one dollar per unit.

If the public enterprise charges a price of $1 per unit of X, 8,000 units of X and 12,000 units of Y will be consumed each period, as D_1 will be the demand curve for good Y. If, instead, the government chooses to subsidize one-half of the cost of good X, the price of X to consumers will be 50¢ per unit. Consumption of X and Y, respectively, will be 9,000 units and 11,000 units per period, as D_2 will be the relevant demand curve for Y. If the government chooses to subsidize the entire cost of good X, consumers will pay nothing for it and will consume 10,000 units of it per period. This will cause the demand curve for Y to shift to D_3 and 10,000 units of Y will be consumed each period. If a government can only choose from among 0%, 50%, and 100% subsidies, which should it choose?

8.2. Demand for the output of a public project has three distinct phases of equal duration over a demand cycle. If each demand function is stated as if it lasted one entire cycle,

$$Q_1 = 2,700 - 100P_1$$
$$Q_2 = 1,500 - 100P_2$$
$$Q_3 = \ \ 800 - 100P_3$$

Short-run marginal cost is $3 per unit, while long-run marginal cost is $5 per unit. Both are assumed to be constant. Capacity output is 1,800 units.

a. What are the socially optimal prices (P_1, P_2, P_3)? Use a diagram to illustrate your answer.

b. Demonstrate that zero profits are earned when these prices are charged.

8.3 Every potential visitor to a theme park has the same demand function for rides given by $R = 20 - 5P$, where P is the price of a ride and R is the number of rides demanded. The owner of the park is a monopolist. The marginal cost to the owner of someone taking a ride is $1.

a. To maximize profits, what prices should this monopolist charge per ride and to enter the park? What is a socially optimal two-part pricing scheme in these circumstances?

b. If the owner were to allow patrons to go on any and all rides for free, what would be the maximum amount any patron would be willing to pay to enter the amusement park?

c. Find the profit-maximizing and socially optimal two-part pricing schemes when two equal-size classes of demanders exist, one with demand given by $R = 20 - 5P$ and the other with demand given by $R = 30 - 5P$.

8.4 Using the same terminology adopted in this chapter on second-best pricing, assume now that goods R and T are complements and that, in the market for good R, $MC_s > MC_p$. Use a diagram to demonstrate how *not* pricing good T at marginal cost may increase social welfare in this situation.

8.5 Using the same terminology adopted in this chapter on second-best pricing, assume now that goods R and T are complements and that, in the market for good R, $MC_s < MC_p$. Use a diagram to demonstrate how *not* pricing good T at marginal cost may increase social welfare in this situation.

ENDNOTES

1. Here, implicitly, we assume that demand conditions are expected to be constant over the life of the facility. The cases where demand is expected to rise or fall over time are treated later in this chapter.

2. In Oi's model, the only attraction in the amusement park is rides. In many theme parks there are also historical displays, concerts, and the like that have the characteristics of public goods and, therefore, should be provided free of charge. However, should the park be required to be self-financing, a lump-sum admission fee may be appropriate.

3. This simple framework may be used for multipart cycles, including situations where capacity output is utilized in more than one part of the cycle. Here, capital costs are shared by the multipeak users. An excellent reference for those who prefer a more mathematical approach is Pressman (1970).

4. This is a result of the assumptions that short- and long-run marginal costs are constant. If LRMC decreases as output increases, as in the case of the natural monopoly, public enterprise output, priced efficiently, will have to be subsidized.

5. Technology has advanced to the point where sensors posted on highways can identify vehicles bearing an electronic "identity tag," making mailed billings for road use possible and tollbooths somewhat obsolete. These sensors make first-best pricing possible without adding to congestion. This technology is not yet in widespread use.

6. See Boadway & Bruce (1984) for a rigorous examination of second-best pricing.

CHAPTER 9

THE VALUATION OF INTANGIBLES

INTRODUCTION

Markets for goods and services accommodate mutually advantageous trades and, in doing so, provide observers with much valuable information. For example, the market price of any good or service reveals the maximum households are willing to pay for the last unit consumed. If the market being examined is competitive, this price also reveals the minimum any firm will be willing to accept for producing the marginal unit. Given enough observations, demand and supply curves can be estimated. Once these are known, consumer and producer surpluses can be calculated, as well as any changes in them should prices change. Thus, when a project either employs a factor of production bought and sold on a competitive input market or produces a good or service for which a competitive output market exists, information required for assessing the costs and benefits of the project is readily available.

However, markets do not exist for all of the things used and produced by public sector projects. For example, markets do not exist for either noise abatement or pollution, yet projects can create either. Airports are built to convenience travellers and cargo movers, but airplanes raise the level of noise in surrounding neighbourhoods. To the extent that noise annoys people, one of the costs of an airport project will be this discomfort. The fact that people cannot buy or sell a decibel of noise in a marketplace does not make this annoyance any less real. Sound barriers along the sides of highways reduce noise. Are they worth what they cost to erect? This question can be answered only if we can put a value on the benefits of noise abatement, even though no market price exists to reveal its value to society.

The principal benefit of many transportation projects is that travellers save time, yet hours per se cannot be bought or sold. "Time is money," but what price time? Similarly, a road-widening project will undoubtedly reduce accidents and save lives, and construction of a subway tunnel will likely involve the sacrifice of lives. To adopt the attitude that life is infinitely precious would automatically qualify all projects that save lives and disqualify all that might take a life. By the same token, to refuse to place a value on life may be to treat it as worthless. Neither extreme is satisfactory.

These are some of the valuation problems analysts must address when a project involves one or more intangibles. As there are no markets to provide information directly and cheaply, it must be obtained by other means. Indeed, valuing "incommensurables" is one of the most challenging and interesting aspects of cost-benefit analysis, and innovative methods have been developed to this purpose. Two basic methods exist.

The first is called *contingent valuation*. This method consists of using surveys to ask the relevant compensating and/or equivalent variation questions. As, ultimately, an analyst wants to know the compensating and equivalent variations of an intangible, directness is a positive feature of this method. One drawback is that individuals may not provide truthful or accurate answers.

The second is the *hedonic price* method. This involves deducing individuals' valuations of intangibles from their behaviour in markets for other goods and services. For example, among the choices available to people travelling between Toronto and Ottawa are air travel and rail travel. Air is faster but rail is cheaper. By their choices, travellers reveal how they assess this time–money trade-off, and thus the value they place on time savings. With enough observations it is possible for analysts to deduce the value (hedonic price) of an hour of time saved. An advantage of this method is that consumers reveal their true preferences in markets. A drawback is the level of sophistication this method requires: to employ this method an analyst must have more than a passing acquaintance with econometric methods.

NOISE POLLUTION AND ABATEMENT

This section considers the valuation of noise and is based on two studies: the first looked at the costs of airport noise pollution near London, England; the second looked at the benefits of noise abatement in Basle, Switzerland. Although the first study has been the target of much criticism, we include it for its historical value and because it illustrates how innovative cost-benefit analysts must be at times. The second study compares hedonic price and contingent valuation techniques. Although its main results apply more broadly, we include it here because it involved measuring the benefits of noise abatement.

The Third London Airport

One of the earliest and most extensive treatments of the cost of noise was found in the Roskill Commission's study of where to construct a third airport near London, England. Its approach is outlined here because it was innovative in its day and laid the groundwork for more modern valuation methods.[1] (The Roskill study also illustrates that economic choices are not always political choices.)

By the early 1960s London's two existing airports, Heathrow and Gatwick, were overcrowded. The government favoured building a third London airport at Stanstead, about 50 kilometres northwest of the city. In 1968, in response to criticism that its choice of Stanstead was arbitrary, the government struck the Roskill Commission and charged it with the task of recommending the best site. A preliminary list of 78 sites was narrowed to four for extensive study: Cublington, Thurleigh, Nuthampstead, and Foulness.

One objective of the study was to determine and compare the social costs of the noise an airport would generate at each of these locations. Affected households were divided into four groups:

Group A: Those who would move away because of the airport noise.

Group B: Those who would move away for other reasons.

Group C: Those who would stay and suffer the extra noise.

Group D: Those who would move into the area.[2]

If we define N, S, D, and R, respectively, as the dollar cost of airport noise, the consumer surplus people enjoy from their homes when no airport exists, the depreciation of housing prices due to noise, and relocation (moving) costs, we can make the following statements regarding the impact of airport noise on each group.

Group A: It must be that N > D + S + R, otherwise these people would stay. Therefore, D + S + R forms a lower bound on their loss.

Group B: These people would be worse off by amount D. Because of the noise generated by an airport, the selling prices of their homes would decrease.

Group C: These people would lose N.

Group D: These people were assumed to be just compensated for the noise they would suffer by the reduced prices they would pay for housing. Therefore, the net cost of increased noise to them would be zero.

For each potential site, an analyst would have to establish N, D, S, and R, and how many households existed in each of Groups A, B, and C.

To assess depreciation (D), real estate agents in the areas surrounding Heathrow and Gatwick were surveyed for their opinions (based on experience) regarding how house prices vary according to noise levels. Eventually, only the results for the Gatwick area were used, because it was judged that the short-listed sites more closely resembled that area than the one around Heathrow. Moving companies provided estimates of R.

The loss of consumer surplus (S) was determined using survey methods. In this context, a household's consumer surplus (without an airport) is the difference between the minimum amount for which it would be willing to sell its dwelling and the market value of the residence. This is the surplus the household would lose if construction of an airport forced it to move. Householders were asked to consider what price they would have to be paid to just compensate them for relocating to a similar (non-airport) area.[3]

The dollar cost of noise (N) was calculated by combining a physical measurement of noise with noise-induced depreciation estimates. The former required formulation of a Noise and Number Index (NNI). This index is a ranking of both the loudness and the frequency of noise caused by aircraft and can be represented on a map. An NNI contour map is very similar to the weather maps you see in newspapers. On a weather map, the reference point is an area of lowest or highest pressure, and the more or less circular contour lines that emanate from it indicate sites of equal barometric pressure. Instead of areas of the same pressure, an NNI contour map shows areas of the same aircraft noise pollution. Devices for measuring noise loudness and frequency record the highest NNI at the site of an existing airport; as the devices are moved farther and farther from the airport, NNI readings decrease. Sites of equal NNI can be plotted to generate a contour map, on which each line indicates a common NNI level. NNI contours resemble concentric cigar-shaped rings because the busiest airport runways are typically parallel. Flowerdew (1972, pp. 438–439) shows the actual NNI map for Heathrow.

Once NNI levels were identified for existing airport sites, households within each NNI contour were surveyed regarding their subjective degree of noise annoyance on a scale from 1 to 5. Using this information, a distribution of noise annoyance was generated for each NNI level. Analysts then assumed that the cost of noise for a given NNI level, N, was equal to the amount by which the median household in this distribution would have to reduce the price of its house to attract the same number of potential buyers that would exist in the absence of an airport. That is, analysts used the depreciation of the median household's dwelling. Given this dollar figure, the entire distribution of noise annoyance (for each NNI level) was converted to dollar values around this median.[4]

With this information and predictions of flight patterns, NNI contours were forecast for each of the four potential sites; investigators were then able to calculate both N for each group and the number of people in each group at each location. Given estimates of N, D, S, and R, analysts were able to predict the costs of noise pollution for each of Cublington, Thurleigh, Nuthampstead, and Foulness.

The Roskill Commission's methodology has been criticized, and with good reason, but it *was* one of the first serious attempts to evaluate an intangible.[5] It may interest the reader that the cost-benefit analysis ranking of the four sites placed Cublington first and Foulness last. However, this ranking was reversed, mainly on distributive grounds: Foulness was preferred because it would most favour low-income travellers, whereas Cublington would favour high-income travellers. In the end, neither facility was built. On Friday, March 13, 1991, Queen Elizabeth II inaugurated Stanstead, the choice the government had made almost 30 years before!

Noise Abatement in Basle

The Hedonic Price Technique

Imagine two houses that are exactly identical except that one is situated closer to a source of noise pollution (such as a factory, busy road, or airport) than the other. If the market-determined rent of the house closer to this disamenity is lower, it must be because its occupants must tolerate more noise.[6] The dollar value of the discomfort this noise causes can be no greater than this rent differential—otherwise its occupants would move. If there are a dozen identical houses, all different distances from the same source of noise, the relationship between house rents and the level of noise can be deduced even more accurately.

For example, suppose that 12 houses, numbered from the closest (#1) to the farthest (#12) from the source, are located at 100-metre intervals and that the average daily noise reading decreases by 5 decibels every 100 metres. If monthly rents increase in increments of $20 per 100 metres, and if residents have voluntarily chosen to pay these rents, we may deduce that people in these houses value noise at $20 per month per 5 decibels. What we have calculated is the hedonic price of noise. People, by their behaviour in a housing market, have revealed that they are willing to accept $20 per month in compensation for tolerating an additional 5 decibels of noise.

Of course, other factors can cause house rents to differ. Suppose that a park is located closest to houses #6 and #7 and thus farthest from houses #1 and #12. The park is an amenity and households will be willing to pay more to be close to it. Still, the rent on #6 should be lower than the rent on #7, because although the same distance from the park, it is closer to the source of noise pollution. Similarly, rents will differ for houses #5 and #8, and so on. Thus, even if there are two factors that cause rents to differ, a hedonic price of noise pollution can still be deduced. In ideal circumstances, this technique can be used to distinguish the impact of every amenity and disamenity on house rents.

Obviously, several other factors determine house prices and rents. Indeed, the market rent of a particular house will be a function of *all* of its characteristics, good and bad. Still, if we call the complete list of a house's characteristics an observation, we can calculate a hedonic price for each characteristic as long as we have a large and varied enough set of observations.

Basically, an analyst discovers why houses rent for the number of dollars per month they do. The econometric methodology consists of using regression techniques to estimate an equation; monthly house rent can then be expressed as a function of a set of characteristics. The partial derivative of rent with respect to a particular characteristic is that characteristic's hedonic price. Thus, the partial derivative of rent with respect to noise (measured in decibels) reveals the value that households attribute to an extra decibel of noise.

Pommerehne (1986) provides an example of this technique. His task was to compare methods of estimating the social value of noise reduction in Basle, Switzerland, using 1983 data. His sample consisted of 223 households throughout that city. For each, he treated monthly rent as a function of a total of 70 characteristics, which he grouped into four broad categories. The first category included interior house-specific characteristics such as the number of rooms, the number of bathrooms, and the age of the structure. The second included exterior house-specific characteristics such as distances to schools and bus stops and whether or not the street was tree-lined. The third dealt with neighbourhood-specific characteristics such as the size of open areas, the existence of recreational facilities, and the quality of schools. The fourth was a measure of noise. Decibels were used to measure road noise, and an NNI, similar to the one used in the Roskill study, was devised to gauge aircraft noise.

Using these 223 observations, Pommerehne regressed all of these 70 characteristics on house rents. A detailed discussion of his econometric methodology and results is beyond the scope of this book. We do, however, provide one of Pommerehne's simpler equations in Box 9.1. Using these results, Pommerehne calculated that an average household would be willing to pay 74.0 Swiss francs (SFr) per month for a 50% reduction in road noise and 32.2 SFr per month for a 50% reduction in aircraft noise.

Contingent Valuation

Pommerehne also determined households' contingent valuations (compensating variations) of noise abatement using the same sample in Basle. Using survey techniques, he determined what each household would be willing to pay for a 50% reduction in noise levels—just as he had using the hedonic price technique.[7]

BOX 9.1

Calculating Hedonic Prices

One equation estimated by Pommerehne is the following:

$$ln\text{MR} = 6.962 + 0.663 \cdot ln\text{NR} + 0.028 \cdot \text{QI} + 0.127 \cdot \text{D}_1 + 0.205 \cdot \text{D}_2 + 0.111 \cdot \text{D}_3 + 0.279 \cdot \text{D}_4 - 0.00049 \cdot ln\text{SC} - 0.00020 \cdot ln\text{PG} - 0.00021 \cdot ln\text{BS} + 0.0010 \cdot ln\text{OA} - 0.0038 \cdot \text{IA} - 0.0125 \cdot \text{RN} - 0.0020 \cdot \text{AN}$$

where

MR $\equiv$ the monthly net dwelling rent (in Swiss francs)

NR $\equiv$ the number of rooms

QI $\equiv$ a dwelling quality index ranging from very poor (-9) to very good ($+9$)

D_1 $\equiv$ a dummy variable; = 1 if the structure is purely a dwelling, = 0 otherwise

D_2 $\equiv$ a dummy variable; = 1 if the structure is a single-family dwelling, = 0 otherwise

D_3 $\equiv$ a dummy variable; = 1 if the dwelling is on an avenue with trees, = 0 otherwise

D_4 $\equiv$ a dummy variable; = 1 if the dwelling is situated on the Rhine, = 0 otherwise

SC $\equiv$ the distance in metres from the nearest shopping centre

PG $\equiv$ the distance in metres from the nearest playground

BS $\equiv$ the distance in metres from the nearest bus stop

OA $\equiv$ the amount of open area in the neighbourhood expressed as a percentage of total space

IA $\equiv$ the amount of industrial area in the neighbourhood expressed as a percentage of total space

RN $\equiv$ road traffic noise measured in decibels (dB)

AN $\equiv$ aircraft noise according to a Noise and Number Index (NNI)

From this equation, the hedonic prices of noise pollution in Basle were calculated. Partially differentiating lnMR with respect to RN yields the hedonic price of road traffic noise: a one-decibel increase in road noise causes a 1.25% decrease in monthly rents. In the case of aircraft noise, partially differentiating lnMR with respect to AN reveals that a one-unit increase in NNI is associated with a 0.20% decrease in monthly rents.

His method was to inform the 223 households that they were part of a larger, general environmental study. Presumably, the rationale for this was that if respondents felt that their answers would be of minor consequence to the overall result, they would be less likely to exaggerate or to answer strategically. Pommerehne (1986, p. 382) provides a description of the interview held with each household:

> In a next step households were informed that they could improve their actual housing situation by moving into another dwelling being identical, but situated in a neighbouring street where traffic noise is reduced by half. Moving costs, it was said, would be financed out of a special fund of city government. After that, households were asked about their actual net rent and the maximum accepted increase for the alternative dwelling.

Using this method, Pommerehne found that an average household would be willing to pay 81.0 SFr per month for a 50% reduction in road noise and 22.3 SFr per month for a 50% reduction in aircraft noise.

Comparing Methods

We note that although these methods yield about the same valuation of road noise, estimates of the social cost of aircraft noise differ by a significant factor. Nevertheless, an important result of Pommerehne's study is that it suggests that it is possible for these methods to yield similar results, not just in the case of noise pollution caused by cars, but more broadly for other public goods and intangibles. This is important, given the advantages and disadvantages of each method.

The principal advantage of the hedonic price method is that it uses market data. This is significant, because people reveal their true preferences when they make consumption decisions in markets. A main disadvantage is that it is sometimes difficult or impossible to amass enough market observations to ensure the econometric validity of the estimates.

On the other hand, the contingent valuation method uses self-generated survey data. Because market data are not required, this method may be applied to all public goods and intangibles. The main disadvantage is that individuals may respond to survey questions strategically. For example, if individuals are asked the minimum amount they would be willing to accept in compensation for some disamenity, they may overstate the true amount if they believe that they will actually be compensated according to their answers. Pommerehne's result may be interpreted to mean that this bias may not be important. If this result can be extended to other intangibles and public goods, it means that although the hedonic price method is more sophisticated and its estimates more dependable, the results of the contingent valuation method may be used with some confidence in circumstances where it is impossible to amass the data required in order to calculate hedonic prices.

THE VALUE OF LIFE

Many projects and policies result in lives either saved or lost. For example, if a roadway is widened, made one-way, or has a centre median installed, we can predict how many fewer road fatalities will occur each year. Similarly, adding a runway to an existing airport or building an additional airport to serve a flight centre will reduce congestion and decrease the likelihood of midair collisions. On the other hand, it is likely that some workers will die in the process of constructing projects like subway tunnels. Also, closing rail lines will expose more people to road hazards, and closing hospitals may result in lives lost that might have been saved had emergency facilities been available.

This raises the question of the "value of life"—of how we put a value on lives saved and lost. This question cannot be avoided in cost-benefit analyses because we must compare all of the costs and benefits of projects in order to determine whether they enhance or diminish social welfare.

Consider a stretch of highway used by one million people each year. On average, traffic accidents claim 100 of them annually. That is, the probability of death along this stretch is 1:10,000, or 0.0001. Suppose that a public project would decrease the number of fatalities to 90, thus saving 10 lives per year and causing the probability of death to decrease to 0.00009. An analyst's quest is to determine the compensating and/or equivalent variations of this obvious benefit. If each of these one million people were willing to pay $50 per year for this 0.00001 reduction in the probability of dying, the total all one million travellers would be willing to pay for this 10-person reduction in fatalities would be $50 million. Here, the value of one life saved is $5 million.[8]

If the above were true, $5 million would be what economists call "the value of life." Notice, however, that it would be more appropriate to call it the value of a *statistical* life, because the identities of the people who will not die if the road project is built are not known. The valuation made is *ex ante*, and the life saved may be thought of as that of a traveller chosen by lot. It would be a very different situation if the policy question concerned a specific living person, or if the valuation were made *ex post*.

The Value of Known Lives

Suppose that Mr. X will die if he does not receive an operation. If the compensating and equivalent variation questions were put to him, they would be, "What is the maximum you are willing to pay for the operation?" and "What is the minimum you are willing to accept to forgo the operation …

and thus die?" Whereas the answer to the first question would be restricted by his wealth, the answer to the second would likely be boundless. If medical care is privately provided, Mr. X will only have the operation if he, and his friends and family, are willing and able to pay for it. In a world of socialized medicine, if the question is put, "What is the maximum we as society are willing to pay to save Mr. X's life?" the answer will likely be very large, because Mr. X's answer will count and because we may want to be accorded the same treatment in similar circumstances. But if society spends $1 million saving Mr. X, it will have $1 million less with which to save other people. If society felt the same way about all people, it would soon become apparent that it does not possess all of the resources necessary to save everyone.

Given the reality of scarce resources, all an economist can offer to the decision-making process is that if $1 million is spent saving Mr. X, society will incur an opportunity cost of that amount. If Mrs. Y also needs the operation, but only one can be performed, who should get it? When the identities of the people affected are known, the ethical dimensions of the decisions that must be made lie beyond an economist's—perhaps anyone's—purview.

Courts, of course, do determine the value of people, but usually only after they are dead—another instance when the individual's identity is known. When liability is judged in the case of the death of a neurosurgeon, the award to the doctor's family is likely to be larger than that to the family of an economics professor killed in the same circumstances. Much of this *ex post* determination is based on what the individual's future earnings would have been had he or she lived. But individuals' earnings measure only what they contribute to society. Perhaps the amount they would have consumed had they lived—the resources they would have used up—should be subtracted from this to yield their net contribution. However, if society based the value of lives on this, it would lead to older people being judged less "valuable" than young people, and so on. Another ethical morass would result.

Fortunately, these kinds of questions usually do not arise in cost-benefit analyses. Usually, a project or policy may either save lives or take them, but the identity of those who will be saved or killed is not known. The victim or person saved is randomly selected and, as such, is simply a statistic. It is this, the *ex ante* valuation of statistical lives, that is ethically defensible and lies within the purview of cost-benefit analysis.[9]

Estimating the Value of a Statistical Life

Of interest to an analyst is not how much individuals are willing to pay to survive (a decrease of the probability of death to zero), but how much they are willing to pay for a marginal decrease in the probability of death. Conversely, it may be the minimum they are willing to accept to bear a marginal increase in the probability of untimely death. Three methods exist for obtaining answers to the compensating and/or equivalent variation questions if construction of a particular road project would, as in the example above, decrease the probability of a fatal accident.

The first is simply to ask those who would be affected. Of course, estimates of compensating and equivalent variations will be suspect if those surveyed respond strategically. It may also be that whereas a person is able to judge the riskiness of what currently exists, he or she may not be able to fully comprehend the potential impact of a policy or project on his or her own probability of survival.

The second method is to deduce the answers by observing consumption patterns. For example, how much people are willing to pay in the marketplace for smoke detectors, seat belts, and the like may reveal their attitudes toward life-threatening risks. However, the value of life that can be deduced when a person buys both cigarettes and a smoke detector is questionable! Notice that people buying life insurance may reveal what they think they *should* be worth to their heirs.

The third method is to note that people reveal how much they are willing to pay for reduced risks of death, and are willing to accept for increased risks of death, in labour markets. Typically, the more dangerous the job, the higher the pay *ceteris paribus*. That is, although a person's wage is a function of many variables, one of them is the risk of death he or she faces on the job. This suggests that if we were to estimate wages as a function of all of these determinants, we could calculate a hedonic price of risk of death.

Indeed, this is how most investigators have addressed this issue. One of the most recent attempts is reported in Meng & Smith (1990), who used data from the 1984 Canadian National Election Study on the earnings of 777 men and women to study this question. The results of one of the equations they estimated are the subject of Box 9.2.

Employing the same methodology as in Box 9.2 but using different variables, Meng & Smith estimate additional values of life of $6,122,717, $4,620,275, $6,971,042, and $7,330,713. Given no way of choosing among these estimates, they settle on a value of life of $5.2 million (measured in 1983 dollars), the average of their five estimates.[10] This means that, on average, a worker requires compensation (through increased wages) of $5,200 dollars per year to accept an additional one-in-a-thousand (0.001) chance of dying on the job.

Clearly, the hedonic price approach for gauging the value of life using labour market data generates wide-ranging estimates. Similar to the variance of results reported by Meng & Smith, Usher (1985) reports estimates (in 1982 dollars) from $170,000 to $6 million per life.[11] Part of the problem is that labour market data will only reveal the true trade-off between money

BOX 9.2

The Value of Life

Meng & Smith (1990) report five regression equations. The simplest is this one:

$$ln Y = 0.4526 \cdot \male + 0.1785 \cdot H + 0.2491 \cdot T + 0.3319 \cdot C + 0.112 \cdot U + 0.04023 \cdot R$$

where

Y $\equiv$ annual earnings ($)

$\male$ $\equiv$ a dummy variable; = 1 if male, = 0 if female

H $\equiv$ a dummy variable; = 1 if the person finished high school, = 0 otherwise

T $\equiv$ a dummy variable; = 1 if the person graduated from a technical school, = 0 otherwise

C $\equiv$ a dummy variable; = 1 if the person obtained a university degree, = 0 otherwise

U $\equiv$ a dummy variable; = 1 if a member of a union, = 0 otherwise

R $\equiv$ the occupational fatality rate per 1,000 workers—the risk variable

When calculating the value of life from this equation, we must first calculate the following partial derivative:

$$\partial Y / \partial R = 0.04023 \cdot Y$$

Using the average income of the sample for Y ($21,125):

$$\partial Y / \partial R = \$849.858$$

This means that the average person requires compensation of $849.858 per year to induce him or her to accept an additional 0.001 (one in a thousand) chance of death on the job. The value of life Meng & Smith calculate from this equation is, therefore, $849.858/0.001 = $849,858.

and risk of death if these markets function perfectly. For example, individuals must actually be able to move from one job to another to effect the money-risk trade-off. However, many people are quite immobile. Government intervention in labour markets may also affect this trade-off. As well, it is likely that very risk-averse people will choose safe jobs, whereas less risk-averse individuals will choose relatively risky jobs. To the extent that risk preferences are not known, and therefore cannot be used as a determinant of wages in regression analyses, these studies do not yield exactly the desired information.[12]

Nevertheless, Usher (1985, p. 91) cautions that it is better for a government to specify a value of life even if it is not correct rather than specify none at all: "A specified value of life maximizes the number of lives saved for any given amount of expenditure and minimizes the extent to which my life is at the mercy of others." Also, there may be merit in an analyst performing sensitivity analysis using different values of life. If a project is viable (or not viable) when the value of life is set at both $1 million and $6 million, any debate concerning which is the more accurate of the two will add little to the analysis.

Two Caveats

We have presented two methods of estimating the value of life. In applying either, much caution is warranted. If a value of life has been calculated from labour market data covering a spectrum of occupations, it would be inappropriate to use it for appraising a road project if the road would be used mainly by either schoolchildren or daredevils. That is, the sample used to calculate the value of life should be somewhat representative of the people who will actually use the project.

Furthermore, even if everyone agrees on the value of life to be used in analyses, it is not always proper to use it as part of the assessment of projects that would cost or save lives. The reason is that it may already have been accounted for in market-determined prices and wages.

Example: A project involves digging a tunnel. Statisticians may be able to tell an analyst that construction accidents are expected to claim the lives of three workers. Using the Meng & Smith (1990) estimate, the analyst may be inclined to assess an additional $15.6 million cost to the project. But if labour markets are functioning well, the tunnel diggers will already be well informed about the hazards of their work, and their wages will include compensation for bearing this added risk of death: if this risk did not exist, their wages would be lower. The value of lives lost—the compensation workers require to accept the additional risks—has already been included in the project's total wage bill. To make a separate entry for the value of three lives would be to double-count this cost to society. Only if this risk has not yet been recognized—and if the wage rate is correspondingly lower—would it be appropriate to make a separate calculation.

Another example: It is proposed to replace a ferry with a bridge. Suppose that the bridge would be safer than the ferry to the extent that the lives of fewer travellers would be lost if they could travel by bridge. We know that the benefit to diverted travellers is the extra amount they are willing to pay to make the crossing by bridge. Presumably, they are willing to pay this premium because travelling by bridge is faster, more convenient, more comfortable ... and safer. That is, what they are prepared to pay for a decrease in the probability of a fatal accident is already included in this premium. Again, to make a separate calculation of the value of lives the bridge would save would be to double-count.

Thus, in project analysis a separate accounting of the value of life is only appropriate if the benefit or cost of a change in the probability of death is neither implicit in market prices or wages, nor included elsewhere. Whether market prices and wages accurately reflect the trade-off of dollars for risk depends on what information is available to consumers and labourers. Only if it is clear that individuals are not fully aware of these risks, and of the trade-offs they entail, can a case be made for an explicit accounting of the value of lives expected to be lost or saved due to a project or policy.

THE VALUE OF TIME SAVED

The main rationale behind many transportation projects is to save travellers time. Whether a project involves adding runways at an airport, building or widening a road, replacing a ferry service with a bridge, constructing a subway system, or adding buses to an existing public-transit system, individuals are made better off because they spend less time travelling and thus have more time—a precious commodity—to pursue other activities. The value they attribute to an hour of time saved depends on the alternative uses they can make of it.[13] Broadly, there are two uses for time saved: work and leisure. To each, cost-benefit analysts attribute a different value of time.

Working Time Saved

The gross wage a competitive firm pays employees of a given type reflects the value of their marginal product.[14] If a project saves one of these workers an hour of travelling time during the workday, he or she can work an extra hour. The value of this hour saved is the worth of what the employee is able to produce in an hour: the wage rate. If the workers whose time is saved by some project are fairly representative of the labour force, it may be acceptable to use published data on average wages as the value per hour of their time saved. In the cost-benefit analysis of the Northumberland Strait Fixed Crossing project, the average hourly industrial wage ($11.38, using 1987 prices) was used for working time saved by nontruckers, and the regional average hourly wage for truckers ($16.24 in 1987) was used for the value of an hour saved by truck drivers.[15] However, there are several reasons to believe that using wage rates in this manner may result in over-estimates of the true value of working time saved.

First, using a wage rate to measure the value of time is only valid if all of the time saved can be used for productive activities. This may be true when the job involves something like delivering messages or parcels within a city. An employee who is constantly on the go can use the travelling time saved to make more deliveries. Indeed, employers may be able to design delivery routes to exploit the particular features of a transportation project. On the other hand, some jobs cannot be broken down into a series of short tasks; that is, some are not divisible. For example, if a delivery job consists of making four two-hour trips every eight-hour shift, a time savings of 15 minutes per trip yields an hour saved per day, but that hour is not long enough to complete another trip. Because nothing extra is produced during the hour saved, using the employee's wage rate as a yardstick will overstate the value of this saved hour to society.

Second, not all time saved is appreciated equally by everyone. An employee travelling on a congested road might appreciate a project that saves time (and the aggravation of rush hours). But suppose that part of a working trip consists of a one-hour ride on a vehicle ferry. If the driver uses this time for leisure, a bridge project that replaces the ferry may decrease his or her utility.[16]

Third, to equate the value of time to a wage rate is to imply that no productive use can be made of travelling time. With the growing use of laptop and notebook computers, this is clearly no longer true, especially for plane, train, and ferry travellers. Also, it is common for people to schedule work-related reading for times when they know they will be travelling. It is white-collar workers and professionals who can most easily adapt their work habits and schedules to this purpose, and who are most likely to use technology to accommodate productive activities while travelling. By using their wages as the value of their time, we may be significantly overstating the value of time saved attributable to a project.

Analysts should assess the value of working time saved with care. Only in certain circumstances will using a wage rate as this value be justified. Indeed, there is no unique value of working time saved that can be applied to all transportation projects; any value applied will be project-specific. Using an average wage rate will likely overestimate the value of working time a project saves and thus the net present value of the project; this is why analysts may wish to subject their calculations to sensitivity analysis using values per hour of time saved that are less than travellers' wage rates.

Leisure Time Saved

If people use time saved for leisure activities (including inactivity!), an analyst will most certainly want to value it at less than gross-of-tax wage rates. Even when a person can trade off leisure and income perfectly, that person will only opt for an extra hour of leisure if its value is at least as much as his or her net-of-tax wage. This offers analysts little guidance. Fortunately, there are situations where people trade off money for leisure time, and a literature exists that is devoted to estimating its value.

Most commuters travel either by car or by public transit. If a project saves commuting time, extra leisure time will result. In mornings, because people don't have to leave for work as early, they will be able to sleep longer or simply dawdle over their coffee and newspaper. They will also arrive home from work earlier and have more time to engage in sports, gardening, and other recreational activities. An analyst's task is to deduce what value people attribute to this extra leisure time. The basic technique is to find circumstances where people face a trade-off between travel costs and commuting time.

Beesley's approach

In 1965, Beesley published an attempt to estimate the value of commuting time saved. Although his methodology has been overtaken by more sophisticated econometric techniques, his model is instructive in that it highlights strongly the basic trade-off that analysts must assess.

In 1963, Beesley surveyed civil servants working for the Ministry of Transport in central London. The data gleaned from each person included the following: address, car ownership, usual mode of travel to work, employment grade, and alternative mode of transportation to and from work. Modes of transportation considered were car travel and an aggregate of all forms of public transit. For each person, the money costs of car and public transit travel were calculated, along with commuting time by both modes.

Beesley grouped respondents according to civil service rank (a proxy for income) and assumed that the value of time saved was identical and constant per minute for people holding the same rank. Possible responses are shown in Figure 9.1.

Responses falling in Quadrant I are for commuters who, for whatever reason, choose to commute by a mode that is both slower and more expensive than the alternative. Others (the majority) face no money-time trade-off,

FIGURE 9.1   Possible Responses

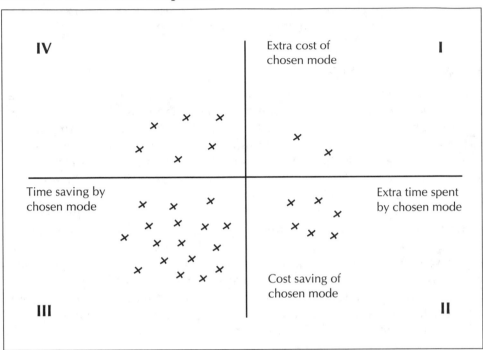

because the mode they use is both faster and cheaper than the alternative (Quadrant III) or because there exists no alternative mode of commuting (either they do not own a car or no public transit exists where they live). Only observations in the remaining two quadrants are of interest, because only these people face the relevant trade-off. The people whose responses fall in Quadrant II have opted to travel to and from work by a slower but cheaper mode of travel. For them, the money saved is treated as the *minimum* amount they are willing to accept in compensation for the extra time they spend commuting. The observations falling in Quadrant IV relate to people who have opted to pay a higher price to be able to travel by a faster mode. For these people, this extra cost is treated as the *maximum* they are willing to pay for the time they save.

Figure 9.2 has been developed from Figure 9.1.[17] Note that all responses falling in Quadrants I and III have been omitted for the reasons given above. Also, by simple transformation, all Quadrant II (minimum) responses have been moved to Quadrant IV; each of these has been marked by a □ . The maximum responses have been left in Quadrant IV, but each has been marked by a ● to distinguish it from the minimum responses. In this way, all relevant responses have been gathered in one quadrant, with maximum

FIGURE 9.2 The Value of Commuting Time Saved

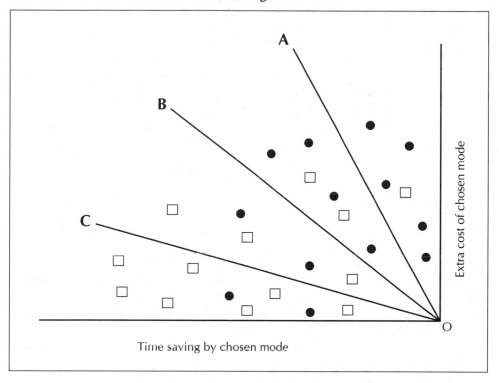

responses clustering more or less above minimum responses. Note that for some numbers of minutes saved, it is possible to read off vertically both the maximum some respondent is willing to pay for this time savings (●) and the minimum amount someone else is willing to accept to tolerate a journey this number of minutes longer than the alternative □ .

Beesley made a similar set of observations for each income class, and made the assumption that all members with the same job rank valued time equally. He then determined the average value of time saved by fitting a line through the observations so that it passed through the origin at a slope that minimized the number of "misclassifications." That is, for a given line fitted through the observations, perfection would require that all maximum responses (●) lie above it and that all minimum responses (□) lie below it. Given his assumptions, the slope of such a line measures the value of time saved per minute.[18]

Note that various sources of error have rendered perfection unattainable. Nevertheless, of lines OA, OB, and OC, the one with the lowest "misclassification count" would be chosen. Eight maximum responses lie below line OA, and 1 minimum response lies above it; this yields a misclassification count of 9. Similarly, the error counts for lines OB and OC are, respectively, 7 (4 below and 3 above) and 8 (2 below and 6 above). Therefore, of the three lines shown, OB is the best fit, given Beesley's crude criterion; and its slope thus measures his estimate of the value of time saved per minute.

Beesley calculated a value of time for each employment rank in this manner. He reported values of time for two ranks: clerical officers and executive officers. As expected, the value of time increased with income, but when expressed as a percentage of wages the results were remarkably similar. Beesley estimated that clerical officers' value of time was 30.8% of their wage rate, whereas executive officers valued their time saved at 35.2% of their wage rate.

More Modern Modal-choice Methods

Beesley's method is attractive because it is simple, and because its results can be derived on a diagram. However, to attain simplicity requires strong and sometimes unrealistic assumptions. A major weakness of his approach is that it ignores a number of other determinants for choosing a mode of travel. Also, his results are suspect because the sizes of the samples of individuals actually trading off money for time (and vice versa) are considered too small to have desirable statistical properties. For example, his valuation of time saved by executive officers was based on only 21 responses. Still, his method is a useful starting point in the development of more sophisticated estimation methods. These techniques are somewhat similar to those used to estimate the hedonic price of noise and the value of life.

Harrison & Quarmby (1972) state the basic model of modal choice where travellers are assumed to choose the mode that causes them the least disutility. If the relative disutility of travelling by a mode is denoted by L(X), and if x_i denotes the relative characteristic of two modes (i = 1, 2, 3, ..., m), it is asserted that

$$L(X) = \emptyset_0 + \emptyset_1 x_1 + \emptyset_2 x_2 + \emptyset_3 x_3 + ... + \emptyset_m x_m.$$

Here, $\emptyset_0$ is the difference in intrinsic attributes of the modes.[19] The list of x_i variables could include differences in travelling time, waiting time, and money cost, and any other differences in measurable characteristics that could influence an individual's choice of mode. The coefficients of these characteristics ($\emptyset_i$) to be estimated are their hedonic prices. If P(X), denoting the probability of a person choosing a particular mode of travel, is a function of L(X), a particular functional form often chosen for estimation is

$$P(X) = e^{L(X)}/[1 + e^{L(X)}]$$

A simple example would be if we were to specify the cost of travelling by Mode 1 as a function of time costs and money costs only. If C_1, T_1, and M_1, respectively, denoted the total cost (\$), time cost (minutes), and money cost (\$) of travelling a particular route by Mode 1, the function could be stated as

$$C_1 = \alpha_1 + \beta \cdot T_1 + M_1$$

In this equation, α_1 denotes the intrinsic utility (or disutility) of travelling by Mode 1 (which need not be measured). The parameter β converts the time cost in minutes of travelling by Mode 1 into a dollar measure. Therefore, β is the value of a minute of time saved.

For an alternative mode of travel between the same two points (Mode 2), we can specify a similar cost function:

$$C_2 = \alpha_2 + \beta \cdot T_2 + M_2$$

Implicit in these equations is that β, the value of time, is mode-independent. The extra cost of travelling by Mode 1 compared to Mode 2, ΔC, is

$$\Delta C = (\alpha_1 - \alpha_2) + \beta \cdot (T_1 - T_2) + (M_1 - M_2)$$

When we substitute this into the general equation for L(X), the specific form of the relative disutility function is, therefore, $L(X) = \emptyset \Delta C$,[20] and the relative probability of a traveller selecting Mode 1 is given by $e^{\Delta C}/(1 + e^{\Delta C})$. Taking the natural logarithms of both sides and rearranging yields

$$ln \ \{P_1/P_2\} = \emptyset \Delta C = \emptyset(\alpha_1 - \alpha_2) + \emptyset \beta \cdot (T_1 - T_2) + \emptyset(M_1 - M_2)$$

which we can estimate when we use the fact that for large samples of travellers, P_1 and P_2 may also be interpreted as the proportion of travellers choosing Modes 1 and 2, respectively. Given data on proportions of people travelling by these alternative modes, time differences, and money-cost differences, estimating this equation will yield values for coefficients $\emptyset(\alpha_1 - \alpha_2)$, $\emptyset \beta$, and $\emptyset$. From these, we can calculate β, the value of time measured in dollars per unit of time, as the ratio of $\emptyset \beta$ to $\emptyset$.

The form of the above equation chosen is quite simple and is almost the equivalent of Beesley's diagrammatic model. Models actually used tend to be much more complex and require knowledge of econometric models of qualitative choice. As well, investigators have distinguished travelling, walking, and waiting time, and have disaggregated money costs into fares, gasoline costs, parking costs, and so on. Because there exist several econometric methods, and so many ways of specifying the function to be estimated, it is not surprising that estimates of commuting time saved vary considerably. For example, Gaudry (1980) estimates per hour values of time saved for Montreal transit users to be $0.85, $1.08, $2.98, and $7.43 (1970 prices) using four different specifications.[21]

Whatever level of mathematical sophistication we apply, the essential method is to draw out statistically what travellers reveal about how they trade off time and money. As a practical matter, when there is little agreement concerning the value of time saved to a particular class of traveller, it may be best to resort to sensitivity analysis using a variety of dollar figures, as proportions of relevant wage rates or not.

SUMMARY

In this chapter we have addressed the problems of how to estimate the values of noise, lives saved or lost, and time saved. Other intangibles exist, but the same principles of measurement as outlined here apply to them. Bear in mind that the basic objective is to obtain answers to the relevant compensating and/or equivalent variation questions.

At first glance, this would seem a difficult task. However, once an analyst finds circumstances where a trade-off between an intangible and money exists, the problem becomes manageable. House rents decrease with proximity to a source of noise pollution or other disamenity; labourers are paid risk premiums; and travellers exhibit their willingness to pay for faster modes of transportation. An advantage to using market data is that people reveal their preferences truthfully in markets. Whether we use simple diagrammatic analysis or complex econometric techniques, our objective is to calculate the value (hedonic price) of the relevant intangible. The greater the number of observations, the more accurate will be our estimate. However, this suggests a weakness of the hedonic price method: sufficient market observations may not be available.

The second method relies on surveys. Pommerehne's contingent valuation method was directed at measuring compensating variation: the maximum people would be prepared to pay for a reduction in noise pollution. Equivalent variation may also be assessed by simple survey methods. An advantage of survey methods is that an analyst can generate a data set regardless of the number of people that would be affected by a project; there is no lower limit on the number of observations required. We realize, however, that answers given to either question may not be truthful or accurate if people respond strategically.

Thus, estimates of hedonic prices are accurate given sufficient observations, but obtaining enough data may not always be possible. At the same time, contingent valuation estimates, although likely to be less accurate, are relatively simple to generate from surveys. Pommerehne's result—that it is possible for contingent valuation estimates to approximate those gleaned from hedonic pricing techniques—is important, albeit optimistic.

Whichever method is used, a caution is in order. It is possible for analysts to become so caught up in putting dollar values on intangibles such as noise, lives, and time, that they lose sight of the fact that separate entries for these things are not always necessary in cost-benefit analysis. In some situations, to do so would involve double-counting the relevant cost or benefit. For example, if it is likely that lives will be lost on a construction project, a separate accounting of the value of the lives expected to be lost should not be made if the wages labourers receive include compensation for the extra risks they take. This cost to a project would already be accounted for in wage bills. Similarly, it is possible to double-count time savings, as noted above. (To reinforce this warning, we provide an example of double-counting time savings in Case 2 concerning the proposed Trans Labrador Highway project.)

KEY TERMS

contingent valuation
hedonic price

EXERCISES

9.1 People living near an airport have won a lawsuit against the airport authority. The judge agrees with them that aircraft make enough of a racket to qualify as "excessive noise pollution." Now the judge must determine what compensation should be awarded to the plaintiffs and wants to know which existed first, the airport or the complainants' houses? Why is this relevant?

9.2 Construction workers died while constructing Confederation Bridge, which links Prince Edward Island and New Brunswick. Even though these tragic events were predictable, the analyst who evaluated the project included no cost for lives expected to be lost. In what circumstances would the analyst be justified? In what circumstances would the analyst's omission not be justified?

9.3 A number of respondents in Beesley's survey answered that they travelled to and from work by slower, more expensive modes than what were available. If these people value commuting time saved, can we conclude that these people are not rational?

9.4 In Box 9.1, partially differentiating *ln*MR with respect to RN yields the hedonic price of road traffic noise. From this, it is concluded that people would be willing to pay 74 SFr per month for a 50% reduction in road noise. Assuming that a one-decibel reduction in road noise is far smaller than the number of decibels required for a 50% reduction, it would appear that constant marginal disutility of noise has been assumed. How would the 74 SFr figure have to be adjusted if marginal disutility of noise were increasing? decreasing?

9.5 Road-widening projects reduce fatal accidents. They also reduce the number of accidents involving injury. Sometimes analysts assess this benefit using wage and salary data. That is, if a project would save one million person-hours of employment per year, and if a representative wage were $15 per hour, the benefit assessed would be $15 million per year. Discuss the validity of this approach.

ENDNOTES

1. More detailed expositions of how the Roskill Commission treated the social cost of noise may be found in Flowerdew (1972) and Pearce (1976).

2. Several critics have noted that the commission ignored a fifth group—people who do not move in because of the added noise.

3. Pearce (1976, p. 23) reports that householders were first asked if they would accept £100 to move. Those refusing were asked: "What would the difference in price have to be to make you seriously consider moving?" Those responding that no amount would induce them to leave were imputed a consumer surplus equal to the house price.

4. The actual distribution also grouped houses according to price range.

5. See Pearce (1976) and Mishan (1970) for criticisms of the Roskill Commission's methodology.

6. If owner-occupied, monthly rents can be imputed from house prices.

7. Road traffic noise and aircraft noise were treated separately. That is, Pommerehne asked households about their willingness to pay for a reduction in traffic noise while maintaining the same level of aircraft noise, and then asked how much they would be willing to pay for a reduction in aircraft noise while maintaining the same level of road noise.

8. Note that this can be calculated either by dividing society's total willingness to pay by the number of lives saved ($50 million ÷ 10 lives) or by dividing what a representative person is willing to pay for the reduction in the probability of death by this reduction ($50 ÷ 0.00001).

9. See Usher (1985) for a discussion of the economic and ethical dimensions of this approach.

10. They regard this as a lower bound on the value of life, arguing that workers may be willing to accept job-related risks that they would not expose themselves or their families to outside the workplace. They do not provide evidence to support this view. Correct or not, it would not accord, for example, with casual observation of the number of people in "safe" jobs who are weekend bungee-jumpers, sky-divers, and hang-gliders.

11. Usher (1985, pp. 176–177) himself puts forward a figure of $750,000. See this article for a rich review of this literature.

12. Behaviour under uncertainty and risk preferences is presented in Chapter 10.

13. Investigations have shown that its value also depends on what kind of time is saved. That is, people value time saved walking, driving, waiting, and riding on public transit differently. See, for example, Gaudry (1980). Also, it seems reasonable that the value of time saved depends on the time of day and/or the season when it is saved.

14. The gross wage rate here is the total cost to the firm of employing a person for an hour. Thus, it includes not only the employee's gross-of-tax wage but also the firm's contributions to (un)employment insurance, Canada or Quebec Pension Plans, other payroll taxes, medical insurance, the firm's own pension plan, and so forth.

15. See Fiander-Good Associates (1987, p. 5.12).

16. For example, truck drivers who travel the Northumberland Strait by ferry use the time required for crossings to eat, play cards, and so forth. People crossing between Yarmouth, Nova Scotia, and Bar Harbour, Maine, sometimes use the time to sleep. Of course, these travellers are aware that a gambling section consisting of slot machines opens once this cross-border ferry enters international waters.

17. Axes and symbols on this diagram have been chosen to closely resemble those of Beesley's Figure 1 (1965, p. 179), a diagram central to his analysis.

18. This line passes through the origin because, presumably, a rational commuter would be willing to pay nothing for no time saving.

19. For example, intrinsic characteristics of train travel not available to automobile drivers include the potential for a passenger to read, write, sleep, or take a walk while travelling.

20. For this simple form, we can think of all but $\emptyset_1$ in the general equation for L(X) being set equal to zero, setting $\emptyset_1 = \emptyset$ because a subscript is no longer needed, and setting $x_1 = \Delta C$ to make clear that it is the total cost differential that determines which mode passengers choose.

21. Readers familiar with econometrics are directed to Gaudry's paper and to an Ottawa study by Gillen (1977).

DEALING WITH RISK
AND UNCERTAINTY

INTRODUCTION

Many projects that analysts are asked to evaluate involve a time-stream of costs and benefits that stretch over many decades. Naturally, analysts do not possess perfect foresight regarding events that will influence the magnitude of future costs and benefits. For example, the viability of a road project depends on future traffic patterns, data that sometimes can be forecast only very imprecisely. Whether a particular dam should be constructed for flood protection depends on the frequency and magnitude of future flooding—information beyond the knowledge of even the most experienced forecasters. Only at the end of a project's life can we look back and assess its merits in any deterministic way. This approach may be valid from a historical perspective, but it provides little guidance for cost-benefit analysts who must advise on economic viability in advance of events.

This is not to say that analysts must work within a state of complete ignorance. Traffic patterns may be predicted on the basis of population trends and other factors that influence the way people travel. Historical data on flooding provide insights as to the likelihood of future flood damage. Information that transforms "guesswork" into "informed prediction" is valuable. Analysts, although they would prefer to evaluate projects within a deterministic framework, must learn to deal in a reasonable, prudent manner with the reality of possessing less than perfect foresight.

The risks and uncertainties that analysts must deal with are not very different from those faced by firms and consumers. An automobile producer that is considering building a new factory must deal with uncertain future demand, costs, government regulations, and tax rules. A married couple contemplating a move to another locale so that one of them can accept an attractive job offer may not know if the other will be able to find suitable employment. The firm, presumably, will forecast demand for its product as best it can, and will try to enter into contracts in order to define costs; it may also seek long-term commitments from various levels of government regarding taxes and regulations. The couple will gather as much labour market information as they can before deciding whether to relocate. In both situations, economic agents are seeking to minimize or eliminate the costs of bearing risk and uncertainty.

Economists have long distinguished between *risk* and *uncertainty*. In a *risky* situation, the possible consequences of an action are known and it is possible to assign a probability to each. For example, when we roll a pair of dice, the sum can be any whole number between 2 and 12. The probabilities of the various outcomes (stated as p_{roll}) are $p_2 = 1/36$, $p_3 = 2/36$, $p_4 = 3/36$, $p_5 = 4/36$, $p_6 = 5/36$, $p_7 = 6/36$, $p_8 = 5/36$, $p_9 = 4/36$, $p_{10} = 3/36$, $p_{11} = 2/36$, and $p_{12} = 1/36$. Note that these probabilities sum to 1, indicating that all possible outcomes have been considered. A flip of a fair coin would be characterized by $p_{head} = 0.5$ and $p_{tail} = 0.5$.

Risk is sometimes dealt with in insurance markets. If enough experience with a phenomenon exists, insurance companies can calculate the probability of it occurring in the general population, and determine premiums; the risk becomes insurable. For example, insurance companies do not know whose house in particular will burn down next year, but they can state with some assurance what proportion of homes will meet this end. In a similar vein, a cost-benefit analyst may be required to choose the size of dam to build, based on historical data that in any given year, no flood occurs with a probability of 0.5, a minor flood occurs with probability 0.35, a major flood occurs with probability 0.13, and a flood of disastrous magnitude occurs with probability 0.02. Another example: A bridge is to be constructed over open water. If enough wind and precipitation data are available, it may be possible to forecast how many days the bridge will be closed to traffic each year, though without knowing in advance which days in particular.

In a situation involving *uncertainty*, the probability of any outcome occurring is not known, either because there is no basis for formulating probabilities or because those probabilities cannot be measured. For example, the present value of net benefits attributable to an airport planned for a Canadian border town depends on future rulings or actions by American authorities, who may choose Policy A, or B, or C, these being assorted tax rulings for American firms that ship freight by air. Policy A would be favourable to Canadian carriers, B so-so, and C unfavourable. The choice of policy could be made at any time in the future, and whether this particular Canadian airport is constructed is irrelevant to the American authorities. The cost-benefit analyst must recommend whether to build, but without being able to form any expectation as to which of the three policies will be chosen. That is, the decision must be made without assigning objective or subjective probabilities.

Similarly, when automobiles were first invented it was impossible for insurance companies to assess accurately the likelihood of males between the ages of 16 and 25 being in an accident within a calendar year; no data existed to guide the calculation. Today, of course, insurers can predict this datum with considerable confidence. Not so many years ago, analysts examining the merits of nuclear reactors—and the probability that they would go the way of Chernobyl—were in a similar situation. Obviously, risk experience and thus the ability to formulate meaningful probabilities does not exist when the phenomenon or object is new.

So far in this book we have incorporated individuals' preferences into public sector investment criteria, and into methods for calculating costs and benefits (when risk or uncertainty is not present). In the same way, our methods in the presence of risk or uncertainty should take into account individuals' risk preferences. If individuals are observed to be willing to incur costs in order to lessen the burden of risk or uncertainty, a cost-benefit analyst should be prepared to account for any costs of taking risks associated with a public sector project. It will become apparent in this chapter, however, that individuals' preferences regarding risk and uncertainty do not translate directly into social preferences. That is, even if every person in society were to view the individual risks they face identically, there may be good reason for an analyst not to adopt this common set of risk preferences for project appraisal.

We deal first with making decisions when risk is present, proceeding from the expected utility hypothesis to a theorem sometimes applicable to public sector decisions involving risk. Making decisions when outcomes are uncertain is dealt with in a quasi-game-theoretic context. This chapter concludes with a discussion of how some analysts have accounted for risk, uncertainty, and imperfect information in their evaluations.

DEALING WITH RISK

Suppose you possess $1,000. You are willing to take a bet on tomorrow's weather. Your wealth will be $10,000 if it does not rain, but if it does you will have to pay someone $600 (and be left with $400). The probability of no rain (and winning) is 10%; therefore, the probability of rain is 90% as determined by a consensus of competent meteorologists in your area, people whose forecasts you accept. Do you feel lucky or do you worry about getting soaked?

Examine the terms of the gamble dispassionately. Denote your wealth if you win by W_1 and the probability of winning by p_1. Corresponding values for losing are W_2 and p_2. Denote your wealth if you do not gamble by W_0.

The expected value of your (uncertain) wealth if you gamble is given by $p_1 \cdot W_1 + p_2 \cdot W_2 = 0.1 \cdot (\$10,000) + 0.9 \cdot (\$400) = \$1,360$, which we will denote by $\hat{W}$. (See Box 10.1.) If you choose not to gamble, your certain wealth, W_0, is $\$1,000$.

Call the above Gamble A. Now consider another, Gamble B. If you win it, your wealth will be $\$272,000$; if you lose, you lose everything—your entire initial wealth of $\$1,000$. The probability of winning is 0.005 (thus, the probability of losing is 0.995). Yet as with Gamble A, your expected wealth ($\hat{W}$) if you accept Gamble B is $0.005 \cdot (\$272,000) + 0.995 \cdot (\$0) = \$1,360$.

Is either of these gambles worth taking? For both, the expected wealth exceeds that which you will have if you do not gamble. If this were the sole criterion, you would gamble. Yet at the same time, none of this helps you determine which gamble to take. The lesson here is that "certain wealth versus expected wealth" and "expected wealth versus expected wealth" comparisons are not especially useful when we are trying to rank our choices. Another consideration is necessary: What level of discomfort do you feel when you take risks? Are those risks worth it?

If asked the difference between Gambles A and B, most people would comment on the difference in the "spreads." Gamble A, in this sense, seems more conservative than Gamble B. To put this feeling into the terminology of statistics, the difference is *variance*. (See Box 10.2.) The variance of the possible outcomes of Gamble A is less than that of Gamble B; in that sense, Gamble A is less "risky" for the same expected value.

There are, then, two criteria for ranking alternatives in risky situations: expected value and variance. If your only choices are between Gamble A and Gamble B, you will make your choice solely on the basis of variance, because the two gambles have the same expected value. However, "not gambling" may also be an option here. Assuming it is, you have three alternatives, which you will rank according to your personal risk preferences.

BOX 10.1
Expected Value

Consider an action that can result in one of five possible outcomes (measured in dollars), which are denoted by W_1, W_2, W_3, W_4, and W_5. The probabilities of them occurring are, respectively, p_1, p_2, p_3, p_4, and p_5 (which sum to 1). The *expected value* of this action, denoted by $\hat{W}$, is $\hat{W} = p_1 \cdot W_1 + p_2 \cdot W_2 + p_3 \cdot W_3 + p_4 \cdot W_4 + p_5 \cdot W_5$.

BOX 10.2
Variance

The general formula for variance when possible outcomes are W_1, W_2, W_3, ..., W_n and the probabilities, respectively, are p_1, p_2, p_3, ..., p_n is $p_1 \cdot [W_1 - \hat{W}]^2 + p_2 \cdot [W_2 - \hat{W}]^2 + p_3 \cdot [W_3 - \hat{W}]^2 + ... + p_n[W_n - \hat{W}]^2$. In the case of Box 10.1, $n = 5$.

Applying this formula to Gamble A, $VAR_A = 0.9 \cdot [400 - 1,360]^2 + 0.1 \cdot [10,000 - 1,360]^2 = 8,294,400$. Compare this to the variance of Gamble B: $VAR_B = 0.005 \cdot [272,000 - 1,360]^2 + .995 \cdot [0 - 1,360]^2 = 368,070,000$.

Another comparison will emphasize the trade-off involved. Let Option J entail wealth of $100,000 with probability 0.1 and wealth of $5,000 with probability 0.9. The alternative, Option Y, entails wealth of $20,000 with probability 0.4 and $3,000 with probability of 0.6. Here $\hat{J}$ = $14,500 and $VAR_J = 812,250,000$, while $\hat{Y}$ = $9,800 and $VAR_Y = 69,360,000$. An individual in facing this choice views expected value positively but variance as a measure of riskiness negatively. It is not clear which of Options J and Y that individual will prefer.

If we are to consider further how to rank alternatives in such circumstances, we will require a formal approach to making decisions when faced with risk. Our objective is to develop an analytical framework for analyzing risk preferences that can be brought to bear on an essential matter for project evaluation—the social costs of risk taking.

THE EXPECTED UTILITY HYPOTHESIS

Suppose an individual must choose between two risky options, G and H. Option G involves possible outcomes expressed in dollars, G_1, G_2, G_3, ..., G_n, with corresponding probabilities of g_1, g_2, g_3, ..., g_n. Option H involves possible outcomes expressed in dollars, H_1, H_2, H_3, ..., H_m, with corresponding probabilities of h_1, h_2, h_3, ..., h_m. A person who is neither risk-averse nor risk-loving will decide on the basis of which option has the higher expected value. Such a person is classified as risk-neutral; the variance of the two options is irrelevant to him or her. This is the kind of person who, if offered a bet involving winning or losing $100 on the toss of a fair coin, will be indifferent between betting and not betting—indifferent to a fair bet. That is, for a particular amount of money W, $U(W) = EU(W)$, where $U(\cdot)$ denotes certain utility and $EU(\cdot)$

uncertain, or expected, utility (to be defined and described below). If offered the chance to win $110 if heads appears but lose $100 if tails appears, a person with these risk preferences will bet, because the expected value of the bet, $0.5 \cdot [\$110] + 0.5 \cdot [-\$100] = \$5$, is positive. He or she will not bet if the terms of the wager are reversed. Expected value is everything to this type of person.

However, not all people are risk-neutral. For this reason, we need a way of characterizing the preferences of those who are not—a way of illustrating how they rank alternatives when risk is present. The expected utility hypothesis allows us to do this. If we can specify an individual's preferences as U(W), where W denotes income (or wealth) and $U(\cdot)$ is the individual's utility function defined over income, we can state the expected utility this person obtains from the two options as $EU(G) = g_1 \cdot U(G_1) + g_2 \cdot U(G_2) + g_3 \cdot U(G_3) + \ldots + g_n \cdot U(G_n)$, and $EU(H) = h_1 \cdot U(H_1) + h_2 \cdot U(H_2) + h_3 \cdot U(H_3) + \ldots + h_m \cdot U(H_m)$. The option chosen will depend on whether EU(G) is greater than, less than, or identical to EU(H)—where both expected values ($\hat{G}$ and $\hat{H}$) and variances (VAR_G and VAR_H) are captured by the form of $U(\cdot)$. That is, an individual's attitude toward taking risks—whether he or she feels discomfort or enjoys gambling—is captured by the properties (including the shape) of his of her utility function.[1]

Risk-averse Behaviour

A risk-averse person will not accept a fair bet. This means simply that he or she will prefer a certain amount of money, say $100, with certainty, rather than a risky prospect with an expected value of $100. Using the terminology developed above, for a particular W, U(W) > EU(W). For this to be the case, the individual's utility function must have the shape shown in Figure 10.1—strictly concave, in the language of calculus.

The slope of the function at a particular level of income (wealth) indicates the individual's marginal utility of income: positive because utility is a positive function of income. Note that the slope of the function decreases as income increases; risk aversion is indicated by diminishing marginal utility of wealth. This has a straightforward interpretation: a gain of x dollars yields less of a utility gain than the loss of utility caused by losing x dollars. (See Box 10.3.)

Figure 10.2 corresponds to Figure 10.1 with some of the labels and measures removed and others added. This individual faces the same risky situation: income level W_1 or W_2 with probabilities p_1 and p_2, respectively. As the expected value of these prospects is $\hat{W}$, the individual's expected utility is given by distance $\hat{W}C$. We know that the individual would be better off if income $\hat{W}$ were certain. A relevant question is, "What level of certain income would cause the individual to be indifferent between it and expected income $\hat{W}$?"

FIGURE 10.1 Risk-averse Behaviour

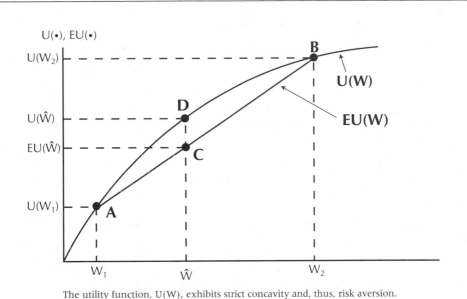

The utility function, U(W), exhibits strict concavity and, thus, risk aversion. For two prospects, W_1 and W_2. $\hat{W}$ is the expected value. Note that the expected utility function, EU(W), is formed by joining points A and B—the linear combination of $U(W_1)$ and $U(W_2)$. That is, $EU(W) = p_1 \cdot U(W_1) + p_2 \cdot U(W_2)$. Note, too, that $U(\hat{W})$, the utility this individual would obtain from certain income $\hat{W}$, —given by distance $\hat{W}$D—exceeds that which he or she would obtain from expected income $\hat{W}$, $EU(\hat{W})$, shown by distance $\hat{W}$C.

BOX 10.3

Strict Concavity and Risk Aversion

Consider a utility function U(W). It should make sense that the first derivative (or partial derivative with respect to wealth, if there is more than one argument) is positive; this indicates that the individual's preferences exhibit a positive marginal utility of wealth (or income). Strict concavity requires that the second derivative be negative, indicating a diminishing marginal utility of wealth (income). Suitable functional forms for risk-averse individuals include $U(W) = W^{1/2}$ and $U(W) = ln\ W$.

FIGURE 10.2   The Cost of Risk-taking

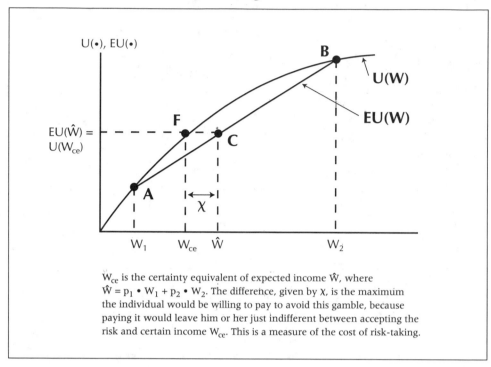

W_{ce} is the certainty equivalent of expected income $\hat{W}$, where $\hat{W} = p_1 \bullet W_1 + p_2 \bullet W_2$. The difference, given by χ, is the maximum the individual would be willing to pay to avoid this gamble, because paying it would leave him or her just indifferent between accepting the risk and certain income W_{ce}. This is a measure of the cost of risk-taking.

This question is answered in Figure 10.2. Proceeding horizontally from point C on the expected utility function, we reach point F on the (certain) utility function. Note that certain utility FW_{ce} is exactly equal to expected utility $C\hat{W}$. Another way to state this is $U(W_{ce}) = EU(\hat{W})$, thus identifying level of income W_{ce} as the answer to the question posed. As the individual would be indifferent between certain income W_{ce} and expected income $\hat{W}$, W_{ce} is called the individual's ***certainty equivalent*** income.

Another relevant question is this: "What is the maximum amount this individual would be willing to forgo in order to avoid the risk associated with uncertain outcomes W_1 and W_2, and thus receive the same level of certain income regardless of outcome?" Again, the answer appears in Figure 10.2. If the individual could escape this risk by forgoing any amount less than the difference between $\hat{W}$ and W_{ce}, he or she would enjoy certain utility greater than $U(W_{ce})$. The individual would not surrender any amount greater than the difference between $\hat{W}$ and W_{ce}, because this would leave him or her worse off relative to the situation where he or she accepts the risky situation. Therefore, the dollar amount $\hat{W} - W_{ce}$, also given by distance FC, is the maximum he or she would be willing to pay to escape the risk. This amount, denoted by χ in Figure 10.2, is, thus, the individual's ***cost of risk-taking***.

BOX 10.4

An Example

Consider again alternative gambles J and Y above, where W_{J1}, W_{J2}, p_{J1}, and p_{J2} are, respectively, $100,000, $5,000, 0.1, and 0.9; and W_{Y1}, W_{Y2}, p_{Y1}, and p_{Y2} are, respectively, $20,000, $3,000, 0.4, and 0.6.

If an individual's utility function is $U(W) = W^{1/2}$, his or her expected utility from Gamble J is $0.1 \cdot (100,000)^{1/2} + 0.9 \cdot (5,000)^{1/2} = 95.26$, and from Gamble Y it is $0.4 \cdot (20,000)^{1/2} + 0.6 \cdot (3,000)^{1/2} = 89.43$. Gamble J is thus preferred to Gamble Y.

To calculate the certainty equivalent income of Gamble J, we must calculate the level of income that would yield certain utility of 95.26. This is the solution to $W^{1/2} = 95.26$. Therefore, W_{ce} for Gamble J is $9,074.47.

The expected value of Gamble J is $14,500 ($0.9 \cdot $100,000 + 0.1 \cdot $5,000). Therefore, the cost of risk-taking associated with Gamble J is, $14,500 - $9,074.47 = $5,425.53.

Risk-loving Behaviour

Consider another possibility. Suppose an individual likes taking risks. Indeed, suppose he or she is willing to pay for the privilege of taking them. The utility function for such an individual is shown in Figure 10.3; this person is facing the same risky prospects as the risk-averse individual above.

This utility function is strictly convex, exhibiting an increasing marginal utility of income. If this person were given the chance of winning or losing $100 on the toss of a coin, he or she would accept the gamble, because the gain in utility from winning exceeds the loss of utility from losing. For any specific positive level of wealth, $EU(W) > U(W)$.

Using the same notation as in Figure 10.2, note that this individual's certainty equivalent income is greater than the expected income from taking the gamble. The difference between the two, denoted here by Ω, is the maximum the individual would be willing to pay to gamble on the risky prospects W_1 and W_2. For this type of person, there is no cost of risk-taking.

Risk-neutral Behaviour

Preferences that exhibit risk-neutrality have been described above. If given the chance of winning or losing $100 on the toss of a coin, this person will be indifferent to the gamble—the gain in utility from winning is exactly equal to the prospective loss of utility from losing. A utility function exhibiting such preferences must be linear; one is shown in Figure 10.4.

FIGURE 10.3 Risk-loving Behaviour

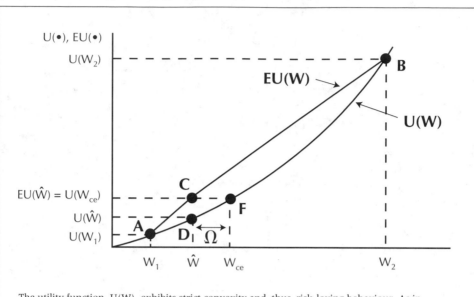

The utility function, U(W), exhibits strict convexity and, thus, risk-loving behaviour. As in Figure 10.2 the expected utility function, EU(W), is formed by joining points A and B—the linear combination of $U(W_1)$ and $U(W_2)$. Note that it is situated above the (certain) utility function. That is, this person would prefer a gamble with expected value $\hat{W}$ to possessing level of income $\hat{W}$ with certainty. Here, Ω is the premium he or she associates with being allowed to take the gamble.

The person whose preferences are illustrated in Figure 10.4 faces the same risky situation addressed by the risk-averse and risk-loving individuals above. When we draw the expected utility function by joining points A and B as before, we find that it is coincident with the certain utility function. Here the certainty equivalent income is identical to the expected value of the prospects. As such, the cost of risk-taking in this context is zero.

Which Preferences Are Representative?

Are people typically risk-averse, risk-neutral, or risk-loving? On the one hand we observe that people are willing to pay premiums to insurance companies for protection against automobile collisions and house fires. While comprehensive automobile insurance is mandatory, collision insurance is not. Mortgagors require house insurance against fire, but even people who own their homes outright usually purchase house insurance. In both cases people exhibit a willingness to pay to lessen the costs associated with risk-taking. This leads us to conclude that people are risk-averse.

FIGURE 10.4 Risk-neutral Behaviour

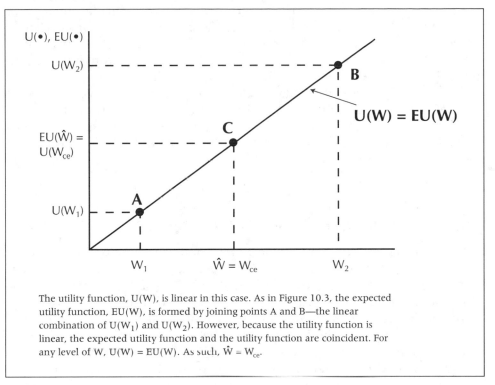

The utility function, U(W), is linear in this case. As in Figure 10.3, the expected utility function, EU(W), is formed by joining points A and B—the linear combination of $U(W_1)$ and $U(W_2)$. However, because the utility function is linear, the expected utility function and the utility function are coincident. For any level of W, U(W) = EU(W). As such, $\hat{W} = W_{ce}$.

On the other hand, people purchase lottery tickets, and governments, especially, operate these schemes precisely because the expected value of the payout is much less than the cost of the ticket. On average, ticket sales exceed prizes. "The house wins" rings familiar with those who have left their shirts behind in Las Vegas or at a racetrack. This suggests that many people are risk-lovers.

What can we say about the many people who purchase both collision insurance *and* lottery tickets? It seems that such people are risk-loving when the stakes are low but risk-averse when something of significant value is at stake, such as a car or house. Cost-benefit analysis is used to evaluate projects such as dams and nuclear power stations. If the relevant risk is flooding, the potential damage to fields and homes is great; if the relevant risk is nuclear meltdown, losing the "gamble" can be catastrophic. Therefore, for the class of events and risks relevant to cost-benefit analysis, it seems appropriate for an analyst to assume that risk aversion is the norm. That is, most individuals incur costs associated with risk-taking and are willing to pay to avoid situations involving risk.

For a cost-benefit analyst examining the viability of a risky project, the decision whether to adopt risk-neutral or risk-averse preferences is an important one. Consider a risky project with n possible outcomes. That is, the net present value of the project could be any of NPV_1, NPV_2, NPV_3, through NPV_n with associated probabilities of p_1, p_2, p_3, through p_n. If risk-neutral preferences are adopted, the project's viability will depend on whether the expected net present value of the project, $p_1 \cdot NPV_1 + p_2 \cdot NPV_2 + p_3 \cdot NPV_3 + \ldots + p_n \cdot NPV_n$, is positive or negative. If, on the other hand, risk-averse preferences are adopted, the analyst will have to assess the social costs of risk-taking. Here the project will be viable only if its expected net present value including these costs is positive. Similar considerations apply to ranking risky projects.

INDIVIDUALS' VERSUS SOCIAL COSTS OF RISK-TAKING

Begin from the premise that a typical individual in society is risk-averse. In Figure 10.2, χ denotes the cost of risk-taking to an individual—the maximum he or she is willing to pay to avoid all risk. This suggests that if a public sector project is risky, an analyst should account for the cost of risk-taking on the debit side. However, collective risk is not simply an aggregate of individuals' risks; there may be good reason to believe that the social cost of risk-taking may be negligible. This is the thrust of the Arrow-Lind Theorem. A formal proof of this theorem requires mathematics beyond the scope of this book; even so, we can demonstrate it by an example using the terminology and concepts already established.

Consider an individual with an income of $50,000 confronted with a risky project, one that will pay a net present value of $20,000 if the outcome is favourable but lose a present value of $15,000 if the outcome is not. For simplicity, assume that the chances of success and failure are identical so that the expected net present value of the project is $2,500. For this project $\hat{W} = 1/2 \cdot \$70,000 + 1/2 \cdot \$35,000 = \$52,500$. If we assume that $U(W) = W^{1/2}$, his or her expected utility is $1/2 \cdot (70,000)^{1/2} + 1/2 \cdot (35,000)^{1/2} = 225.829$, and his or her certainty equivalent wealth is the solution to $W_{ce}^{1/2} = 225.829$, therefore $50,998.737. The cost of risk-taking to this individual is, thus, $\hat{W} - W_{ce} = \$1,501.263$.

To keep track, let us rewrite the essentials of the above paragraph and subscript the main variables with a "1" to indicate that it is a single individual undertaking the risky project. That is, $\hat{W}_1 = \$52,500$; $EU(W_1) = 225.829$; $W_{ce1} = \$50,998.737$; and $\chi_1 = \$1,501.263$.

Now suppose the project is shared by ten identical people. From a single person's perspective the project will either add $2,000 to his or her income or cost $1,500. Going through the relevant calculations in the same order, and using the subscript "10" to indicate the number of people in society, $\hat{W}_{10}$ = \$50,250; $EU(W_{10})$ = 224.13112; W_{ce10} = \$50,234.759; and χ_{10} = \$15.240945. This, of course, is for just one of the ten people sharing the project. Note that the expected net present value of the project has not changed from a social perspective: the project either adds \$20,000 to society or costs \$15,000. Instead of the expected net present value accruing to just one person, it is now shared among ten people. Nevertheless, observe what has happened to the social cost of risk-taking. It was \$1,501.263 in a one-person society. The social cost of risk-taking to the ten-person society is \$152.40945 ($\chi_{10} \times 10$).

Consider now a 100-person society, all sharing the same project. Here, $\hat{W}_{100}$ = \$50,025; $EU(W_{100})$ = 223.66235; W_{ce100} = \$50,024.847; and χ_{100} = \$0.153054. The social cost of risk-taking is, thus, \$15.3054 ($\chi_{100} \times 100$).

Expanding the population further, so that 1,000 people share the project, should provide enough of a trend to establish our point. Here, $\hat{W}_{1,000}$ = \$50,002.50; $EU(W_{1,000})$ = 223.61238; $W_{ce1,000}$ = \$50,002.496; and $\chi_{1,000}$ = \$0.004. The total cost of risk-taking is, thus, \$4 ($\chi_{1,000} \times 1,000$).

The expected net present value of the project does not change—only the degree to which it is shared among members of society. The important phenomenon is that as more and more people share in the proceeds and costs of a risky project, the social cost of risk-taking shrinks. This phenomenon is called **risk spreading**, and it is the basis of the Arrow-Lind Theorem. The same shrinking phenomenon, using variance as a measure of riskiness, is shown in Table 10.1.

Recall that the individual starts with \$50,000 and that the project has two possible net present values: +\$20,000 with probability 0.5, and −\$15,000 with the same probability. Recall also that the formulae for expected value and variance are, respectively, $\hat{W} = p_1 \cdot W_1 + p_2 \cdot W_2$ and $VAR = p_1 \cdot (W_1 - \hat{W})^2 + p_2 \cdot (W_2 - \hat{W})^2$.

TABLE 10.1   Variance and Population

Number of People	W_1	W_2	$\hat{W}$	Variance per Person	Total Variance
1	\$35,000	\$70,000	\$52,500.00	306,250,000.00	306,250,000
2	\$42,500	\$60,000	\$51,250.00	76,562,500.00	153,130,000
10	\$48,500	\$52,000	\$50,250.00	3,062,500.00	30,625,000
100	\$49,850	\$50,200	\$50,025.00	30,625.00	3,062,500
1,000	\$49,985	\$50,020	\$50,002.50	306.25	306,250

Note the impact of doubling the size of the population from one to two. The expected net present value of the project per person decreases by half, from $2,500 to $1,250, while the variance per person is quartered from 306,250,000 to 76,562,500. This is rather like the area of a square—when you double the length of a side, you quadruple the area. Because variance per person is quartered, while the population has only doubled, total variance must fall by a factor of 2.

Similarly, increasing the number of people who share the project by a factor of 10 decreases the variance per person by a factor of 100. Together, this means that total variance must decrease by a factor of 10. This phenomenon is much akin the "Central Limit Theorem" featured in most elementary statistics textbooks. An analyst invoking the Arrow-Lind Theorem would treat the social cost of risk-taking as negligible and would simply calculate the expected net present value of projects in order to determine viability and/or ranking. Still, invoking this theorem requires care. Three conditions must be satisfied:

1. The population sharing the costs and benefits of the project must be large.[2]

2. The project must be small relative to GDP.

3. The probabilities of the possible net present value outcomes must not be correlated with GDP.

It is important that the Arrow-Lind Theorem not be invoked indiscriminately—it requires justification. Below we suggest practical ways of dealing with the costs of risk-taking when these conditions are not satisfied.[3]

DEALING WITH UNCERTAINTY

When the probabilities associated with all potential net present values of a proposed project are known, it is usual to calculate the expected net present value to determine the project's viability—with or without an allowance for the social cost of risk-taking, as warranted. However, sometimes it is impossible to assign probabilities to the possible outcomes, perhaps because they are not knowable. That is, the analyst can calculate the net present value of the project if X happens, or if Y happens, or if Z happens, but can do nothing to establish which of these is most likely to happen. Events X, Y, and Z could be as simple as three possible wind conditions over a year that will affect crop yields: little wind, moderate wind, and hold-on-to-your-hat wind.

When organizing an evaluation in these circumstances, it is helpful to prepare a table such as Payoff Matrix 10.1.[4] Here the analyst is to choose a project from among six alternatives. The net present value of each depends

PAYOFF MATRIX 10.1

	Outcome I	Outcome II	Outcome III
Project A	10	0	2
Project B	3	4	6
Project C	2	8	5
Project D	5	5	2
Project E	−6	11	3
Project F	8	−2	0

on which of three possible future events happens; these events provide the outcomes, each stated in billions of dollars. For example, if Project B were chosen the outcome—depending on future events—could be a net present value of $3 billion, $4 billion, or $6 billion.

The first step is to eliminate *dominated* projects (or strategies) from consideration. Note that regardless of the outcome, Project A generates a net present value greater than Project F. That is, Project F would never be chosen over Project A, and because only one project can be chosen, it does not make sense to include F among the alternatives. Project F is said to be "dominated" and is dropped from the menu of potential projects.

The same cannot be said about any of Projects A through E. For example, C is superior to A if either of Outcome I or II occurs, but is inferior to A should I be the outcome. *A priori*, it is impossible to rank these projects. To proceed further, we must formulate a decision rule. Five are presented below.

The Bayes Criterion

Application of the Bayes criterion involves treating outcomes as if they were equally probable, calculating (pseudo-)expected net present values, and choosing the project that yields the highest. In Payoff Matrix 10.2, Project F has been eliminated, and the expected net present values using equal probabilities of 1/3 are shown in the last column.

Thus, if this criterion were adopted, Project C would be chosen. However, there is no rationale for believing that the three outcomes are equally likely to occur. In a sense, the Bayes criterion requires that the analyst deny his or her ignorance. Indeed, this criterion is based on the "Principle of Insufficient Reason." Although it may appear that the analyst is adopting risk-neutral preferences, this is not so. An analyst applying the Bayes criterion is simply being arbitrary—perhaps for the sake of expediency.

PAYOFF MATRIX 10.2

	Outcome I	Outcome II	Outcome III	Expected NPV
Project A	10	0	2	12/3
Project B	3	4	6	13/3
Project C	2	8	5	15/3
Project D	5	5	2	12/3
Project E	−6	11	3	8/3

The Maxi-Min Criterion

To apply the maxi-min criterion, an analyst chooses the project that has the best "worst possible" outcome of all the other projects (this is akin to choosing the "lesser of two evils"). The first step is to identify the worst possible outcome in each case; these are shown in the last column of Payoff Matrix 10.3.

Here, the best "worst possible outcome" is that of Project B. That is, a net present value of $3 billion is the maximum of the minima—hence maxi-min. It represents the best guaranteed outcome if chosen.

Because only the worst possible outcomes are relevant to this criterion, the analyst who adopts it is being very pessimistic, perhaps risk-averse in the extreme. We can imagine circumstances where fear of the worst may be warranted. Still, we note that if the potential payoffs to Project C, for example, were $2 billion, $800 billion, and $500 billion instead, Project B would still be chosen according to this criterion.

PAYOFF MATRIX 10.3

	Outcome I	Outcome II	Outcome III	Minima
Project A	10	0	2	0
Project B	3	4	6	3
Project C	2	8	5	2
Project D	5	5	2	2
Project E	−6	11	3	−6

The Maxi-Max Criterion

The maxi-min criterion is consistent with extreme pessimism; the maxi-max criterion is associated with unbridled optimism. Its application involves choosing the project that has a best possible outcome larger than those of all of the other projects. The best possible outcomes are shown in the last column of Payoff Matrix 10.4. By this criterion, Project E would be chosen.

Like the maxi-min criterion, the maxi-max criterion can lead us away from what most people would consider to be reasonable behaviour, because not all of the available information is used to make decisions. For example, we note that if the possible payoffs to Project E were −$999 billion, $11 billion, and −$999 billion instead, it would still be chosen.

PAYOFF MATRIX 10.4

	Outcome I	Outcome II	Outcome III	Maxima
Project A	10	0	2	10
Project B	3	4	6	6
Project C	2	8	5	8
Project D	5	5	2	5
Project E	−6	11	3	11

The Mini-Max Regret Criterion

Examine Payoff Matrix 10.2 again. Assume that Outcome 1 occurs and that you had chosen Project A. In retrospect, you would be quite happy. You would have no regret concerning your decision. On the other hand, had you chosen Project C you would not be as pleased, since it has a net present value of $2 billion, as opposed to $10 billion for Project A. It follows that a measure of your regret is the difference, $8 billion. Similarly, had you chosen B or E your regret would now be $7 billion or $16 billion. "Regret" values can also be calculated for Outcomes II and III. These amounts are shown in Payoff Matrix 10.5.

PAYOFF MATRIX 10.5

	Outcome I	Outcome II	Outcome III	Maxima
Project A	0	11	4	11
Project B	7	7	0	7
Project C	8	3	1	8
Project D	5	6	4	6
Project E	16	0	3	16

Of course, an analyst must choose projects without the benefit of hindsight. The mini-max regret criterion is simply a way, beforehand, of making a number of if/then statements regarding how "worse off" we would be relative to what we would have gained had we chosen with perfect foresight. The last column of Matrix 10.5 is formed by asking, for each project in turn, "What could be the maximum possible regret if this project is chosen?" In the case of Project A the most regret, or highest net present value forgone, is $11 billion if Outcome II occurs; in the case of Project B the answer is $7 billion; and so on. Applying this pessimistic criterion requires an analyst to choose the project that minimizes the maximum possible regret. Here the choice would be Project D.

The Hurwicz Criterion

The maxi-min and mini-max regret criteria may appeal to pessimists; the maxi-max criterion to optimists. A major problem with all three is that information is ignored; only the worst or the best scenarios are considered. Moreover, extreme risk-averseness or -loving may not represent the risk preferences of the population or a client. Some middle ground, some way of taking into account (perhaps) more realistic risk preferences, would be useful. The Hurwicz criterion provides this by allowing the analyst to determine weights to impute to the worst (pessimistic) and best (optimistic) outcomes. Examine Payoff Matrix 10.6.

Suppose the individual or agency who must ultimately make the decision is asked to choose a value for "x" in the above payoff matrix that would make him or her just indifferent between alternatives 1 and 2. If the person chooses "0," the maxi-min criterion will yield the same answer and the person will be revealed to be extremely risk-averse. If the person chooses "1," it is the maxi-max criterion that will yield the same answer, and the person will be revealed to be risk-loving. The closer x is set to 0, the more risk-averse he or she is. Note that $0 \leq x \leq 1$.

This suggests that answers falling between the two extremes can be used to assess an individual's risk preferences and to establish a weighting scheme for best and worst outcomes. To establish the latter, simply set the weight of

PAYOFF MATRIX 10.6

	Outcome 1	Outcome 2
Alternative 1	0	1
Alternative 2	x	x

the worst outcome equal to $1 - x$. Thus, an answer of 0.6 would mean that worst outcomes should be imputed a weight of 0.4 and that the best outcomes should be given a weight of 0.6.

Once established, these weights are used much as probabilities are used to calculate expected net present value. The difference is that here, only the best and worst outcomes of each project are considered. Examine Payoff Matrix 10.7, which is Payoff Matrix 10.2 without the final column.

Applying the above weights to the worst and best possible outcomes of each project yields the following results:

Project A: $0.4 \cdot (0) + 0.6 \cdot (10)$ = $6 billion
Project B: $0.4 \cdot (3) + 0.6 \cdot (6)$ = $4.8 billion
Project C: $0.4 \cdot (2) + 0.6 \cdot (8)$ = $5.6 billion
Project D: $0.4 \cdot (2) + 0.6 \cdot (5)$ = $3.8 billion
Project E: $0.4 \cdot (-6) + 0.6 \cdot (11)$ = $4.2 billion

Thus, if this rule were applied, and if the above weights were chosen, Project A would be selected.

PAYOFF MATRIX 10.7

	Outcome I	Outcome II	Outcome III
Project A	10	0	2
Project B	3	4	6
Project C	2	8	5
Project D	5	5	2
Project E	−6	11	3

Summary

What has been presented above is a simplistic quasi-game-theoretic framework for organizing one's thoughts when confronted by the kind of ignorance that uncertainty entails.[5] At the other extreme might be mindless "flipping of coins" or writing A, B, C, D, and E on slips of paper and pulling one out of a hat to select a project.

Those looking for a definitive rule to apply to project selection in these circumstances will be disappointed. Five criteria were presented: the Bayes criterion, the maxi-min criterion, the maxi-max criterion, the mini-max regret criterion, and the Hurwicz criterion; each resulted in a different project being chosen: C, B, E, D, and A, respectively. This result, of course, was manufactured to make the point that decision-making in this context is neither straightforward nor unambiguous.

Ultimately, it is the government agency charged with making the decision that will choose among potential projects, including whether to proceed with none of them. Through its choices, the agency will reveal its risk preferences, or those it imputes to society. It may be that the best an analyst can do in these circumstances is present the alternatives, with costs and benefits in various scenarios measured as accurately as possible. In these circumstances, the analyst's role is to provide accurate information, not to impose his or her own preferences by advocating a particular criterion.

OTHER METHODS

Uncertainty, measurement error, and risk when the Arrow-Lind Theorem cannot be invoked have been accounted for in a number of ways in actual analyses. Some of these methods seem reasonable; others are not recommended.

Augmented Discount Rates

It is a reasonable assumption that costs and benefits that will accrue far into the future are known with less certainty than ones that will occur in the near future. Therefore, an analyst may wish on these grounds to give the former more weight in project evaluation than the latter. The discounting of future costs and benefits already achieves this to some degree, but the rationale behind such discounting is society's rate of time preference, not risk or uncertainty. To account separately for risk or uncertainty, some analysts add a risk premium to the "riskless" social discount rate. For example, if 7% is the norm, analysts may augment it by, say, 4% to reflect the riskiness of the project, thereby discounting all future costs and benefits at a higher rate than usual, here 11%.

This approach is *not* recommended. If, indeed, an analyst is able to calculate that the relevant risk premium is 4%, he or she should be able to state the dollar cost of risk-taking for the project being evaluated. It is the latter that is relevant to project analysis, and a separate accounting of it will require justification in terms of the maximum society would be willing to pay to avoid the risk.

Moreover, if some projects are riskier than others, applying a single risk-adjusted discount rate to all projects being considered makes little sense. Also, whereas interest compounds on financial assets, it is unclear why risk would compound over time. Note, too, that if all future costs and benefits are discounted using a risk-adjusted rate, no accounting is being made for a resolution of the uncertainty at a future date. In the example that introduced this chapter, after the American aviation authorities make their decision, there is no uncertainty in this regard; so costs and benefits from that time forward should not be discounted at the higher rate.

Cut-off Period and Pay-back Period Criteria

In Chapter 3 we described the cut-off and pay-back period criteria. When the former is used, only costs and benefits accruing within a set number of years from t = 0 are examined. The project is rejected if its costs will not be recovered within that period. The pay-back criterion ranks projects according to which will recover its costs in the fewest years.

These seem to be extreme reactions to uncertainty. Say that we know that the annual net benefit accruing to a project will be either $60 million or $80 million one decade after it is constructed. It hardly makes sense to discount this information entirely simply because we don't know which figure is correct. Yet this is what would be expected of us if the cut-off period were set at seven years. As the person employing such a decision rule is likely to be very risk-averse, applying the maxi-min criterion may be more appropriate.

Insurance Premiums

Corporations purchase insurance to protect themselves against any number of risks. Even small retailers can purchase insurance policies that guarantee a stream of profits should they have to close their stores because of fire, flood, and the like. The insurance premiums these firms pay are entered in their books as costs.

In a risky situation where the Arrow-Lind Theorem cannot be invoked, there is a cost of risk-taking: the difference between the expected net present value of the project and its certainty equivalent (χ in Figure 10.2). However, measuring this cost requires more information than is usually available. Note that this amount is the maximum a public sector agency would, on behalf of society, be willing to pay for an insurance policy that would guarantee that the net present value of the project is at least as great as the certainty equivalent net present value regardless of future events. The agency could, then, behave as if the insured value were certain, and the policy premium would be treated as a cost of the project.

The problem, of course, is that insurance markets do not exist for most of the risks that public sector agencies would like to insure against. Indeed, there are a number of reasons why insurance markets fail. Still, many risks are insurable, and it may be possible to glean some information from the market data.

For example, if a project involves a seagoing vessel, considerable information is available concerning insurance premiums paid by private sector freighters and ferries. If the public sector project is a nuclear reactor, it is worth noting that there are private sector reactors that face the same types of risk.

In situations involving risk when the Arrow-Lind Theorem cannot be invoked legitimately, it may be necessary to estimate a cost of risk-taking. We are not suggesting that imputing a figure from private sector insurance data is an optimal approach; having said that, some reasoned, perhaps inventive, approach to assessing the cost associated with risk is better than no assessment at all.

Sensitivity Analysis

One of the most practical and popular ways of dealing with the unknown is to create a series of net present value scenarios based on "what if" questions. *What if* the capital cost of a dam is 25% higher (lower) than what the architect has estimated? *What if* traffic across a bridge grows at a rate less (more) than what the traffic engineers predicted? A specific example of this kind of sensitivity analysis appears in Case 1 on the Northumberland Strait Fixed Crossing project. Here we outline the general principles.

Let us suppose that there are five main elements of a particular project that must be evaluated: (1) the capital cost; (2) operating costs; (3) initial benefits; (4) the rate of growth of net benefits; and (5) the social discount rate. It is likely that engineers, contractors, and/or architects will have provided estimates of capital and operating costs, and they will (probably) have based their estimattes at least partly on the actual costs incurred on similar projects elsewhere.[6] As we have seen, there are ways of calculating and estimating benefits. When all is said and done, however, they are still only estimates. Also, it is not unusual to expect net benefits to increase or decrease over time, especially in line with predictable demographic trends. The final item is the social discount rate.

The first step is to use these capital cost, operating cost, initial benefit, and growth of net benefit estimates to establish a *base-case scenario*. If we accept Burgess's advice (1981), the net present value for this case will be calculated using a discount rate of 7%.[7]

The next step is to create alternative cases. If we accept the base-case assumptions as the "middle ground," we can calculate net present values for capital costs higher and lower than what was estimated, thus expanding the number of cases from 1 to 3. We can then try operating costs both higher and lower than estimated, raising the number of cases to 9. If additional high and low initial-benefit figures are used, the number of cases increases to 27. Two alternative rates of benefit growth raise the total to 81; and alternative social rates of discount of 4% and 10% raise the total number of cases to be examined to 243.[8] At each step, some effort should be made to keep the alternative cost and benefit values within reasonable bounds.

There will be 243 net present values to calculate in this example. This may sound daunting, but any popular spreadsheet software package will be able to accomplish the task within seconds once the base-case figures are entered.

If the net present value estimates are all negative or all positive, the decision regarding viability will be straightforward. Typically, however, this is not so, and there is no rule for determining viability when the results are mixed. At this stage, assuming that no combinations can be discarded with cause, the full set of results should be presented to those who must make the final decision.

SUMMARY

Cost-benefit analysts have to deal with the unknown—with situations involving risk and uncertainty. When delving into the unknown, analysts should proceed in an orderly fashion. We offer three suggestions:

1. If the Arrow-Lind Theorem is to be invoked, be prepared to justify its use in the circumstances.
2. If the problem involves uncertainty rather than risk, a quasi-game-theoretic approach is useful for defining and refining the parameters of the decision-making process.
3. Sensitivity analysis is a valuable tool in these circumstances, even if its role is limited to providing decision-makers with base-, best-, and worst-case scenarios.

KEY TERMS

certainty equivalent
cost of risk-taking
risk spreading

EXERCISES

10.1 Mr. Alpha's utility function defined over wealth is given by $U = lnW$. He has \$50,000 but faces a risk of an accident that could cost him \$20,000. The probability of the accident is 30%. How much will he be willing to pay to shed this risk, to have a certain level of wealth whether the accident happens or not?

10.2 Mr. Alpha (of Question 10.1) has a twin brother who has the same utility function and the same level of wealth, and who faces exactly the same risk. Still, the risks they face are independent in the sense that the probability of Mr. Alpha having an accident has no bearing on the probability of his brother having or not having an accident, and vice versa. His brother suggests that they co-operate. That is, if one of them has an accident and one does not, they will share equally the $20,000 loss. If both have accidents, each will bear the full loss; if neither has an accident, there will be no loss. If the deal is acceptable to one, it must be to both, as they are identical twins. Would it be to Mr. Alpha's advantage to enter into this agreement with his brother?

10.3 Ms. Beta's utility function defined over wealth is given by $U = W^{1/2}$. She has $1 million and is considering the purchase of a racehorse. The horse would cost $400,000, but has the potential of winning $3 million with a probability of 20%. Would she buy the horse? Would she buy this horse if she had a partner who would share equally in the cost and the winnings?

10.4 Ms. Gamma has a utility function defined over wealth described by $U = W^2$. She has initial wealth of $20,000 and has an opportunity to enter into a business agreement that would leave her with $10,000 or $30,000 with 50-50 odds. Will she forgo the business opportunity or not?

10.5 An analyst must choose one of projects A, B, C, D, and E, but the net present value of each is not known with certainty. For each project, three outcomes are possible, but the likelihood of a particular outcome is unknown. The payoff matrix for these projects is shown below. For each project, the net present value (in millions of dollars) of every possible outcome is shown.

   a. Which project would be selected if the analyst were to adopt the Bayes criterion?

   b. Which project would be selected if the analyst were to adopt the maxi-min criterion?

   c. Which project would be selected if the analyst were to adopt the maxi-max criterion?

PAYOFF MATRIX 10.8

	Outcome I	Outcome II	Outcome III
Project A	17	1	16
Project B	15	6	10
Project C	18	0	3
Project D	12	9	9
Project E	9	7	17

    d. Which project would be selected if the analyst were to adopt the mini-max regret criterion?

    e. Which project would be selected if the analyst were to adopt the Hurwicz criterion in a situation where the weight placed on the worst possible outcome is 2/3?

ENDNOTES

1.   Note that if a person is risk-neutral, $U(W) = EU(W)$ for a particular level of wealth or income. If he or she were asked to choose between a certain level of income of $100,000 and a gamble involving payoffs of $0 and $1 million with probabilities 0.9 and 0.1, respectively, the individual would be indifferent.

2.   The theorem proper requires an infinitely large population; that is, as the size of the population approaches infinity, the social cost of risk-taking tends to zero. Obviously, this condition can never be satisfied. In practice, analysts are not strict in their interpretation of what constitutes a "large enough" population.

3.   Another justification for ignoring the risk associated with a particular project is risk-pooling. This is akin to diversifying a financial portfolio to reduce overall risk. In the context of public sector projects, it may mean that if some event occurs to reduce the net benefits of one risky project, the same event may enhance the net benefits of another risky project—although the principle of diversification goes beyond this.

4.   By doing so the analyst is putting the choice problem into a quasi-game-theoretic framework. To students who wish to delve more deeply into game theory, we recommend Osborne & Rubinstein (1994).

5.   For a fuller exposition, see Chapter 8 of Dasgupta & Pearce (1972). Also, Dorfman (1972) is a popular source.

6.   If these estimates appear unreasonable, the analyst may wish to adjust them. Analysts who opine that there is a bias toward accepting projects because of unrealistically low cost estimates provided by project proponents may have a case. For example, the capital cost of the English Channel tunnel project was several times higher than first estimated, as was that of the Point Lepreau nuclear generating station in New Brunswick. This phenomenon seems to be not unusual—indeed, it would be an interesting exercise to determine what proportion of recent public-sector projects cost *less* than estimated.

7.   See Chapter 6.

8.   For n elements, each with x alternative values, the total number of distinct combinations is x^n. In our example, $n = 5$ and $x = 3$; thus, $3^5 = 243$.

PART IV

CASES

THE NORTHUMBERLAND STRAIT FIXED CROSSING PROJECT

INTRODUCTION

On May 31, 1997, vehicular traffic began to flow across the 13.5 kilometre Confederation Bridge between Prince Edward Island and New Brunswick, and the existing year-round ferry service between Borden, P.E.I., and Cape Tormentine, N.B., shut down.[1] Even naming the bridge caused controversy: many insist on calling it Abegweit Crossing, using the traditional Micmac name for the island; others have become used to saying "the Fixed Link"; and, some have dubbed it Anne's Span, in reference to Lucy Maud Montgomery's *Anne of Green Gables*. Less complimentary names exist.

The idea of a fixed crossing linking P.E.I. to the mainland is not new. A proposal to construct either a rail tunnel or a subway along the seafloor of the Northumberland Strait was put forward by Senator George Howland in 1885—obviously an idea that would never float. Construction of a combined causeway-tunnel-bridge was approved and actually began in 1966, but was halted in 1969 before much was accomplished (Perchanok, 1988, pp. 17–18).

In 1986 the federal government gave Public Works Canada permission to commission investigations into various aspects of a proposed fixed link crossing between Borden and Tourimain Island. In 1987, one of these, an analysis of the economic feasibility of a fixed link, was completed by Fiander-Good Associates Limited (FGA hereafter), a firm of consulting engineers based in Fredericton. That same year, seven consortia were invited to submit proposals for the construction, operation, and maintenance of a fixed link crossing (Perchanok, 1988, pp. 7, 18).

In February 1990, Public Works Minister Elmer MacKay announced that the project would proceed, "provided it gains the necessary environmental approvals" (MacDonald, 1990). That August an environmental review panel ruled that "the proposal to build a fixed link ... was environmentally unacceptable" (Peters, 1990a). However, the project was not scrapped. Three months later, in November, another environmental review panel was struck. In April 1991, this panel reversed the decision of the first by ruling "that a bridge would not create any serious environmental problems" (MacNeill, 1991). In May 1991, Public Works Canada invited three (of the original seven) firms to submit specific bridge proposals.

People concerned about the environmental impacts of a bridge across the Northumberland Strait were, quite naturally, upset. Certainly there was wonderment expressed that the two environmental assessment panels could reach opposite conclusions using "basically the same data" (McCoag, 1991). Perhaps environmentalists should have anticipated this kind of manœuvring. As early as 1988, then–Environment Minister Tom McMillan argued against a full-scale environmental study because it would "put construction back a couple of years and may ultimately kill the idea" (Canadian Press, 1988b).

The fixed link project is controversial. A legal action against it succeeded in court but lost on appeal, and residents of P.E.I. are still divided on it. Those in favour of the project include trucking firms, tourism operators, and people who place a high priority on short-term job creation. Arguments against it include those based on environmental concerns, and on fears that a fixed link will change Islanders' way of life. While some bewail the long-term job losses that will result from closure of the Borden–Tormentine ferry service, others view the transportation cost savings of a bridge as essential to the island's economic future. The economic question—"Would a fixed link be economically viable?"—received only minor attention until 1992.

In the summer of 1992, a critique of FGA's analysis was published and presented to the Minister of Public Works Canada.[2] The next several sections of this chapter are based on that critique. Later we will chronicle subsequent events, including the minister's reaction to criticisms of FGA's methodology.

THE PROJECT

Prior to June 1997, a subsidized year-round ferry service operated between Borden, P.E.I., and Cape Tormentine, N.B. An alternative ferry service between Wood Islands, P.E.I., and Caribou, Nova Scotia, continues to operate in ice-free months. It was determined in the planning stage of the project that any bridge or tunnel would follow approximately the Borden–Tormentine ferry route. The Borden and Wood Islands routes are shown on the accompanying map.[3] For 35 years after construction, the fixed link operator is to receive the federal subsidy the ferry service would have received, and to collect about the same tolls as would have been charged for the ferry crossing.[4]

MAP C1.1 Prince Edward Island

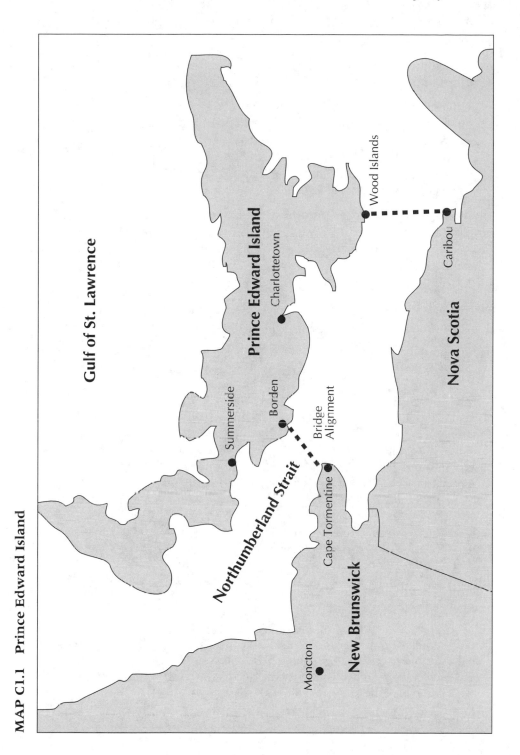

FGA'S ANALYSIS

At the outset of its report, FGA made clear what Public Works Canada required of it by reproducing the terms of reference for the analysis:

> The economic feasibility study is to be of the benefit-cost type wherein all capital costs, public facility maintenance and operating costs and economic development costs are to be expressed in present value terms for each alternative, including the sensitivity to changes in assumptions. The Stanford and the DRIE-TC-PWC analyses are of the type expected. (1987, p. 1.2.)

Why Public Works Canada did not suggest that the methodology employed be that used for evaluating the tunnel link between England and France (Ministry of Transport, U.K., 1963) is not known. (See Box C1.1 regarding other studies.)

BOX C1.1

Other Studies

FGA does not include a bibliographical entry for either a "Stanford" or a "Department of Regional Industrial Expansion–Transport Canada–Public Works Canada" study. However, there does exist a 1968 evaluation of a causeway-bridge proposal, which was prepared for Canada's Department of Transport by the Stanford Research Institute of Menlo Park, California, and Acres Research and Planning Limited of Toronto.

This analysis is titled *Benefit/Cost Evaluation of a Proposed Fixed Crossing of the Northumberland Strait* and is stamped CONFIDENTIAL. We know of no reason why this report was given this or any other security classification. (There is no indication on the report as to when this classification was ordered, nor is it known if the document has been declassified.)

In any case, it would appear that FGA did not follow the methodology of the Stanford study too closely. At the same time, there may exist a DRIE-TC-PWC study that it did emulate.

We note, first, that Public Works Canada suggested—to some extent—the cost-benefit methodology to be used. Thus, PWC may be somewhat responsible for the errors in the FGA study. Also, because of these terms of reference, the errors made may be the result of FGA applying *or* misapplying the methodology of the "model" analysis.

Provision of year-round communication between P.E.I. and the mainland was a condition of the Island joining Confederation in 1873. This is why FGA's task was to examine what kind of transportation service should be provided, not whether any should be provided at all. The five alternatives examined were as follows:

1. The status quo.
2. A bridge replacing both ferry services.
3. A bridge replacing the Borden–Tormentine ferry service, with the Caribou–Wood Islands ferry service to be retained.
4. A rail tunnel replacing both ferry services.
5. A rail tunnel replacing the Borden–Tormentine ferry service, but with the Caribou–Wood Islands ferry service to be retained.

Although bridge and rail tunnel options were assumed to have an economic life of 100 years (after construction), the time horizon used for the analysis was limited to 40 years—1987–2027—and the "continuation of the existing ferry services and the associated costs were considered the base case from which the four remaining options were compared with respect to their present worth costs and incremental benefits" (FGA, 1987, p. 1.2). The objective, then, was to identify the alternative that would minimize net social costs.

The categories of benefits that FGA attributed to a fixed link were travel time savings, corporate income taxes raised, reduced vehicle operating costs, the salvage value of the infrastructure, and economic development. Regarding this last item, FGA attributed zero developmental benefits to a fixed link, because the main impact would be on tourism and FGA concurred with the advice of another advisory group that "a tourism gain by one province generally results in a loss by another province, thus resulting in benefits being netted out from a global perspective" (1987, p. 5.17).

This view was supported in a later report prepared for Public Works Canada. In its investigation into the impact of a fixed link on tourism, Smith Green & Associates reported: "Reverse tourism is largely a reflection of the fact that the Maritime Provinces continue to be their own best customers with the Island residents travelling to the mainland and vice versa" (1989a, p. 34). In other words, any gain Prince Edward Island might reap from increased tourism because of a fixed link would be at the expense of tourism operators in Nova Scotia and New Brunswick.

Costs were separated into capital, operating, and maintenance, and estimates of these were provided by Public Works Canada. The capital costs of the bridge and rail tunnel options used for the base case were $630 million and $543.5 million, respectively.

FGA set base-case (Case 1) assumptions and then performed sensitivity analyses. Nine cases in total were examined. The base-case assumptions were these:

1. A real discount rate of 10%.

2. Commercial traffic would increase by 2% annually with or without a fixed link.

3. Passenger-related traffic would increase by 2.5% annually with or without a fixed link.

4. Induced traffic due to construction of a bridge would be 25%, and the same datum due to construction of a tunnel would be 15%.

5. The shadow wage rates for permanent jobs and short-term jobs associated with the project would be, respectively, 65% and 75% of wages paid.

6. Real ferry operating costs would increase by 1% annually.

7. Corporate income taxes generated by either a rail tunnel or a bridge would be treated as a benefit.

8. Time saved by business travellers would be valued at the hourly average industrial wage in the Maritimes ($11.38 in 1987), time saved by occupants of trucks would be valued at the average truck-driver wage ($16.24), and time saved by nonbusiness travellers would be assumed to be half that of business travellers.

FGA then altered the above assumptions (separately) to form an additional eight cases:

Case 2: The real discount rate is 4%.

Case 3: Shadow wages are assumed to be equal to those paid.

Case 4: Capital costs of the rail tunnel and bridge are 20% higher than those used in the base case.

Case 5: Capital costs of the rail tunnel and bridge are 20% lower than those used in the base case.

Case 6: Real ferry operating costs are constant.

Case 7: The value of time saved is 20% higher than in the base case.

Case 8: The value of time saved is 20% lower than in the base case.

Case 9: Corporate income taxes raised by operation of either a rail tunnel or a bridge are not to be treated as a benefit.

Table C1.1 provides a summary of FGA's calculations. The least costly option in each case is marked by an asterisk. These data reveal that the rail tunnel option (with or without the Caribou–Wood Islands ferry) was never

TABLE C1.1 **Net Present Value of Social Costs**
(millions of 1987 dollars)

Case	Status Quo	Bridge Only	Bridge and Ferry	Rail Tunnel Only	Rail Tunnel and Ferry
Case 1	528.2	* 491.8	492.7	528.4	523.8
Case 2	1,085.0	318.6	* 267.5	519.2	454.0
Case 3	647.5	* 589.8	606.5	632.0	643.0
Case 4	* 528.2	577.8	578.7	602.8	598.2
Case 5	528.2	* 405.8	406.7	454.0	449.4
Case 6	489.6	487.7	* 482.0	524.3	513.0
Case 7	528.2	455.0	* 453.7	508.5	502.2
Case 8	* 528.2	528.6	531.7	548.3	545.4
Case 9	* 528.2	554.7	555.6	582.3	577.7

the least costly option, and that any of the other three alternatives might be favoured depending on which set of assumptions was adopted.[5] The existing ferry service option—the status quo—was favoured only in Cases 4, 8, and 9.

FGA concluded:

> In summary, the economic results indicate that a fixed crossing, more specifically a fixed crossing involving a bridge, will be similar to the existing ferry services with respect to the net present value of society costs. A lower discount rate [than 10%] would favour the fixed crossing alternatives. (1987, p. 2.3)

Public Works Canada signalled its interpretation of FGA's conclusion by proceeding with the project. Eventually, Strait Crossing Incorporated was contracted to build and operate a bridge (with the intention of retaining the Caribou–Wood Islands ferry service).

METHODOLOGICAL INADEQUACIES

This section is concerned mainly with a number of fundamental errors in methodology. Our objective is to establish sufficient grounds to dismiss FGA's analysis; for this reason, we ignore its failure to investigate shadow-pricing (except of labour), the roles of second-best and peak-load pricing schemes, and so on—the kinds of considerations we would expect in a more rigorous study. Also, we devote little effort to challenging the actual data used. Indeed, investigators are constrained, because FGA does not report all of the data required to redo the analysis.

Inclusion of Corporate Income Taxes

For the base case and Cases 3 through 8, FGA includes benefits attributed to increases in corporate tax revenues of $62.9 million and $53.9 million to either bridge option and to either rail tunnel option, respectively. In Case 2, these benefits are $161.1 million and $138.1 million, respectively. No benefit is attributed to corporate tax increases in Case 9. Only Case 9 is correct.

Certainly, there is nothing wrong with including corporate taxes as a benefit to government—which is part of society—as long as they are also counted as a cost to the bridge or rail tunnel operator, which is also a part of society. FGA includes corporate taxes as a benefit but not as an offsetting cost, and in doing so biases the results of the first eight cases in favour of construction.

Most economists would simply ignore changes in corporate tax revenues, as they would any transfer, because transfers represent a cost to one party and a benefit to another, and thus cancel. Indeed, FGA reported that it was aware of this problem, and that it was the reason it did not include corporate income taxes as a benefit in Case 9. In the context of toll revenues, FGA stated clearly the case against including such transfers:

> In keeping with the objectives of the economic analysis, which is to compare society's costs and benefits attributable to each of the transportation alternatives, toll revenues have been excluded from the economic analysis. It should be clearly understood that from society's perspective, the collection of toll revenues does not represent a benefit. Rather it represents a transfer of funds from individual motorists (who are members of society) to the crossing operator (another member of society). No net gain or loss is realized by the transaction. (1987, pp. 3.2–3.3)

Calculation of Salvage Values

The following is a statement of how FGA calculated salvage values:

> The bridge is expected to have a 100 year life, and thus has a salvage value equal to the ratio of the remaining useful years (65) to the expected life (100) times the initial cost ($630 million), which results in a salvage value of $409.5 million in the year 2027. This value must be discounted to 1987. The rail tunnel only option would have a similar salvage value as above, but based on the initial cost of $543.5 million. (1987, p. 5.14)

Thus, the salvage values of the bridge and rail tunnel, respectively, were calculated to be $9.1 million and $7.8 million in all cases except Case 2 (which is odd, given the assumptions of Cases 4 and 5). FGA calculated values of $85.3 million and $73.3 million, respectively, in Case 2.

As explained in Chapter 7, the principal implication of using this method is an absurdity. If a bridge, for example, with a life of 100 years is worth 65% of its original cost after 35 years of use, then, logically, it must be worth 80% of its original cost after 20 years—and worth 100% of its original cost at the beginning of the project. To calculate salvage values this way is to assume that the structure is worth its cost, and is thus economically viable. The economic viability of a bridge or rail tunnel is something to be *determined*, not assumed.

The proper way to proceed would have been to align the time horizon of the project with that of the assumed economic life of a bridge or tunnel, which is 105 years—5 years for construction and 100 years for use. Indeed, this was the methodology used in the financial analysis of the fixed link performed by Woods Gordon Management Consultants in 1987 for Public Works Canada. Woods Gordon stated: "The bridge is constructed over the 1988-92 period, and has a life span of 100 years (with regular maintenance). There is no salvage value at the end of the 100 year period" (p. 2).

However, using a 105-year time horizon would have called into question the plausibility of FGA's assumptions regarding traffic growth. Peters (1990b) reports that 686,500 passenger-related vehicles and 153,000 commercial vehicles made the ferry crossing between Borden and Cape Tormentine in 1989. To examine how plausible FGA's assumptions were, assume that these figures are roughly the relevant traffic data in the year immediately before the bridge is completed. Given FGA's base-case assumption 4—that induced traffic because of a bridge will be 25%—the number of passenger-related and commercial vehicles, respectively, will increase to 858,125 and 191,250 in the first year of bridge operation. Base-case assumptions 2 and 3 are that passenger-related and commercial traffic will increase annually thereafter by 2.5% and 2%, respectively. FGA's assumptions thus require that after a further 99 years of bridge use, in the last year of its economic life, about 9,890,385 passenger-related vehicles and 1,358,371 commercial vehicles will cross the bridge. Forecasts of an almost nine-fold increase in commercial traffic and of a more than fourteen-fold increase in passenger vehicle traffic over the life of a bridge both seem quite farfetched, especially when we consider that most of the forecasted traffic will occur in July and August. After all, P.E.I. is an island.

FGA's analysis required that for either option, salvage values be calculated before the end of the project's economic life. The question: What should those values be? That is, what is the (economic) value of a bridge or tunnel in its next-best alternative use after 35 years? We presume that the only alternative use of a bridge is as scrap, which has a salvage value near zero. We make the same presumption for a tunnel.[6] Obviously, it would be not be sensible to decommission a bridge or tunnel in this manner, but this is the implication of the methodology FGA chose or was instructed to choose.

Table C1.2 is a revised table of FGA's results when salvage values are assumed to be zero and corporate taxes are treated as a transfer. Once again, for each case an asterisk indicates the least costly option. Note that when these corrections are made, the status quo dominates all other options in all cases except 2, 5, and 7—and each of these three cases is based on a questionable assumption.

In Case 2, FGA used a real discount rate of 4%, which exaggerated the relative merit of a fixed link project. To conform with Treasury Board recommendations (1976, p. 26), FGA should have used a discount rate of 10%, and then performed sensitivity analyses using 5% and 15%. Note here also that many economists would agree with Burgess's conclusion (1981) that 7% is a more appropriate social discount rate, and should be supported by sensitivity analyses using 4% and 10%. However, without access to FGA's full data set, it is impossible to perform these calculations. As low discount rates tend to favour a fixed link, and high ones to favour the status quo, a full reporting of results for a justifiable range of discount rates is necessary.

It was assumed in Case 5 that capital costs were 20% lower than in the base case, yet the cost of a bridge has been estimated elsewhere (Calhoun, 1989, p. 14) to be $1 billion (1989 dollars)—that is, over $900 million (1987 dollars) compared to FGA's base-case estimate of $630 million (1987 dollars). (Indeed, Strait Crossing Incorporated's own estimate of $840 million has been cited on many occasions during the past several years.) Therefore, using the Case 5 assumption that the capital cost of a bridge is $504 million (1987 dollars) seems quite unrealistic.

The assumption of Case 7 is that the value of time saved is 20% higher than that assumed for the base case. We comment on this matter below.

**TABLE C1.2   Net Present Value of Social Costs
(millions of 1987 dollars)**

Case	Status Quo	Bridge Only	Bridge and Ferry	Rail Tunnel Only	Rail Tunnel and Ferry
Case 1	* 528.2	563.8	564.7	590.1	585.5
Case 2	1,085.0	565.0	* 513.9	730.6	665.4
Case 3	* 647.5	661.6	678.5	693.7	704.7
Case 4	* 528.2	649.8	650.7	664.5	659.9
Case 5	528.2	* 477.8	478.7	515.7	511.1
Case 6	* 489.6	559.7	554.0	586.0	574.7
Case 7	528.2	527.0	* 525.7	570.2	563.9
Case 8	* 528.2	600.6	603.7	610.0	607.1
Case 9	* 528.2	563.8	564.7	590.1	585.5

The Value of Time Saved

The Dollar Value of Time Saved

In its base case, FGA used values of time saved that seem quite high. Indeed, because it assumed (implicitly) that business travellers and truck drivers would be able to make full productive use of every minute of time saved, its base-case assumptions in this regard should have been treated as maximum values. Quite possibly, it was not necessary to *assume* dollar values of time saved at all: given its access to the various roadside surveys it referred to, it seems that FGA possessed the data (not published in its report) required to *calculate* these amounts. Travellers of all types were already facing a time-distance-money trade-off on the island when both ferry systems were operating in the ice-free season. The methods by which such data could have been used to estimate more precisely the value of time saved to all classes of travellers are well known. (See Chapter 9.)

Benefits to Generated (Induced) Traffic

FGA calculated the value of time saved, and any increase (or decrease) in vehicle operating costs, to be the same for all fixed link travellers regardless of whether they would be diverted from the existing ferries or counted as generated traffic. This was a faulty approach. This method is appropriate for diverted traffic; but "generated" travellers' willingness to pay for rail tunnel or bridge trips should be assessed in its entirety as their benefit.[7] Whether FGA's method overestimated or underestimated the benefit of a fixed link to generated traffic depends on the exact characteristics of generated travellers' demand for this service. The first generated traveller's benefit from a trip via a fixed link alternative is equal to his or her willingness to pay for that trip. This amount will exceed the toll charged by whatever extra value this traveller places on a trip by bridge or tunnel. The value of the same trip to the last generated traveller is simply the toll he or she pays—he or she is the *marginal* traveller. The value of a bridge or rail tunnel trip to other generated traffic lies between these extremes. (Whether proper calculation of this item would change the ranking of options given in Table C1.2 cannot be determined without access to FGA's data.)

Actual Minutes Saved

Beyond the issue of the dollar value of time per hour saved for each class of traveller, there is an important matter concerning how many minutes a bridge will save each type of traveller per trip. FGA stated: "Presently at the Borden–Cape Tormentine ferry crossing, an average crossing time, including delays and waiting time, has been estimated to be 100 minutes" (1987, p. 5.11). As a bridge trip will take approximately 15 minutes, FGA used a time savings per bridge trip of 85 minutes *for all types of traffic*.

However, this method of calculation overestimates the time savings for commercial traffic. Travellers in automobiles may find their trips delayed, especially in July and August, because they must wait for a ferry with sufficient space; but commercial traffic is given boarding priority. It seems that FGA's 100-minute average trip time applied to vehicles of all types; as a result, this figure overestimated the minutes saved by commercial traffic and underestimated the minutes saved by passenger vehicles. By assuming that the dollar value of time saved per hour would be much higher for truck drivers than for other travellers, FGA exaggerated the total dollar value of time saved. To avoid seriously overestimating this benefit, a more appropriate method would have been to calculate the average number of minutes saved by each different class of vehicle, convert each to a dollar value separately, then aggregate.

OTHER ISSUES

Job Creation—Shadow Wages

One of FGA's base-case assumptions was that the shadow wage rates for permanent jobs and short-term jobs associated with the fixed link project would be, respectively, 65% and 75% of wages paid. This was to assume that significant numbers of those employed by the project would come from the ranks of the unemployed. In Case 3 it assumed shadow wages equal to actual wages paid. This was to assume that a fixed link project would only hire people away from other employment. Which assumption was more realistic?

FGA reported that "discussions with DRIE [Department of Regional Industrial Expansion] officials in Prince Edward Island indicated that they believe the social opportunity cost of labour is closer to 100 percent rather than 65 and 75 percent" (1987, p. 5.11). That is, the project would hire people away from other employment for the most part. This was especially true of bridge construction, as it would take place mostly during good-weather months, when employment in fishing and tourism industries is high. It was likely to be less true for tunnel construction, which could proceed year-round.

Three conclusions may be drawn if we take the DRIE officials at their word. First, the base-case assumptions biased the analysis in favour of construction of a fixed link of either type relative to the status quo. Second, using the same shadow wage rate for both bridge and tunnel options ignored the lower social costs of labour associated with tunnel construction relative to bridge construction. Third, there would be no significant impact on the unemployment rate on P.E.I. during construction of a bridge.

Ferry Operating Costs

FGA made the base-case assumption (6) that real ferry operating costs would increase by 1% annually over the life of the project. Thus, these costs would increase by 1% plus the rate of inflation in nominal terms. In Case 6 it was assumed that these costs would not increase in real terms, but only by the rate of inflation in nominal terms. In this way, the base-case assumption made retaining the existing ferry service expensive relative to the bridge and tunnel options and relative to the Case 6 assumption. Certainly, the larger the costs attributed to operating the Borden–Tormentine ferry, the less likely it was that the status quo would be seen as the least costly option.

The 1990 Report of the Environmental Assessment Panel (FEARO) stated: "Between 1979 and 1989, operating costs for the Marine Atlantic vessels crossing the Strait have decreased" (p. 9). From this, it follows that the base-case assumption, especially, seemed to bias the analysis against the status quo.

Other Options

Base-case assumptions were that a bridge would generate 25% more traffic than the existing ferry service. This figure for a rail tunnel was 15%. This difference was, presumably, attributable to FGA's calculations that a bridge would save 85 minutes of travelling time per trip on the Borden–Tormentine run, whereas a rail tunnel would save only 55 minutes because part of the trip by train would involve time spent loading and unloading vehicles. Aside from the matter of how accurate these figures were, one option FGA did not consider—it was not asked to—was a highway tunnel. If it had, and if it had made the same time saving and generated traffic assumptions for it as for a bridge, a highway tunnel would have dominated the bridge option in all cases using FGA's methodology (unless the extra costs associated with a highway tunnel and not with a rail tunnel—such as providing greater ventilation capability—exceeded $86.5 million, the difference between FGA's estimates of bridge and rail tunnel capital costs). (See Box C1.2 regarding the feasibility of tunnel construction.)

Moreover, there were other reasons besides lower capital, maintenance, and operating costs to prefer a highway tunnel to a bridge. (Although FGA attributed higher operating costs to a rail tunnel than to a bridge, it seems unlikely that it would cost more to maintain a highway tunnel than a bridge.) First, a tunnel is safer for travellers and far less prone to being closed in bad weather. No accounting was made of this. Second, a major environmental danger of a bridge across the Strait is its potential to impede ice break-up each spring, and in so doing, harm the fishing and agricultural industries. Another problem with a bridge relates to its impact on silting. Marine populations are, obviously, especially sensitive to this. Whether fears of these impacts were

---

BOX C1.2

The Tunnel Option

Harris & Billard (1988) were concerned mainly with the impacts of a fixed link on commercial marine life. In their Executive Summary, they noted the following:

> The commercial fishing industry of the Northumberland Strait is capable of producing over $70 million in landed value, annually and providing employment for 10,000 persons. Of greatest value are the shellfish (lobster and scallops) which account for almost 75% of the total annual value. These species are slow-moving and bottom-dwelling, and therefore the most susceptible to the negative factors which would result from most forms of fixed links planned for the Northumberland Strait … In fact, it is likely that a causeway, bridge, an immersed tube tunnel, or a combination of any of these, would result in significant, long-term damage to shellfish grounds, the species themselves and, as well, the other marine species which support the commercial fishery.

Regarding the feasibility of constructing a tunnel under the strait, they stated (italics added):

> A deep level tunnel under the Strait would constitute the most desirable form of crossing. With access portals located on land at both ends, there would be minimal effect upon existing environmental conditions within the Strait, if affected at all. *In view of the basically favourable geology (uniformity of rock conditions, lack of faulting and presence of dykes and other intrusives), rock conditions are considered to be most favourable for tunnelling* (1988, p. 6).

---

exaggerated or not, they would not have held for a tunnel, the choice of environmentalists—both in Canada and abroad—and some engineers. (See Land [1989], Staff [1990], and Dyck [1991] regarding this matter.) Indeed, even the generic "Initial Environmental Evaluation" conducted in compliance with federal environmental assessment regulations awarded the bridge a much higher risk-score than the tunnel: 547,443 to 139,102 (Perchanok, 1988, p. 14). Although the costs of uncertain environmental damage and risk to life and limb may be difficult to measure, analysts can appeal to substantial literatures on the theory and measurement of both. There was no justification for ignoring them in a study meant to assess *all* social costs and benefits. This more thorough approach would have been especially prudent, given the August 1990 "Report of the Environmental Assessment Panel." FEARO stated:

The Panel agrees that there is a need for an improved transportation service between Prince Edward Island and New Brunswick. After careful consideration, however, the Panel concludes that the risk of harmful effects of the proposed bridge concept is unacceptable. The Panel recommends, therefore, that the project not proceed. (1990, p. 1)

This is not to say that a highway tunnel would have been preferred to the status quo. The estimated cost (in 1987 dollars) of a 17 kilometre railway tunnel between Malmö and Copenhagen was over $1.8 billion (Land, 1989). Although many factors can account for cost differences, FGA's estimate of $543.5 million for a slightly shorter tunnel seems optimistic. In any case, a more complete study would have considered as many technically feasible options as possible, including, as Peters (1991) details, the use of faster vessels. (See Box C1.3 regarding some reservations expressed concerning construction of a tunnel.)

BOX C1.3

Tunnels and the Environment

The only specific objections to a tunnel we can find reported were made by Bill Casey, then Member of Parliament for the Nova Scotia riding of Cumberland-Colchester. He provided two.

The first was that construction of a tunnel "would make it hard to nail down costs" (MacDonald, 1991). We find this objection unreasonable. FGA was given construction cost estimates by Public Works Canada; planners of a proposed Malmö-to-Copenhagen tunnel did not hesitate to forecast construction costs (Land, 1989); and regardless, Canadian analysts were in a position to learn from the experience of the builders of the English Channel tunnel.

Casey's second objection was that digging the tunnel between England and France "resulted in amounts of fill being dumped in the English Channel and similar amounts being spread over valuable farmlands in France (MacDonald, 1991)." This may be true, but it would seem simple enough to instruct Canadian tunnel diggers not to emulate their European counterparts.

Perchanok (1988, p. 13) reported that digging a tunnel would produce 3 million cubic metres of rock. Possibly, this mass could have served a useful purpose on the Island. One notes that the rate of erosion along the north shore of P.E.I. is a major problem, and this rock might have been suitable for slowing it. Others, perhaps tongue-in-cheek, once advocated its use to construct what would have been the Island's only resort for downhill skiers.

SUMMARY AND RECOMMENDATIONS

Regarding the FGA study, Townley (1992, p. 18) concluded:

> Given the above methodological errors, one cannot conclude that construction of a bridge between New Brunswick and Prince Edward Island is justified on economic grounds. Indeed, when FGA's errors concerning corporate income taxes and salvage values are corrected, and when the extreme assumptions of cases 2, 5 and 7 are dismissed, the *status quo* dominates in all scenarios examined. That is, construction of a fixed link would impose a net loss on society. From this perspective, any debate concerning the magnitude of any environmental damage a bridge might cause would seem moot: *any* damage at all would simply magnify this social loss.
>
> If Public Works Canada is not prepared to let current proposals for a fixed link go the way of Senator Howland's 1885 proposal, it would be well-advised, at the very least, to commission a more complete and methodologically sound cost-benefit analysis of this project.

REACTION

The Honourable Elmer MacKay, then Minister of Public Works, was made aware of the Townley (1992) critique of FGA's analysis. Mr. MacKay responded on September 14, 1992, by letter:

> Although differences of opinion can exist on the methodology of economic analysis, the conclusion I reach is that the analysis that was undertaken to assess the social costs and benefits of the Fixed Link Crossing was sound.

Later that autumn, a legal action against the project was initiated in Federal Court by Friends of the Island, a group based on P.E.I. It came to light in the discovery part of that action that Public Works Canada had commissioned a review of the FGA study and Townley (1992) by Gardner Pinfold Consulting Economists Limited of Halifax. Its report is dated September 1992. (We find it odd that this report was commissioned, given the minister's statement.) Gardner Pinfold agreed with Townley's conclusions: "The Fiander-Good study does not establish the economic viability of the fixed crossing. If economic viability is an important criterion for proceeding with the project, then it would be advisable to conduct a more rigorous analysis" (p. 8).

In March 1993 the House of Commons committee charged with considering *Bill C-110, An Act respecting the Northumberland Strait Crossing*, heard testimony. One recommendation the committee heard was that a proper cost-benefit analysis be commissioned and that additional options, including extra ferries, faster ferries, the bridge option, and a highway tunnel option, be considered. Perhaps as a result of these hearings, Gardner Pinfold Consulting Economists was commissioned by Public Works Canada to prepare a new cost-benefit analysis. Unfortunately, only the bridge project was to be considered.

THE GARDNER PINFOLD ANALYSIS (1993)

Gardner Pinfold reworked the FGA analysis in light of criticisms of FGA's methods. Some observers were surprised by its conclusion: that construction of a bridge would result in a positive net present value.

Key assumptions made were as follows:

- All traffic would grow at a rate of 2.5% annually.
- Induced passenger-related and commercial traffic, respectively, would be 25% and 5% of the volumes found immediately prior to opening.
- Shadow wages would be 32% of wages paid for ferry workers and for those engaged in operation of the bridge, and 36% of wages paid for bridge construction workers.
- The value of time saved to working people would be 100% of their wage rate per hour.
- The capital cost of the bridge would be $515.5 million (1993 dollars).

Shadow Wage Rates

The shadow wage rate assumptions Gardner Pinfold used were even more at odds with DRIE than FGA's. Any authority holding actual employment records of those hired by the project should be able to determine which assumption was closest to being correct, admittedly *ex post*. In any case, it seems that unemployment will increase because of the project, perhaps reducing the shadow wage rate to be used on future island projects below 100% of actual wages paid, depending on exact labour requirements. (See Box C1.4 for other analyses of employment impacts.)

Traffic Growth Projections

Gardner Pinfold's induced traffic and traffic growth assumptions were, like FGA's, somewhat suspect. According to Gardner Pinfold's assumptions, passenger-car and commercial traffic volumes will grow by factors greater than 14 and 12, respectively, over the life of the project. (We note that even Stanford [1968] assumed that there existed a carrying capacity for tourists to P.E.I.)

BOX C1.4

Employment

Regarding ferry jobs, Jacques Whitford states: "Marine Atlantic employs a total of 656 employees on the Borden-Cape Tormentine Ferry Service. Of these, 402 (61%) are full-time employees" (1993, p. 5–16).

Assuming that the remaining 254 part-time positions are literally half-time, 529 full-time (or equivalent) positions will be lost when the ferry service is eliminated. Now assume that these jobs will not be lost until year 6 of the project (allowing 5 years for construction). As one person-year is roughly 250 person-days, the annual loss will be 132,250 person-days of employment. As the bridge is expected to last 100 years, the total loss of ferry jobs because of the bridge will be 13,225,000 person-days of employment (from year 6 to year 105).

Regarding bridge construction jobs, (also from Whitford), "The construction of the bridge will generate approximately 600,000 person days of employment" (1993, p. 7-33).

Regarding employment on the bridge, Smith Green & Associates state: "Based on preliminary analysis the operation of the bridge crossing may require up to 60 to 80 full-time staff" (1989b, p. 13). If we adopt the assumption that the bridge will create 80 full-time jobs per year from year 6 to year 105, this is 20,000 person-days per year, or 2,000,000 person-days over the life of the project.

Therefore, the net job loss due to the bridge is (13,225,000 − 600,000 − 2,000,000 =) 10,625,000 person-days (42,500 person-years) over the 105-year life of the project. Another way of expressing this is that, on average over the 105-year project life, over 400 jobs (42,500 ÷ 105 = 404.76) will be lost each year.

Therefore, according to the above estimates, building the bridge will create fewer than 500 full-time jobs per year for five years, and shutting down the ferry will cause the loss of more than 500 full-time jobs per year for 100 years.

The implications of these assumptions raise a number of practical questions:

- Why will tourists want to go to such a crowded place?
- What will all these commercial vehicles be carrying? What physical output will have increased?
- How much of P.E.I. will have to be paved over to create the necessary parking lots?

- Given that P.E.I. motels and hotels already serve capacity volumes every summer, where will additional ones be built?
- What extra water and sewer services will these extra millions of people require? What will happen to peak-load demands for water provision, and will the municipalities of P.E.I. be able to cope with them?

It is unfortunate that these traffic growth assumptions were not scrutinized more carefully. However, they are quite common in this type of study, and it seems that after they are used several times their use becomes accepted. In some situations these assumptions may be reasonable; in others, especially where the relevant land mass is fixed because it is an island, they are unreasonable. To the extent that FGA's and Gardner Pinfold's traffic growth assumptions drove their results, it is prudent to assess how realistic they were.

Tourist Expenditures

Tourism operators view the fixed link as good for business. If FGA's and Gardner Pinfold's traffic growth assumptions prove realistic, these operators will have ever-growing numbers of customers. There is a factor, however, that does not seem to have been appreciated: although it is true that a bridge will make it easier for tourists to come to the Island, it will also make it easier for them to *leave*.[8]

The bulk of tourist expenditures are made after 5 p.m. daily on accommodations, evening meals, and entertainment. If, because of the bridge (and thus easy evening exit from the island), tourists turn two-night trips into overnight trips, four-night trips in three-night trips, and so on, average tourist expenditures may decrease markedly. Therefore, it is possible that while the number of tourists will increase, their expenditures will *fall*.

Construction Costs

Finally, there is the matter of bridge construction costs. FGA was given a bridge construction cost figure of $630 million (1987 dollars) by Public Works Canada. By applying the Consumer Price Index, we can convert this estimate to $780 million 1993 dollars. Gardner Pinfold used a base-case construction cost figure, in 1993 dollars, of $515.5 million.[9]

Thus, the estimated cost of constructing the bridge was $264.5 million (1993 dollars) less—33.9% lower—in the Gardner Pinfold study than in the Fiander-Good analysis. It is unfortunate that Gardner Pinfold was not instructed to assess other options; we could then have observed whether estimated tunnel construction costs would have decreased by a similar factor.

POST MORTEM

Confederation Bridge is a reality. Economically viable or not, this project will afford students of Canadian project evaluation an opportunity to conduct a *post mortem* analysis. In a few years, if the authorities and Strait Crossing Incorporated co-operate, the information required to conduct such analyses will be available. The question will be this: "Was the fixed link worth building?"

In some ways this procedure will not be fair to FGA or Gardner Pinfold, who conducted their analyses from an *ex ante* perspective. On the other hand, it will be interesting to assess the reasonableness of their assumptions and cost estimates with the advantage of hindsight.

ENDNOTES

1. A first: Cornelius Van Ewyk of Cavendish, P.E.I., walked across Confederation Bridge on February 8, 1997 ... but was caught. According to the Canadian Press (1997a, A2), "Police met Mr. Van Ewyk on the P.E.I. side, where they fined him $110 under the Trespassing Act for entering enclosed premises."

2. See Townley (1992).

3. Adapted from Harris & Billard (1988).

4. What future ferry subsidies would be was a matter of some debate in the House of Commons. The annual ferry subsidy at the time of the debate (1993) was slightly over $20 million. The contracted annual subsidy to the fixed link operator is in excess of $40 million. Also, it may be worth noting that Woods Gordon (1987) based its financial analysis of the fixed link project on the operator receiving both subsidy and tolls for 100 years after construction.

5. The "Chunnel Project," the tunnel under the English Channel linking England and France, is a railway tunnel project. Those travelling by automobile or truck drive their vehicles onto flatbed rail cars at one end and off-load at the other. Given the length of the trip, loading and off-loading vehicles is a minor part of the trip's duration. This would not be so if a rail tunnel were constructed under the Northumberland Strait. Loading and off-loading vehicles would take longer than the time spent crossing. This lack of time savings relative to the bridge option caused this option to pale in comparison.

6. We ignore at our peril notions of a tunnel being converted into the world's longest poolhall, the Maritimes' answer to the West Edmonton Mall, or a bomb shelter.

7. FGA's explanation as to why toll revenues should be treated as a transfer reveals that it adopted the "change in total benefits minus change in total costs" method rather than the "party by party" approach.

8. It is not clear whether the bridge will attract more tourists. Ferry ridership increased dramatically in 1996, because people wanted to watch the bridge being built. These travellers from the mainland took the two-way trip without visiting P.E.I. Japanese tourists—who appear quite enthralled with *Anne of Green Gables*—think the link will diminish P.E.I. as a tourist destination. Still others view ferry rides as part of their vacation and are rather relieved that the Caribou–Wood Islands ferry will continue to run.

9. Regarding bridge construction costs, Gardner Pinfold states: "An overall cost figure of $747.0 million and a construction schedule of September, 1993, to May, 1997, are used and conform to the most recent estimates of the contractor and Public Works Canada" (1993, p. 11). Apparently the shadow wage assumptions used caused the reduction from this figure to the base-case estimate of $515.5 million.

THE TRANS LABRADOR
HIGHWAY PROJECT

INTRODUCTION

The Project

In January 1993, Fiander-Good Associates Limited of Fredericton (FGA hereafter) completed the *Trans Labrador Highway Social and Economic Project Feasibility Analysis* for the Province of Newfoundland's Department of Works, Services and Transportation.[1] FGA's objective was

> to establish a reasonably accurate forecast of the social and economic impacts of a Trans Labrador Highway, constructed and maintained at national highway policy standards. The impacts on tourism, resource development and other economic development are to be quantified, translated to dollars, and used in a cost benefit analysis with a thirty year life for the highway. (1993, p. 1.2)

Three options were considered (shown on Map C2.1[2]):

- **The *Coastal Access* option** (1,804 kilometres). This option would involve upgrading the existing highway between Baie Comeau and Happy Valley-Goose Bay, building a new road corridor from Happy Valley-Goose Bay to the Straits that would connect to the existing road network at Red Bay, and providing connectors from this network to the coastal villages of Cartwright, Charlottetown, Port Hope Simpson, and Mary's Harbour.

- **The *No Link* option**. This option would involve merely upgrading the existing 1,134 kilometres of highway between Baie Comeau and Happy Valley-Goose Bay.

MAP C2.1

- **The *Direct Link* option** (1,513 kilometres). This option would involve upgrading the existing highway between Baie Comeau and Happy Valley-Goose Bay and connecting Happy Valley-Goose Bay to the Strait of Belle Isle by constructing a single road between Muskrat Falls and Forteau (and to the ferry at Blanc Sablon).

Construction would proceed in phases. Phase 1 would involve developing a 9-metre-wide gravel road; Phase 2 would involve paving this road; and Phase 3 would involve upgrading the entire road to National Highway Systems Standards (so that motorists would be able to travel year-round at speeds between 90 and 100 kilometres per hour in reasonable comfort). Total time to completion was estimated as 23, 11, and 18 years for the *Coastal Access*, *No Link*, and *Direct Link* options respectively.

The Setting

According to the 1991 census, there were 30,375 residents of Labrador that year. Along the proposed routes, beginning at the Quebec end, available census data are the following: Baie Comeau (26,012), Labrador City (9,061), Wabush (2,331), Happy Valley-Goose Bay (8,610), North West River (528), Cartwright (611), Charlottetown (292), Port Hope Simpson (614), Mary's Harbour (470), Red Bay (288), West St. Modeste (202), L'Anse-au-Loup (630), L'Anse-au-Clair (263), and Forteau (518). The data reveal that southern Labrador is sparsely populated, with only a few towns and a series of coastal villages.

Highway 389 links Baie Comeau to Labrador City. Those who have driven it advise the use of a four-wheel-drive vehicle. The road from about Labrador City to Happy Valley-Goose Bay is named the Trans Labrador Highway on some maps, but is more usually called "Freedom Road"—with good reason, some say. Depending on the season, striking out along it, even in an FWD, may not be wise. There is no highway between Muskrat Falls (near Happy Valley-Goose Bay) and the coast. It is bushland, populated by caribou, moose, and other wildlife. Ferry services connect the coastal villages to the island of Newfoundland. Most air traffic passes through Goose Bay, but smaller airports dot the area. Rail service from Quebec ends at the western border of Labrador.

The Results

For each option, FGA estimated construction and maintenance costs and, using discount rates (denoted by "i" below) of 5% and 10%, calculated the present values of these costs for a 30-year time horizon. These costs (expressed in 1992 dollars) are shown in Table C2.1 (FGA's Table 6.1, page 6.2).

Also, for each option FGA calculated "user," "mode shift," and "economic" benefits (to be described below) attributable to Labrador. The results are shown in Table C2.2 (FGA's Table 6.2, page 6.3).

Given the information in Tables C2.1 and C2.2, FGA calculated both the net present value (NPV) and the benefit-cost ratio (B/C) for Labrador of each option.[3] These are presented in Table C2.3 (FGA's Table 6.3, page 6.5), again measured in 1992 dollars and discounted at 5% and 10%.

TABLE C2.1   Present Value of Highway Costs

Option	Type of Cost	i = 10%	i = 5%
COASTAL ACCESS	Construction	$967,115,000	$1,389,337,000
	Maintenance	31,690,000	58,192,000
	Total	$998,805,000	$1,447,528,000
NO LINK	Construction	$703,629,000	$859,293,000
	Maintenance	14,959,000	24,824,000
	Total	$718,588,000	$884,116,000
DIRECT LINK	Construction	$907,615,000	$1,228,978,000
	Maintenance	31,088,000	54,823,000
	Total	$938,703,000	$1,283,801,000

TABLE C2.2   Present Value of Highway Benefits to Labrador

Option	Type of Benefit	i = 10%	i = 5%
COASTAL ACCESS	User	$330,986,000	$715,364,000
	Mode shift	342,213,000	619,522,000
	Economic	620,675,000	1,225,906,000
	Total	$1,293,873,000	$2,560,792,000
NO LINK	User	$232,568,000	$453,185,000
	Mode shift	93,616,000	165,439,000
	Economic	227,163,000	385,480,000
	Total	$553,346,000	$1,004,104,000
DIRECT LINK	User	$234,293,000	$482,755,000
	Mode shift	310,816,000	531,969,000
	Economic	528,782,000	1,003,413,000
	Total	$1,073,891,000	$2,018,137,000

TABLE C2.3   Net Present Value of the Trans Labrador Highway to Labrador

Option	Measure	i = 10%	i = 5%
COASTAL ACCESS	NPV	$295,068,000	$1,113,264,000
	B/C	1.30	1.77
NO LINK	NPV	−$165,242,000	$119,988,000
	B/C	0.77	1.14
DIRECT LINK	NPV	$135,187,000	$734,336,000
	B/C	1.14	1.57

Based on these estimates, FGA concluded as follows:

- The *Coastal Access* option ranks highest overall.
- All options are economically viable at a discount rate of 5%.
- Only the *No Link* option is not economically viable at a discount rate of 10%.

According to FGA's analysis, the *Coastal Access* option is economically viable and, of the options examined, the one that would generate the largest net benefits.

FUNDAMENTAL METHODOLOGICAL ERRORS

FGA's analysis is instructive because of its flaws. Its fundamental errors—that is, FGA's departures from standard cost-benefit analysis methodology—included (but are not limited to) the following:

- Counting as benefits items that ought not to be counted as benefits.
- Counting as benefits items that ought to be counted as costs.
- Not counting items that ought to be counted as costs.
- Double-counting benefits.
- Failing to subject estimates to extensive sensitivity testing in the presence of substantial uncertainty.

We deal with these errors below, in a much-condensed version of Locke and Townley's 1993 critique of FGA's analysis.[4]

THE TREATMENT OF COSTS

There are two principal criticisms concerning how FGA treated project costs.

Construction and Maintenance Cost Estimates

The first problem is that according to FGA's own discussion, its estimates for maintenance and construction costs were quite preliminary. There was some uncertainty concerning routes; average maintenance cost data from other highways were used to forecast those for the three options; the timing of construction phases was not definite; and so on.

Given this uncertainty, a suitable procedure would have been to subject these cost estimates to a sensitivity analysis similar to the sensitivity analysis that FGA applied in its evaluation of the P.E.I. Fixed Link project (see Case 1). Estimates 20% higher and lower than the base-case estimates would have been appropriate. (We note that the *Coastal Access* and *Direct Link* options have negative net present values, using a discount rate of 10%, when costs are 30% and 15% higher, respectively, than those appearing in Table C2.1.)

Environmental Costs

The second problem, methodologically, is much more serious. As we have noted, the human population of Labrador is small. This cannot be said of other members of the Animal Kingdom. Hooved, winged, and finned species abound, and construction of a highway, especially between Happy Valley-Goose Bay and the coast through what is now wilderness, would cause considerable disruption to the environment and these wildlife populations. FGA acknowledged that these populations would be affected by the project.

Waterfowl

Regarding waterfowl, FGA stated:

> These birds have a tendency to lift off at the slightest disturbance. This activity uses up already depleted energy reserves, making these birds susceptible to other forms of mortality; and staging areas are popular areas for hunting which is positive for residents, but generally negative for waterfowl and waterfowl managers ...
>
> Construction and operation activities in or adjacent to either of these habitats would be a concern due to possible disturbance and avoidance or abandonment. The proximity of the road would increase access by hunters. At the same time, this would increase the accessibility by enforcement officials, as long as the appropriate increases in the level of enforcement staffing are provided. (1993, p. 4.3)

Moose

Regarding moose, FGA reported:

> Streeter *et al.* (1979) and Klein (1979) stated that the clearing of vegetation and associated construction of roads and facilities are considered to have the most serious effects on moose and other ungulates during the life of a project. These effects may be more serious if such activities are adjacent to or within important habitats such as wintering areas.
>
> The proposed project may displace moose during winter if the routing is within or nearby these areas of concentration. Although experience in other areas indicates that highways may not necessarily displace these animals, it would increase the risk of animal road kills. The highway would improve access for hunting and there would be an increased likelihood of moose-vehicle collisions (and its inherent impact on vehicular safety). (1993, p. 4.4)

Indeed, it is because of the "increased likelihood of moose-vehicle collisions" that FGA acknowledged that the proposed highway would require more police services to be allocated to it than otherwise. However, this extra policing was not counted as a cost to the project.

Caribou

According to FGA, "the Mealy Mountain caribou herd is the largest herd in southern Labrador and of important regional significance" (1993, p. 4.5). This herd occupies about 22,000 square kilometres and has been off limits to hunters since 1975 because of overhunting. A highway would improve access to this herd, thus making illegal hunting easier. To prevent or to control this would require additional expenditures on wildlife protection.

As well, FGA reported that the George River herd—the largest in the world—is often observed crossing the existing "Freedom Road" near Churchill Falls, and that the Lac Joseph herd roams the area between Baie Comeau and Labrador City. Like the Mealy Mountain herd, these other herds would cross the proposed highway, and there would be a number of collisions. Although FGA later took into account the costs of these collisions and lives lost, it did not count as costs the extra financial commitments required to enforce wildlife and traffic laws.

Freshwater Fish

There are some concerns regarding the impact of the construction and operation of a Trans Labrador Highway on freshwater rivers. FGA described these as "downstream effects to spawning and other types of habitats from siltation, hydrocarbon spills, river fordings and unplanned events [and] enhanced access for anglers, natives and poachers which have positive or negative aspects depending on who is being interviewed" (1993, p. 4.6). The magnitude of these environmental impacts is not known. FGA noted: "At the implementation stage, there will be a need for development of an Environmental Protection Plan to identify required precautions associated with specific sites and specific construction stages/activities" (1993, p. 4.18).

Summary—Environmental Costs

Clearly, there will be environmental costs, but FGA did not include them in its calculations. Instead, it stated: "To reduce effects to wildlife and freshwater [fish,] it is important to ensure that government allocate additional funding for wildlife and fisheries patrol officers along the alignment" (FGA, 1993, p. 4.18). Because the costs of the negative environmental impacts of a Trans Labrador Highway were not assessed (or at least counted as costs), FGA's estimates understated the true cost of this project to society.

We might argue that this "additional funding" required of government might serve as a proxy for environmental costs to be included in the calculation of total project costs. Although imperfect, this approach would be better than assessing no cost when very real environmental costs may be incurred. (Paradoxically, as we shall note below, these extra expenditures were actually counted as benefits by FGA.)

THE TREATMENT OF BENEFITS

FGA separated the benefits it attributed to the Trans Labrador Highway project into three categories: highway user benefits, transport mode shift cost savings, and economic benefits. We shall consider these in order.

Highway User Benefits

To calculate highway user benefits, FGA employed Transport Canada's *Highway User Benefit Assessment Model* (HUBAM). FGA provided the following description of HUBAM:

> A benefit-cost approach is used in the HUBAM model which calculates the expected benefits to road users in terms of time savings, vehicle operating cost savings and accident reduction, as well as highway maintenance cost savings over the lifetime of the project. The model is sensitive to changes in traffic volumes and vehicle operating speeds, as well as highway geometric characteristics, surface conditions, and expected maintenance requirements. (1993, p. 5.6)

Essentially, the HUBAM methodology requires a projection of traffic volumes on the Trans Labrador Highway over the project's time horizon. After these have been estimated, assumptions are made regarding the values of time savings, lives saved, vehicles collisions, and so on. With all of this information, aggregate time savings, vehicle operating cost savings, accident cost savings, and highway maintenance savings can be calculated.

We shall examine first how FGA generated the necessary traffic data, then how it determined the total benefit or cost produced by HUBAM in each category. Note that although we do not have access to the HUBAM model, we can still identify some results of this "black box" approach that are most peculiar.

Traffic Data

For its calculations, FGA required data in four categories: (1) existing traffic, (2) latent resident travel demand traffic, (3) passenger travel and freight transportation mode shift traffic, and (4) traffic growth.

Existing traffic   In the absence of traffic counts in Labrador, FGA based its estimate of existing traffic on

> traffic counts along Route 389; truck traffic levels into Labrador West and on to Goose Bay, as established through interviews of trucking firms and major freight handling businesses; Strait of Belle Isle Ferry counts of passenger vehicles and trucks travelling between the Labrador Straits and the Island of Newfoundland; and estimation of existing auto travel between communities connected by all season or summer seasonal roads utilizing the Atlantic Region Auto Travel Gravity Model ... for existing travel times and adjusted for seasonality, as necessary. (1993, pp. 5.9–5.10)

It would appear that its calculations of existing average daily traffic were as follows: slightly more than 200 vehicles along each of Highway 389 and the Red Bay–Blanc Sablon road; and a handful of vehicles between Labrador City and Happy Valley-Goose Bay.[5]

Latent Resident Travel Demand Traffic   According to FGA:

> Latent resident travel demand traffic is an estimate of normal automobile travel traffic, generated by residents who would take trips to other communities and centres, if a highway were available. That is, it reflects a latent unfulfilled demand for automobile travel due to lack of an all-season fully serviced highway connection, which is not fulfilled by other alternative modes. (1993, p. 5.10)

To calculate this latent demand (to the Island of Newfoundland and the Canadian highway network at Montreal), the Atlantic Provinces Auto Travel Gravity Model calibrated with 1979 Atlantic Provinces Origin-Destination Survey data was used. It seems that traffic is expected to increase along the entire highway by approximately 200 vehicles per day because of latent demand.

Passenger Travel and Freight Transportation Mode Shift Traffic Basically, FGA has predicted that if a Trans Labrador Highway were constructed, people now travelling by train, ferry, and/or airplane would switch to automobile travel. In the same vein, freight currently being shipped by other means would also be switched to the highway. The reason in both cases being, of course, time and cost savings.

Regarding marine-to-highway passenger and freight shifts, rather than report FGA's calculations, we note that they were based on a peculiar set of assumptions. The first was that "marine services would be continued only where highway access is not provided" (FGA, 1993, p. 5.29). The second was that passengers and freight from all modes would shift to the highway because highway transportation costs would be lower than those of other modes *if subsidies for the other modes were not taken into account.*

However, we note that passengers and shippers do not choose a particular mode of transportation based on unsubsidized prices; they make their choices on the basis of what they actually have to pay. Indeed, according to C.K. MacLeod (1992) of National Defence's Project Management Office in Goose Bay, regarding shifting to road transport from other modes:

> A superficial check on land transportation rates with *local* carriers indicates a ten-fold increase in shipping costs. This does not take into account the effects of any economic subsidies that may be in place for current air and marine modes, nor the effects of competitive bidding by regional or national carriers.

Therefore, unless all subsidies were removed (so that fares increased) or unless marine transportation were terminated, we cannot assume that any marine passengers or freight would shift to the highway. Below, we present evidence which suggests that the federal government intends neither to reduce subsidies nor to terminate ferry service, and that this source of highway traffic may be greatly overstated.

Traffic Growth FGA assumed that traffic would grow at 3% per annum. That is, traffic increases would be 3% each year over the project's 30-year life, augmented by discrete jumps each time a phase of the road was completed. (We commented on the credibility of such compounding traffic growth rates in Case 1.)

The Value of Time Saved

The values that were used in the FGA study are presented in Table C2.4.[6]

FGA combined these data with its traffic projections to calculate overall travel time savings for the three options. These are presented in Table C2.5.[7]

Vehicle Operating Cost Savings

It is less expensive to operate a vehicle on a good road than on a poor one. FGA thus entered costs for fuel, oil, tires, depreciation, and maintenance and repair into the HUBAM model. How HUBAM processed these data into cost savings was not explained in the FGA study. Nevertheless, we present HUBAM's estimates of vehicle operating cost savings in Table C2.6.[8]

TABLE C2.4   Travel Time Savings

Vehicle Type	Persons per Vehicle	Time Value ($/person/hour)
Automobile	2.6	5.04
Single unit truck	1.3	11.68
Semi tractor-trailer	1.4	13.27
Bus	33.0	2.89
Recreational vehicle	4.4	2.61

TABLE C2.5   Present Value of Travel Time Savings

Option	i = 10%	i = 5%
Coastal Access	$168,407,000	$367,198,000
No Link	$124,512,000	$242,772,000
Direct Link	$137,493,000	$279,952,000

TABLE C2.6   Present Value of Vehicle Operating Cost Savings

Option	i = 10%	i = 5%
Coastal Access	$122,249,000	$251,114,000
No Link	$107,219,000	$201,139,000
Direct Link	$106,273,000	$203,926,000

Accident Cost Savings

If any of the Trans Labrador Highway options were constructed, the number of highway accidents in Labrador would increase. For this reason, when the relevant data were processed by HUBAM, negative savings—or simply extra costs—were calculated. Besides traffic data, calculation of this cost requires assumptions regarding the costs of various sorts of accidents. The costs per accident used by FGA were $1.5 million per fatal accident, $13,000 per personal injury accident, and $3,300 per property damage accident. The aggregate estimates appear in Table C2.7.

TABLE C2.7   Present Value of Increased Accident Costs

Option	i = 10%	i = 5%
Coastal Access	$28,996,000	$43,024,000
No Link	$28,679,000	$46,903,000
Direct Link	$32,714,000	$50,308,000

Highway Maintenance Cost Savings

The final category of highway user benefits that FGA considered was highway maintenance savings. FGA's calculations of these savings are shown in Table C2.8.[9]

TABLE C2.8   Present Value of Highway Maintenance Cost Savings

Option	i = 10%	i = 5%
Coastal Access	$69,326,000	$140,076,000
No Link	$29,516,000	$56,176,000
Direct Link	$23,240,000	$49,185,000

Phantom Savings—A Puzzle

We suppose that FGA's traffic projections (and assumptions) could be challenged. They seem quite arbitrary, but we note that they were based on existing models, and we also appreciate that insufficient data were available.

To obtain more reliable data would have been expensive for the proponent of the project. Still, the inadequacy of data from interviews and from other possibly flawed studies and models should be acknowledged.

Time savings, vehicle operating cost savings, accident cost savings, and highway maintenance cost savings are, of course, legitimate benefits to be attributed to the project. However, there seems to be a major problem regarding how these were calculated.

Note that the *No Link* option is part of both the *Coastal Access* and *Direct Link* options. Note also that the *Coastal Access* option is 670 kilometres longer than the *No Link* option and that all of the extra proposed road lies between Happy Valley-Goose Bay and the coast. Of these 670 kilometres, only 76 kilometres currently exist as a road (from Red Bay to near L'Anse-au-Clair). The balance, the 594 kilometres between Red Bay and Muskrat Falls, is wilderness—no highway exists.

Now examine Table C2.8 again. At discount rates of 10% and 5%, respectively, by subtracting the benefits attributed to the *No Link* option from those of the *Coastal Access* option, we can deduce that FGA attributed highway maintenance cost savings of $39,810,000 and $83,900,000 to these 670 kilometres—594 kilometres of bush and 76 kilometres of road. Note also that FGA (1993, p. 2.14) stated that along the Red Bay–L'Anse-au-Clair route, "from the Quebec border to Pinware the road has a good asphaltic surface," and that from Pinware to Red Bay the road "was paved during the past few years."

This raises a major question regarding the 594 kilometres that are part of the *Coastal Access* option but are currently roadless wilderness: As current expenditures on maintenance for this non-road are zero, how can highway road maintenance cost savings be realized by building a highway where none existed? A highway costs money to maintain, whereas it costs nothing to maintain a highway that does not exist. Maintenance costs along this stretch of wilderness can only increase—not decrease—going from a state of "no highway" to one of "highway."

Similarly, currently no one is travelling on this roadless part of the proposed *Coastal Access* option. No person can save time by travelling on a road after it is built; he or she can only spend time. Yet according to Table C2.5, time savings of $43,895,000 and $124,426,000 at discount rates of 10% and 5%, respectively, are attributed to this nonexistent (other than the stretch from Red Bay to near L'Anse-au-Clair) portion of the *Coastal Access* option.

In Table C2.6, that part of the *Coastal Access* option that is not part of the *No Link* option accounts for vehicle operating cost savings of $15,030,000 and $49,975,000 (at 10% and 5%, respectively). Again, people do not drive on nonexistent highways. If one is built, vehicle operating costs will have to increase. We note, as well, that it is along this stretch of the proposed project that we would expect many collisions with moose and caribou. To this extent, the extra costs of accidents attributed to this option are understated in Table C2.7 (as it is our understanding that a highway is required for a person to become involved in a highway traffic accident with a moose).

None of this makes sense. When we go from a situation of "no road" to one where a new road is built, there can be no time savings, or vehicle operating cost savings, or road maintenance cost savings, or accident cost savings, because obviously, a person cannot drive (or die) on a road that does not exist. If no time is being spent, and if no operating cost or highway maintenance cost is being incurred, and if no life (human or otherwise) is being lost on a nonexistent highway, there can be no savings should a road be constructed—only extra expenditures.

Therefore, something is very wrong with either the HUBAM model or with how it was applied when the point is missed that society can have none of these savings from building a highway where one does not now exist. It is worth noting that this problem relates to the "virgin bush" part of the *Coastal Access* option more than to the similar stretch of the *Direct Link* option. (We leave the corresponding subtraction exercise to the reader.) Certainly, it seems that highway user benefits attributed to the *Coastal Access* option have been overstated. However, without further details concerning HUBAM and what variables were entered into this model, we are unable to trace the source of this anomaly.

Transport Mode Shift Cost Savings

FGA's predictions of the volumes of rail, air, and ferry traffic that would switch to a Trans Labrador Highway were summarized earlier. FGA defined what it meant by transport mode shift cost savings:

> Highway mode transport cost savings are distinct and independent from the highway user benefits generated by the HUBAM model. Highway user benefits apply only to the cost savings to highway users, as a consequence of improvements made to the existing highway system. On the other hand, transport mode shift cost savings benefits apply only to the cost savings which are attained from the cost differential of using the highway mode in place of an existing, more costly, alternate mode of transportation. (1993, p. 5.19)

Table C2.9 summarizes FGA's Tables 5.9 and 5.10, which were its estimates of current passenger (round trips) and freight (tonnes) costs in Labrador.

TABLE C2.9   Passenger and Freight Costs in Labrador

TYPE	Highway	Rail	Marine	Air
Passenger	—	6,600	9,050	110,600
Travel	—	$4,905,000	$5,921,000	$72,644,000
Freight	41,950	55,700	58,100	4,815
Transport	$6,228,000	$7,498,000	$50,589,000	$7,043,000

Unit costs for each mode of transportation may be calculated from this table. FGA's basic assumption was that if transportation or travel costs per unit on a Trans Labrador Highway turned out to be lower than those for the currently used mode, some or all passengers and freight would switch to the highway. Unfortunately, the costs stated earlier are not those that travellers and freight companies actually face, as we noted above. These people and firms pay lower prices because of subsidies. FGA states (italics ours):

Tables 5.9 and 5.10 [Table C2.9 above] provide the existing annual passenger travel and freight transportation volumes and costs esti-mates, respectively. The tables include all existing modes as available in each region, ie. highway, rail, marine and/or air. All transportation mode costs presented in the tables include any subsidies or service to the mode. This is fundamental to this transport mode shift cost sav-ings analysis because the levels of subsidization, particularly in the marine passenger and freight services, are such that based on fares or freight rates alone, *mode shift upon construction of a TLH would not occur.* In other words, the subsidized marine fares and freight rates paid by users at present are lower than would be the costs of highway trans-portation once the TLH was built. *Only when the true total cost of mode transport operations are considered, which must include the consideration of operating subsidies, can modal shift to the TLH be assumed.* (1993, pp. 5.20–5.23)

Therefore, travel and transportation on the Trans Labrador Highway would only be cheaper than by air, ferry, or rail if all subsidies were removed. If air, rail, and ferry subsidies did not change, there would be little or no shift of traffic to the Trans Labrador Highway, because it would be a more expensive way both to travel and to transport goods. (We noted earlier the letter from C.K. MacLeod of National Defence's Project Management Office at Goose Bay regarding what such a mode shift would cost his office.)

All of this raises a relevant question: Would the government remove subsidies for ferry and air travel so that the mode shifts FGA predicted would actually occur? Unless they do, passengers and freight firms will make their mode choices based on *the prices they actually face*—not on the unsubsidized prices FGA assumes are relevant.

A second question arises because of assumptions FGA made with regard to the shutting down of other modes of transport should a highway be built. In the case of marine traffic, FGA stated: "A conscious decision would have to be made to curtail marine services, before the complete mode shift to the TLH highway would take place" (1993, p. 5.28). But would the government in fact eliminate this alternative mode of transport?

A third question arises because of the way FGA calculated the actual cost savings. Take, for example, how FGA calculated marine-to-highway freight and passenger cost savings. It stated:

> Subsequent to the completion of the second phase of the TLH *"Coastal Access"* Option 1 and continuing on through the rest of the planning period, approximately 5,500 marine passenger trips and 44,500 tonnes of marine freight would be shifted to the TLH. At this stage, the combined costs of the remaining marine passengers and former marine passengers now travelling on the TLH in Labrador would be $4,176,000 per annum. When this is subtracted from the existing marine passenger service costs of $5,921,000 [see Table C2.9], annual cost savings would be $1,745,000. Similarly, the combined costs of $20,353,000 per annum of the remaining marine freight services and trucking services of the freight shifted to the TLH subsequent to the completion of Phase 2, when subtracted from existing marine freight costs of $50,589,000, would result in annual cost savings of $30,236,000 [see Table C2.9]. (1993, p. 5.30)

Note that FGA included the costs of providing subsidies in its cost estimates. This was tantamount to saying that if, say, 80% of travellers on a particular mode shifted to the highway, then the government would save 80% of the total subsidy it currently pays for that alternative mode. For example, if half the freight currently being transported by ferry shifted to the highway, then half the cost of operating the ferry would be saved. But was this method of calculating cost savings valid?

The answers to the above questions may be gleaned from a statement by the Honourable Jean Corbeil (1993), former Minister of Transportation:

> It should be borne in mind, however, that Transport Canada's obligations with respect to the provision of marine services to coastal Labrador communities would not be terminated by the construction of the Trans-Labrador Highway. Although a consulting study has been completed, the proposed highway has several possible configurations, none of which provide road linkages to all of the 51 communities

served by Marine Atlantic in 1993. In the absence of a road link, the federal government would remain obligated to provide a marine service to these communities.

Transport Canada will provide a subsidy of approximately $20 million to Marine Atlantic in 1993 to operate the Coastal Labrador Service. Even if the Trans-Labrador Highway were to be completed, such that Goose Bay, Cartwright, Mary's Harbour and a few other major centres were linked to the Island of Newfoundland, the communities of Northern Labrador would still require a marine service, as would a large number of communities on the south coast of Labrador. While it is likely that some reduction in subsidy could be achieved by constructing a road, a significant proportion would likely remain.[10]

The minister did not foresee the same reduction in subsidy (and operating) costs that FGA did. Clearly, FGA's estimates of transport mode shift cost savings were overstated. It would seem, too, that the only reason passengers and freight carriers would switch to a Trans Labrador Highway would be if other services shut down; fare and price differentials would not be a reason. But this does not make economic sense either. If ferries would still have to serve communities on southern and northern coasts even *with* a Trans Labrador Highway, then the extra cost of Marine Atlantic continuing to serve the communities in between these coasts would be a pittance compared to the cost of building a Trans Labrador Highway. And if subsidies were not eliminated, then according to FGA's own analysis, passengers and freight would not shift to the highway in any case, because it would be a more costly mode of transportation.

In summary, FGA based its estimates of transport mode shift cost savings on assumptions that were inconsistent with official policy and rational economic behaviour. As such, these benefits were overstated.

Economic Benefits

According to FGA:

Economic benefits are benefits from productivity gains and industry sectoral growth achieved by the highway development. Productivity gains arise as a consequence of business improvements through inventory and warehousing cost savings, as well as the purchasing savings from the availability of lower cost commodities from new alternative sources of suppliers and distributors. Economic benefits also include those occurring from industry and business sector developmental growth derived improved resource accessibility and generally enhanced business opportunities. (1993, p. 5.4)

We note the importance of these benefits to FGA's main conclusions. For example, for the *Coastal Access* option—using a discount rate of 10%—highway user benefits, transport mode shift cost savings, and economic benefits accounted for 25.58%, 26.45%, and 47.97%, respectively, of the total benefits attributed to this option (see Table C2.2).

However, as we shall argue below, it would be more appropriate to attribute zero "economic benefits" to the proposed Trans Labrador Highway options, even if we are prepared to accept FGA's estimates of "highway user benefits" and "transport mode shift cost savings." The basic reasons are these: FGA's methodology involved double-counting of benefits; it failed to attribute opportunity costs to the increases in activities it predicted; and it failed to avoid what is described in the Treasury Board's *Benefit-Cost Analysis Guide* as "one of the oldest fallacies in economics" (1976, p. 24).

FGA's Method

FGA separated economic benefits into what it called *direct*, *indirect*, and *induced* benefits. For *direct* benefits, FGA forecasted the impact of a Trans Labrador Highway on the following sectors: mining, fishing, fish processing, the freshwater fishery, forestry, tourism, trade, construction, hydroelectricity, other services and utilities, and government. For each, it calculated "business development" and "business improvement" benefits. *Indirect* benefits were calculated by applying sector-specific multipliers to the direct benefits in each sector. To calculate *induced* benefits, the sum of direct and indirect benefits was multiplied by a factor of 0.53. The sum of direct + indirect + induced benefits was then calculated for each sector. Finally, these sums were totalled to arrive at FGA's total "economic benefits" of the project to Labrador.

For example, attributable to the *Coastal Access* option, FGA (1993, p. 5.73) calculated that there would be direct benefits of $14,818,000 a year as a result of business development in the forestry sector. It then multiplied this figure by 1.22 to calculate $18,143,000 of indirect business development benefits, thus bringing the total of direct and indirect business development benefits to $32,961,000 a year. FGA then calculated savings to this sector because of business improvements to be $1,256,000 a year, thus raising the total of business development and business improvement savings in this sector to $34,217,000 a year. This figure was then multiplied by 0.53 to calculate induced benefits of $18,135,000 a year. Summing direct, indirect, and induced benefits yielded a total of $52,352,000 in "economic benefits" each year to the forestry sector. The same procedure was carried out for each sector. From all of this, FGA calculated that total economic benefits to Labrador would be $125,068,000 a year under the *Coastal Access* option.

Of course, the use of multipliers is more than questionable.[11] Moreover, there is more than the use of multipliers that is incorrect about FGA's approach. Before we turn to more general problems of methodology, it would be instructive to examine FGA's treatment of selected sectors of the Labrador economy.[12] As FGA concentrated on its preferred option, the *Coastal Access* option, so shall we.

Mining   FGA determined that a Trans Labrador Highway would not have an effect on current mining activities but would generate more exploration. Indeed, it assumed that a highway would induce increased expenditures (business development) of $2 million a year, and that the value-added of this in Labrador would be $1 million a year. Note that FGA counted this *expenditure* as a benefit. Regarding business improvement benefits, FGA stated:

> New exploration attributed to the road, added to the historical average level of $1.07 million gives a new annual level of about $3.0 million. Based on estimates of reduced mobilization/demobilization and drilling costs, average savings of 25 percent on exploration costs overall have been assumed, leading to an annual savings estimate of $750,000. (1993, p. 5.51)

Aside from the specific way it made the calculation, note that FGA did not state the basis for this estimate. Presumably, these cost savings would arise because employees would be able to travel from one point to another faster by the highway, and because supplies would be cheaper if freight firms passed on their transportation cost savings to their customers. Both of these, however, were accounted for in FGA's calculations of "highway user benefits" (as travel time savings) and/or "transport mode shift cost savings."

For example, assume that FGA's analyses of "highway user benefits" and "transport mode shift cost savings" were correct. Now, suppose that the price of a particular product a mining firm requires is $150 per unit, including a $70 shipping cost, when it must be transported by air or sea. Suppose, also, that because of a highway, the cost of shipping this product falls to $20. Here the difference in transportation costs, $50, would be counted in the FGA study as "transport mode shift cost savings." Now assume that because transportation costs have decreased, the mining firm can now purchase this good for $130 per unit, $20 less than before (although any deduction in price up to $50 would serve the purpose of this example). That is, the trucking firm passes along $20 of its $50 cost saving to the mining firm. Using FGA's methodology, this $20 saving would also be counted as a benefit, yielding a total benefit of $70 ($50 in "transport mode shift cost savings" to the trucking firm and a price saving of $20 to the mining firm). This, however, is not correct. What has happened is that the benefit to the trucking firm is now only $30 because of the $20 cost saving it passed along to the mining firm.

Summing the trucking and mining firms' benefits—$30 and $20, respectively—yields the $50 benefit that has already been counted as a "transport mode shift cost saving." How these savings are distributed is not relevant to the analysis, and to count the mining firm's $20 benefit separately is to ignore the fact that it has already been counted in another category, "transport mode shift cost savings."

FGA's methodological error was that it double-counted benefits. It took a benefit that had already been counted as a transport mode shift cost saving and redistributed it among firms. The price (or cost) saving had already been accounted for elsewhere. New benefits had not been generated; rather, old ones were redistributed and thus counted twice.

The same is true for consumer goods. For example, suppose the price of a can of beans in Cartwright falls from $2 to $1.25 because transportation costs fall by 75¢ per can. We could count this as a 75¢ per can time savings to the trucking company, a 75¢ per can saving to the wholesaler, a 75¢ per can saving to the retailer, or a 75¢ per can saving to the customer who eats the beans—as long as the benefit is attributed to *only one party*. Otherwise, it would be possible to engage in double-, triple-, or even quadruple-counting of the same benefit. The point is that the same benefit can appear in many guises, but it is still only one benefit.

Forestry A Trans Labrador Highway would make forests between Happy Valley-Goose Bay and the Straits more accessible to harvesters. FGA stated:

> The annual value of the pulpwood at dockside, plus the cost of loading the vessels, would be approximately $30 million, and the value attributed to fuelwood, plus spending on silvaculture and road building would add in the order of $1.0 to $1.5 million. In this sector, a factor of approximately 0.5 is used to estimate the value-added in the Labrador economy, so that ultimately benefits of about $16 million per year would be attributed to the road. Virtually all these benefits are in the category of business development. (1993, p. 5.55)

However, we note that FGA's notion that forestry in this area is economically viable flies in the face of government- and non-government-commissioned reports. (See Silva [1993] for a survey of these studies.) As well, it has not been substantiated that harvesting these forests would be environmentally sound. These realities aside, another basic economic point is that FGA counted transportation and loading expenditures as benefits rather than as costs. Moreover, FGA counted the value of the lumber as a benefit without assessing any cost to the resources that would have to be allocated to harvesting it. When lumber firms hire labour and machinery to harvest a forest, very real costs are incurred. FGA attributed zero opportunity cost to these inputs, and this is not valid.

Tourism FGA stated: "Estimating the possible effects of the completed TLH on tourism is an exercise in futurism" (1993, p. 5.57). Even so, it did forecast tourist movements into, out of, and within Labrador arising from a Trans Labrador Highway under the categories of "personal and pleasure," "business," and "passing through." The total numbers for nonresidents and residents are shown in Table C2.10.[13]

Regarding the "economic benefit" attributable to increased tourism because of a Trans Labrador Highway, FGA concluded:

> On the above basis, our estimate for the net increase in expenditure, ultimately attributable to the TLH by travellers and visitors in all areas of the food and accommodations sector, is $13.4 million per year and the value-added in Labrador is $9 million. (1993, p. 5.63)

How FGA reached that conclusion is our concern. The following excerpts from the FGA study summarize its assumptions.

A. Regarding Island resident travel to Labrador: "An expenditure of $155 is assumed per trip of average three days' duration, for a blend of VFR [Visiting Friends and Relatives] and other Island residents touring by car for personal reasons and pleasure. Two thirds of this time and expenditure would be in Labrador" (1993, p. 5.60).

B. Regarding Labrador resident travel outside Labrador: "It is assumed that [these residents] will spend an average of $30 each either on the outward or return legs of their trip on food and/or accommodations while travelling within Labrador, and that [they] previously would have spent nothing" (1993, p. 5.62).

TABLE C2.10   Incremental Annual Tourism Expenditures in Labrador

Origin	Number of Visitors	Annual Expenditure
Nonresident	18,650	$5,150,000
Resident: Island	28,000	$2,480,000
Resident: Labrador Out (net)	10,000	$210,000
Resident: Labrador Internal (net)	268,500	$4,100,000
Total: Resident + Non-Resident	325,150	$11,940,000
Outfitting		$1,500,000
Grand Total		$13,440,000

C. Regarding Labrador resident travel within Labrador: "On the above assumptions, net new spending in the food and accommodations sector within Labrador, by Labrador residents, including travellers leaving Labrador and returning, would be $4,300,000 per year" (1993, p. 6.62).

D. Regarding the outfitting (wilderness camp) industry: "Based on the current total level of outfitters' business as $2–$3 million, the TLH could engender $1.5 million of additional business annually" (1993, p. 5.63).

Consider statement A. Island residents are expected to travel to Labrador and to spend money on food, accommodation, and the like, and these expenditures are designated as benefits by FGA. Will innkeepers and restaurateurs not incur any costs when they serve these visitors? The point is that revenues may increase, but so will costs. No accounting has been made of these incremental costs.

Consider now statements B and C. The expenditures of Labrador residents on trips in or through Labrador are counted as benefits. Thus, if a family from Goose Bay eats in a restaurant in Red Bay on its way to or from the ferry, the cost of the meal will be counted as a benefit of the Trans Labrador Highway. This raises the same question regarding the cost of food in Labrador. And it raises another: Do people in Labrador not eat when they stay at home? Surely if restaurant expenditures in Red Bay increase, expenditures on groceries or at restaurants in Goose Bay or elsewhere will decrease. The only impact of the highway is that it may determine *where* one eats, not *whether* one eats. This expenditure is irrelevant to the analysis, as it is made whether the highway is constructed or not.

Regarding statement D, it is our understanding that one of the principal attractions of wilderness camps in Labrador is that they are isolated. A Trans Labrador Highway, obviously, would make them less isolated and thus less attractive.

Government   FGA noted that added government expenditures on health care, transportation, justice, wildlife, forestry, education, fisheries, and tourism would be required if a Trans Labrador Highway were built. These expenditures would be for additional personnel, services, and supplies. FGA concluded:

Total annual wages and salaries for these staff additions are estimated at about $2.5 million and services and supplies, assumed to be supplied from within Labrador, add an additional $1.1 million per year. (1993, p. 5.71)

As we noted above regarding environmental costs, counting these expenditures as benefits does not make sense. FGA acknowledged that additional wildlife officials would be required in order to mitigate the adverse impacts of the highway on wildlife populations. This is a direct cost—not a benefit at all. If extra government monies are spent on wildlife protection, less will be available for expenditure on other goods and services. In other words, there is an opportunity cost involved. To count these expenditures as benefits, and then apply multipliers to them, is quite extraordinary.

The same applies to the extra law enforcement officials and other personnel who would be required, to deal with the inevitable increase in collisions between caribou and moose and cars. Yet not only did FGA count their salaries as benefits rather than as costs, but it counted multiples of their salaries as benefits.

This point is worth emphasizing. Suppose the project results in the need to hire extra wildlife enforcement or police officers, who would be paid annual salaries of, say, $40,000 a year. Instead of counting this item as a cost, FGA's study treated it as a $142,576 annual benefit for the duration of the project. Note that the *Coastal Access* option is expected to cost $100 million per year for each of 23 years. If we were to accept FGA's method, hiring approximately 700 officers at $40,000 each per year annually would generate an annual benefit great enough to pay for the highway. We hope that this does not make sense to you!

Summary: Economic Benefits

FGA's calculation of "economic benefits" was not correct. Some of the benefits it attributed to a Trans Labrador Highway (such as lower prices) were already accounted for either as "highway user benefits" or as "transport mode shift cost savings," and thus were double-counted. In other matters, such as providing meals and accommodation to nonresident travellers and building new gas stations, the benefit was calculated as the expenditure on the item, as if providing these goods, services, and structures would entail no resource cost. And the matter of counting the expenditure of a resident on restaurant meals as a benefit ignored the fact that expenditures elsewhere in the Labrador economy would have to fall. Still other matters, such as expenditures on the extra wildlife, fisheries, and police personnel that a highway would require, would be direct costs of the project, yet were counted as benefits. Moreover, treating the multiplier effects of these extra expenditures as benefits is not acceptable (See Chapter 7).

Therefore, it would be appropriate to ignore the "economic benefits" that FGA has attributed to the Trans Labrador Highway project. Of course, there is a question of why they were included in the first place. To this, the Treasury Board suggests the following answer:

> The continued enthusiasm for secondary benefits and multipliers in benefit-cost analyses may represent a misplaced endeavour to incorporate effects which are entirely relevant in a different context. We have

seen that these effects are often pecuniary effects, involving transfers of income from some areas and persons to others. We are therefore not indifferent to such pecuniary effects, although they are irrelevant in estimating what the implications of a project are for *total* production and consumption opportunities in the economy (that is, the efficiency effects of a project). (1976, p. 24)

SUMMARY

We have identified a number of fundamental methodological errors, errors of omission, and errors of commission in FGA's analysis of the proposed Trans Labrador Highway. Indeed, it is evident from Tables C2.3 and C2.4 that even if only "economic benefits" were removed from the calculus—as they should be—the net present value of every option would be negative at both discount rates used; this signifies that the project should not proceed because it is not economically viable. We may conclude that FGA's estimates of costs understated true costs, and that its estimates of highway user benefits and transport mode shift benefits were overstated; this weakens still further any claims that the Trans Labrador Highway project is economically viable.

Still, sorting through this kind of analysis is instructive. Returning to FGA's terms of reference quoted at the beginning of this chapter, we observe that the project proponent asked for both an economic impact study and a cost-benefit analysis. We wonder if confusion between the two was a major cause of the methodological problems noted in this chapter. We discuss this matter in a broader context in the conclusion of this book.

POSTSCRIPT

According to the *Canadian Press* (1997b), Premier Brian Tobin of the Province of Newfoundland and Labrador announced on April 3, 1997, that the federal government had agreed to provide the province with $340 million to construct a highway through southern Labrador. Part of this highway would pass through an area that is part of a land claim by the Innu Nation.

ENDNOTES

1. FGA prepared its report in association with the following consultants: Atlantic Consulting Economists Limited, Hector Blake Associates, Labrador Consultants Limited, LeDrew Fudge and Associates Limited, and R.J. Noah & Associates Limited.

2. Adapted from the cover page of FGA's "Condensed Final Report."

3. FGA also calculated net present values and benefit-cost ratios for Newfoundland, Quebec, and Canada as a whole.

4. The author expresses his thanks to Wade Locke of Memorial University of Newfoundland for permitting inclusion of this version. The original critique was prepared for Innu Nation.

5. We can find no statement of existing or latent demand traffic figures in the FGA document. Nevertheless, the report does contain graphs (FGA's Figure 5.1), from which we have made approximations.

6. FGA, Table 5.3, page 5.14.

7. FGA, Table 5.5. page 5.16.

8. FGA, Table 5.4, page 5.15.

9. FGA, Table 5.7, page 5.18.

10. Letter of June 28, 1993, written by the Honourable Jean Corbeil. The name of the addressee has been erased.

11. FGA uses multipliers in this analysis, but did not in its 1987 economic evaluation of the Northumberland Strait Fixed Crossing project (see Case 1). Note that high unemployment is often used as a justification for counting secondary effects, but the unemployment rate in Labrador is much less than on P.E.I.

12. For a more thorough examination of FGA's treatment of all sectors, see Locke & Townley (1993).

13. FGA, Table 5.16, page 5.64.

THE RAFFERTY-ALAMEDA DAMS PROJECT

INTRODUCTION

The Rafferty-Alameda Dams project, like the Northumberland Strait Fixed Crossing, Great Whale, Trans Labrador Highway, and Oldman River Dam projects, is one of the most controversial in recent times. Below we describe the cost-benefit analysis of this project. Except where noted, the discussion is based on the following four parts of Rafferty-Alameda Project: Environmental Impact Statement, prepared by the Souris Basin Development Authority (Regina, 1987): Executive Summary, Chapter I—Project Description, Chapter II—Social and Economic Characteristics, and Chapter III—Benefit Cost Analysis.[1]

A number of legal challenges and provincial–federal disputes arose because of this project, and these have international and interprovincial dimensions. Although some critics have noted that this project does not make economic sense, the major battles were fought over the environmental impacts of the project.

It is not our intention to stray from the economic aspects of the project into the legal ones. While we point out a number of shortcomings, it is not our objective to offer an exhaustive critique. The cost-benefit analysis of this project is presented so that readers can reflect—especially in light of Chapter 7—on the methodology employed by the Souris Basin Development Authority, the proponent of the project.

This focus on basic methodology is also dictated by the content of the report. A major problem confronting reviewers of this project's cost-benefit analysis is that the proponent failed to explain clearly how it derived many of the benefits and costs used in this study.

THE PROJECT

The setting of the Rafferty-Alameda Dams project is shown on Map C3.1.

The 700-kilometre-long Souris River originates in Saskatchewan north of Weyburn and flows in a southeasterly direction past Weyburn and Estevan before crossing the international border just south of Oxbow. In the United States the river continues in the same direction until just southeast of Minot, North Dakota, where it turns north and recrosses the border, to join the Assiniboine River southeast of Brandon, Manitoba. The 29,600-square-kilometre Saskatchewan portion of the Souris River Basin—the project area—consists of the Souris River and its three main tributaries: Moose Mountain Creek, Long Creek, and Roughbark Creek.

Principal economic activities in this area include oilfield development, mining, and agriculture, although the quality of the agricultural land is low. The population in the Saskatchewan portion of this area in 1986 was 29,361.

MAP C3.1

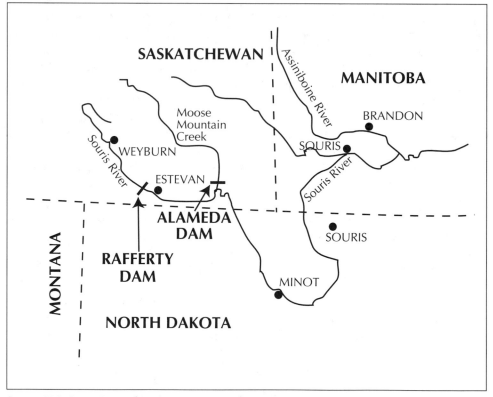

Source: U.S. Army Corps of Engineers Report, July 1988
Bernard Bennell, *The Globe and Mail*, (Canadian Press, 1991b)

Although groundwater is plentiful in the region, it is of poor quality. The Souris and its tributaries are the basin's sources of surface water. This area is considered dry at best and drought-stricken at worst; at the same time, it is prone to floods roughly one year in five because of spring runoff.

In February 1986 the government of Saskatchewan announced its plans to proceed with a multi-objective project, to consist of the following:

1. The Rafferty Dam and Reservoir, to provide the following: cooling water for a 300-megawatt thermal power unit at the Shand Generating Plant; flood protection for the communities of Estevan, Roche Percée, and Oxbow in Saskatchewan and for Minot, North Dakota; irrigation for 5,000 acres by means of downstream channelization; municipal water supplies; and water-based recreation facilities consisting of parks as well as sites for about 175 cottages adjacent to the reservoir. Construction was to begin in April 1988 and to be completed by October 1990.

2. A diversion channel from the Rafferty Reservoir to the existing Boundary Dam and Reservoir (on Long Creek). Construction work on this channel was to begin in the spring of 1989 and to be completed later that same year.

3. The Alameda Dam and Reservoir, to provide recreation (including about 100 cottage sites) and the potential to irrigate 4,000 upstream acres and 3,000 downstream acres. The same reservoir would be used to satisfy Saskatchewan's water apportionment obligation to the United States in accordance with an international treaty. This part of the project was to be constructed between the spring of 1989 and the fall of 1990.

The Souris Basin Development Authority was formed as a Crown corporation to act as the project's proponent.

The Rafferty part of the project would be built 6 kilometres northeast of Estevan and would consist of a zoned, earth-filled dam, a concrete service spillway, a low-level outlet, an emergency outlet, and a reservoir. The reservoir would have a full supply level (FSL) of 550.5 metres and a maximum flood level (MFL) of 554.0 metres, but would be operated initially at 549.5 metres so as to allow extraction of some oil reserves that would otherwise be inundated.[2] At MSL the reservoir would have a surface area of 15,320 acres, be 57 kilometres long with a maximum width of 1.2 kilometres, and have a volume of 443,000 cubic decametres.[3]

The Alameda site would be 14 kilometres north of Oxbow on Moose Mountain Creek and would consist of a zoned, earth-filled dam, a concrete service spillway, a low-level outlet, and a reservoir. The reservoir would have an FSL of 574 metres and an MFL of 589 metres. At MFL the reservoir would occupy 5,313 acres and have a volume of 130,000 cubic decametres. Both dams would have an expected life of between 50 and 100 years.

Construction of the reservoirs would entail the loss of 10,100 acres of natural grazing land, 3,126 acres of hay lands, and 1,468 acres of cultivated land. Inundation would also involve the loss of some critical wildlife habitat, a long-established church camp, and the Dr. Mainprize Regional Park (to be relocated to the Rafferty Reservoir). The reservoirs would also inundate several roads and bridges and make it necessary to divert power lines. Finally, they would flood several archaeological sites that had not yet been catalogued.

COSTS

Table C3.1 summarizes the project's capital costs, to be borne by the province of Saskatchewan, expressed as present values in 1986 dollars. Omitted from this summary is the capital cost of downstream channelization. The proponent estimated this cost to be $3 million, but concluded that

TABLE C3.1   Summary of Capital Costs to Be Incurred by the Government of Saskatchewan (1986 dollars)

Site	Alameda	Rafferty	Total
AGRICULTURE:			
Land lost	4,310,000	6,600,000	10,910,000
Dugouts & fencing	100,000	400,000	500,000
DAM:			
Dam construction	28,350,000	23,940,000	52,290,000
Diversion channel		9,525,000	9,525,000
Valley clearing	100,000	300,000	400,000
Engineering & administration	2,677,500	2,677,500	5,355,000
RECREATION:			
Dr. Mainprize Park relocation		1,720,000	1,720,000
Recreation site development	1,200,000	2,690,000	3,890,000
MITIGATION:			
Oil well mitigation	4,055,000	18,165,000	22,220,000
Power line relocations	600,000	300,000	900,000
Transportation	2,885,000	9,240,000	12,125,000
Heritage site mitigation	520,000	780,000	1,300,000
Water supplies	60,000	365,000	425,000
Fisheries		650,500	650,500
Wildlife		3,789,500	3,789,500
TOTALS	44,857,500	81,142,500	126,000,000

Sources: Table 12, Chapter III, p. 6.27, and Chapter I, p. 37.

more analysis of this item was required. Also omitted is the cost of mitigation associated with the inundation of a bible camp located at the Alameda site.

It is not clear whether the proponent considered additional or all relevant costs, nor is it obvious how it derived some of these figures. Cost summaries appear in different parts of the report, but ascertaining whether they are consistent with each other is a daunting task, because they are not identical. Although not stated, it would appear that figures in Table C3.1 were calculated using a discount rate of 5%. Under these informational constraints, we present next a description of capital and operating costs for an assumed 50-year time horizon.

Agricultural

The cost per acre of converting dryland into irrigated land was calculated for two scenarios depending on whether the irrigated Alameda uplands would be used for grain production or for livestock. These capital costs included expenditures on the farm machinery, vehicles, buildings, and storage sites that would be required to handle the increased production. Cost per acre for the upland grain scenario was assessed to be $387.10, and for the livestock scenario, $293.03. The cost of converting any lowland acre from dry to irrigated was calculated to be $355.12. The breakdown of this calculation is shown in Table C3.2.

Annual operating and maintenance costs, excluding on-farm costs for the project, were assumed to be $184,400 for the 4,000 upland acres and $9,900 for the 8,000 lowland acres.

Some agricultural land would be flooded by the reservoirs or taken over by service and recreational facilities. The distribution of the acreage lost in these ways is shown in Table C3.3.

In calculating the value of this lost agricultural land, the proponent estimated the current average annual net return (over current farm operating costs) from the 15,200 acres to be $6.68 per acre. It then calculated:

> If this return were expected over the 50-year life of the project, at a discount rate of 5%, the present value per acre for the lost agricultural land is $122.00. The present value should reflect the current economic market value of the average acre of land lost to agriculture. Given the combinations of valley slopes and better bottom lands, this appears to be a reasonable estimate. (III, p. 6.20)

That is, the proponent used the capitalized value of farm profits per acre as defined, to calculate the value of the land lost. It is not explained why the proponent did not take a more direct approach: that is, surveying real estate agents in the area to determine the current market value of each parcel lost. Also, although some 1,960 already-irrigated acres would be inundated, it appears that no cost was attributed to this loss, because "creation of the reservoirs will relocate irrigable acreage, rather than decrease them" (III, p. 6.20).

TABLE C3.2 Marginal Cost of Converting an Acre of Dryland into Irrigated Land by Economic Development Scenario ($/Acre)

Scenario	Farm Machinery	Buildings & Storage	Vehicles	Total
Grain	261.97	73.73	51.40	387.10
Livestock	156.08	66.84	70.11	293.03
Lowlands	225.97	71.39	57.76	355.12

Source: Table 5, Chapter III, Appendix 2, p. 13.

TABLE C3.3 Agricultural Acreage Lost

Reason	Acres Lost
Rafferty Reservoir	9,670
Alameda Reservoir	4,830
Dr. Mainprize Park	320
Rafferty recreation sites	160
Alameda recreation sites	160
Services and miscellaneous	60
TOTAL	15,200

Source: Table 11, Chapter III, p. 6.19

The other expenditures shown in this category relate to accommodating livestock grazing on land bordering the reservoirs. Fencing would be required to keep the cattle out of the reservoirs proper. (A dugout consists of a channel from a reservoir to a constructed watering hole for cattle.) The (joint) capital cost of these items is shown in the table. Their annual costs would be $10,000 and $40,000 for the Alameda and Rafferty reservoirs, respectively.

Recreation

About $600,000 would be required to replace the deteriorating facilities of the Dr. Mainprize Regional Park; a further $90,000 per year would be needed to prevent further depreciation. Capital costs to rehabilitate this park would amount to $920,000, with a further $138,000 per year in operating and maintenance expenditures.

Recreation sites would be developed and operated at both reservoir sites. The one at the Rafferty Reservoir would cost $2,609,000 to develop and $403,500 per year to operate and maintain. The corresponding costs at the Alameda Reservoir would be $1,200,000 and $180,000 per year.

Cottage sites would be developed on the shores of both reservoirs, although no costs associated with this activity are shown in Table C3.1. Land development and cottage construction costs, respectively, were assumed to be $7,000 and $30,000 per site for a total capital expenditure of $10,175,000. Annual operating and maintenance costs were calculated to be $1,100 per cottage.

Mitigation Expenditures

The project would have a number of impacts requiring mitigation (see Table C3.1). Both reservoirs would inundate existing oil wells, and the placement of the dams and reservoirs would make it necessary to relocate and reconfigure power lines. Another impact is that some (water) wells would be contaminated. These costs are shown in Table C3.1.

As a result of the project, some roads would have to be closed and others upgraded. Capital costs associated with this impact are shown in Table C3.1. The associated annual costs would be $29,000 and $92,000 for the Alameda and Rafferty sites, respectively.

At both sites are aboriginal campsites that would be inundated by the reservoirs. Archaeological work is proceeding, but at too slow a pace to protect the area's cultural heritage. The purpose of the expenditure in this category in Table C3.1 is to accelerate this research.

Construction of the Rafferty Dam and Reservoir would damage existing wildlife habitats and local fishing. The proponent listed the total of these costs ($4,440,000) as mitigation expenditures in Chapter I, but listed the same total expenditure as being for "fish and wildlife enhancement" in Chapter III.[4]

The proponent did not explain how it calculated the dollar estimates of these mitigation expenditures, and there is obvious disagreement regarding the impact of the project on wildlife especially. According to Environment Canada, a federal department, "Unless corrective measures are taken, the twin dams near Estevan, Sask., could cause the loss of 30,700 migratory birds annually."[5] Others have called the project "an environmental disaster,"[6] and elsewhere it is reported that proposals by the U.S. Army Corps of Engineers to build a dam on the Souris in North Dakota to afford Minot flood protection were blocked in the 1970s by protests from property owners and environmentalists. Note that a moratorium on dams in this area (in the United States) was declared in the mid-1980s.[7]

Dam and Reservoir Construction

In this category the proponent listed total engineering and administration costs. In Table C3.1 we have simply divided them equally between the two sites. In addition to the capital costs shown, annual operating and maintenance costs are $107,000 and $156,000 for the Alameda and Rafferty sites, respectively.

Irrigation System and On-farm Costs

Table C3.4 shows the expenditures that would be required to irrigate the 12,000 acres in the project area that are considered suitable for this kind of development. Capital costs for irrigation development (including main pump stations, distribution systems, and on-farm irrigation equipment) were assessed at $10,587,000 for the 4,000 Alameda upland acres to be irrigated and at $7,173,000 for the 8,000 acres (total) downstream from the dams.

TABLE C3.4   Capital Cost Estimates for Irrigation Development

Location	Alameda Upland	Lowlands
Area (acres)	4,000	8,000
Main pump station ($)	3,604,000	1,312,000
Irrigation systems ($)	4,185,000	
On-farm irrigation equipment ($)	2,798,000	5,861,000
TOTAL ($)	10,587,000	7,173,000

Source: Table 4, Chapter III, Appendix 2, p. 12.

BENEFITS

Agriculture

Irrigation would increase the productive capabilities of 12,000 acres of land: 5,000 acres below the Rafferty Reservoir, 3,000 acres below the Alameda Reservoir, and 4,000 acres above the Alameda Reservoir. The magnitude of the benefits to be gleaned from this irrigation would depend on how farmers employed the 3,000 upland acres. Alternative-use scenarios are shown in Table C3.5.

In assigning dollar values to the extra production that irrigation would generate, the next step the proponent took was to make the price and yield assumptions shown in Table C3.6.

The yields in Table C3.6 (presumably per acre) were based on 100% water availability. The justification for this assumption was as follows: "It is assumed that the farm operators are able to anticipate [any] water shortage and alter their planting and crop management strategies to account for it" (III, p. 6.7). We find this odd. If this were true, presumably farmers could also predict water surpluses—flooding. But if local farmers can do this, why does the flooding of the Souris cause so much damage? After all, fore-warned is supposed to be fore-armed.

Regarding the assumed prices, the proponent states:

These prices are based on mid-range historical commodity prices in 1984 dollars. The prices were derived to reflect long-range prices over the life of the project. Agricultural commodity prices have continued

TABLE C3.5   Expected Use of Irrigated Acreage by Percentage

Use	Grain Scenario	Livestock Scenario	Lowlands
Forages and pasture	14	27	28
Wheat	53	36	45
Other cereals	9	24	5
Oilseeds	14	5	14
Specialty & vegetable	6	6	0
Summer fallow	4	2	8
TOTAL	100	100	100

Source: Table 3, Chapter III, p. 6.6.

TABLE C3.6   Assumed Agricultural Commodity Yields and Prices

Commodity	Yield	Price ($)
Soft wheat (bu)	76	4.90
Barley (bu)	87	2.60
Canola (bu)	39	7.50
Alfalfa (ton)	3.95	87.00
Slaughter beef (cwt)		79.00

Source: Table 4, Chapter III, p. 6.7.

to feel downward pressure and the agricultural community appears to have become more pessimistic. In light of this pessimism, 1984 commodity dollar values were not indexed to 1986 dollars as per the other components of this analysis. (III, p. 6.6)

Increased production results in higher revenues and costs. The costs used in the analysis were "cash" costs, which excluded capital costs. Using this definition, net revenues were "a measure of return for family and operator labour, management and capital investment."[8] Returns per acre were calculated for the two possible production scenarios; these are shown in Table C3.7. Throughout, no attempt was made to calculate shadow prices.

Table C3.7   Irrigation Benefits ($ per acre)

Dollar Item	River Valley Lands	Alameda Lands Grain Scenario	Alameda Uplands Livestock Scenario
Gross revenue	354	315	596
Cash costs	238	189	438
Return over cash costs	116	126	158
Return over cash costs including government subsidies for irrigation	168	178	212

Source: Table 5, Chapter III, p. 6.8.

Recreational Benefits

Table C3.8 shows, by site and activity, what the number of visitor-days per year would be for the project area after all facilities had been developed. The proponent states: "All recreational and wildlife enhancement benefits are measured by the increase in visitor days" (III, App. 6, p. 28). However, this would not appear to be so. Although the figures used—55,000, 1,500, and 3,000 visitor days for the Dr. Mainprize Regional Park, nonconsumptive use (sightseeing), and hunting, respectively—are clearly projected increases over pre-project uses in these specific categories; but it is not clear that they represent increases in overall recreational activities in Saskatchewan. If these visitors were drawn from other sites or activities, they would represent a *reallocation* of recreational consumption, not an increase. Similarly, the figures for the other five categories (Rafferty South Recreation through Alameda Cottaging) do not show overall increases. Although it is true that the figures shown for each site are increases, this is only because none of

TABLE C3.8 Recreation Days per Annum After Full Development

Site or Activity	Visitor Days
Dr. Mainprize Park	80,000
Rafferty South recreation	120,000
Alameda recreation	70,000
Dr. Mainprize cottaging	15,000
Rafferty cottaging	37,000
Alameda cottaging	30,000
Nonconsumptive use	1,500
Hunting	3,000
Total	356,500

Source: Table 6, Chapter III, p. 6.12.

those sites existed before the project. It may well be that some or most of these recreation days were spent at other existing sites or in other activities. Realistically, the extent to which people can trade off leisure and nonleisure activities would be more limited than what the proponent assumed.

Clearly, the analysis failed to distinguish between diverted and generated visitors. This is not to say that the new facilities would bestow no benefit on diverted recreationalists—after all, these people could have continued to choose their pre-project activities. By rejecting those in favour of project-related activities, they would be signalling an increase in utility, and their benefit would be the extra amount they would be willing to pay for these utility-enhancing facilities.

How the value of an outdoor recreation day is calculated in the study is quite confusing. When we sum daily cash expenditures and an imputed daily capital (recreational equipment) cost from survey data at nearby sites, we find that $21 per day is the amount that people spend on average for a recreation day. The proponent notes: "Expenditures per visitor day for various activities, sales of recreational equipment, travel costs, and hunting and fishing license sales are all used as indicators of the public's value or willingness to pay for recreational facilities" (III, p. 6.12). As such, this figure seems to be an estimate of the maximum an average person would be willing to pay for a recreation day—his or her gross benefit.

However, this same figure, $21, also shows up as a net benefit in the study. The proponent, citing other studies, assumes a gross benefit of $39 per day, subtracts the above $21 expenditure, and adds a $3 daily park entrance fee to be levied, thus calculating a net benefit of $21 per recreation day.

There are problems with this method regardless of which $21 is which. If a visit to one of the project's recreation sites is truly generated, one would wish to calculate the maximum an individual is willing to pay for that recreation day. But if a visit to one of these sites comes at the sacrifice of an existing recreational activity or a visit to an existing site, one would want to measure the extra amount a person would be willing to pay to visit the new site. It is unclear whether the $21 per day used measures either of these. (It is not clear whether the proponent meant to take the *party by party* or the *change in total benefits minus change in total resource costs* approach.)

Benefits to Thermal Generating Plants

It is cheaper to operate a water-cooled thermal generator than an air-cooled one. Therefore, the project would result in a resource saving at the Shand Generating Plant. (Moreover, surface water from the reservoir would not require the same expensive treatment before use as pumped groundwater would.) Although it may be possible for water from the project to cool both power units proposed for this plant, it was assumed that the second unit would be air-cooled. The benefit figure used for this cost saving was based on the following:

> As the air-cooled process is less efficient, the Saskatchewan Power Corporation has discounted to present value, the savings in coal fuel, considering all other costs, which would accrue back to a water-cooled power unit over an air-cooled one for an assumed future power demand scenario. Saskatchewan Power Corporation estimates the value in savings of the one technology over the other for one power unit is $20.3 million dollars. (III, p. 6.14)

Flood Control

According to the report, flooding in this basin results in lost production as well as damage to dwellings and other structures. Based on average damage data, an annual cost saving in Saskatchewan attributable to the project was calculated to be $139,200. Similarly, the project would reduce flooding in the United States, especially near Minot, N.D. Given this benefit, the American Congress allocated US$41.1 million to the project, and this amount was assumed to be the present value of their benefit from flood control.

DIRECT COSTS AND BENEFITS

Table C3.9 provides a summary of the above costs and benefits measured in 1986 dollars. Net present values and benefit-cost ratios are shown for discount rates of 5% and 10%. The proponent notes that the "quantified benefits and costs indicate a direct benefit-cost ratio of slightly less than unity" (III, p. 7.2). Nevertheless, the proponent did not recommend that the project be rejected on the basis of these negative net present values. The proponent's arguments in favour of proceeding rested on a number of questionable grounds.

Table C3.9   Direct Benefits and Costs of the Souris River Development Project

Category	Present Value (5%)	Present Value (10%)
BENEFITS		
Agriculture – Grain scenario	68,140,000	32,168,000
Agriculture – Livestock scenario	96,574,000	45,591,000
Recreation & tourism	62,695,000	20,691,000
Flood control – U.S.A.	60,000,000	60,000,000
Flood control – Canada	2,541,000	1,380,000
Power generation	20,300,000	20,300
TOTAL BENEFITS – Grain scenario	213,676,000	134,539,000
TOTAL BENEFITS – Livestock scenario	242,110,000	147,962,000
COSTS		
Agriculture – Grain scenario	72,550,000	40,594,000
Agriculture – Livestock scenario	96,782,000	51,918,000
Dam construction	56,539,000	44,355,000
Diversion channel construction	10,693,000	9,399,000
Recreation facilities	29,372,000	17,807,000
Water supply	625,000	430,000
Land, fencing, and dugouts	12,118,000	11,622,000
Other items	28,335,000	27,424,000
Administration	3,718,000	3,470,000
TOTAL COSTS – Grain scenario	213,950,000	155,102,000
TOTAL COSTS – Livestock scenario	238,182,000	166,426,000
NET PRESENT VALUE – Grain scenario	-274,000	-20,563,000
NET PRESENT VALUE – Livestock scenario	3,928,000	-18,464,000
BENEFIT-COST RATIO – Grain scenario	0.999	0.867
BENEFIT-COST RATIO – Livestock scenario	1.016	0.889

Source: Table 1, Chapter III, Appendix 8, p. 7.

Precedent

It was argued that similar projects had been constructed despite calculated negative net present values; Lake Diefenbaker was cited as a prime example of this. Of course, if this was the thinking of the analyst at the outset, expending resources to prepare an economic evaluation of this project was also a (justifiable!) waste of resources. We note here the contribution of such thinking to the state of project evaluation in Canada.

Nonquantified Benefits

The proponent notes the existence of nonquantified benefits such as "the relative scarcity of water in the basin, combined with the desire to develop local aesthetics, community pride, community stability and local economic development" (III, p. 7.2). The following two statements were used to promote the notion that these nonquantified benefits would be sufficiently large to justify the project:

- "Water is so critical to the survival and development of an arid region that water inspires an elevated status of emotional or spiritual respect" (III, p. 5.2).
- "Several communities, including Regina, have been stigmatized for their poor water quality. Removal of these stigmas allows a flowering of community pride, which can lead to several important benefits. Releasing the negative self-images associated with drought and poor water quality, especially when those stigmas have become widely acknowledged, releases a great deal of optimism and enthusiasm, through the process of eliminating or reversing a deeply felt weakness" (III, pp. 5.5–5.6).

These references are rather amusing, although we doubt that the analyst meant them to be. Regarding the first, even though we appreciate that the term "holy water" was not used, we note that if water were priced, its price would be relatively high in this area to reflect its scarcity. That is, this benefit would be quantifiable. Indeed, its value in uses such as irrigation has already been counted in the analysis. The second reference is included here partly for comic relief. Although we hesitate to dismiss the role of mass psychoanalysis in cost-benefit analysis, the citizens of southeastern Saskatchewan might wish to take issue with the proponent's diagnosis of their common state of mind.

Some nonquantified costs were also noted:

The construction period will increase traffic flows and the presence of non-locally oriented populations. There are costs to these increased activities such as accelerated deterioration of road services and decreased regard for community values. (III, p. 5.3)

We suppose that "non-locally oriented populations" refers to construction workers working on the project from outside the project area—strangers. Still, if public sector resources such as additional police would have to be diverted to the project sites to deal with increased traffic and the like, this cost could be quantified.

Secondary and Indirect Impacts—Linkages

A *forward linkage* (secondary stemming benefit) is an economic activity that is an indirect result of a project. For example, increased livestock production may lead to the establishment or expansion of meat processing plants. With construction activity in the area, the demand for other goods and services such as restaurant meals and motel rooms may increase. The principal forward linkage noted in this study is the potential for meat processing. Although it is not clear how they were calculated, forward linkages total $3,371,000 for the livestock scenario using a discount rate of 5%, and $1,860,000 using 10%.

Backward linkages (secondary induced benefits) are defined in the report:

> Purchases by the primary beneficiaries, by the forward beneficiaries and for the project development itself are made from the provincial and national economies. A purchase made by one economic entity is a sale for another economic sector. As each sector increases production activities to meet increased sales, the impact of its production oriented purchases are trickled back through its suppliers until virtually all sectors of society are affected. (III, p. 6.29)

For example, increases in grain output would cause the demand for inputs such as herbicides to increase. In turn, demand for the components of herbicides would increase, and so on.

The proponent included as backward linkage expenditures (indirect benefits) arising from

> agriculture on farm and irrigation system development, recreation visitor day expenditures, recreation site removal and redevelopment, cottage development, wildlife enhancement and fishery development, rural water mitigation, Hitchcock community water intake facilities, oil well mitigation, power line and phone line relocation, road mitigation, and administration fees ... dam construction, fencing and reservoir clearing. (III, p. 6.32)

The dollar values of these backward linkages are shown in Table C3.10.

TABLE C3.10   Net Benefits of Backward Linkages

Secondary Net Benefits (backward linkages)	Rate 5%	Rate 10%
Agriculture – Grain scenario	26,197,000	14,780,000
Agriculture – Livestock scenario	41,439,000	21,874,000
Recreation and tourism	748,397,000	15,972,000
Dam construction	37,007,000	27,723,000
Diversion channel	6,678,000	5,868,000
Water supply	273,000	154,000
Recreation facilities	14,644,000	8,816,000
Other	17,680,000	16,769,000
Land lost	−913,000	−496,000
Power generation	−575,000	−575,000
Administration	4,562,000	4,258,000
TOTAL – Grain scenario	153,950,000	93,269,000
TOTAL – Livestock scenario	169,192,000	100,363,000

Source: Table 4, Chapter III, Appendix 8, p. 11.

In Chapter 7 we argued that such benefits—which are akin to multiplier effects—should not be included. Part of the argument against their use is that their values have already been counted in another form. For example, the value of increased farm production has been counted. To count the value-added of all the inputs necessary for increased farm production would be to double-count. Also, it is clear that some of the items counted as benefits are actually costs. In some cases, even if the argument is put forward that the resources used would be otherwise unemployed, it would be necessary to net out all "induced and stemming" opportunity costs from the benefits calculated. In any case, for many of the above activities described as linkages by the proponent, any increase most likely represents a transfer of economic activity only.

Table C3.11 shows benefit-cost ratios when forward and backward linkages are included. According to the proponent:

> The benefit/cost ratio (Direct + Forward + Backward) ... represents the total impact that will be felt through the economy from all direct beneficiaries, from their expenditures from the opportunity to invest in a livestock processing industry and the livestock processing industry's purchases. (III, p. 6.34)

TABLE C3.11   Direct + Forward + Backward Benefit-Cost Ratios

Scenario (discount rate)	Livestock (5%)	Livestock (10%)
Forward linkages	$3,371,000	$1,860,000
NPV (direct & forward)	$7,299,000	−$16,604,000
B/C (direct)	1.031	0.900
B/C (direct & forward & backward Linkages)	1.741	1.503

Source: Table 15, Chapter III, p. 6.33.

Only when these linkages are incorrectly included does the project have the appearance of being economically viable. Moreover, the analyst's statement reveals that the difference between a cost-benefit analysis and an economic impact assessment is not recognized.

TWO OPINIONS

The proponent recommended that the project proceed:

> The quantified benefits and costs indicate a direct benefit/cost ratio of slightly less than unity. Other issues such as indirect benefits beyond the project and non-quantified issues such as the relative scarcity of water in the basin, combined with the desire to develop local aesthetics, community pride, community stability and local economic development opportunities continue to press for continued water development opportunities such as the Rafferty-Alameda project. (III, p. 7.2)

An alternative view is that because of a number of methodological errors and omissions that exaggerate the net benefits of the project, the proponent did not establish the economic viability of the Rafferty-Alameda Dams project. Indeed, using the analyst's own figures, but making only a few corrections, it may be concluded that the project was not viable.

EPILOGUE

The Saskatchewan government proceeded with the Rafferty and Alameda Dams, although construction of both was stalled by various legal battles. The Rafferty Dam was completed first. It was reported that in the summer of 1991 the reservoir amounted to "a puddle behind tons of concrete."[9] Indeed, so little water was captured in the Rafferty Reservoir that groundwater had to be pumped to the Shand Generating Plant at a cost of $2 million per year and treated (unlike surface water) for an additional $18 million before it could be used for cooling.[10]

Critics note that the power generated at Shand costs some four times what it would have cost to import electricity from North Dakota. Questions concerning whether nuclear power could be produced more cheaply, and whether it would be more economical to purchase hydroelectric power from Manitoba, were not addressed by the proponent.[11]

Construction of the Alameda Dam proceeded, but additional construction of berms was required to correct slippage, at a cost of $1.827 million.[12] This extra construction was necessary because the dam was built on clay shale, which lacks shear strength.

Construction costs for the Rafferty-Alameda project ran $58 million over budget. To this should be added the extra costs incurred at the Shand Plant. In the end, the president of the Souris Basin Development Authority stated that "the benefit-cost ratio for the entire project was 0.44."[13] If those who protested the project on environmental grounds prove correct, the realized benefit-cost ratio will turn out to be lower still.

ENDNOTES

1. To avoid riddling the discussion with chapter and page references for many of the facts and dollar figures taken from these documents, we do not provide citations, other than those for direct quotations. However, they are available from the author on request. A short form for citations within the text has been adopted. For example, (III, p. 4.4) means that the passage cited can be found in *Chapter III—Benefit Cost Analysis* on page 4.4.

2. FSL is the maximum level at which the reservoir would normally be operated, and MSL is the maximum elevation before the reservoir would overflow unless the emergency spillway were activated.

3. One cubic decametre is equal to 0.8 acre-feet, 35,314 cubic feet, or 219,969 gallons.

4. See page 37 in Chapter I and Table 12 on page 6 in Chapter III.

5. Canadian Press, "Dams said threat to migratory birds," *The Chronicle-Herald* (Halifax), July 5, 1991a, C15.

6. Canadian Press, "Dam project labelled an environmental disaster," *The Chronicle-Herald*, November 29, 1991c, D15.

7. Bueckert, Dennis, "De Cotret may appeal court decision in Rafferty dam dispute," *The Chronicle-Herald*, November 17, 1990, C8; and, May, Elizabeth, "A tangled tale set on a tiny river," *The Globe and Mail*, November 6, 1990, A17.

8. Chapter III, page 6.7. On the same page, the proponent states: "For the sake of convenience the above measure is estimated as the incremental change under irrigated conditions over and above that under dryland conditions."

9. Editorial, "A dam without water,"*Winnipeg Free Press*, June 29, 1991, p. 6.

10. Doskoch, Bill, "Dams and politics," *The Leader-Post* (Regina), August 21, 1993, A9.

11. In 1991, Saskatchewan was a net importer within Canada of only 1.9% of its electricity consumption and was a net exporter to the United States of 0.14% of what it consumed (Statistics Canada, "Electric power statistics," Catalogue 57-202, 1992).

12. Doskoch, Bill, "Alameda dam slips slightly," *The Leader-Post*, August 7, 1993. A1.

13. Doskoch, Bill, "Dams and politics," *The Leader-Post*, August 21, 1993, A9.

PART V

CONCLUSION

C O N C L U S I O N

ERRORS AND CONFLICTS

INTRODUCTION

The three projects presented in the preceding section were chosen because of the variety of errors made in them. Neither the type of project nor the identity of the analyst was a criterion for inclusion. Similar and additional types of errors can be found in analyses of other dam projects, waste-to-energy projects, health projects, and so on. Although not all cost-benefit analyses conducted in the past many decades to evaluate Canadian projects suffer from major methodological flaws, there are enough like the ones presented that concern is justified. We can only conclude that there is considerable potential for error (and improvement) in the practice of cost-benefit analysis, and note that most of the errors made in actual studies are quite basic.

ACCEPTED PRACTICE?

Fundamental errors, such as treating costs as if they were benefits, double-counting benefits, and counting as benefits items that are not benefits, bias project evaluation in favour of construction. This, of course, may lead to social losses. That the same errors are made over and over again is worrisome.

One cause of *common errors* may be that poor methodology is somewhat self-perpetuating. An analyst who bases his or her approach to an evaluation problem on previous studies, perhaps not realizing that they are flawed, ends up adding to the body of flawed precedents, which come to be viewed as *accepted practice*. It follows that to refute a specific study one may have to refute dozens. It can be difficult to convince decision-makers—who often have little or no background in economics—that errors are, in fact, errors.

ECONOMIC DEBATES

This raises a question: Do economists not disagree about the methodology of cost-benefit analysis? Indeed they do, but far less often than those not wishing to accept an economist's judgment would suggest, and at a theoretical level not readily appreciated by some decision-makers and practitioners.

Areas for debate include (but are not limited to) the following:

- Choice of technique—that is, whether or not cost-benefit analysis is the appropriate tool for investigating a particular project or policy. The crux of this issue usually is the potential impact of the project or policy on relative prices throughout the economy.

- The treatment of (income) distributional impacts. Consideration of this requires an analyst to tread carefully into the intricacies of advanced welfare economics.

- Matters econometric with respect to estimating hedonic prices, calculating social discount rates and shadow wage rates, and so on.

- Options available to deal with aggregating costs and benefits over time. This includes discussions of the opportunity cost of capital, and of the deadweight losses of taxation.[1]

We note that debates on such matters are ongoing, and usually conducted at a level of considerable theoretical sophistication. Readers wishing to go beyond the introductory treatment of cost-benefit analysis presented here will be required to investigate some highly sophisticated topics. That being said, it is one thing for two economists to disagree about the econometric merits of alternative methods for estimating the environmental costs of a proposed project; it is quite another for an analyst to count expenditures incurred to prevent environmental damage as a benefit of a project. Refinements and theoretical advances are important, but they lack the urgency of those violations of basic economic principles which have made their way into the practice of cost-benefit analysis.

THE ECONOMIC PERSPECTIVE

Economists seek to ascertain whether public sector projects and policies will enhance or diminish social well-being. If it is determined that cost-benefit analysis is the appropriate tool, economists apply it well aware of its limitations, especially those which relate to the underlying assumptions vis-à-vis interpersonal comparisons, quantification, aggregation of welfare change, and the potential Pareto improvement criterion. Benefits and costs are identified and measured from a social perspective, with an appreciation that observed prices do not always accurately reflect social marginal benefits and costs.

From an economic perspective, a viable project is one in which scarce resources are used to produce something with a value to society greater than that of the constituent resources. In other words, there is a social dividend.

If benefits and costs are not weighted in any manner, to whom in society benefits flow and costs accrue is irrelevant. A project that is not economically viable will waste scarce resources if it is built; this is a social loss. Again, and importantly, the distribution of costs and benefits across the citizenry would not be relevant in the absence of some explicit weighting scheme.

OTHER PERSPECTIVES

The economic perspective, however, is not the only one. Distributional concerns, with respect to incomes and regions, often outweigh efficiency concerns when final decisions are made. Economists may not worry about who in particular gains or loses if a project proceeds (or doesn't proceed); but many people and decision-makers *do* care. Analysts should be aware of the extent to which alternative perspectives and criteria for project selection conflict with economic ones.

Voting

In the absence of actual compensation to them, losers actually lose, and we should not expect them to accept gladly the dictates of the potential Pareto improvement criterion. Moreover, this criterion is based on relative magnitudes of gains and losses, not numbers of gainers and losers. It is quite conceivable that if "majority rule" were the decision criterion, nonviable projects might be favoured and viable ones rejected by a majority of voters in a plebiscite or referendum.

Plebiscites and referenda are rare in Canada at the federal and provincial levels, although issues of local importance are sometimes included on municipal election ballots. Note that the question asked typically requires a yes-or-no answer, and does not at all resemble the willingness-to-pay or -accept questions used in compensating and/or equivalent variation surveys. (For a description of the plebiscite that was held on Prince Edward Island regarding the fixed link, see the box on the following page.)

Equity

Criticisms that a project should not proceed because its impacts would vary with individuals' income levels ought to be assessed. When the benefits of a project will accrue mainly to the wealthy and the costs will be borne mainly by the poor, this phenomenon will not be accounted for in the net present value of the project unless distributional weights are used.

Trade-offs between efficiency and equity are common in policy-making. Of course, what constitutes an acceptable trade-off is a normative judgment,

The PEI Plebiscite[2]

On January 18, 1988, Prince Edward Islanders were posed the following question: "Do you favour a fixed link crossing between Prince Edward Island and New Brunswick?" 59.4% responded in the affirmative. "Yes" and "No" votes tallied 33,167 and 22,655, respectively.

Two features of the Prince Edward Island plebiscite illustrate the difference between economic and political decision-making. First, we note that not all affected citizens were asked to consider the fixed link question. Given how federal revenues are raised, a national plebiscite might have been more appropriate.

Second, from an economic perspective, these people were not asked the relevant compensating and equivalent variation questions. Pro-link Islanders would have been asked, "What is the maximum you are willing to pay for a fixed link to the mainland?" The question for anti-link Islanders would have been, "What is the minimum you are willing to accept to tolerate a fixed link?" The premier, the late Joe Ghiz, stated, "This is a clear indication of Prince Edward Islanders' support of a fixed link." Obviously, had the compensating variation questions been asked and their answers tallied, the result might have been quite different.

and economists are reluctant to impose their preferences on society. If it is likely that the distributional impacts of a project would be important, an analyst can provide some of the relevant information to decision-makers (assuming that official distributional weights have not been dictated).

For example, the *party by party* approach yields information concerning the distributional impacts of a policy that the *change in total benefits minus change in total resource costs* approach does not. Once the net benefit or cost in each category is calculated, it may be possible to assess differential impacts according to income for each party. If there is to be a trade-off, it would be prudent that it be determined using the fullest and most accurate information available.

If an objective of a project is to redistribute income, it is important to advise decision-makers that there are likely better ways to achieve this objective. A government that proceeds with an otherwise nonviable project because it will mainly benefit the poor, is courting a significant efficiency loss. If the tax-and-transfer system can achieve the same distributional objective at less cost to society, surely the preferred option is clear.

Job Creation and Regional Economic Development

Quite often, a project judged "not viable" in a cost-benefit analysis is defended on the basis of its potential to create jobs. The same argument is used to defend government loans and grants to business. Those favouring such expenditures often speak of "spin-off" effects. A number of points should be made.

Labour

Unemployment rates are already accounted for when shadow wage rates are used in project evaluation. To give regional unemployment further weight is, in a sense, to double-count.

Confusing Economic Viability and Local GDP Impacts

Spin-off effects are multiplier impacts. We have discussed why multipliers should not be used in project evaluation, but note further that their popularity may be a result of confusing social well-being with GDP, and of limiting the geographical range of inquiry. An increase in the level of economic activity in one location may be welfare-diminishing—and in any case, it may be offset (or more than offset) by decreases in levels of economic activity elsewhere.

For example, consider a patently ludicrous project: building another bridge right beside the P.E.I.–N.B. Confederation Bridge, to be financed by higher federal income taxes. (Indeed, to avoid any misunderstanding that this would be an absolute waste of resources, let us specify that the centre section of the bridge will *not* be constructed—no one could cross it.) What would happen?

The level of economic activity in the area would increase, and there would be spin-off effects in the region. It may be that local politicians would support the project because of its job-creation potential. GDP in the area would rise. On the other hand, the higher tax rate would diminish the level of economic activity across the country and, in any case, overall social well-being would be diminished. (Similarly, demolishing GM Place in Vancouver and the SkyDome in Toronto, then rebuilding them, may raise levels of economic activity in these cities, but it would be difficult to argue that these acts would contribute to social well-being.)

Winners and Losers According to Region

We suppose that the heart of the problem is that projects necessarily have a geographical dimension that is specific and limited. This may mean that those who reap the benefits of a project are not those who pay for it; typically, federally financed projects built in "have not" provinces are financed by taxpayers in "have" provinces. It would seem rather easy to support projects for which one does not pay—especially those with perceived job-creation potential. Regional economic development would appear to be the objective, and regional gains at the expense of national losses would appear to be an acceptable trade-off to some people—at least politically. Of course, such policies could be challenged on economic grounds. Even if regional development were the objective, it still makes sense to favour a project with a positive net present value over one with a negative net present value. Indeed, if society is truly concerned with incomes in relatively depressed regions, direct transfers may be the least costly option.

A FINAL WORD

Analysts face two general problems. The first is that the economic criteria used for determining a project's viability may not be accepted by decision-makers and others. The second is that economically valid procedures may not be viewed by affected individuals and decision-makers as correct because error-making has become accepted practice.

Regarding the first problem, other criteria for accepting and rejecting projects and policies exist and may conflict with economic criteria. We can offer little guidance in this regard other than to note than these conflicts are sometimes more perceived than real, perhaps arising from a lack of appreciation that economic evaluations are to account for *all* social costs and *all* social benefits. For example, some environmentalists may not be aware that environmental costs and benefits are included by economists as social costs and benefits. Equally, it would be surprising if many politicians appreciated that shadow pricing of labour takes into account regional employment conditions. When conflicts are based on ignorance or misunderstanding, there is potential for resolution. Acceptance of the notion that resources are scarce would be a major step in this process. Ideally, any remaining arguments would be concerned with the validity of assumptions and not with methodology.

It is the second general problem that is our principal concern: the making of errors seems to have become accepted practice. Obviously, a first step toward improving this situation is to identify those errors. To this end, we conclude with a list of 20 errors, warnings, and suggestions. This list could have been longer.

*Do*s and *Don't*s

1. Use *all* real values or *all* nominal values, not a mix of them.
2. Do not include explicit depreciation or interest charges.

3. If it is necessary to report internal rate of return and/or benefit-cost ratio information, report also net present values (with an explanation).

4. Do not use rule-of-thumb shadow wage formulations because labour—and thus its shadow wage—is project-specific, not region-specific.

5. Be prepared to defend whatever base-case discount rate is used and to support the results with sensitivity analysis.

6. Align a project's planning horizon with its economic life.

7. For transportation projects, resist the use of compounding traffic-growth-rate assumptions.

8. Do not cause the capital cost of a project to be counted as a benefit either explicitly or implicitly through the use of historical accounting methods.

9. Optimal prices—even when they are zero—exist and should be used in project evaluation in order to maximize net present value.

10. Use both *party by party* and *change in total benefits minus change in total resource costs* approaches when possible. If they yield different answers, at least one error has been made.

11. A job created by a public sector project should not be treated as a benefit.

12. Use marginal (incremental) cost estimates rather than average ones. When this is not possible, report any perceived direction of bias.

13. Do not make separate provision for lives expected to be saved or lost due to a project if the phenomenon is already accounted for in market prices and/or wage rates.

14. Be wary of benefits and costs that can appear both as flows and as stocks (e.g., a stream of annual profits accruing to an asset and the value of the asset itself). Count one but not both.

15. Be wary of benefits and costs that can appear both explicitly and as price effects (e.g., as time saved and as price changes due to altered transportation costs).

16. Do not confuse a cost-benefit analysis with an economic impact study.

17. Ignore intergovernmental grants.

18. Regarding secondary impacts, be aware of what to count and what not to count (see Chapter 7).

19. Double-counting, especially of benefits, occurs in many forms. Care is required.

20. Abstain from the use of multipliers.

ENDNOTES

1. Readers wishing to review this rich literature are advised to begin with the relevant chapters in Layard (1972).

2. *The Charlottetown Guardian*, January 4, 1988, p. 1, is the source of the plebiscite question. The later Premier Ghiz's reaction was reported in *The Winnipeg Free Press*, January 19, 1988, pp. 1, 4.

GLOSSARY

Annual amortization schedule
An amortization schedule sets the dollar amount consisting of principal and interest that must be paid at regular intervals (usually each month or year) in order to retire a sum at a specified future date that is borrowed at a stated rate of interest.

Backward linkage See Secondary induced benefit.

Baseyear The year to which all dollar values are discounted is the baseyear of a project. Although arbitrary, usually the year the policy or construction of a project begins—the present—is chosen. This year is also called "the present."

Benefit-cost ratio A benefit-cost ratio is the present value of a project's benefits divided by the present value of its costs. If this ratio is greater (less) than one, the project is deemed viable (not viable).

Certainty equivalent income (or wealth) Certainty equivalent income is the level of riskless income that would leave an individual just indifferent between it and taking a gamble (accepting risk).

Compensating variation Given some event (such as project, policy, or price change), compensating variation is the dollar amount that would have to be given or taken away from an individual in order to leave his or her utility at its pre-event level.

Consumer surplus Consumer surplus is the difference between what consumers are willing to pay for a specific quantity of a good or service and what they actually pay for this quantity.

Contingent valuation An individual's contingent valuation is his or her willingness to pay (compensating variation) for a project or policy; this willingness is revealed in response to survey questions.

Corrective subsidy A corrective subsidy placed on a good or service is one that lessens or eliminates an efficiency (net welfare) loss caused by some form of market failure (e.g., an external benefit or monopoly power) by causing consumption and production of the good or service to expand.

Corrective tax A corrective tax levied on a commodity is one that lessens or eliminates an efficiency (net welfare) loss caused by some form of market failure (e.g., an external cost) by causing consumption and production of the commodity to contract.

Cost of risk-taking For an individual, the cost of risk-taking is the difference between his or her expected income and certainty-equivalent income.

Cut-off period A cut-off period is a specific length of time, usually expressed in years. If the costs of a project are not recovered within this period of time, it is rejected.

Discounting Discounting is the act of transforming dollar values accrued in one year into dollar values as of an earlier year using an interest (discount) rate. It is the opposite of compounding dollar values into the future.

Discount rate A discount rate is the rate of interest used to transform dollar values through time so that they may be expressed as of any given year.

Economic life   The economic life of a project or policy extends from its beginning to its termination. While some projects or policies may last forever (have an infinite economic life), the economic life of a finite-lived project is usually determined according to when its usefulness is expected to end.

Economically viable   An economically viable project is one whose economic benefits to society exceed its economic costs to society.

Efficient   The quantity of a good or service produced is efficient if all units for which marginal benefit to society exceeds marginal cost to society are produced and consumed, and no units for which marginal social cost exceeds marginal social benefit are produced.

Equivalent variation   Given some potential event (such as project, policy, or price change), equivalent variation is the dollar amount that would have to be given or taken away from an individual in order to yield him or her the level of utility at the level he or she would have enjoyed had the event occurred.

External benefit   An external benefit is not captured by market prices. It is not taken into account by consumers and producers in their market decisions because it is bestowed on an economic agent who is not a direct party to the transaction and, who, therefore, does not pay for it. Competitive markets produce too little of goods and services with external benefits to be efficient.

External cost   An external cost is not captured by market prices. It is not taken into account by consumers and producers in their market decisions because it is incurred not by them but, rather, by some economic agent who is a third party to the transaction. Competitive markets produce too much of goods and services with external costs to be efficient.

Financially viable   A financially viable project is one that is profitable.

Forward linkage   See secondary stemming benefit.

Free rider   A free rider is a person who consumes a public good without paying for it.

Future value   A dollar amount allowed to compound over time at a rate of interest grows to its future value expressed as of some future date.

Hedonic price   The hedonic price of an intangible, for which no market price exists, is imputed by observing trade-offs between the quantity and/or quality of a related commodity and money.

Inferior good   An inferior good is characterized by a negative income elasticity of demand; *ceteris paribus*, as income rises (falls), demand for an inferior good falls (rises).

Internal rate of return   The internal rate of return of a project is the discount rate that causes its net present value to be zero.

Law of diminishing productivity   As additional units of a variable input are combined with a fixed input in order to expand output, eventually the marginal product of the variable input must decrease.

Marginal cost   Marginal cost is the amount by which total cost increases when output expands by one unit. *Short-run marginal cost* can never be less than *long-run marginal cost* because, in the long run, a firm may choose the least-cost combination of inputs with which to expand output whereas, in the short run, the existence of at least one fixed input restricts the firm's input choice.

Marginal rate of time preference
An individual's marginal rate of time preference is the rate at which he or she is *willing* to trade off present and future consumption. This is to be contrasted with the relevant interest rate, which is the rate the individual *can* trade off present and future consumption by borrowing or saving.

Marginal value product of labour
The marginal value product of labour is the dollar amount the incremental output produced by an additional worker can be sold for in a competitive market.

Net present value   The net present value of a project is equal to the present value of its benefits minus the present value of its costs. If this amount is positive (negative) the project is deemed viable (not viable).

Nonexclusion   A good or service exhibits nonexclusion if individuals cannot be prevented from consuming it even if they pay no price for it (e.g., a streetlight).

Nonrivalry   A good or service exhibits nonrivalry if one person's consumption of units of it does not detract from another person's consumption of the same units (e.g., national defence).

Normal good   A normal good is characterized by a positive income elasticity of demand. *Ceteris paribus*, as income rises (falls), demand for a normal good rises (falls).

Opportunity cost   The opportunity cost of using a resource in a particular application is the value forgone by not employing it in its next-best alternative use.

Pareto improvement   An event generates a Pareto improvement if it causes at least one person to be made better off *and* no person to be made worse off.

Pareto improvement criterion
An act satisfies the Pareto improvement criterion if it would cause a Pareto improvement.

Pareto inferior   An allocation of resources is Pareto inferior if it is possible to reallocate these resources so that a Pareto improvement will result. The resulting allocation is deemed **Pareto superior** to the first.

Pareto optimal   An allocation of resources is Pareto optimal if it is impossible to make any change that will cause at least one person to be made better off and no person to be made worse off.

Pareto superior   See Pareto inferior.

Pay-back period   The pay-back period criterion requires an analyst assessing projects to rank first the one with costs that are recovered in the shortest period of time.

Potential Pareto improvement
An act causes a potential Pareto improvement if those who gain from the act would be able to compensate those who would lose yet still be left better off. Only hypothetical compensation is necessary.

Potential Pareto improvement criterion   The single criterion is that an act satisfies it if it would cause a potential Pareto improvement. The double criterion is satisfied if it would be possible for gainers from the act to compensate losers and not possible for those who would lose to compensate others for forgoing the act.

Present value   The present value of a dollar amount to be realized in the future may be expressed as of an earlier date (the present) by discounting it backward through time using a discount (interest) rate.

Price elastic   Demand for a good or service is price elastic if a price change, *ceteris paribus*, causes a proportionately larger change in the quantity demanded. Consumers are relatively sensitive to price changes, and the absolute value of the price elasticity of demand is greater than one.

Price inelastic   Demand for a good or service is price inelastic if a price change, *ceteris paribus*, causes a proportionately smaller change in the quantity demanded. Consumers are relatively insensitive to price changes, and the absolute value of the price elasticity of demand is less than one.

Producer surplus   Producer surplus is the difference between what firms actually receive in revenues for producing a specific quantity of a good or service and the least amount they would have been willing to accept. For a specific quantity, it is total revenue minus total variable cost.

Public goods   A public good is a good or service that exhibits nonexclusion and nonrivalry in consumption.

Risk   A risky situation is one where the possible consequences that can arise from an action are known and it is possible to assign a probability to each of them. This is to be contrasted to a situation involving **uncertainty**, where it is not possible to assign probabilities to possible outcomes.

Risk pooling   Risk pooling occurs when similar risks (e.g., fire) faced by many people are aggregated and mutually insured, in some circumstances in insurance markets.

Risk spreading   Risk spreading occurs when the consequences of a single risk are shared by more than one person.

Secondary induced benefit   When a project causes a direct impact on the production of some commodity, a secondary induced benefit occurs when the demand for inputs used in the production of this commodity expands. It is a movement backward in the production process.

Secondary stemming benefit   When a project causes a direct impact on the production of some commodity that is an input in a production process, a secondary stemming benefit occurs when the demand for other inputs in the process expands. It is a movement forward in the production process.

Shadow price   The shadow price imputed to a commodity is the unit opportunity cost of it to society. It need not be the market price of the commodity.

Shadow wage rate   The shadow wage rate imputed to a project is the opportunity cost per worker to society of employing labour. It need not be the wage rate actually paid labour to work on the project.

Sinking fund   A sinking fund is the dollar amount that must be saved at regular intervals (usually a week, month, or year) to earn a specific rate of interest so that the accrued principal and interest accumulate to a predetermined target sum at a specified future date.

Social surplus   Social surplus is the sum of consumer surplus and producer surplus.

Technological spillover   A technological spillover is an indirect impact of a project on other productive capabilities. If positive (negative), it enhances (diminishes) the production possibilities of the indirectly related activity.

Uncertainty   See Risk.

BIBLIOGRAPHY

Arrow, K.J. (1951), *Social Choice and Individual Values* (Washington: Brookings Institute).

Arrow, K.J., & R.C. Lind (1970), "Uncertainty and the evaluation of public investment decisions," *American Economic Review LX*: 364–378.

Beesley, M.E. (1965), "The value of time spent travelling: Some new evidence," *Economica XXXII*: 174–185.

Blackorby, C., & D. Donaldson (1990), "A review article: The case against use of the sum of compensating variations in cost-benefit analysis," *Canadian Journal of Economics XXIII*: 471–494.

Boadway, R.W., & N. Bruce (1984), *Welfare Economics* (Oxford: Basil Blackwell).

Boadway, R.W., & D. Wildasin (1984), *Public Sector Economics*, 2nd ed. (Toronto: Little, Brown and Company).

Boardman, A.E., D.H. Greenberg, A.R. Vining & D.L. Weimer (1996), *Cost-Benefit Analysis: Concepts and Practice* (Upper Saddle River: Prentice Hall).

Bueckert, Dennis, "De Cotret may appeal court decision in Rafferty dam dispute," *The Chronicle-Herald*, November 17, 1990, C8.

Burgess, David F. (1981), "The Social Discount Rate for Canada: Theory and Evidence," *Canadian Public Policy VII(3)*: 383–394.

Calhoun, C. (1989), "When P.E.I. joins the mainland: How much will a fixed link change Island life?" *Canadian Geographic 109(2)* (April–May): 12–21.

Canadian Press, "P.E.I. residents favor fixed link to mainland," *Winnipeg Free Press*, January 19, 1988a, 1, 4.

——————— "Nova Scotia joins clamor for details on fixed link,"*The Chronicle-Herald*, January 22, 1988b, A17.

——————— "Dams said threat to migratory birds," *The Chronicle-Herald*, July 5, 1991a, C15.

——————— "Saskatchewan dam to go ahead," *The Globe and Mail*, August 21, 1991b, A5.

——————— "Dam project labelled an environmental disaster," *The Chronicle-Herald*, November 29, 1991c, D15.

——————— "PEI man fined for bridge walk," *The Globe and Mail*, February 15, 1997a, A2.

——————— "Trans-Labrador Highway," *The Globe and Mail,"* April 4, 1997b, A4.

Corbeil, The Honourable Jean (1993), Letter of June 28, addressee unknown.

Curry, Steve, & John Weiss (1993), *Project Analysis in Developing Countries,* (Toronto: McClelland & Stewart).

"A dam without water" (editorial), *Winnipeg Free Press,* June 29, 1991, p. 6.

Dasgupta, Ajit K., & D.W. Pearce (1972), *Cost-Benefit Analysis: Theory and Practice* (London: Harper and Row).

Dorfman, R. (1972), "Decision rules under uncertainty," pp. 360–392 in R. Layard (ed.), *Cost Benefit Analysis* (Harmondsworth: Penguin).

Doskoch, Bill, "Alameda dam slips slightly," *The Leader-Post,* August 7, 1993, A1.

Doskoch, Bill, "Dams and politics," *The Leader-Post,* August 21, 1993, A9.

Dyck, H. (1991), "Despite calls for tunnel option, MacKay backs idea of bridge to P.E.I.," *The Chronicle-Herald,* January 2, 1991, C12.

FEARO (Federal Environmental Review Office) (1990), "Report of the Environmental Assessment Panel" (Ottawa).

Feldstein, M.S., "The Inadequacy of Weighted Discount Rates," pp. 311–332 in R. Layard (ed.) (1972), *Cost-Benefit Analysis* (Harmondsworth: Penguin)

Feldstein, M.S., & J.S. Flemming (1964), "The problem of time-stream evaluation: Present value *versus* internal rate of return rules," *Bulletin of Oxford University Institute of Economics and Statistics XXVI*: 79–85.

Fiander-Good Associates Limited (1987), *Draft Final Report: Economic Feasibility Assessment for the Northumberland Strait Crossing,* (Fredericton).

————— (1993), *Trans Labrador Highway Social and Economic Project Feasibility Analysis,* (Fredericton).

Fisher, Irving (1930), *The Theory of Interest* (New York: Macmillan).

Flowerdew, A.D.J. (1972), "Choosing a Site for the Third London Airport: the Roskill Commission's Approach," pp. 431–451 in R. Layard (ed.) (1972), *Cost Benefit Analysis* (Harmondsworth: Penguin).

Gardner Pinfold Consulting Economists Limited (1992), "A Review of the benefit-cost analysis of the Northumberland Strait Crossing Project" (Halifax).

————— (1993), *A benefit-cost analysis of the Northumberland Strait Crossing Project* (Halifax).

Gaudry, M.J.I. (1980), "Dogit and logit models of travel mode choice in Montreal," *Canadian Journal of Economics XIII*: 268–279.

Gillen, D.W. (1977), "Alternative policy variables to influence urban transport demand," *Canadian Journal of Economics X*: 686–695.

Harberger, A.C. (1971), "On Measuring the Social Opportunity Cost of Labour," *International Labour Review CIII*: 559–579.

————— (1972), "The Opportunity Costs of Public Investment Financed by Borrowing," pp. 303–310 in R. Layard (ed.), *Cost-Benefit Analysis* (Harmondsworth: Penguin)

Harris, Graham, & Allan Billard (1988), *The Northumberland Strait Crossing: The Fishing Industry's Viewpoint Favouring a Deep-Level Tunnel*, (Dartmouth: Eastern Fishermen's Federation).

Harris, John R., & Michael P. Todaro (1970), "Migration, Unemployment and Development: A Two-Sector Model," *American Economic Review LX*: 126–142.

Harrison, A.J., & D.A. Quarmby (1972), "The value of time," pp. 173–208 in R. Layard (ed.), *Cost Benefit Analysis* (Harmondsworth: Penguin).

Haveman, Robert H. (1977), "Evaluating Public Expenditure under Conditions of Unemployment," in Robert H. Haveman and Julius Margolis (eds.), *Public Expenditure and Policy Analysis* (Chicago: Rand McNally).

Haveman, Robert H., & John V. Krutilla (1968), *Unemployment, Idle Capacity and the Evaluation of Public Expenditures* (Baltimore: Johns Hopkins Press).

Hughes, Walter G. (1981), "Benefit-Cost Analysis for RDIA Projects," (Moncton: Department of Regional Economic Expansion).

Jacques Whitford Environment Limited (1993), *Environmental Evaluation of SCI's Proposed Northumberland Strait Crossing Project* (Fredericton).

Jenkins, Glenn P. (1973), "The Measurement of Rates of Return and Taxation from Private Capital in Canada," in W.A. Niskanen et al. (eds.), *Benefit Cost and Policy Analysis* (Chicago: Aldine).

————— (1977), "Capital in Canada: Its Social and Private Performance 1965 74," Economic Council of Canada Discussion Paper No. 98.

Land, T. (1989), "Greens may dictate Baltic fixed link," *The Chronicle-Herald*, August 7, 1989, A7.

Layard, R. (1972), "Introduction," pp. 395–428 in R. Layard (ed.), *Cost-Benefit Analysis*, (Harmondsworth: Penguin).

Little, I.M.D., & J.A. Mirrlees (1968), *Manual of Industrial Project Analysis for Developing Countries* (Paris: OECD).

Locke, L. Wade, & Peter G.C. Townley (1993), "A Critical Review of the `Trans Labrador Highway Social and Economic Project Feasibility Analysis'" (Sheshatiu: Innu Nation).

Loeb, M., & W.A. Magat (1979), "A Decentralized Method for Utility Regulation," *Journal of Law and Economics*, 22: 339–404.

MacDonald, D., "Fixed link still in works—MacKay," *The Chronicle-Herald*, February 5, 1990.

————— "Fixed link remains a reality says Conservative MP Casey," *The Chronicle-Herald*, February 21, 1991: A11.

MacLeod, C.K. (1992), Letter of 10 June to T. Murphy, Government of Newfoundland and Labrador.

MacNeill, P., "Fixed link seen as boon to N.S.," *The Chronicle-Herald,* May 4, 1991, C1.

McCoag, T., "Cynicism greets fixed link debate," The *Chronicle-Herald,* April 20, 1991, A15.

Marglin, S.A. (1963), "The Opportunity Costs of Public Investment," *Quarterly Journal of Economics LXXVII:* 274–289, reprinted pp. 284–302 in R. Layard (ed.), *Cost-Benefit Analysis* (Harmondsworth: Penguin).

May, Elizabeth, "A tangled tale set on a tiny river," *The Globe and Mail,* November 6, 1990, A17.

Meng, R.A., & D.A. Smith (1990), "The valuation of risk of death in public sector decision-making," *Canadian Public Policy XVI:* 137–144.

Ministry of Transport, U.K. (1963), Proposals for a Fixed Channel Link, HMSO: Cmnd. 6137 (London).

Mishan, E.J. (1972), "What is wrong with Roskill?" *Journal of Transport Economics and Policy IV:* 221–234, reprinted pp. 452–472 in R. Layard (ed.), *Cost-Benefit Analysis* (Harmondsworth: Penguin).

———— (1976), *Cost-Benefit Analysis* (New York: Praeger).

Musgrave, R.A., & P.G. Musgrave (1984), *Public Finance in Theory and Practice,* 4th ed. (New York: McGraw-Hill).

Oi, Walter Y. (1971), "A Disneyland dilemma: Two-part tariffs for a Mickey Mouse monopoly," *Quarterly Journal of Economics 85:* 77–96.

Osborne, M.J., & A. Rubinstein (1994), *A Course in Game Theory* (Cambridge: MIT Press).

Pearce, D.W. (1976), "Social Cost of Noise," (Paris: Environment Directorate, Organisation for Economic Co-operation and Development).

Pearce, D.W., & C.A. Nash (1981), *The Social Appraisal of Projects: A Text in Cost-Benefit Analysis* (London: Macmillan).

Perchanok, N. (1988), Backgrounder: The P.E.I. Fixed Link Project (Ottawa: Science and Technology Division of the Library of Parliament).

Peters, T., "Firm raps panel's fixed-link decision," *The Chronicle-Herald,* August 29, 1990a.

———— "Island ferry service in question," *The Chronicle-Herald,* June 2, 1990b.

———— "High speed vessels seen as replacements for existing ferries," *The Chronicle-Herald,* March 2, 1991, A16.

Pommerehne, Werner W. (1986), "Measuring environmental benefits: A comparison of hedonic technique and contingent valuation," pp. 363–400 in D. Bös, M. Rose, & C. Seidl (eds.) *Welfare and Efficiency in Public Economics* (Berlin: Springer-Verlag).

Pressman, I. (1970), "A mathematical formulation of the peak-load pricing problem," *Bell Journal of Economics and Management Science* (Autumn): 304–326.

Privy Council of Canada (1984), Environmental Assessment and Review Process Guidelines Order, *Canada Gazette* Part II, Vol. 118, No. 114, pp. 2794–2798 (July 11, 1984).

Raynauld, J., Y. Stringer, & P.G.C. Townley (1994), *Markets and Prices: A Policy Perspective* (Toronto: Prentice Hall).

Scitovsky, T. (1941), "A note on welfare propositions in economics," *Review of Economic Studies IX*: 77–88.

Sen, A.K. (1961), "On optimizing the rate of saving," *Economic Journal LXXI*: 479–496.

Silva Ecosystem Consultants Limited (1993), *Initial Study of Ecological and Economic Viability of Commercial Timber Management in Labrador* (Winlaw, B.C.).

Smith Green & Associates Inc. (1989a), *Bridge Concept Assessment Supplement: Effects on Tourism and Associated Development Strategies — Support Document for Question J* (Ottawa: Public Works Canada).

————— (1989b), "Northumberland Strait Fixed Crossing Imapcts: Employment Opportunities and Social Environment—Background Document for Question K-1(g)" (Ottawa: Public Works Canada).

Souris Basin Development Authority (1987), *Rafferty-Alameda Project: Environmental Impact Statement*—"Executive Summary," "Chapter I: Project Description," "Chapter II: Social and Economic Characteristics," and "Chapter III: Benefit Cost Analysis" (Regina).

Staff (1990), "Consultant forecasts P.E.I. tunnel link," *The Chronicle-Herald*, December 24, 1990, A2.

Stanford Research Institute and Acres Research and Planning Limited (1968), *Benefit/Cost Evaluation of a Proposed Fixed Crossing of the Northumberland Strait* (Menlo Park).

Statistics Canada (1992), *Census Divisions and Census Subdivisions: Population and Dwelling Counts* (Ottawa).

Stiglitz, J.E. (1986), *Economics of the Public Sector* (New York: W.W. Norton).

Sugden, R., & A. Williams (1978), *The Principles of Practical Cost-Benefit Analysis* (Oxford: Oxford University Press).

Sumner, M.T. (1980), "Benefit-Cost Analysis in Canadian Practice," *Canadian Public Policy VI(2)*: 389–393.

Townley, Peter G.C. (1991), "Reversing the Scitovsky reversal: The case of compulsory annuities," *Papers and Proceedings of the Atlantic Canada Economics Association XIX*, 110–124.

————— (1992), "The weakest link: The economic viability of a Northumberland Strait crossing," *Policy Options XIII(6)*: 15–18.

Treasury Board of Canada Secretariat (1976), *Benefit-Cost Analysis Guide* (Ottawa: Minister of Supply and Services Canada).

Usher, D. (1985), "The value of life for decision making in the public sector," *Social Philosophy and Policy II*: 168–191.

Weisbrod, B.A. (1968), "Deriving an implicit set of government weights for income classes," pp. 395–428 in R. Layard (ed.), *Cost Benefit Analysis* (Harmondsworth: Penguin).

Williamson, Oliver E. (1966), "Peak-load pricing and optimal capacity under indivisibility constraints," *American Economic Review LVI*: 810–827.

Willig, R.D. (1976), "Consumer's surplus without apology," *American Economic Review LXVI*: 589–597.

Woods Gordon Management Consultants (1987) *Financial Analysis of the Northumberland Strait Crossing Project* (Toronto).

Zerbe, R.O., Jr., & D.D. Dively (1994), *Benefit-Cost Analysis* (New York: HarperCollins).

AUTHOR INDEX

SUBJECT INDEX